MW01089591

CRIME PREVENTION THROUGH ENVIRONMENTAL DESIGN

CRIME PREVENTION THROUGH ENVIRONMENTAL DESIGN

Third Edition

TIMOTHY D. CROWE
REVISED BY LAWRENCE J. FENNELLY

AMSTERDAM • BOSTON • HEIDELBERG • LONDON • NEW YORK • OXFORD
PARIS • SAN DIEGO • SAN FRANCISCO • SINGAPORE • SYDNEY • TOKYO
Butterworth-Heinemann is an imprint of Elsevier

Acquiring Editor: *Brian Romer*
Editorial Project Manager: *Amber Hodge*
Project Manager: *Punithavathy Govindaradjane*
Designer: *Maria Inês Cruz*

Butterworth-Heinemann is an imprint of Elsevier
225 Wyman Street, Waltham, MA 02451, USA
The Boulevard, Langford Lane, Kidlington, Oxford, OX5 1 GB, UK

Library of Congress Cataloging-in-Publication Data
Crowe, Timothy D.
Crime prevention through environmental design / Timothy D. Crowe ; revised by Lawrence Fennelly. -- Third edition.
pages cm
Includes bibliographical references and index.
ISBN 978-0-12-411635-1 (alk. paper)
1. Crime prevention and architectural design. I. Fennelly, Lawrence J.,
1940- II. Title.
HV7431.C79 2013
364.4'9--dc23

2013017276

British Library Cataloguing-in-Publication Data
A catalogue record for this book is available from the British Library.

ISBN: 978-0-12-411635-1

For information on all Butterworth-Heinemann publications
visit our website at store.elsevier.com

Transferred to Digital Printing in 2014

Dedication

It is my personal pleasure to dedicate this book to Leslie N. A. Cole, Sr. CPP, CST. Mr. Cole is currently a regional vice president of ASIS 2013. He is a security professional who has gone far beyond the call of duty in mentoring and helping ASIS members in their advancement of our profession. He is an active crime-prevention practitioner, one who, I'm sure Tim Crowe would agree, is worthy of this dedication.

Timothy D. Crowe

Tim passed away on February 21, 2009. Needless to say, it was a shock to the international community. He was an international crime-prevention expert, criminologist, and author of the first and second editions of *Crime Prevention Through Environmental Design*. This book has become the standard textbook in the field of CPTED. Mr. Crowe was formerly the director of the National Crime Prevention Institute. He alone trained over 6,000 professionals in CPTED. He was a person of great humility, professional integrity, and a sharp mind. He was also our friend.

The CPTED concept, *is the proper design and effective use of the built environment can lead to a reduction in the fear of crime and the incidence of crime, and to an improvement in the quality of life.*

~Dr. C. Ray Jeffery

CONTENTS

ACKNOWLEDGMENTS

Larry is extremely grateful to Rick Draper in Australia for all the hard work he and his team put into this book. He would also like to thank:

Jill Fechner, Administration and Marketing Manager, Amtac Professional Services Pty. Ltd. (Illustrations)
Tony Lake, Senior Crime Prevention Advisor, Amtac Professional Services Pty. Ltd. and Chair of the International CPTED Association
Jessica Ritchie, Security and Crime Prevention Support Officer, Amtac Professional Services Pty. Ltd.
Judy Draper, Quality Assurance Manager, Amtac Professional Services Pty. Ltd.
Siobhan Allen, student, School of Criminology and Criminal Justice, Griffith University, Australia

FOREWORD

Crime prevention through environmental design (CPTED) is not a new concept. The phrase was coined by C. Ray Jeffery in 1971, but a significant contributor to the concept of CPTED was renowned criminologist Timothy D. Crowe, a legend in the security industry. His book, *Crime Prevention Through Environmental Design* (1991), is a primary resource for crime-prevention practitioners in the security industry to help them better understand the relationship between design and human behavior. CPTED is not a reactive discipline. Rather, it is a proactive approach to manipulate the physical environment and bring about the desired behavior of reduced criminal activity as well as reduced fear of crime.

While director of the National Crime Prevention Institute, Tim Crowe began the CPTED Training program in Louisville, Kentucky, where thousands of crime-prevention practitioners, law enforcement officers, and security professionals still proudly say that they attended classes.

This updated edition of Tim Crowe's book is a CPTED milestone, both nationally and internationally, and is long overdue. It was imperative that the second edition of Crowe's book be written by someone with the experience level that is gained only by years of working as a security professional. Larry Fennelly understands what being proactive truly means. This edition discusses how to reduce criminal opportunity and reduce risk. This is the essence of what crime prevention is about.

Schools are operating today by "surviving one major disruption after another," and CPTED is an approach that may help to harden these "soft targets" and keep our children safe. We want our schools to be open, caring places that are conducive to learning and achieving success for our children, not "educational prisons" that stifle growth and instill fear. CPTED concepts are part of a holistic approach to security and are easily incorporated into physical security measures in an effort to lessen the likelihood that crime will occur and also help to alleviate the fear of crime. The CPTED concepts of natural access control, natural surveillance, and territorial reinforcement work well in the school environment and encourage a well-cared-for space that is used for its intended purpose: education. CPTED is not the only answer to preventing crime and other illegal activity; instead, it is one of the approaches that that can be combined with other components of a total security process. CPTED objectives specifically designed for the school environment can be applied to address the issues facing our schools today.

Larry Fennelly has taken CPTED to a new, more modern level by updating Tim Crowe's original text and using success stories that prove CPTED strategies work. The scope of the text takes the reader from the early beginnings of CPTED, architectural design, and urban planning to training outlines and applications—proving that CPTED strategies are even more relevant today than they were when Tim Crowe wrote his book in 1991.

—Marianna Perry, M.S., CPP
Former Director, National Crime Prevention Institute

PART 1

1

INTRODUCTION TO CPTED

CHAPTER OUTLINE

The theory of Crime Prevention Through Environmental Design is based on one simple idea: that crime results partly from the opportunities presented by physical environment. This being the case, it should be possible to alter the physical environment so that crime is less likely to occur.

—**Ronald V. Clarke**

Background

The purpose of this book is to provide challenging questions and practical advice to people who make decisions that affect the physical environment and human functions in the community. This book is not intended to be an academic study of the environment, of crime prevention, or of environmental psychology; however, it does offer practical insights into the application of the theories that underpin crime prevention through environmental design (CPTED) concepts and principles. Because of the pervasiveness of CPTED's potential influence, it would be impossible for this book to be a complete study of all of the fields and disciplines that CPTED topics encounter.

A practical guide to the use of CPTED concepts is necessary because the research literature has yet to thoroughly investigate the considerable small-scale applications of the CPTED concept. Controlled research and evaluation activities are required to make CPTED a fully definitive concept. However, buildings must be built, major events must be conducted, and communities must continue to grow without the benefit of perfect scientific knowledge. Accordingly, this book contains some simple concepts and a variety of examples to assist the builder, planner, architect, or police and security consultant who will be making decisions about individual projects and human functions.

The intention of this book is not to tell people how to design buildings or what decisions to make about the future of the properties that they manage. It is rather to share concepts and ask questions that may never have been asked, with the hope that these concepts and questions will improve decisions and stimulate greater creativity in designing for and managing human activities.

This third edition builds on the author's life work with the concept of crime prevention through environmental design. The CPTED concept, coined by Dr. C. Ray Jeffery in his book by the same title, expands on the assumption that *the proper design and effective use of the built environment can lead to a reduction in the fear of crime and the incidence of crime and to an improvement in the quality of life.* This idea translates to many practical and useful applications in a wide range of settings.

The contents bring together the observations, consulting work, and lectures and teaching materials from the first two editions of this book, along with new material written by the author before his sad passing on February 21, 2009. This third edition also includes updated chapters and fresh contributions by other CPTED practitioners who knew and worked with him.

Asking the Right Questions

CPTED concepts, at least as used in this work, are largely self-evident. Most of the time recipients of CPTED assistance exclaim, "I should have thought of that!" Too often, after it is too late to undo the damage, an individual will say, "I thought of that, but I was afraid to ask." It is quite common for police officers and security consultants to withhold their comments in various situations because they feel that they would be overstepping the boundaries of their security role. Yet the performance of architects, developers, and facility managers can only be as good as the information they are given from all quarters. Once the basic principles of CPTED are understood, it is difficult to look at the environment again without asking, "What if …?" At the beginning of CPTED seminars and training programs, it is common for the following three points to be stressed by the instructors:

1. Never look at the environment the same way again.
2. Question everything, no matter how trivial.
3. Learn the language of the professions you are working with and you will understand their motivations.

Elizabeth Meehan, a color and light consultant and a visiting lecturer of the National Crime Prevention Institute (NCPI), summarized the problem with interior design. She said that illumination consultants are always looking up. Floor-covering consultants are always looking down. Wallpaper consultants are always looking at the walls. But no one usually looks at the whole interior as the sum of its parts. Each profession is trained to focus attention on its unique objectives. For instance, police officers are trained to look at openings—doors and windows. Not until they have had CPTED training do they begin to see the property as a whole, as it was intended to be. And it is not until this happens that a good crime prevention officer or security consultant can contribute to meeting the objectives of the human function. *Never look at the environment the same way again.* The old expression "If I had a nickel for every time something happened that I knew would happen and didn't stop, I'd be rich" too often applies in CPTED experience. Designers and planners need help in identifying the little problems, which are often their undoing. For instance, many years ago the city of Louisville, Kentucky, replaced a portion of the failed River City pedestrian mall with a cobblestone street that was intended for people to walk on. Instead, people fell down. Similarly, in Jacksonville, Florida, a River Walk project with a pier was installed along a transitional site across from its downtown riverfront improvement program. But the designer got so involved in the aesthetics of his boardwalk that he installed boards that were separated to allow the pedestrian to see, as well as hear, the water lapping underneath. This was great for water drainage, but not for high-heeled shoes! *Question everything.*

Many agencies and professions learn to stick to their own bailiwick and avoid direct conflict. At least in direct conflict they are still talking, albeit somewhat loudly. It is not until someone is able to cross over the disciplines that common interests are found. This is perhaps the hardest lesson for law enforcement officers and security consultants to learn. It is too easy to allow buildings to be built and events to be planned before thinking about security. There is a tendency to feel out of place in insisting that security be considered in the design and layout of an environment where a human function or activity will take place. Conversely, event managers, architects, and planners often view security and law enforcement consultants as myopically concerned with what can go wrong, not with what can go right. CPTED enthusiasts know that planning ahead to make things go right is the key to reducing or eliminating security problems. *Learn the language.*

The Need for CPTED

Do you currently have review and approval authority for all physical changes occurring in your jurisdiction? Are you involved at the concept stage in event planning, or are you last in line to comment on a completed plan? Are you tired of hearing about new crime prevention efforts that are abandoned after several years? Are you willing to take a calculated risk, one that presents great promise for the future role of your organization or community?

It's been a mere 40 years since C. Ray Jeffery coined the term, but any analysis of CPTED concepts and principles reveals a long and ancient tradition of leveraging the environment to support and influence human behavior. After initial awareness of CPTED began in the 1970s, there was a surge of interest again in the late 1980s and early 1990s. With CPTED-related policies and ordinances in place in some communities for more than 20 years, trends are pointing to another resurgence of interest in CPTED. CPTED practitioners are being asked to consider how previous implementations of the fundamental CPTED principles can be refreshed in an environment that is evolving to respond to the needs of the uses of these spaces. Consequently, CPTED is again being seen as a featured topic at numerous conferences and seminars around the world. For example, the American Society for Industrial Security (ASIS) featured a CPTED session in its store security segment at the 2012 convention in Philadelphia. In addition, the ASIS publication *Facilities Physical Security Measures* (ASIS GDL FPSM-2009) includes CPTED as a key consideration.

Since some of the earliest implementations of CPTED-related laws and ordinances in Florida, literally thousands of jurisdictions around the world have followed suit, establishing policy, passing laws and regulations, and implementing guidelines to ensure that CPTED concepts and principles are followed in a wide range of contexts. The CPTED-related ordinance passed by the city of Gainesville, Florida, so many years ago in relation to convenience stores demonstrated at the time that there were wider benefits to be gained through following the principles. That ordinance required, among other things, that the stores provide security training, remove signs from windows, increase the number of store employees after 9:00 P.M., and increase internal lighting at night. At the time, the implementation of this ordinance was credited with a reduction of robberies alone of more than 65 percent. Other studies over time have reportedly shown links between the implementation of CPTED principles and increases in productivity and profitability and, of course, an enhanced quality of life for people living and working in those communities.

Since the first edition of this book was published, downtown pedestrian malls and those horrible downtown one-way street systems have been under the gun. In the latter case, critics continue to find that the one-dimensional value of enhanced traffic flow is not worth the loss of traditional business areas. The loss of on-street parking and the diversion of traffic have hurt many business areas. We have given up a lot for the sake of moving commuters through traffic a little faster. Why don't we just divert them instead? NCPI's CPTED Studio and one- and two-week courses present an excellent opportunity to initiate a team approach to CPTED, even for the corporate businessperson. Bring your facility planners and designers with you to a class that could change the way you do business. Learn how to merge your common interests and objectives, thus helping each member of the team do a better job of attaining his or her own goal. One strong admonition is, "Don't hide CPTED from your boss, like you do everything else that you want to control."

A friend of the author is known to have complained that his boss had "gone off half-cocked and shot his mouth off about CPTED." The official complaint was that the boss couldn't be protected unless what he saw was controlled. Perhaps the real problem was that *the boss couldn't be controlled when he understood what was going on.*

Both you and your bosses need to understand and practice CPTED. It will take all the support you can get to make it a success. Of course, you are only looking at something that has the potential, for the first time, of achieving some results over the long term for your community or organization. What we do right or wrong with our human and physical resources produces a lasting legacy.

Competing Crime Prevention Strategies

A number of related concepts have become confused with the CPTED operating theories and applications. Although some of these concepts overlap with CPTED, others are very different in that they attempt to repackage and redefine the commonsense approach of CPTED. An explanation of some of these related concepts follows:

- *A CPTED-organized and mechanical approach versus a natural approach.* There is some confusion and competition within the CPTED movement itself that boils down to one group that casually blends the three strategy areas (organized, mechanical, and natural approaches) as opposed to another group of specialists whose principal emphasis is on natural approaches. The former is more of a crime-control model; the latter may be conceived of as a planning model.

- *Defensible space.* This concept was developed in the public housing environment and is attributed to the work of Oscar Newman. It is similar to CPTED in that it shares the basic characteristics of natural surveillance, natural access control, and territorial concern. CPTED, in its narrowest form, can be seen as an extension of defensible space concepts to commercial retail, industrial institutional, and low-density residential environments.
- *Environmental security.* This concept was developed on a parallel basis to CPTED. It was initially used in residential settings. Environmental security differs from CPTED in that it contemplates the use of a broad range of crime-control strategies, including social management, target hardening, activity support, and law enforcement.
- *Security by design.* This concept is best understood as a repackaging of solid security engineering, physical security, and procedural security measures to provide improved emphasis on the design process.
- *Natural crime prevention.* This concept grew out of the CPTED emphasis on natural strategies, those that factor behavior management and control into the design and use of the built environment.
- *Safer cities.* This is another spin-off of CPTED that attempts to define an approach to crime prevention that incorporates traditional crime prevention and law enforcement strategies with CPTED. Of course, CPTED planners know that CPTED does not replace other crime prevention strategies but that a high priority should be placed on natural strategies that take advantage of how human and physical resources are being expended.
- *Situational crime prevention.* This concept is much more comprehensive than CPTED because it incorporates other crime prevention and law enforcement strategies in an effort that focuses on place-specific crime problems.
- *Place-specific crime prevention.* This is just another name for situational crime prevention and environmental security. It is clear from a review of these apparently competing concepts that they actually overlap and are extremely compatible with CPTED. Many were developed to provide a vehicle for incorporating organized and mechanical strategies into a free-standing model. However, most long-time CPTED planners have always viewed CPTED as a small subset of the total set of measures required for effective crime prevention and control. Criminologists know that a comprehensive system must include strategies on a continuum that ranges from prenatal care to dementia among elderly persons. It would be unconscionable for anyone to think otherwise.

- *Second-generation CPTED*. The authors of this term suggest that "second-generation CPTED is a new form of ecological, sustainable development." It includes a focus on building neighborhoods on a small, local scale and incorporates community building and the social aspects of the environment. To a large extent this revisits C. Ray Jeffery's CPTED model, which included engineering the social environment and the built environment as well as recognizing the importance of rewards and disincentives for behavior (including the role of enforcement).

CPTED and Contemporary Planning Models

There have been some controversy and misinformation about the role of CPTED in contemporary planning models. These contemporary models include the urban village, transportation-oriented development, neotraditional planning, livable cities, and New Urbanism. Supporters of these planning approaches will often cite conflict with CPTED based on a narrow perception that all CPTED planners do is "close streets and cut bushes."

A study of the concepts and beliefs associated with these contemporary planning models and the natural approaches to space management and design emphasized in CPTED reveals that there is very little conflict. Moreover, there is an overwhelming amount of compatibility. Perhaps an increase in education about all of these planning approaches will help eliminate the myths. The key to overcoming the concern about conflicts is to understand that *CPTED is a process for improving planning decisions*. Once the critic understands that CPTED is a process and not a belief system, it will be easy to use CPTED to improve on decisions within the framework of whatever planning model that is adopted.

CPTED in the United States

Early interest in what has become known as CPTED began with the research of Jane Jacobs. Her book, *The Death and Life of Great American Cities*, published in 1961, described many observations of the relationships between urban design and crime. Jacobs's work stressed the importance of increasing territorial identity and natural surveillance. Oscar Newman demonstrated the importance of natural surveillance, access control, and territorial concern in his 1972 book, *Defensible Space*. Newman proved that a relationship exists between space management and design and crime in public housing environments.

As mentioned earlier, Dr. C. Ray Jeffery coined the phrase *crime prevention through environmental design* in his 1971 book by that title, in which he described the relationship between urban design and crime. His book included excerpts from a 1968 report from the National Commission on the Causes and Prevention of Violence that warned the American public of the direct relationships between urban design and crime. This commission studied the massive urban violence and racial unrest that occurred in U.S. cities between 1964 and 1968. Richard Gardiner, a landscape architect and developer, successfully demonstrated the use of CPTED concepts in residential areas. His 1978 manual, *Design for Safe Neighborhoods*, presented the results of a successful project in a Hartford, Connecticut, neighborhood that significantly reduced crime and improved the quality of life. The most significant CPTED developmental effort in the United States to date was conducted in the 1970s by the Westinghouse Electric Corporation through a massive contractual effort funded by the U.S. Department of Justice. Westinghouse managed a large group of consultants and subcontractors who were responsible for adapting CPTED concepts that had been proven effective in public housing environments to retail, transportation, and school environments.

Much was learned from these efforts, which formed the basis of current efforts in the United States. Interest in CPTED at the federal government level waned during the 1980s. However, state and local units of government took the lead and produced a large number of successful projects. These led to the incorporation of CPTED principles into local building codes. Design review ordinances have been modified to require the use of CPTED in building design. Several state governments have passed legislation and developed new regulations governing the design and management of schools and the convenience-store industry. The state of Florida has taken the most steps by passing legislation and actively conducting training for the public and private sectors.

NCPI at the University of Louisville created the first CPTED training program in 1985. A design studio was created to assist in teaching CPTED concepts. To date this training program has been attended by several thousand participants who have spread the use of CPTED concepts in their communities throughout the world. The content of this training program formed the basis of the first edition of this book in 1991, *Crime Prevention Through Environmental Design: Applications of Architectural Design and Space Management Concepts*, by Timothy D. Crowe. This book is still the most widely used manual for CPTED at the present time in the United States.

CPTED Worldwide

Many of the concepts of CPTED are being practiced in countries throughout the world. It is interesting to note that the process in most cases is an evolution toward a simple model of CPTED that becomes integrated as part of a comprehensive planning process for crime control. It is impossible to describe all of these activities, let alone attempt to list them or identify all the individuals involved. Accordingly, the following is a sample of many of the outstanding activities that are now being implemented.

Canadian provinces and cities have been very active in CPTED. In 1992, the city of Toronto published a manual for planners, *A Working Guide for Planning and Designing Safer Urban Environments*. The Peel Regional Police in the suburbs of Toronto implemented CPTED in housing guidelines, school site plans, and commercial and industrial site improvements. The city of Calgary, located in the province of Alberta, has used CPTED in downtown and transit improvements. Vancouver, British Columbia, has a formal CPTED program that has involved police and planning activities for many years. The British Home Office conducted many demonstrations and evaluations in housing programs concurrent with the early efforts of the U.S. planners. Guidelines were developed for architectural liaison officers in late 1987. The British Crime Prevention Center, in Stafford, U.K., has provided CPTED training to these officers since approximately 1980. A special instructor exchange program between the British Crime Prevention Center and the National Crime Prevention Institute, in Louisville, Kentucky, occurred between 1987 and 1990.

Architect Barry Poyner published *Design Out Crime* in 1983 and engineer Graham Underhill published *Security of Buildings* in 1985. Dr. Ronald Clarke published *Situational Crime Prevention* in 1982. These books added to the wealth of research and developmental efforts that have been contributed by U.K. writers and designers.

The Japanese Ministry of Justice has conducted CPTED research in housing and transportation. The privately funded Japanese Urban Security Research Institute has published a number of CPTED journal articles and conducted two major national symposia on CPTED. The first edition of this book, published in 1991, was republished in 1994 in a Japanese language translation. There is much interest in using CPTED concepts in the promotion of three-generation housing to increase territoriality and stability in neighborhoods.

A group of researchers in the Netherlands is actively involved in using CPTED to overcome high-crime problems and poor quality-of-life issues in low-income housing and small neighborhoods. The firm of Van Djk, von Soomeren, and Partners, located in Amsterdam, has had considerable success in obtaining acceptance of CPTED in the community-planning process.

The Australian Institute of Criminology has conducted numerous research projects involving CPTED. This organization produced a 1989 manual entitled *Design Out Crime*. The city of Waverly published its CPTED planning guidelines in the early 1990s, and since then every state and territory in Australia now has some form of regulatory guidance for developments that requires consideration of CPTED principles. In 1995 the railway authority in the state of New South Wales conducted CPTED reviews of almost 200 railway stations in the Sydney metropolitan area and then followed that up just over 15 years later with audits of a subset of those locations, this time with the review team using iPads to plot CPTED-related observations in real time in the field.

Results of CPTED

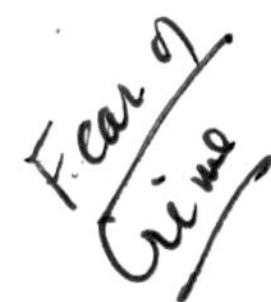

There are many case studies that demonstrate how the application of CPTED concepts has reduced the incidence of crime and fear of crime. Significant results have been produced in many places, including residential areas, convenience stores, malls and shopping centers, transit stations, and parking structures. Journal and newspaper articles have reported on these successes. Descriptive studies have reported on historical relationships between crime and the environment. The U.S. Department of Justice has published a number of bibliographies and documents about these observational studies.

Small-to medium size cities have also reported on considerable crime and fear reductions directly attributable to CPTED traffic management strategies. The pertinent statistical results documenting the impact of CPTED are too numerous to list in this book; any attempt to provide detailed case studies and research results would not only take up this whole volume but would duplicate many other published studies and annotated bibliographies. For example, the National Criminal Justice Reference Service in Rockville, Maryland, maintains an active database. Additionally, Internet sites provide access to public and private information sources worldwide. Finally, the historical basis of CPTED makes the success of the concepts self-evident.

The following is a sample of the many success stories that have resulted from the use of CPTED concepts:

- Convenience stores have used CPTED to increase sales and reduce losses from thefts by up to 50 percent and losses from robberies by 65 percent.
- Malls in Sacramento, California, and Knoxville, Tennessee, have reduced incidents by 24 percent and noncrime calls to police by another 14 percent using CPTED parking management concepts. The largest mall in the world, located in West Edmonton, Alberta, Canada, has used CPTED concepts with well-documented success. The Mall of America in Bloomington, Minnesota, used CPTED from the initial conceptual stage of design. The same or better results have been obtained by many other malls.

- Corporations, including Westinghouse, Mobil, Trinova, Macy's, Disney World, and Sam's/Pace, have reduced losses and improved productivity using CPTED strategies.
- Neighborhoods in Ft. Lauderdale, Tallahassee, Bridgeport, Knoxville, Jacksonville, Dayton, North Miami Beach, Calgary, Toronto, and many other cities have produced dramatic reductions in drug sales, burglaries, and general crime by 15–100 percent.
- Schools using CPTED throughout the world are reducing construction costs, lowering conduct and crime violations, and improving achievement and matriculation levels.
- Design research on office environments has determined that the lack of territorial identity in the office space contributes to lower morale, less productivity, and greater tolerance of dishonesty among fellow workers.
- Transportation authorities in Washington, D.C., Houston, Toronto, Sydney (Australia), the Canadian Pacific Railway, and many other entities have produced cost savings, crime reductions, and improved passenger perceptions of safety using CPTED principles.
- Various levels of government in the United States, Canada, Japan, France, Germany, Australia, New Zealand, Turkey, United Kingdom, and many other countries have initiated CPTED programs. Provincial and state governments have developed legislative requirements. Many cities throughout the world have adopted ordinances or bylaws in which CPTED design review processes were established.

Scope and Content of this Book

The goals of this book are to alter and expand the reader's perception of the immediate physical environment. This, in turn, increases the capacity to understand the direct relationship of the environment to human behavior and to crime. An increase in this basic understanding should result in greater likelihood of the individual confidently questioning or challenging decisions that affect her immediate environment—particularly those that may have a direct bearing on the safety of that individual, her family, her neighborhood, or her place of business.

An understanding of the direct relationship of the design and management of the environment to human behavior is a prerequisite to increasing the success of efforts in crime prevention. It is the key to effective community organization because it gives the citizen the power to protect and control the physical environment and quality of life. CPTED is not the total answer to community problems, but it does provide a community with the means to eliminate or reduce environmental obstacles to social, cultural, or managerial control. Productivity and profit in the commercial and industrial sectors cannot be separated from the design and use of the environment and human reactions to that environment. Loss prevention and profit are quite obviously linked. Loss prevention as a concept goes far beyond crime prevention and its focus on legally defined criminal behavior.

The contents of this book largely represent the author's own observations and experiences. Most of the historical discussions are composed of generally accepted knowledge. A selected bibliography is included for the reader who seeks additional research support. As a practical guide to CPTED concepts, the book has been written in an open narrative style. It is intended to challenge many notions of security and loss prevention and to stimulate a reassessment of space management and design concepts, about which it shares a variety of strategies that may be useful to the reader. The book contains many down-to-earth observations about the interaction between human behavior and the environment. It is the reader's task to relate these examples and ideas to his own life experiences and observations and to determine their usefulness and application to his vocation or professional activity.

2

TWENTY MOST FREQUENTLY ASKED QUESTIONS

Question 1: What is CPTED and how does it differ from traditional approaches to crime and loss control?

CPTED is a natural approach to crime and loss control. CPTED differs from traditional approaches by placing most of its emphasis on human activities and how they become exposed to crime and loss. Traditional approaches to crime control center on the offender, the offense, and the offender's background. The objective has been to control crime by identifying and apprehending the offender. Moreover, most basic approaches to crime prevention focus on the offender by trying to deny access to a victim through physical barriers.

It has been argued that for the past 180 years, criminology has failed to deal effectively with crime because of criminology's limited emphasis on the criminal event, the criminal, and the criminal's behavior. Criminologists attempted to explain crime through legal, social, psychological, biological, and political theories, all of which dealt with the offender as the focal point. It is now commonly accepted that there are many causes of crime but few successful approaches to treating offenders. However, it is also commonly accepted that most criminals commit crimes based on opportunity that is inherent in how human space is designed or used.

By placing a primary emphasis on the human activity and its objectives, CPTED generates a greater interest among residents, business, government and community leaders. Crime prevention, security and law enforcement professionals find that their efforts are more readily accepted when they use CPTED to help improve the quality of life and attainment of the objectives of human activities, while reducing their exposure to crime and loss victimization.

Question 2: How does the CPTED concept differ from the other approaches to procedural and physical security?

The simplest response to this question is that CPTED differs from procedural and physical security by its primary emphasis on natural strategies. Natural strategies are aimed at integrating and incorporating behavior management into the design and management of human and physical resources by whatever means necessary to carry out the human function. Procedural and physical security are well defined and sophisticated processes, but they rely on the expenditure of resources that are intended solely to protect people, information, and property in place of helping to attain their objectives.

Question 3: Do CPTED concepts conflict with building code requirements for life safety and accessibility for physically challenged people?

The answer is no! This is, perhaps, the most misunderstood concept among the lay public as well as public safety professionals. It is often used to avoid dealing with security and safety issues. A fundamental understanding of concepts and requirements of CPTED, security, life safety, and accessibility reveals that there are many solutions that are compatible among these programs.

One common misinterpretation of life safety codes is that it is illegal to secure exit doors in schools, malls, and office buildings. A legal solution in some jurisdictions is the use of magnetic locks that delay egress for a defined period (e.g., 15 seconds), depending on the occupancy and fire codes. Once an attempt is made to exit, an alarm is activated locally and optionally sent to a monitoring facility. The door will not open until the preprogrammed delay has expired, unless there is a general fire alarm, a power failure, or the magnetic lock mechanism detects smoke.

Another common misinterpretation, in this case, of accessibility requirements, is that ramps have to be enclosed with opaque walls. Such walls isolate the legitimate user of the accessibility ramp and actually contribute to more discomfort for the user because of the tendency for the walls to accumulate waste materials and debris along the lower edges, where wheelchairs have to pass or crutches and canes have to establish a secure hold. Finally, there are many people who think that it is illegal to install maze entrances in public or school toilets because the trash bins have been sources of fire and smoke. Subject to local code requirements, these facilities may have open, maze-type entrances if they have, for example, sprinkler systems, fire-retardant walls, or magnetic holders that allow fire-rated doors to close when there is a smoke source present.

Question 4: Is there a relationship between the design and use of space and the opportunity for criminal activities?

Yes! Criminals or improper users of space look for opportunities to commit unwanted acts based on opportunity that is inherent in the way the space is designed and used. Human history is replete with examples of how the environment was used to affect certain behaviors or to prevent undesired acts. The early Mayan civilizations built zigzag walls around their habitats to discourage intruders. The walls required intruders to expose their backs to the opposite elevation from which they were attempting to climb. The Washington, D.C., Metro subway system stations have curved walls next to the pedestrian platforms that are impossible to reach, thus preventing graffiti. Studies of criminal assaults and rape show that predatory offenders are known to exploit heavily landscaped pathways that provide concealment and the element of surprise.

Question 5: How does the design and use of the physical environment affect the behavior of normal and abnormal users of space?

In opposite ways. The environmental cues that make a normal user feel safe have the opposite effect on abnormal users. These cues will make the abnormal user feel at greater risk of detection or apprehension. The users of space react to how others are behaving or to the presence or absence of others. They also react to perceptions of barriers, to entrapment, and to evidence of ownership. The only environmental cue that has the same effect on normal and abnormal users of space alike is distance. The further one is from a potential threat, the easier that threat is to manage. This is why CPTED planners will generally try to give the normal or desired user of space more distance in which to make choices. Conversely, the CPTED planner tries to take distance away from abnormal or undesired users of space, to reduce their choices and to make them feel more conspicuous and susceptible to identification and intervention.

Question 6: What is the difference between organized, mechanical, and natural approaches to crime and loss control?

Organized approaches to security are labor-intensive; they require the use of people to protect other people and property. These approaches may be characterized by the use or hall monitors or guards in schools and shopping centers. The personnel costs for these security methods are extracurricular to the normal human resource costs of human activities. These people are there to protect, not to carry out the human function. Mechanical approaches are hardware- or capital-intensive. Such security approaches rely on barriers, alarms, and camera systems to protect people and property. In contrast, natural approaches merely factor behavior management into what was going to be done anyway. The smart planner tries to make the maximum use of natural strategies first, before automatically relying on the additional cost of organized and mechanical approaches. It is clear that organized and mechanical approaches to security and safety work better in an environment that has made the most of incorporating natural strategies into the design and use of the space.

Question 7: In what ways will natural approaches to crime and loss contribute to the attainment of profit, productivity, and quality of life?

The answer is that by focusing efforts on using natural strategies to increase the attainment of the objectives of the human activity, profit, productivity, and quality of life will increase. Human activities that are meeting their objectives most always experience a reduced exposure to crime and loss. Why? Because space and human resources are better managed, which increases supervision and control, thus decreasing opportunity for abnormal behavior or undesired activities.

Question 8: Are there historical precedents for the use of CPTED concepts and strategies?

Yes! Archeological evidence demonstrates that Germanic tribes used hierarchies of space to defend habitats nearly 200,000 years ago. The ruins of Pompeii and similar ruins in the American Southwest from a civilization that existed more than a 1,000 years later reveal that hierarchies of space were well defined. Clear transitions from semiprivate to public space were very important to security by defining who belonged when and in what spaces. The archeological and historical planning reveals that tribes or communal groups recognized that there was an appropriate number of people who could live together in harmony. Too few could not survive the rigors of nature; too many resulted in a breakdown of social control. Native Americans realized that too great a concentration of people in one place rapidly diminished natural resources, so they went through a constant process of winnowing down large assemblies to workable sizes.

Question 9: Will concerns about aesthetics or appearance be sacrificed by the use of CPTED concepts and strategies?

Of course not! One major misconception is that all CPTED planners do is cut bushes and close streets. On the contrary, CPTED planners introduce new dimensions in the planning of aesthetics by incorporating behavior management into design and space use plans. Good horticulture has turned out to be a major CPTED tool that is used to define space and to promote desired behaviors. The effective use of color and light can enhance behavior management in positive ways.

Question 10: Does it cost a lot of money for a building owner or manager to use CPTED concepts and strategies?

No. Experience has demonstrated that CPTED concepts can save money and resources when they're incorporated into conceptual plans for facilities. Many design efficiencies are inherent in the use of the CPTED process to help determine what is appropriate for spaces.

Natural strategies reduce the extra costs of organized and mechanical security. Retrofit strategies have helped reduce management and security costs. Where the use of a CPTED strategy results in an increase in cost, usually during the initial investment, there is always a significant return on investment due to increased profitability and reduced liability.

Question 11: Is CPTED limited in value to only the planning of new facilities?
No! It has proven its usefulness in all types of facilities. Since CPTED relies on good common sense, it is clear that it may be useful in nearly every human endeavor.

Question 12: May CPTED concepts be used in planning major events, or are these strategies limited to the built environment?
CPTED strategies have been used, sometimes without formal attribution, in the management of events throughout human history. CPTED has been used in major events since the 1972 Republican and Democratic political conventions in the United States. CPTED has been part and parcel of almost every major event since the late 1970s. CPTED was used during the 1979 Pan American Games and in the 1982 World's Fair in Knoxville, Tennessee. The 2000 Olympic Games held in Sydney, Australia, very carefully and cleverly incorporated CPTED into nearly every phase of planning for transportation, housing, and athletic venues. The successes have been measured in increased profits, reduced incidents, and an improvement in accessibility and enjoyment of the events. It is a documented fact that the careful incorporation of CPTED and planning of law enforcement services for the World's Fair in Knoxville resulted in a savings of approximately $750,000 in the law enforcement services budget of $835,000. Similar dramatic savings were experienced wherever CPTED was used appropriately. How can this be? It is simple: CPTED is founded on good planning and a commitment to doing what is appropriate in place of what is believed! Experience has demonstrated that major breakdowns in security at major events have been a direct result of poor event planning and poor management.

Question 13: How does CPTED relate to local government functions of planning, housing, traffic control, and downtown revitalization?
It totally does. CPTED is a benign approach to improving good planning. Accordingly, CPTED is compatible with every type of planning model, including functional planning, livable cities, urban villages, neotraditionalism, New Urbanism, and transportation-oriented development.

In addition, many cities have introduced CPTED into their Creating Safer Communities programs. The city of Cincinnati, Ohio, for example, put together a program titled Tactics to Reduce Crime Through CPTED.

Question 14: Are CPTED concepts of value in the design and management of interior spaces?
Yes! It is another common misconception that CPTED is strictly an outdoor- or site-planning concept, perhaps because its contemporary stimulus has come from urban planners. However, the interior design of workspaces and schools has often been successful in improving quality of life, productivity, and safety. Convenience stores have been leaders in the interior use of CPTED. Malls and shopping centers have dramatically altered interior uses. Sales have been enhanced and losses reduced. Many designers and decorators have discovered that *feng shui*, the Chinese art of promoting harmony in space, is closely aligned with CPTED concepts in that it acknowledges users' reactions to the spaces they occupy and visit. Interior design research has demonstrated that the more employees who share a common workspace and the less differentiated it is, the lower will be their morale, the lower the productive output, and the greater the tolerance of dishonesty.

Question 15: Do CPTED concepts have any value in dealing with concerns about youth development and delinquency prevention?
Very much so! CPTED principles in public housing, building on the concept of defensible space, have demonstrated that children who grow up in large, undifferentiated spaces are less likely to develop respect for property values and rights; they exhibit more disruptive behavior in school, and they experience more maladaptive behavior as adults. CPTED in school design and management has had a dramatic impact on increased achievement and reduced behavioral problems. CPTED has worked in parks, recreation facilities, and retail environments where children spend a considerable amount of time, often unsupervised by their parents.

Question 16: Who should use CPTED concepts?
Everyone! Everybody has to be concerned about the effective and productive use of space. Almost everyone should be concerned about safety and security. Interestingly, CPTED is very important in the design and management of juvenile detention, group home, and correctional facilities. It would be hard to identify a profession or a human activity that does not have a responsibility for and interest in safety and security. There is no one "CPTED profession," but professionals across all disciplines have the opportunity to use and adapt

CPTED concepts within their own areas of expertise and in their interactions with other professionals.

Question 17: What are the important steps required in conducting a CPTED review of proposed site plans or of existing facilities?

The "Three-D" approach to the assessment of the built environment or proposed events has proven to be the most straightforward and simplest to use. This process starts with *designation* of purpose. It is not enough to name the human function; the behavioral objectives of the function or activity must be clearly articulated. Once the behavioral objectives are clear, the designated purpose must be *defined* in terms of rules, laws, signs, and cultural practices to reinforce the desired behaviors. Designation and definition lead to the *design* phase, in which decisions have to made along two dimensions. These are physiological and psychological functions. Physiological functions support and facilitate the carrying out of the human function. The psychological dimension focuses on controlling behavior. The Three-D process is divided into a series of diagnostic questions that may be used to assess proposed plans as well as existing facilities.

Question 18: What types of data are required to conduct CPTED assessments?

Five types of data are required: crime/incident, demographics, land use, observations, and user or resident input. Each of these types of data has strengths and weaknesses. All are required to provide a clear picture of the extent to which the basic concepts of CPTED are operating as desired. Observations conducted in a systematic manner by a team composed of a mixture of professions are of immeasurable value. With a minimum of training and orientation, an interdisciplinary team can conduct an adequate CPTED assessment.

Question 19: Can CPTED concepts and strategies be used to help eliminate or control problem businesses and high-crime housing locations?

Yes! CPTED concepts rely on the effective use of ordinances and codes to maintain territorial control and order. Zoning, business regulation, architectural guidelines, traffic laws, housing codes, and life-safety requirements are all tools that can be used to control problem situations. For example, a building's history of code violations can open the door for an interdisciplinary team to exercise powers of local government in a process that is referred to as *intrusive code enforcement*. There are literally thousands of examples of the successful use of local codes and ordinances by CPTED teams to clean up problem neighborhoods and businesses.

Question 20: Do CPTED concepts conflict with the increasingly popular planning processes identified as New Urbanism, neo-traditional planning, livable cities, and transportation-oriented development?

The answer is an emphatic no! The key is to understand that CPTED is linked to a commitment to good planning, to using a process for determining what is appropriate for an individual site or human activity. The CPTED process relies on the requirement to carefully orchestrate planning activities and to integrate the best of all planning models. Contemporary misconceptions have been instigated by conflict over strategies and the failure to recognize that CPTED is a planning process. Strategies will change as new technologies and methods are developed, but the process has been and will always be the same. Community planners and builders 5,000 years ago were using the same commonsense process that is inherent in contemporary CPTED programs. This process is based on an understanding of human nature and how people respond to the environment.

3

CPTED CONCEPTS AND STRATEGIES

CHAPTER OUTLINE

I think one of the things that everyone liked about Tim's work was that he always promoted using a commonsense approach to security and working efficiently as possible to achieve the desired results.

—Marianna Perry, MS, CPP, former director of the National Crime Prevention Institute

Background

Do you know that the signaling of the traffic light at the end of your block or just down the street from the intersection near where you live has a lot to do with the amount of control you and your friends have over your neighborhood? Are you concerned with the scheduling of park programs for youth and the locations of these activities? Were you aware of the fact that the placement of bus stops can help make or break the businesses nearby, thus contributing to the perception that an area is either safe or unstable and unsafe?

Everyone knows that zoning and business regulation contribute to a more controlled and safe community, but do they know that the size, shape, landscaping, and exterior design of local buildings have an impact, too? The design and management of parking lots, storefronts, parks, schools, and just about everything in your community have important connections to the problems of crime and the fear of crime. What can you do about it? Does it take a lot of expertise to understand the relationship among the environment, the roles of noncriminal justice agencies, and crime? The answers to these questions are simple: All it takes is an awareness that there is a relationship between the things that people do naturally—just everyday things—and the amount of surveillance and access control that exists. Both offenders and normal users of space recognize the environmental cues that say, "This is a safe place—or an unsafe place." A lot of experts and sophisticated technology are not required to think about what is going on and to take advantage of natural opportunities to make your community safer. All that is required is good sense.

Environmental approaches to crime prevention and security were made popular by Oscar Newman in his book *Defensible Space*. These concepts have been successfully demonstrated in schools and commercial, residential, and transportation areas. They are now being widely adopted by industry because they contribute to productivity. City governments are finding out that it is a lot less expensive to design crime prevention into the way things are done than to hire extra police or to pay for extra protection that can make the community look like a fortress instead of a nice place to live. For several thousand years, an awareness of how the environment shapes human behavior has been used by architects, city planners, and residential dwellers to elicit desired behaviors. Greek temples in the large

Sicilian colony were designed to produce fear through the absence of light. Early city-states, such as the Italian city of Florence, designed assembly chambers to create the impression that the roof would cave in, literally, to speed up the legislative process. Modern-day commercial establishments use sound, color, and furniture design to create the illusion (if not the reality) of fast service. McDonald's restaurants and numerous other stores use their physical environments to manipulate our senses and behavior to enhance their sales.

At the national level, the CPTED Program is a synthesis and extension of reports, investigations, studies, and initial demonstrations sponsored by the National Institute of Law Enforcement and Criminal Justice (NILECJ). In turn, many of those activities trace their conceptual content to a variety of NILECJ-sponsored crime prevention and environmental design-related documents, texts, and articles that date back many years. The most significant antecedents of the CPTED Program, dating from 1969, related to the following areas:

- *Studies.* Crimes against small business, neighborhood design techniques for crime prevention, burglary prevention studies, public safety in urban dwellings, architectural design for crime prevention, private police, public housing, patterns of robbery and burglary, street lighting, hardware performance and standards, and "defensible space."
- *Programs.* The Federal Crime Insurance Program, development of Model Security Codes and Guidelines, equipment standards program, vertical policing programs in public housing, architectural design experiments in public housing and residential areas, and training in crime prevention.

These prior efforts led the NILECJ to initiate the CPTED program as a comprehensive effort to create physical and social conditions through environmental design demonstrations in selected environments (residential, school, commercial, transportation) aimed at reducing crime and fear of crime and at improving the quality of life in these environments. A selected bibliography, sources of information, and related research are found at the end of this volume.

CPTED Concepts

The conceptual thrust of the CPTED programs that the physical environment can be manipulated to produce behavioral effects that will reduce the incidence and fear of crime, thereby improving the quality of life. These behavioral effects can be accomplished by reducing the propensity of the physical environment to support criminal behavior. Environmental design, as used in the CPTED program, is rooted in the design of the human/environment relationship. It embodies several

concepts. The term *environment* includes the people and their physical and social surroundings. However, as a matter of practical necessity, the environment defined for demonstration purposes is that which has recognizable territorial and system limits. It is critical to note that the term *design* includes physical, social, management, and law enforcement directives that seek to affect positively human behavior as people interact with their environment. Thus, the CPTED program seeks to prevent certain specified crimes (and the fear attendant on them) within a specifically defined environment by manipulating variables that are closely related to the environment itself.

The program does not purport to develop crime-prevention solutions in a broad universe of human behavior but rather solutions limited to variables that can be manipulated and evaluated in the specified human/environment relationship. CPTED involves design of physical space in the context of the physical, social, and psychological needs of bona fide users of the space, the normal and expected (or intended) use of the space (the activity or absence of activity planned for the space), and the predictable behavior of both bona fide users and offenders. Therefore, in the CPTED approach, a design is proper if it recognizes the designated use of the space, defines the crime problem incidental to and the solution compatible with the designated use, and incorporates the crime-prevention strategies that enhance (or at least do not impair) the effective use of the space. CPTED draws not only on physical and urban design but also on contemporary thinking in behavioral and social science, law enforcement, and community organization.

The emphasis on design and use deviates from the target-hardening approach to crime prevention. Traditional target hardening focuses predominantly on denying access to a crime target through physical or artificial barrier techniques such as walls, fences, gates, locks, grilles, and the like.

Target hardening often leads to constraints on use, access, and enjoyment of the hardened environment. Moreover, the traditional approach tends to overlook opportunities for natural access control and surveillance. The term *natural* refers to deriving access control and surveillance results as a byproduct of the normal and routine use of the environment. It is possible to adapt normal and natural uses of the environment to accomplish the effects of artificial or mechanical hardening and surveillance. Nevertheless, CPTED employs pure target-hardening strategies, either to test their effectiveness compared to natural strategies or when they appear to be justified as not unduly impairing the effective use of the environment.

For example, a design strategy of improved street lighting must be planned and evaluated in terms of the behavior it promotes or deters and the use impact of the lighted (and related) areas in terms of all users of the area (offenders, victims, other permanent or casual users). Any strategies related to the lighting strategy (e.g., block watch, 9-1-1 emergency service, police patrol [COPS]) must be evaluated in the same regard. This reflects the comprehensiveness of the CPTED design approach in focusing on both the proper design and effective use of the physical environment. Additionally, the concept of proper design and effective use emphasizes the designed relationship among strategies to ensure that the desired results are achieved. It has been observed that improved street lighting alone (a design strategy) is ineffective against crime without the conscious and active support of citizens (in reporting what they see) and of police (in responding and conducting surveillance). CPTED involves the effort to integrate design, citizen and community action, and law enforcement strategies to accomplish surveillance consistent with the design and use of the environment.

CPTED Strategies

There are three overlapping strategies in CPTED:

1. Natural access control
2. Natural surveillance
3. Territorial reinforcement

Access control and surveillance have been the primary design concepts of physical design programs. At the outset of the CPTED program, access control and surveillance—preexisting as conspicuous concepts in the field of crime prevention through environmental design—received major attention. Access control and surveillance are not mutually exclusive classifications, since certain strategies achieve both and strategies in one classification typically are mutually supportive of the other. However, the operational thrust of each is distinctly different, and the differences must be recognized in performing analysis, research, design, implementation, and evaluation.

Access control is a design concept directed primarily at decreasing crime opportunity. Access control strategies are typically classified as organized (e.g., security officers), mechanical (e.g., locks), and natural (e.g., spatial definition). The primary thrust of an access control strategy is to deny access to a crime target and to create a perception of risk in offenders. Surveillance is a design concept directed primarily at keeping intruders under observation. Therefore, the primary thrust of a surveillance strategy is to facilitate observation, although it may have the effect of an access control strategy by effectively keeping intruders out because of an increased perception of risk.

Surveillance strategies are typically classified as organized (e.g., police patrol), mechanical (e.g., lighting), and natural (e.g., windows).

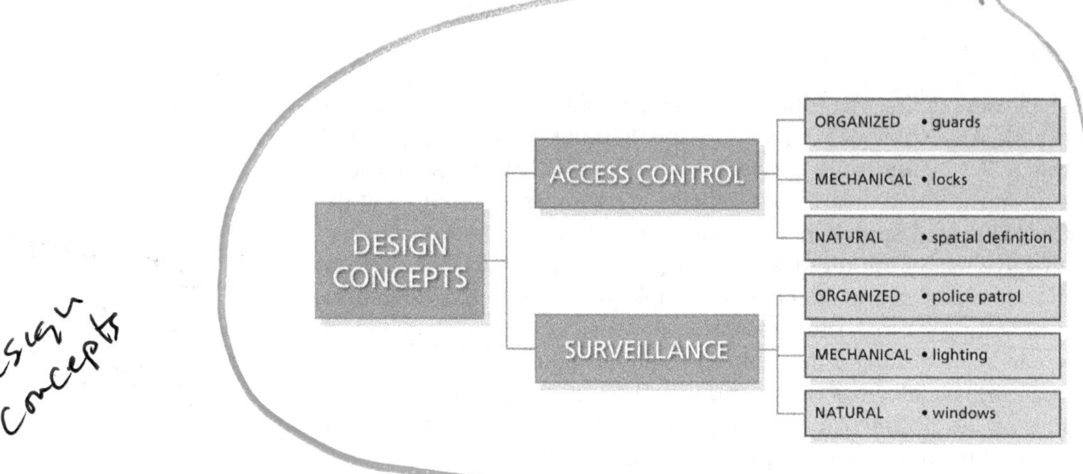

Figure 3.1 Typical access control and surveillance concepts and classifications.

These typical concepts and strategies are illustrated in Figure 3.1. Traditionally, access control and surveillance, as design concepts, have emphasized mechanical or organized crime-prevention techniques while overlooking, minimizing, or ignoring attitudes, motivation, and use of the physical environment. More recent approaches to physical design of environments have shifted the emphasis to natural crime-prevention techniques, attempting to use natural opportunities presented by the environment for crime prevention. This shift in emphasis led to the concept of territoriality. The concept of territoriality (elaborated most fully to date in the public housing environment) suggests that physical design can contribute to a sense of territoriality. That is, physical design can create or extend a sphere of influence so that users develop a sense of proprietorship—a sense of territorial influence—and potential offenders perceive that territorial influence.

At the same time, it was recognized that natural access control and surveillance contributed to a sense of territoriality, making it effective for crime prevention. Natural access control and surveillance will promote more responsiveness from users in protecting their territory (e.g., more security awareness, reporting, reacting) and promote greater perception of risk by offenders.

Maintenance

Finally, care and maintenance allow for the continued use of a space for its intended purpose, as well as contributing to territorial reinforcement. Deterioration and blight indicate less concern and control by the intended users of a site and indicate a greater tolerance of disorder. Proper maintenance protects the public health, safety, and welfare in all existing structures, residential and nonresidential, and on all existing premises by establishing minimum requirements and acceptable standards. Maintenance is the responsibility of the owners, operators, and occupants.

Furthermore, the effort to achieve a balance between design for crime prevention and design for effective use of environments contributed to the shift in focus from organized and mechanical strategies *per se* to natural strategies. This was because natural strategies exploited the opportunities of the given environment, both to naturally and routinely facilitate access control and surveillance and to reinforce positive behavior in the use of the environment. The concept reflects a preference, where feasible, to reinforce existing or new activities or to otherwise reinforce the behavior of environment users so that crime prevention flows naturally and routinely from the activity being promoted.

The conceptual shift from organized and mechanical to natural strategies has oriented the CPTED program to develop plans that emphasize natural access control and surveillance and territorial reinforcement. The conceptual relationship suggested by this shift is reflected in Figure 3.2.

Although conceptually distinct, it is important to realize that these strategy categories tend to overlap in practice. It is perhaps most useful to think of territorial reinforcement as the umbrella concept, comprising all natural surveillance principles, which in turn comprises all access control principles. It is not practical to think of territorial reinforcement, natural surveillance, and access control as independent strategies because, for example, access control operates to denote transitional zones, not necessarily impenetrable barriers. If these symbolic or psychological barriers are to succeed in controlling access by demarcating specific spaces for specific individuals, potential offenders must perceive that unwarranted intrusion will elicit protective territorial responses from those who have legitimate access. Similarly, natural surveillance operates to increase the likelihood that intrusion will be observed by individuals who care but are not officially responsible for regulating the use and treatment of spaces. If people observe inappropriate behavior but do nothing about it, then the most carefully planned natural surveillance tactics are useless in terms of stopping crime and vandalism.

The Three-D Approach

For CPTED to be a success, it must be understandable and practical for the normal users of the space. That is, the normal residents of a neighborhood and the people who work in buildings or commercial areas must be able to use these concepts. Why? Because these people know more about what is going on in that environment and they have

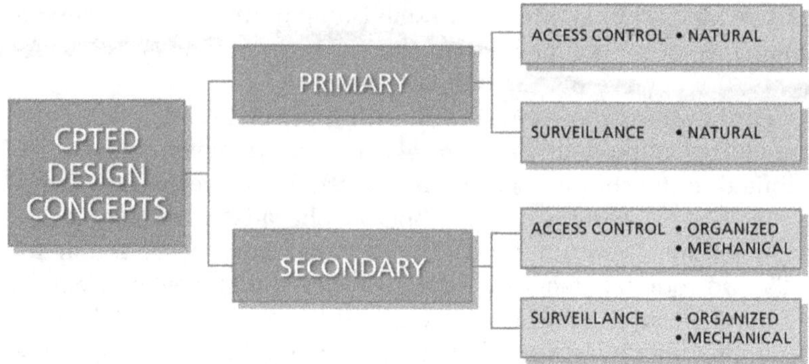

Figure 3.2 The conceptual shift from organized and mechanical concepts has led to the natural CPTED concepts.

a vested interest (their own well-being) in ensuring that their immediate environment operates properly. The technologist or specialist, who may be a traffic engineer, city planner, architect, or security specialist, should not alone be allowed to shoulder the responsibility for safety and security. The specialist needs to follow the dictates of the users of the space, because he can often be swayed by misperceptions or by the conflicting demands of his professional competition.

The Three-D approach to space assessment provides a simple guide for the layperson to use in determining the appropriateness of how her space is designed and used. The Three-D concept is based on the three functions or dimensions of human space:

1. All human space has some designated purpose.
2. All human space has social, cultural, legal, or physical definitions that prescribe the desired and acceptable behaviors.
3. All human space is designed to support and control the desired behaviors.

Using the Three-D approach as a guide, we can evaluate space by asking the following types of questions.

Designation

- What is the designated purpose of this space?
- What was it originally intended to be used for?
- How well does the space support its current use? Its intended use?
- Is there conflict?

Definition

- How is the space defined?
- Is it clear who owns it?

- Where are its borders?
- Are there social or cultural definitions that affect how that space is used?
- Are the legal or administrative rules clearly set out and reinforced in policy?
- Are there signs?
- Is there conflict or confusion between the space's designated purpose and its definition?

Design

- How well does the physical design support the intended function?
- How well does the physical design support the definition of the desired or accepted behaviors?
- Does the physical design conflict with or impede the productive use of the space or the proper functioning of the intended human activity?
- Is there confusion or conflict in terms of the manner in which the physical design is intended to control behavior?

The three CPTED strategies of territorial reinforcement, natural access control, and natural surveillance are inherent in the Three-D concept. Does the space clearly belong to someone or some group? Is the intended use clearly defined? Does the physical design match the intended use? Does the design provide the means for normal users to naturally control the activities, to control access, and to provide surveillance?

Once a basic self-assessment has been conducted, the Three Ds may then be turned around as a simple means of guiding decisions about what to do with human space. The proper functions have to be matched with space that can support them—with space that can effectively support territorial identity, natural access control, and surveillance—and intended behaviors have to be indisputable and be reinforced in social, cultural, legal, and administrative terms or norms. The design has to ensure that the intended activity can function well, and it has to directly support the control of behavior.

Examples of Strategies in Action

There are hundreds of examples of CPTED strategies in practice today. In each example there is a mixture of the three CPTED strategies that is appropriate to the setting and to the particular security or crime problem. Some of the examples were created in the direct application of CPTED concepts. Others were borrowed from real-life situations. The common thread is the primary emphasis on naturalness—simply doing things that you already have to do, but doing them a little better. Some examples of CPTED strategy activities are:

- Providing clear border definition of controlled space
- Providing clearly marked transitional zones that indicate movement from public to semipublic to private space
- Relocating gathering areas to locations with natural surveillance and access control or to locations away from the view of would-be offenders
- Placing safe activities in unsafe locations to bring along the natural surveillance of these activities and to increase the perception of safety for normal users and of risk for offenders
- Placing unsafe activities in safe spots to overcome the vulnerability of these activities with the natural surveillance and access control of the safe area
- Redesignating the use of space to provide natural barriers to conflicting activities
- Improving scheduling of space to allow for effective use and appropriate critical intensity
- Redesigning space to increase the perception or reality of natural surveillance
- Overcoming distance and isolation through improved communications and design efficiencies

Use of Information

It goes without saying that all important decisions should be based on good information. Especially where the design and use of the physical environment is at stake, it is imperative that at least five basic types of information be collected and used. Unless we have a rational basis for making informed decisions, the same mistakes that generated the original problem will continue to be made.

The five basic types of information needed for good CPTED planning are crime analysis information, demographic information, land-use information, observations, and resident or user interviews. This information does not have to be sophisticated. It exists in a fundamental form in every community or location. Moreover, unless it can be presented in its most basic form, it is of little value. For instance, very little can be done with a statistical measure that says burglaries are up by 5 percent. Much more can be done with a crime map that shows a clustering of burglaries in a specific block (see Figure 3.3).

Even more can be done when one finds that the burglar used an alleyway as his approach to a series of related offenses because it afforded a good cover for his vehicle. The other bits of information

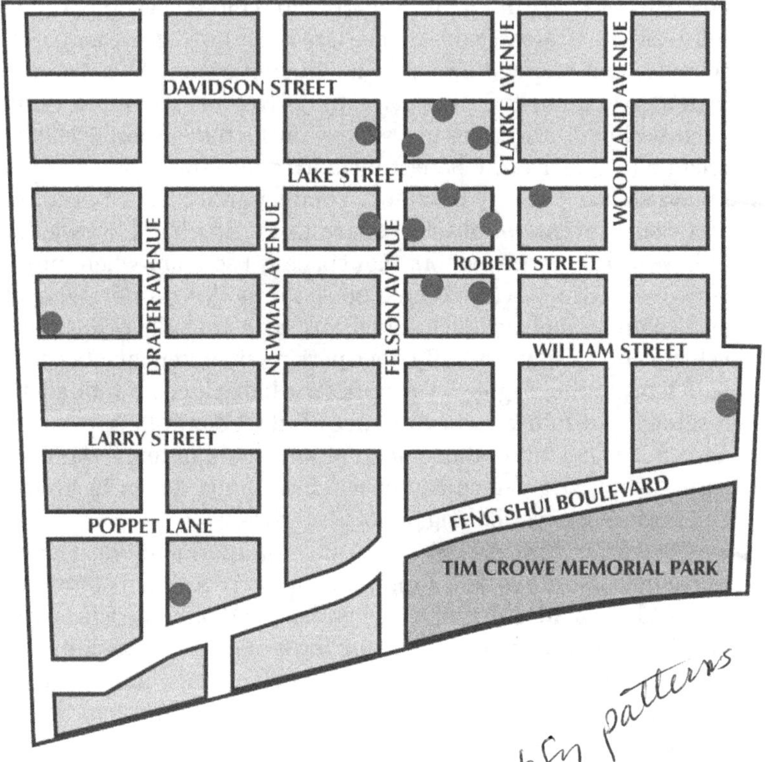

Figure 3.3 A geographic concentration pattern.

that are needed should be available in simple, usable formats. The following is a simple guide to each type of information:

- *Crime analysis*. This type of information is available in every police department; it is obtained by plotting offenses on a wall map and organizing the information on crime reports for the major purpose of identifying patterns of criminal activity. There are two basic types of patterns: geographic and similar offense.
- *Demographic*. This is information that describes the nature of the population for a given city, district, or neighborhood. It is available through city planning departments or the city manager's or mayor's office. Another source of this type of information is the census bureau and the city and county data books that can be found in most public libraries.
- *Land use*. City planning departments, zoning boards, traffic engineering councils, and local councils of government have information and maps that describe and depict the physical allocations

and uses of land. Simple wall maps with colored sections showing residential areas, commercial areas, industrial areas, parks, schools, and traffic flows can be of immeasurable assistance in understanding the physical setting. Natural boundaries and neighborhoods are easier to visualize on such maps, especially in relation to land use and pedestrian and traffic flows.

- *Observations*. It is very helpful to conduct either formal or informal visual reviews of physical space to get first-hand knowledge of how, when, and by whom that space is used and where problems may arise. Environmental cues are the key to normal user and offender behavior. Observations may include pedestrian/vehicle counts, on- and off-street parking, maintenance of yards and fences, the degree of proprietary behaviors prohibited by residents and/or users, the presence of either controlling or avoidance behaviors, and other potential indicators of territorial concern such as the percentage of window blinds drawn in homes and businesses overlooking parks or schools.
- *Resident or user interviews*. This source of information is needed to balance the other data sources. People's perceptions of where they feel safe and where they feel endangered often vary from the locations on crime maps where the most offenses occur. It is vital to determine the residents' or users' perceptions and extent of identity with the surrounding space, what affects their behavior or reactions as they move about, and what they think the needs are.

Any attempt to skip the basics in favor of more complex forms of information gathering or analysis often obscures the picture. Professionals often suppress the active participation of residents or space users by relying on complex modes of analysis. This is dangerous because it can cause some very basic ideas or explanations to be overlooked. It is axiomatic that very little good will be accomplished without the full and active involvement of the users of space.

The best way to understand the information and present it to others is through visual means. Maps and transparent overlays are useful means of comparing the five types of information that are needed in CPTED planning. Figure 3.4 presents an example of a time-of-day crime map.

Some Benefits of CPTED Planning Activities

In addition to dealing with the reduction of crime and fear problems, other benefits of CPTED planning include the following:

- *Treatment of crime problems at various environmental scales*. The CPTED process for identifying crime/environment problems, selecting CPTED strategies, and initiating, implementing, and

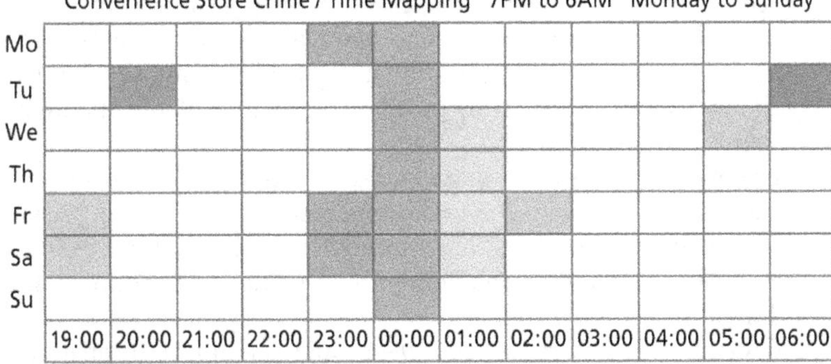

Figure 3.4 Time-of-day analysis.

evaluating anticrime projects can be applied to entire neighborhoods or types of institutional settings within a city, such as secondary schools, or the process can be applied equally well to a small geographic area or to one particular institution.

- *Integration of prevention approaches.* CPTED principles are derived from an opportunity model of criminal behavior that assumes that the offender's behavior can be accounted for by understanding how and under what circumstances variables in the environment interact to induce crime. Once an assessment of the opportunity structure is made, appropriate strategies can be designed and integrated into a coordinated, consistent program.
- *Identification of short- and long-term goals.* Comprehensive, broad-based programs like CPTED have ultimate goals that may take years to accomplish. Unlike CPTED, however, many programs fail to develop short-term or proximate goals and adequate ways to measure their success. The CPTED approach includes an evaluation framework that details proximate goals relating to increased access control, surveillance, and territorial reinforcement. The rationale is that the ultimate program success is directly related to its success in achieving the proximate goals.
- *Encouragement of collective responses to problems.* The CPTED emphasis is on increasing the capacity of residents to act in concert rather than individually. Strategies are aimed at fostering citizen participation and strengthening social cohesion.
- *Interdisciplinary approach to urban problems.* An explicit policy of interdisciplinary teaming ensures effective cooperation among diverse city departments such as public works, social services, economic development, police, and so forth. Each participant benefits from exposure to the responsibilities, jurisdiction, and skills of the others.

- *Encouragement of better police/community relations.* A key strategy is to coordinate law enforcement and community service activities with the result of improving police/community relations and developing an anticrime program that is not solely dependent on enforcement agencies.
- *Development of security guidelines and standards.* CPTED programming can lead to the creation of security criteria for newly constructed or modified environments to avoid planning and design decisions that inadvertently provide opportunities for crime.
- *Assistance in urban revitalization.* Through its impact on physical, social, and economic conditions, CPTED can be instrumental in revitalizing communities, including downtown areas. Once business leaders, investors, and other citizens perceive that a comprehensive effort is underway to reduce crime and fear, there will be an improvement in community identity and cohesiveness.
- *Acquisition of development funds.* The incorporation of CPTED into existing programs can provide additional jurisdiction for awarding grants, loans, and community development funds.
- *Institutionalization of crime-prevention policies and practices.* CPTED projects can create a local management capability and expertise to maintain ongoing projects. This capability can be incorporated into existing citizen organizations or municipal agencies. Not all of these situations will apply to every local jurisdiction, and there may be additional applications not covered by the preceding examples. It is important that local decision makers establish objectives that they hope to achieve through a CPTED project. These can range from a narrowly drawn focus that aims at a single purpose to a broad and comprehensive goal with multiple benefits. Hence, a decision about the project and its objectives will be an important determinant of the type of CPTED project to be initiated, its management requirements, its resource commitments, and similar policy decisions.

An Ounce of Prevention: A New Role for Law Enforcement Support of Community Development

The well-worn cliché coined by Benjamin Franklin, "An ounce of prevention is worth a pound of cure," seems an appropriate way of introducing a new role for law enforcement agencies in supporting the public and private activities of communities. Law enforcement agencies are the only major community and governmental services that are not included in the review and approval process of planning, zoning, traffic, and environmental design decisions. Why is it easy for a law enforcement officer who is visiting another city to pick out the problem neighborhoods and business areas? The answer is, because she has learned to associate certain environmental conditions with social, economic, and crime problems. The same is often true for non-law enforcement visitors.

The degree of attractiveness of any location says a lot about its owners and the type of people who frequent the place. But it can also say a lot about the mistakes committed by public agencies and private developers—mistakes that end up making victims (and sometimes hostages) out of the residents. Whatever the interpretation, the atmosphere of any area gives off environmental cues that tell an individual whether he is safe or unsafe.

Consequently, there is a resurgence of interest in the concept of CPTED. The state of Florida has gone so far as to pass a law entitled the Safe Neighborhoods Act, which provides legal authority and funding for the implementation of CPTED strategies. The CPTED concept calls for integrating natural approaches to crime prevention into building design and neighborhood planning rather than responding to crime problems after they materialize. But what has this got to do with law enforcement? What right has law enforcement to be involved in planning, zoning, and architectural design decisions? Is it not true that law enforcement agencies are already too overburdened with calls for service and for investigations to take on another function? Isn't this really someone else's job? Couldn't law enforcement get sued for suggesting a change that does not work?

There are a number of compelling reasons for law enforcement to be involved in CPTED:

1. CPTED concepts have been proven to enhance community activities while reducing crime problems.
2. CPTED concepts are fundamental to traditional law enforcement values in terms of helping the community to function properly.
3. CPTED requires the unique information sources and inherent knowledge of the community that is endemic to the law enforcement profession.
4. CPTED problems and issues bear a direct relationship to repeat calls for service and to crime-producing situations.
5. CPTED methods and techniques can directly improve property values, business profitability, and industrial productivity, thereby enhancing local tax bases.

Law enforcement agencies, regardless of size, must be involved formally in the review and approval process of community and business projects. Their participation must be active and creative rather than passive and reactive. Moreover, any such involvement should not be understood to expose the agencies to possible litigation, since it is the role of law enforcement in CPTED to provide additional information and concerns that may not have occurred to the persons who are responsible (and qualified) to make changes to the environment. The expression "Pay me now or pay me later" conveys the idea that the early involvement of a knowledgeable law enforcement agency in the conceptualization and planning of community projects can lead to improvements in the quality of life and to reductions in the fear and incidence of crime. This early involvement is one of the most cost-effective methods of crime prevention.

CPTED Definitions

The concise description of CPTED, based on the definition used by the National Crime Prevention Institute (NCPI), is "the proper design and effective use of the built environment can lead to a reduction in the fear and incidence of crime, an improvement in the quality of life, and enhanced profitability." This description says, basically, that the better we manage our human and physical resources, the better the outcomes for everyone. In a residential neighborhood, profitability also translates to the protection of property values and enhanced conditions for residents. In a business neighborhood, profit translates to economic growth opportunities, employment, and overall attractiveness (as well as tax benefits). In both situations the byproduct is crime prevention and, quite simply, better communities.

CPTED Problems

One problem with all this is that even today some members of the public and some law enforcement administrators assume that the role of the police is limited to "trail them, nail them, and jail them." Public administrators sometimes find it expedient to limit each local government agency to its most visible task, thereby reducing interagency conflict and avoiding consolidated or collective actions that may be hard to control. Crime and crime prevention cannot be restricted to the law enforcement function unless we want to perpetuate the practice of closing the barn door after the horse gets out. Instead, we must acknowledge the necessity for integrated program planning and support.

Reported crime figures are always just the tip of the iceberg regarding the true extent of crime, fraud, cheating, and dishonesty in any jurisdiction that you might want to name. Any reasonable analysis can't help but conclude that purely reactive law enforcement responses are inappropriate. Something more fundamental than public education and gadget-oriented crime-prevention programs is required. Many environmental issues have surfaced over the past 40 years that led to the conclusion that CPTED will remain one of the more important (but not exclusive) crime-prevention initiatives for the foreseeable future.

Perhaps the most basic of these issues is the discovery that so many of the environmental factors that we take for granted have something to do with crime. Moreover, it has been observed that many community and government functions seem to exist or coexist in a mutually exclusive manner, even while appearing to cooperate. For instance, urban planners and traffic engineers are involved in approving new commercial construction projects. It has been found that many of their standards and requirements have gone unchallenged. Sometimes they agree on the same standard but for different reasons. Over many years of attempted collaboration, it has become commonplace for planners, transportation engineers, developers, public housing officials, and code enforcement authorities to seem to coordinate and cooperate through subtle conflict. That is, instead of openly fighting, they establish territories and stick to them, keeping their noses out of each other's bailiwicks.

Consequently, many fundamental errors slip through, resulting in failed business areas and declining neighborhoods that stand as a permanent legacy to a failure to communicate.

Following are some environmental problems and issues that are a small sample of areas in which a CPTED effort may help:

- *One-way street systems* have been found to improve traffic flow, but they can also create dead zones for business, with resulting crime or fear of crime that deters development efforts.
- *Through traffic in neighborhoods* has been found to be detrimental to residential housing values, stability, and crime rates.
- *Downtown projects* continue to fail by making fundamental errors that reduce natural surveillance and natural access control, resulting in the loss of desired users and domination by unwanted users.
- *Fortress effects* are produced by designers of convention centers, hotels, banks, senior citizen housing, and parking-lot structures. These destroy the surrounding land uses and create a "no-man's land."
- *Bleed-off parking* enhances conflict between commercial and residential land uses; both lose.
- *Store design and management,* if done poorly, can actually reduce business and increase victimization of employees and customers.
- *Mall and major event facility parking* areas with poorly planned access control and layout can produce traffic congestion and become magnets for undesirable activity.
- *School and institutional design* can inadvertently create unsurvivable and dysfunctional areas, resulting in increased behavioral

and crime problems and overall impediments to successful operations (e.g., student achievement in schools).

- *Public housing and affordable housing* can become projects that serve as magnets for transients, as opposed to local poor, with further detrimental effects on existing neighborhoods.

Nearly every environmental situation or location is amenable to the application of CPTED concepts. The law enforcement agency can assist in asking the right questions and in supplying the right kind of information to help the community to make more informed decisions.

Someone has to politely challenge the one-dimensional decisions that are too often made by those individuals with the responsibility to develop, manage, and control our environment. Someone also has to challenge the foundation for many of these decisions. An example of this occurred many years ago in a northern Midwest community. The police department had been incurring excessive overtime costs for a number of years as a result of the popularity of jogging and bicycle events. Event organizers planned the routes and activities, then relied on the police to secure the routes. Nobody questioned the basic routing until a police sergeant who was trained in CPTED asked the question, "Why are you racing on this street pattern?" The sergeant who asked this question had a personal motivation: He wanted to run in the planned event but could not because the chief of police had assigned him to extra duty to supervise a team of officers assigned to the race. The response to his question was, "It seems to be a good idea." After the initial shock of realizing that the police had been holding the bag for a number of years, the sergeant helped the event planners select a route that reduced police personnel requirements by one-half. The race was still a success!

What does a law enforcement agency have to do to conduct CPTED reviews without embarrassing itself? How does the agency go about getting anyone to listen or even to allow the agency to get involved in the first place? First, the head of the agency needs to make the commitment. Second, someone has to study the CPTED concept. CPTED is much easier than it appears initially; many excellent training and orientation programs are available. Third, the agency head has to sell the concept and request formal involvement in the local review and approval process. This is the tricky part! It is easy to sell CPTED if it appears that it will help the other agencies or developers meet their own objectives. It is hard to sell if it appears to be simply another type of crime-prevention activity. The law enforcement administrator must adopt the attitude and priority system reflected in these basic CPTED questions:

1. What are you trying to accomplish in this space or project?
2. How may we help you do it better?

The law enforcement agency is not in the business of telling other professionals how to do their jobs. The role of law enforcement in CPTED is to ask questions, share ideas, and provide information that would otherwise be unavailable to builders, designers, and planners.

"Clean and Well-Lighted Places": A Natural Approach to Retail Security

"One to show and one to go" is a maxim of merchandising and good business accounting. Materials management experts have developed the art of knowing just how much inventory to order to meet merchandising needs while holding down carrying costs. It has also been a common assumption that merchandising and security concepts are contradictory. But is it good business to have a dirty, cluttered store with poor visibility and lighting? Do high gondolas and shelves actually increase sales, or are they really for employee convenience? After all, the job of constantly replenishing inventory is a boring and tedious task. Everyone knows that you have to store the inventory somewhere, so why not on the sales floor? In some retail sectors there is an almost unquestioned acceptance of shrinkage (the theft of merchandise), often justified on the basis of trade-off analysis and risk retention. Young businesspeople working in this type of environment can develop a strong belief that good business and good security are incompatible. Nobody really wants a costumer frisked every time he comes in to buy a gallon of milk (or a fur coat). Many retailers are worried that the presence of armed guards and extensive security measures will turn away customers—and they are probably right.

Years of experiments and practical applications in the field have continually demonstrated that the CPTED concept works in all environmental scales. That is, it has direct applications to commercial, residential, transportation, recreational, and institutional environments. It has worked at scales as small as a single room and as large as an entire community. Its commercial and industrial uses have repeatedly supported the traditional notion that the better one manages human and physical resources, the greater the profit and the smaller the losses. Clearly, effective resource management, which leads to increased profitability, results in fewer security problems.

A store that is attractive, well lighted, and open is more appealing to customers, especially in the convenience industry, which thrives on impulse stopping and buying. A store that is profitable has to depend on the enthusiastic and dedicated support of its staff. Pride in one's work and environment stimulates extended territorial concern. Honest customers and employees feel safer and more visible in clean, well-lighted places. They feel the presence and controlling behaviors of others. Conversely, a dirty and poorly managed store engenders little pride on the part of the honest employee, which reduces territorial concern and promotes avoidance behaviors.

A poorly managed and unkempt store also introduces the possibility of civil negligence. The failure of proprietors to establish reasonable measures to protect their products, employees, and customers will be used against them in determining out-of-court settlements as well as in trials. Poor inventory control and accounting may even suggest some liability in the area of product tampering or poisoning. A clean, well-lighted store in which the proprietors and customers are actively exhibiting controlling behaviors simply tells others that only accepted behaviors will be tolerated.

CPTED is a small part of the total set of concepts involved in loss prevention and asset protection, but it is an important concept for the business community because it emphasizes the integration of security concepts into what has to be done anyway, before additional funds are expended on security officers or security devices.

CPTED planners classify security strategies into three categories:

1. *Organized.* Labor-intensive security whereby the cost is extracurricular to the normal functions and requirements of human space (e.g., security officers).
2. *Mechanical.* Capital- or hardware-intensive security whereby the cost is, once again, extracurricular to the normal functions and requirements of space (e.g., fences, alarms, cameras).
3. *Natural.* The integration of security and behavior concepts into how human and physical resources are used (e.g., spatial definition, placement of workstations, location of windows).

The CPTED planner merely tries to maximize the use of natural strategies before using the more costly organized and mechanical ones that may actually serve as impediments to profitable operations. The conventional security concepts of access controls and surveillance are enhanced by the emphasis on natural approaches, with the added feature of increased territorial behavior and expanded proprietary concern.

It is fundamental to this behavioral approach that the CPTED planner seek to expand the territorial concern of the owner and normal user of space. It is equally important to present behavioral and environmental cues that tell normal users of space that they are safe. The same cue has an inverse effect on the abnormal user or potential offender by increasing her perception of risk. That is, the design of the space and the way people are behaving gives the impression that the abnormal user will be observed, stopped, or apprehended. Accordingly, the CPTED planner learns to differentiate among the unique differences and values of various users. In the design or redesign of store layouts, the owner must focus on several kinds of individuals:

- *Normal users,* or people whom you desire to be in a certain space
- *Abnormal users,* or people whom you do not desire to be in that space
- *Observers,* or people who have to be in that space to support the human function

Strategies are aimed at only one, or sometimes all, of these categories of users, depending on the circumstances. Conditions that make the normal user feel safe make others feel at risk of detection. Conversely, conditions that make the normal user feel unsafe make the abnormal user feel at low risk of detection. The CPTED planner must try to determine how space is defined for each of these groups. Values can shift. For instance, when school lets out in the middle of the afternoon, three or four boys coming into a shopping mall would be desirable visitors. If the same boys came back at 9:30 P.M. when the mall was closing, and they'd taken off their school clothes, were dressed in strange ways, and had dyed their hair orange, they would be less than desirable. Another example: Suppose you are a casual shopper at a convenience store. At one store, you see a group of kids with orange hair in the parking lot. You look down the street and see a well-lighted and appealing store with no one outside. Is there any doubt which store you would patronize?

This shows how the environment can affect the way people feel about your place of business. The physical environment affects people's behavior and perceptions, which not only impact attitudes but also impact productivity and loss prevention. Commercial and retail establishments have always used the physical environment to affect customer perceptions and behavior. CPTED adds a new dimension by incorporating these elements into space design and management:

- *Natural access control.* Your space should give some natural indication of where people are allowed and are not allowed. Don't depend just on locks and guards, but make security part of the layout.
- *Natural surveillance.* Again, traditional factors like good lighting are important, but don't overlook a natural factor such as a strategically placed window or the placement of an employee workstation.
- *Territorial reinforcement.* This is an umbrella concept, embodying all natural surveillance and access control principles. It emphasizes the enhancement of ownership and proprietary behaviors. These concepts can be more important than you suspect. There is one individual, for instance, who has owned five convenience stores for about 20 years. He always felt that environmental concepts were a lot of hogwash. But the neighborhood changed and

disintegrated, and he failed to keep up with it. Now, almost too late, he realizes that you must design your space to cope with your environment.

There are many applications of CPTED to commercial environments. Perhaps the greatest and most valuable lesson being learned is that good store design and merchandising are not incompatible with effective security. Both objectives may be achieved and enhanced through space planning and behavioral concepts. Some examples:

- The convenience industry is using new building shapes to attract, but separate, the construction worker, the juvenile, and the adult impulse buyer.
- Gondolas, shelves, racks, and displays are being dropped to enhance visibility from and into the store as well as within, to improve attractiveness and perceptions of security.
- Parking is being located in front of stores and shops, with good landscaping to screen the unsightliness of autos and pavement but improve perceptions of safe access for people and protection of vehicles.
- Illumination is being increased inside stores at night to suggest a more welcoming atmosphere for the customer who is driving or walking by.
- The location of employee workstations is being selected strategically to increase the perception of surveillance, improved customer convenience, and employee productivity. Employee workstation location and orientation can help increase proprietary concern and cut employee theft.
- Special lease and business license incentives may be used to extend a business owner's and employees' proprietary concern for multiple-purpose or adjacent public space and to increase sales during special events.
- Shopping centers are enclosing parking areas with curbing and landscaping to make them more attractive while limiting the number of access points to those that are perceived to be under surveillance or that may be sealed off, thus cutting off perceived escape routes for abnormal users.
- Shopping centers and adjacent office complexes are using zoned parking based on user need, with systematic closings of zones by time of day, day of week, and other special factors. This increases the probable scrutiny of vehicles that are there at the wrong times.
- Business areas are getting local government to reroute excessive rush-hour or through traffic that bleeds through nonarterial or high-capacity streets. Through traffic has been found to suppress impulse buying (slow driving and parking) because of

higher-speed pressure and driver behavior, and it results in higher numbers of police service calls and crimes.
- Some excessive use of downtown one-way street systems and overemphasis of street design for vehicle movement capacity is being questioned, with an emphasis on providing a more effective balance between the desire to protect business areas versus the need to move commuter traffic.
- Social policies requiring the excessive use of amenities and landscaping in open downtown pedestrian malls is being questioned in view of their tendency to attract unsightly vagrants and associated vandalism as well as to reduce the amount of potential business space.

The list of CPTED applications to the retail environment is potentially endless. Design and use strategies may be employed at any scale if there is the potential for positive effects on employee and customer behavior. Productivity and profit will be enhanced while abnormal users are more visible and aware that they are under greater control and risk. CPTED concepts, creatively applied, can and will improve business, and they may just make it a lot more fun!

CPTED in Low-Income, Public, and Three-Generation Housing

Most concerns about crime problems relate to a high degree of accessibility to housing communities from outside areas. Lighting has been identified as a potential problem, as have space management and design deficiencies that may contribute to the perception of apathy on the part of management and residents. CPTED concepts have been proven to reduce crime and increase the quality of life in many public housing communities. They also are effective in removing many obstacles that prevent law enforcement and social control mechanisms in communities from working effectively to control crime and drug abuse.

Low-income housing communities are victims of community attitudes. Many of the drug dealers and criminals who operate at housing locations are not residents there. The buyers of stolen products and drugs are attracted to public housing sites because of the general perception that these areas are associated with and tolerant of criminal activities.

The following examples of CPTED strategies for low-income and public housing are grouped under the three primary CPTED concepts of natural surveillance, natural access control, and territorial reinforcement (Figure 3.5).

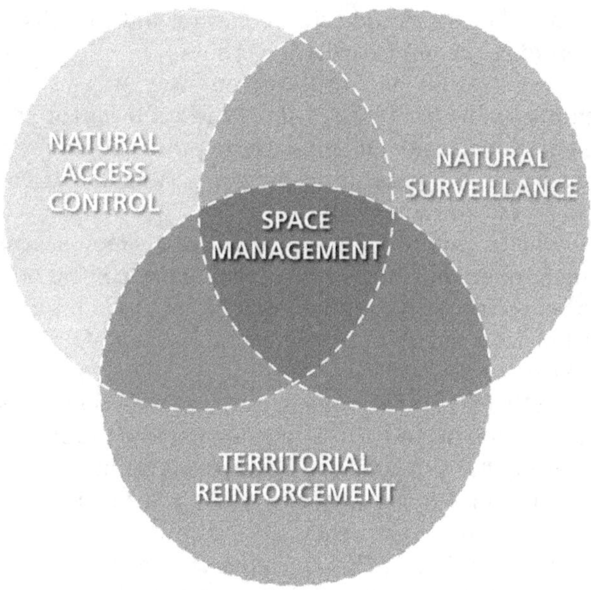

Figure 3.5 When implemented in tandem, natural surveillance, natural access control, and territorial reinforcement create the space management necessary in low-income and public housing.

Natural Surveillance

- Provide magnets for watchers or gatekeepers by increased outdoor use of space (e.g., porches, yard assignment, and gardening).
- Reduce light pollution on bedroom windows to influence residents to leave curtains and blinds open or partially open to create the reality and perception of surveillance.
- Install windows in dead walls on the sides of buildings.
- Install automatically controlled porch lights to create a sea of light at the human scale to allow for better visual identification of faces and to reduce light pollution through the reduction of the use and intensity of overhead mast-mounted lights.
- Place car parking in line-of-sight of residential units or, preferably, immediately in front.
- Install central heating, ventilation, and air conditioning (HVAC) to eliminate the use of window units that block natural surveillance and audio monitoring of outdoor activities. This also significantly improves residents' quality of life.
- Remove walls and hedgerows that produce impediments to natural surveillance. Replace dumpster enclosures and perimeter fencing with transparent materials.

Natural Access Control

- Control vehicle traffic to reduce nonresident through access. This may include closures, one-way streets, or other designs.
- Install traffic chokers and speed bumps to reduce speed and to improve pedestrian safety.
- Install entry monuments to celebrate the identity of the community and to signify the movement from public to private space, as a warning to potential abnormal users.
- Segment parking areas to create enclaves for fewer cars in each and to create one way in and out to promote the perception of potential entrapment for abnormal users of space.

Territorial Reinforcement

- Reduce the number of people sharing a common entrance or stairwell.
- Reduce the number of people sharing a common balcony or gallery.
- Reduce the number of people sharing a common green area.
- Reduce the number of people sharing a common parking area.
- Increase the assignment and active use of yard space.
- Relocate parallel sidewalks away from close proximity to individual units, to create more defensible space for the residents.

Results of CPTED Projects in Neighborhoods[1]

It is important to note that CPTED has had many successful demonstrations in most all environmental settings. These include schools, convenience stores, fast-food restaurants, malls, shopping centers, hospitals, stadiums, transit centers, public housing, hotels, motels, parks, museums, and major event facilities. CPTED has a worldwide success and acceptance rate that is impressive, particularly since it is based on common sense and not some complex theoretical design.

A number of books, journal articles, and publications chronicle CPTED successes. The U.S. Department of Justice has published manuals and guideline reports on the use of CPTED in neighborhood revitalization, parking structures, malls, and small retail stores. The Occupational Safety and Health Administration (OSHA) has adopted advisory guidelines for small businesses that incorporate the CPTED requirements found in the laws of the State of Florida, which provide the minimum standards for store security.

The U.S. Conference of Mayors conducted a major survey of its membership and documented that CPTED has been used in neighborhood revitalization to achieve the following general results:

- Stabilization of property values, including retention and growth
- Increases in owner occupancy

[1] CPTED, *General Guidelines for Designing Safer Communities,* Jan. 20, 2000, City of Virginia Beach, VA, USA.

- Increases in the number of second- and third-generation families
- Increases in the mix of owner occupancy with opportunities for low-income housing
- Increases in average lease terms for residential property rentals
- Increases in business activities
- Reductions in crime and traffic accidents/complaints

The reason CPTED has been so successful in helping to revitalize neighborhoods is that it emphasizes good planning as the means to achieve crime prevention. The key to CPTED is that it is not aimed merely toward crime prevention. Moreover, it is designed to improve the decisions that are made about how a community, organization, or business operates. Good planning helps achieve the objectives of the human activity, which produces the side benefit of reducing exposure to crime and loss.

Numerous additional resources published on the Internet provide insights into CPTED projects, including the extensive Website maintained by the Center for Problem-Oriented Policing (www.popcenter.org/tools/cpted/).

General Liability

In many jurisdictions, responsible governments have kept public housing at an "arm's distance" as a matter of policy to reduce their involvement in the issue over ownership of, and hence responsibility and liability for, properties that are now reaching the end of their useful lives. Many of these properties were built over 80 years ago. Deferred maintenance and capital improvement requirements present some major cost issues that have often resulted in a low priority for budget and policy concern for public housing.

Figure 3.6[2]

[2]Diane Zahm, *Using Crime Prevention Through Environmental Design in Problem Solving*, Funded by COPS, Tool Guide No. 8, 2007.

Housing Recipients

U.S. public housing has focused on the needs of low-income earners throughout most of its history. Other countries provide public housing for working families as well as the poor, which produces more social stability. In some areas, housing authorities have expanded services to include moderate-income earners and working families, which requires more attention to community livability and security to attract these working families.

Neighborhood Planning

Public housing communities and the immediate neighborhoods adjacent to them are linked economically and in quality-of-life issues. In spite of this link, public housing has quite often been viewed as "islands of despair" that divide neighborhoods and areas of cities. Many neighborhood improvement programs have functioned independently and, at times, competitively with public housing communities. Independent agencies within local governments have separate funding sources that they tend to protect. Public sentiment is often misguided regarding the plight of low-income neighborhoods, which can be reflected in local government's policies that do not incorporate public housing concerns within the broader investment in community development.

Law Enforcement

Domestic violence incidents are one of the most frustrating and dangerous events for police intervention. Civil unrest and urban violence have continued to occur in inner cities, producing the perception that police are "occupying forces" in low-income and public housing neighborhoods. It is hard for police officers to feel that they are welcome in these communities, even though they perceive that they are exposing themselves to hazard by the very act of attempting to provide service and to protect the innocent in these areas. Accordingly, stereotypical images of public housing and of those who live there are common among police professionals, which results in slow responsiveness to and even avoidance of these communities.

Density

It is a general principle in the planning for all types of housing that densities should be limited to provide for the following:

- Adequate daylight, sunlight, air, and usable open space for all dwellings
- Adequate space for all community facilities

- A general feeling of openness and privacy
- A reasonable relationship to land and improvement costs
- A relationship to scale of the site, the neighborhood, and the geographic area

High densities are to be avoided because the problems of crowding are self-evident. However, the importance of density has to be assessed on a site-by-site basis. The orientation and relationship of buildings in a low-density environment can be a problem. Conversely, a high-density environment can be livable when the buildings are placed appropriately in relation to human activities.

Three-Generation Housing

It is difficult for extended families to live in close proximity in public housing environments. Young families may have to move across town to another site to find an apartment. As the young family grows in number of children, it is common for them to have to move several times to find more bedroom space. Over time the same families need less space as older children leave the home. A new concept of three-generation housing is actually a rebirth of the pre-World War II practice of providing room for boarders within the existing house design.

Three-generation housing concepts include the planning of architectural options to modify existing structures to increase apartment size or to provide for rental opportunities within one structure. That is, the apartment is designed to be broken into two apartments of various sizes. Conversely, an apartment could be designed to provide for an attic or attached efficiency that could be used for short-term rentals by college students or single tenants who can provide the adult presence needed to support a lone parent. Public housing applications will vary only to the extent of who serves as the landlord.

Three-generation planning for public housing provides architectural options that make it possible for extended families to stay close. Apartments may be modified or originally designed to allow for either upsizing or downsizing the number of bedrooms. One-bedroom flats may be joined or separated as families change. Two kitchens in one large apartment may be useful in promoting harmony among an extended family. This apartment could be split when the large family moves out. Such flexibility allows the apartment to undergo many changes over the years to accommodate the needs of various and changing families.

The value of three-generation housing is potentially enormous. The lone parent will benefit from the potential support of other adults within the home. Child supervision will improve, which may result in less delinquency and vandalism. Higher achievement levels in school may result from improved attendance and study habits that will be influenced by increased parenting and supervision. Finally, it should be expected that quality-of-life issues will be affected in positive ways, thus making the housing community more popular for working families.

CPTED Planning and Design Review

Planning

One of the first priorities for implementing CPTED is to place it in the planning process of the organization or jurisdiction. School districts, housing authorities, transportation systems, and local government all have fundamental responsibilities for public safety. It is necessary that a formal relationship between crime prevention and planning be established. Private companies and public utilities control extensive properties and huge labor forces. Each has a process for making decisions about new development and investment. The CPTED concept and process must be incorporated into these ongoing processes.

For communities and organizations, the CPTED process relates to and must be part of the following functions:

- *Comprehensive plans.* These plans determine the future patterns of land use and development. Comprehensive plans present the values of a community and a vision of what it will look like in the future. These plans establish goals and objectives for up to 50-year time periods.
- Crime-prevention elements are clearly necessary in a community's comprehensive plan. Day-to-day decisions about problems and needs are improved by ensuring that those decisions are consistent with comprehensive plans.
- *Zoning ordinances.* These are established to promote the health, safety, and welfare of residents by formally identifying the locations of land uses to ensure that activities are compatible and mutually supportive. Zoning regulations affect land use, development densities, yard setbacks, open space, building height, location and amount of parking, and maintenance policies. These, in turn, affect activities and routines that concern exposure to crime, surveillance opportunities, and the definition of space for territorial control.
- *Subdivision regulation.* This includes lot size and dimension, street and right-of-way locations, sidewalks, amenities, and location of utilities. These elements directly influence access to neighborhoods, reduction of pedestrian and vehicle conflict, street lighting, and connections with other parts of the community.

- *Landscape ordinances.* These govern the placement of fences, signs, and plant materials. They may be used to improve spatial definition, surveillance, access control, and wayfinding. Hostile landscaping can make unwanted access to parking lots and private property less desirable. Landscape planting materials may also help reduce graffiti by making large areas of walls inaccessible. Good horticulture improves the quality of life and helps reduce exposure to crime.
- *Architectural design guidelines.* These guidelines specify goals and objectives for site and building performance. They affect the location of activities and the definition of public and private space. The site decisions and plans for a building will directly affect opportunities for natural surveillance, pedestrian and vehicle access, wayfinding, and links to adjacent neighborhoods or land uses.
- *Access for physically and mentally challenged persons.* These requirements generally improve accessibility and wayfinding, but they rarely consider the risk of victimization that may be created by use of out-of-the way doors, hallways, or elevators.

Review Process

The work of builders, designers, and planners has long been affected by codes that govern nearly every aspect of a structure, except for security. Historically, a few jurisdictions enacted security ordinances, but most of these related to windows, doors, and locking devices. It is now becoming more common to find a local law or procedure calling for a full security or crime-prevention review of building plans before they are finalized. Nevertheless, it is still generally true that more attention is placed on aesthetics, drainage, fire safety, curb cuts, and parking access than on gaining an understanding of how a building or structure will affect the area in terms of security.

A CPTED design review process must be established within communities and organizations to ensure that good planning is being conducted. The manner in which physical space is designed or used has a direct bearing on crime or security incidents. The clear relationship between the physical environment and crime is now understood to be a cross-cultural phenomenon, since recent international conferences on CPTED have disclosed the universal nature of human/environment relations. That is, despite political and cultural differences, people basically respond the same way to what they see and experience in the environment. Some places make people feel safe and secure; others make people feel vulnerable. Criminals or other undesirables pick up on the same cues. They look at the environmental setting and at how people are behaving. These factors tell them whether they can control the situation or run the risk of being controlled themselves.

Someone has to question design, development, and event-planning decisions. Do you think that anyone from the police department, or the fire department for that matter, asked the builder of a major hotel in Kansas City whether they had extra steel reinforcing rods left over when they built the cross-bridge that fell and resulted in many deaths and injuries? Did anyone ask the planners what effect the downtown pedestrian malls would have when that fad swept the country in the early 1970s? No! Major planning mistakes were made then and now because no one is asking the hard questions.

The real tragedy is that when we make a design or planning decision, it will stay with us for many years. The U.S. Internal Revenue Service (IRS) generally sets depreciation schedules for buildings at 67 years, so it takes a long time to undo our mistakes. Commenting on design and development plans relevant to crime prevention is a crucial step that must be taken by police agencies.

Each building plan must be viewed as a potential legacy for the community. Traffic flow and routing decisions must be done in the context of preserving private neighborhoods. These decisions will be made in every community, whether or not a crime-prevention survey is conducted. It is a question now for communities to try to have a positive impact through an interagency design review process. It requires law enforcement and crime-prevention specialists to learn about the building and design trades and professions to enhance their ability to communicate CPTED ideas. It also requires a primary commitment from the top executives of every agency. The chief of police must take this seriously. The days of attempting to blindly lead the police function while clinging to a badge, a gun, and a Bible are past. The CPTED design review process is the key to effective community development and management.

Are there any compelling reasons other than pure logic for communities and organizations to get involved in a CPTED design review process? Litigation and money are two big ones. Many lawsuits are being decided not on whether a security officer or alarm system was present but on design and management decisions. Questions are being raised about the foreseeability of problems and the reasonableness and adequacy of design and management responses.

Perhaps the greatest future emphasis of security and security-related lawsuits will be on natural security. The courts' understanding of security is expanding beyond organized or mechanical methods to include the natural approaches that are inherent to managing human and physical resources.

CPTED could be viewed as a major escape route for the beleaguered property manager. And that includes just about everyone. City parks, public buildings, schools, shopping centers, small businesses, industrial plants, and hospitals are all fair game when it comes to lawsuit.

But what if logic and lawsuits do not get the attention of community and corporate leaders? How about money? The better one manages human and physical resources, the greater the profit and productivity and the lower the security problems. It is axiomatic that problems emanate from sloppy or bad business management. CPTED concepts in their basic form are oriented primarily around natural approaches to making things work better. A well-run school or office building requires less space and operating cost and has fewer security or crime problems. There is a direct link among good management, profit, and crime prevention. They contribute to each other.

Liability

The case law in general and premises liability have increased the responsibilities of property and business owners. Liability has been extended to architects, engineers, lending companies, and security contractors in wrongful injury or death suits. Courts have found parking lots to be *inherently dangerous,* which means that an owner or operator is liable even when there have been no prior incidents. Likewise, the isolation of restrooms by location and by design has been determined to be inherently dangerous.

The standard by which a property owner or operator is judged is based on proof of *due diligence,* or having done *all things reasonable* to prevent injury. Schools bear an additional duty—*in loco parentis,* literally serving in the place of the parents—which places a burden of responsibility for the protection of students from *portal to portal,* a seemingly impossible task.

The focus of this responsibility, however, is the actual school campus. Employee, student, and parent convenience is perhaps the greatest obstacle to maintaining safety and security. More accidents and victimizations are caused by the defeat of good security practices due to the interest in convenience than any other hazard. It is worse to have procedures that are not followed than to have none at all. New properties and operations are held to a different standard than existing ones. The designer, planner, and owner of a new property or operation will be held accountable for *conscious decisions* that affect the propensity for subsequent injury. Accordingly, a final decision about the design and use plan for a property must be *defensible.* The opinions of a recognized expert in the substantive area of the loss, peril, and hazard establish *proximate cause,* which then implicates foreseeability.

The so-called test of reasonableness that is the backbone of civil liability allows for the support of many factors in making conscious decisions. Aesthetics, educational mission, life safety, accessibility, feasibility, and environmental factors are weighed in the final determination of the adequacy of a school's duty and responsibility in the care and protection of students and staff. This is why CPTED has become so important to civil law: because it allows for the blending of good aesthetics, profitability, and safety.

The willingness to compromise is an admirable trait, one that is essential in any human endeavor. But compromise in making decisions about the design and use of a physical structure must not be arbitrary or carelessly thought out merely for the sake of achieving harmony. A tragic accident involving a rear-end collision of a vehicle with a fire truck provides a chilling example of compromising decisions. The local fire department waited to replace its only truck with one that provided safe jumpseats for the firefighters, despite the fact that their current vehicle violated national safety standards. This saved the department a $200,000 expenditure, although it was one that would have to be made sooner or later. Unfortunately, two firefighters died and two were critically injured in the accident. It is estimated that the settlement on the wrongful death suits may have been $6–7 million and the wrongful injury suits much higher. A new truck that meets safety standards will also have to be purchased.

A Western city experienced the worst nightmare of any community in 1993. The vehicle drop-off zone for an elementary school was located on a public street. It was a common practice for parents to pull up to a specific location to let off their child. A teacher routinely waved each parent ahead after the child exited the vehicle and slammed the door. This helped decrease congestion on the public street. This process apparently, and tragically, became too routine: A fifth-grade girl jumped out of her mother's car and the teacher waved the mother on after hearing the car door slam. But the little girl's coat was caught in the car door and she was dragged to her death by the unknowing mother. Would the cost of creating a proprietary drop-off lane have ever amounted to this one loss?

Is the preceding example merely an isolated freak accident? Or does it have the potential to be repeated elsewhere? Does the cost of prevention, or at least doing all that is reasonable, offset the potential loss?

Four elements are involved in the determination of liability. These are:

- Duty
- Breach of duty
- Injury/harm
- Causal link

These are the factors the court will use in assessing a school system's obligation in the event of a tragic accident like the one described. For its part, the basic requirements any school system must meet to establish a reasonable attempt to provide for safety and security are the following:

- Conduct a threat or problem analysis.
- Adopt a formal plan for safety and security.
- Prove that the plan was/is implemented.
- Document efforts to evaluate the plan.

The greatest protection for liability, crime prevention, and *peace of mind* is the presence of a plan of action that meets these criteria.

Achieving the Right Perspective

One mistake made by some less experienced people attempting to use CPTED concepts is getting the objective wrong. They attempt to apply CPTED concepts solely for security reasons. It does not take them long to find out that no one is interested in listening to them, particularly businesspeople, who justifiably have to concern themselves with profit and loss.

For instance, a crime-prevention officer from Bossier City, Louisiana, conducted a security survey of a luxury-clothing store. He recommended that the owner move the display of furs within the line of sight of one cashier, to keep the patrons from stealing them. The owner was not interested and refused on the basis of concern about insulting his special customers. The officer returned to the store after attending a CPTED course and made the same recommendation. This time, the purpose of the recommendation was primarily to enhance sales by improving clerks' ability to make immediate sales pitches to customers they observed entering the display area. By switching furs with a lingerie display that was in direct view of the clerk, the store enhanced sales *while* reducing the potential for losses.

CPTED's underlying objective is to help the various disciplines do a better job of achieving their primary objectives, with the added byproduct of improved security and loss prevention. The CPTED planner must ask the questions: What are you trying to do? How can we help you do it better? A successful use of these concepts will always result in this sequence of events:

1. Careful design and use of physical space
2. Resulting human decisions and behavior
3. Improved productivity and profit
4. Byproduct of loss prevention or loss reduction

There are many examples of people's tendency to overlook obvious solutions to problems. We have all heard someone who is having difficulty finding an object that turns out to be right in front of him say, "If it had been a snake, it would have bitten me!" CPTED concepts help us look at the environment in a different light to take advantage of solutions that are often inherent in what we are doing anyway. Consider the following somewhat far-fetched but true example:

A school principal told the story that during the early part of the 1980s, during the popularity of the rock group KISS with big red lips on its record album, young ladies in school began to smear on red lipstick and put the imprint of their lips on the mirror of the restroom. When a janitor complained, the principal said, "Don't worry. It's a fad and will go away."

But it didn't. Soon the kiss imprints were on the walls and doors, despite repeated warnings. Some young men, walking down hallways, would feel a pressure on the shoulder or back and find they had been given a big red kiss. Morale among teachers suffered. It was open warfare between young ladies versus boys and teachers. Then a woman who had worked for 30 years as a janitor knocked on the principal's door and said she had an answer. She explained it, and the principal agreed it was worth a try.

What was the solution? The next morning the janitor arrived in the girls' restroom with a bucket. She made a point of filling it with water from the toilets and she used that water to clean the mirrors. Students saw her doing this all day, using toilet water to wipe the mirrors and doors. The problems ceased. Although the final solution to the problem might have been extreme, it shows how the use of physical space and the environment has a direct impact on people's perceptions and thus on security.

4

BEHAVIORAL PRECEDENTS OF CPTED: FROM CAVES TO FAST FOOD

CHAPTER OUTLINE

Behavioral presedents

The attractiveness of big cities causes a drift from rural areas to the cities; legal and illegal immigrants from abroad are attracted by economic possibilities. Political and administrative management capabilities have to keep up pace and create proper administrative responses and strategic plans. Otherwise overpopulation, disorder, higher crime rates, and uncontrolled growth of problematic areas may arise.

—**Paul van Soomeren, Seoul, Korea, 2008**

Caves

Cave dwellers did what we do today when we move into new housing or offices: They cleared areas in front of their caves. They stacked rocks along the periphery of the area that they claimed. They painted the entrances and the interiors to reflect ballads or stories about their past. Why did they do this? Obviously, to mark their space. They did not have alarms, fences, or other home-security devices. They had to ensure that a passerby would observe that the forest or jungle was somehow differentiated from surrounding space, thus indicating ownership. The intruder, who had learned territorial behavior from her antecedents, knew that this was controlled space. If she was going to violate it, she had better do it quickly.

How does this behavior relate to contemporary society? Why is it that the home team has an advantage over visiting teams in any sport? Is it just because the fans cheer louder, or is it because they are defending their turf? It is common for teams to be excused for their road losses, because everyone knows how tough it is to win on the road. Moreover, it is becoming clear that employees are more likely to take care of property that is assigned to them personally than that which is generally available to anyone.

The first thing most people do when they move into a new apartment or office today is to personalize the space. One's belongings have to be unpacked and personal items put out for the new occupant to be comfortable. Everyone is different in this regard. Some people move into an office and reorient their workstation toward the window. Others are wall facers. Still more are door facers. Some don't like to face anything directly, so they place their desk on a diagonal line. The open-space office designers really missed this point during the early 1970s, when they put everyone in the open with the same desk, the same colors, and facing the same direction.

Border definition and symbolic barriers were important to early humans. Sticks with skulls atop them were strategically placed to signify entrance to controlled space. Drums were beaten constantly to define closed space by the distance to which the sound would travel. Similarly, contemporary humans feel the need to identify with space, both permanently and semipermanently. Later chapters of this book deal with territorial behavior, but it is important to note here that the fundamental territorial nature of human beings has changed little in the last 5,000 years and remains a powerful factor in behavioral control.

Greek Temples

During the early period of the Greek empire nearly 2,700 years ago, temple designers used environmental concepts to affect and control behavior. Greek temples built in Sicily, the largest Greek colony at the time, were constructed of stone dug from quarries that were below sea level and as near as possible to the sea. Designers found that this stone contained high levels of phosphorous from thousands of years of decay of sea animals. When this stone was used to form columns, it reflected light in such a manner as to appear golden immediately after dawn and preceding dusk.

These designers were using the environment to affect human behavior. They knew that people would notice and be impressed by the golden spectrum of the temple as they approached it for services—which were naturally scheduled at dawn and dusk. This golden effect elicited a psychological effect, reinforcing the powers of the faith and of the priests, who, the worshipers thought, clearly must have turned the temple to gold just for the services.

The designers also knew that people would focus on the golden aura emanating from the columns, which would have a physiological effect on the eye. Even though the ambient light level was reasonably low at dawn and dusk, the reflected light from the columns would cause the worshipers' eyes to react. The pupils of the eyes would contract as a response to the intensely focused light, thus robbing worshipers of their night or low-light vision. Guess what happened when they entered the temple? It was the same effect as entering a movie theater on a hot summer afternoon. You can't even see your feet, let alone a priest who has been strategically stationed to literally scare the daylights out of you.

Light is important to human beings. Sunlight is a source of vitamin D. Light is used psychologically and physically as a therapy. We refer to smart people as being *bright*. We have bright ideas. We *shed light* on problems. We tell people to sleep on problems, because things are better in the morning—when it is light. We tell people to *lighten up* when they are in dark moods. Ernest Hemingway described light as a remedy for depression in his short story, "A Clean, Well-Lighted Place."

Humans are so oriented to light that it is significant in the "fight versus flight" protective response, which we all possess. A person's reaction to being pinched surreptitiously in the dark will be radically different from the same event occurring in broad daylight. Don't we keep people *in the dark* when we want to keep them guessing?

Medieval Cities

Building height was used as a defense throughout early history. Normal people went to bed when the sun went down, and they got up when the sun came up. Only abnormal people went out at night, so natural barriers were used for personal defense. The ground floors of dwellings were designed only for daytime activities. Ladders were used to go to upper floors so that they could be pulled up at night, denying vertical access to sleeping and high-value areas. Stairs were only used to connect the upper floors.

Height has always been used on the macro scale to protect whole communities. Any tourist who has scaled the many steps to cities and castles in medieval Europe understands this. The tiny country of San Marino, located in northeast Italy, is a classic example. It covers less than a square mile, but it is perched on top of a mountain. Accordingly, it has never been conquered.

How is height used in contemporary society? Church steeples and ministers' pulpits are high. Judges in courtrooms and desk sergeants in police departments have traditionally sat on high benches. The convenience industry has discovered an advantage to elevating the position of cashiers, not only so they can see well but also so they command respect and attention throughout the store.

Height is important socially. Kings did not allow anyone to rise beyond the level of their heads, so people had to kneel to demonstrate subservience. A common expression is that some people "look down on others" as a means of demonstrating their perceived superiority. Lifeguards at swimming pools sit up high, and so do judges at professional tennis matches (possibly for their own safety).

It is certain that in many situations, height is used to facilitate visibility. But do not overlook height's value in terms of symbolic power and superiority. A security guard who is standing on a platform or looking down from a gallery onto a parking lot has a lot more power than one who is standing in the midst of the vehicles parked there. A prison guard may control many more prisoners from her perch in a tower than when she stands on the ground. Is this only because she can see more people, or does it have something to do with advantage? Which rooms cost the most in hotels?

Height is used symbolically in building design and urban planning. The height standard for buildings in Washington, DC, is the Capitol. It would be against local standards, mostly unwritten ones, to build a structure higher; but, realistically, it would probably sink anyway in the swampy geological make-up characteristic of the DC area. After all, the place had no real land value, so they made it into the nation's capital.

Height is used symbolically to denote authority and position. Kids are moved to the *head* or *top* of their class. Executives move to the *top* of the organizational chart. People who are successful generally *move up* in life. They move *up the ladder* of life. Other people get *down on their luck*.

Baroque Mannerism

Artists and philosophers were no different hundreds of years ago than they are now. It is impossible for one human being not to compete with another. During the period between the Renaissance and the development of baroque styles of architecture, art, and classics (1500 to 1700 A.D.), a few artists said, "The heck with this balance stuff!" They broke conventional rules of style and balance by leaving parts of their works in disarray or out of balance. Previously, musical compositions always ended on a consonant chord. Stories were supposed to end happily ever after. Plays were supposed to have some redeeming value. Paintings were supposed to be two-dimensional depictions of the subject, which was usually religious.

But the Mannerists established their own personal styles or they simply went beyond convention. The more radical sought to achieve dissonance where there was once consonance. Paintings and frescoes (painting in wet plaster) were designed to create anxiety as a message or pedagogical device, to convey a new attitude or philosophy. Modern psychologists refer to similar effects as *cognitive dissonance*, which are attempts to disrupt balance in cognitive perceptions as a basic step in attitude reformation.

In this period, Machiavelli was a famous writer and political adviser to the king of the city-state of Florence. An old story that was told in Florence was related by Dr. Frederic Licht, who happened to be the author's professor during his stay in Italy in 1968. He told of a situation wherein the famous Machiavelli assisted the king in handling a serious problem. Apparently the king had to give up some voting power to the local merchant guild because they controlled the money that he needed to run the little country. So he went to Machiavelli with his political problems. He said, "Mach, I am in deep trouble. I had to give the vote to those merchants."

Machiavelli was not to be outdone by a group of merchants. After all, he had achieved great fame as a behind-the-scenes expert in political maneuvering. So he recommended two strategies to the king. One was to use rules of order. This gets everyone, because everyone seems to lose equally, so they are happier. The second strategy was to design meeting chambers that created so much stress that people came in, voted fast, and got out quick. How did he do it? He hid the standard ceiling support columns behind false walls and installed narrow fake columns. This made the walls appear to be weak. He then installed additional beams in the ceiling to make it appear heavy. He added to this additional statuary and violent frescoes painted into the ceiling to convey the impression of heaviness. Hence the person sitting in a meeting was bound to become anxious. Vote quickly and get out before the ceiling falls on your head!

This ploy set a design standard that is commonly used in church sanctuaries, courtrooms, public meeting facilities, legislative chambers, and hotel ballrooms. Many of the contemporary designers of these facilities are vague about the origin of this design practice. They just do it because that is the way it has always been done. This could present a problem in current design if the architect used a heavy ceiling design over a location intended for relaxation and contemplative activity. A poorly used space is costly, nonproductive, and prone to security problems.

Dissonance in music has been used in contemporary society to affect public attitudes. The antiwar period in the late 1960s produced dissident music that was intended to upset listeners, not to please them. Screeching sounds were combined with lyrics that threatened traditional standards and beliefs. Dissonance in art has been used since before World War II to upset and to scare. Nazi Germans were depicted as craven monsters. The Japanese were portrayed as bloodthirsty animals. German posters presented the American as an oversized degenerate who enjoyed torturing prisoners. Posters during the Vietnam War period contained strange and foreboding caricatures of the Uncle Sam image and the US flag.

The artist, sculptor, musician, and architect consciously use their media to achieve the psychological and behavioral effects that they desire. Others copy these patterns without consciously acknowledging the original purpose or intended effect. People react positively or negatively to these designs without consciously questioning their purpose. A state police academy in the northeast United States was constructed using the most up-to-date concepts for training. The interior designers purposely used a high-stress-producing color on the accent walls behind the instructors. The students facing these walls were kept awake and more attentive. But the desire for uniformity in decoration overpowered the thought process of the interior designer, so the same color was used as the accent wall in each instructor's office. Yet the behavioral requirements of these offices were the exact opposite of the classroom. Instructors' offices were for contemplative work, principally in developing lesson materials, so a color scheme was needed that allowed the instructors to pass time more effectively and work calmly.

It did not take long for the staff of the academy to know that something was wrong. No one was ever in his office when you needed him. Eventually it became clear that if you wanted to find anyone, you had to look in the cafeteria or the library. People who had to complete any major project ended up going to these places to find the peace and calm required to be productive.

Louis XIV

Louis XIV, a king of France (1643–1715), introduced what would later be called *urban renewal* to the streets of Paris. He installed broad boulevards and extensive landscaping. Louis was proud of his beautification efforts—until he found them defaced by vandals during his morning rides. So he embarked on a massive security program that culminated in the installation of nearly 7,000 street lamps from 1700 to 1701.

This was the first wide-scale use of outdoor lighting in history. But this lighting was installed primarily to protect property. Normal people got up when the sun came up and went to bed when the sun went down. People were afraid of night air, thinking that it carried more diseases, so they were not out and about on the streets at night. They closed up their homes at night, even in hot weather. It is interesting that a Johns Hopkins University study in the mid-1980s confirmed the suspicion that night airs do carry more viruses.

Contemporary outdoor lighting is viewed popularly as a fundamental device for protecting people. Louis XIV's lighting initiative may have changed the course of human history because he introduced outdoor lighting as a means of protecting property, since normal people did not go out at night. The widespread credibility of and confidence in the technology of outdoor lighting must have planted the seed of change that has irreversibly affected the quality of life to this day.

People now go out at night. They go to church and to school at night. They go to athletic events at night, and they play golf at driving ranges that are open all night. People jog at night for convenience and comfort. People prefer nighttime for many outdoor functions. Technology and the willingness to use it, even for Louis XIV's somewhat selfish and costly reason, significantly changed the course of human history.

Yet most people take the presence of light for granted. Lighting engineers have learned a lot about the effects of light on human behavior. Indoor lighting was designed traditionally to provide a balance of natural and manmade lighting at the floor level. Lighting sources were placed in hallways and foyers at the center of ceilings, so that the cones of light would cover the floor. But people's eyes are not on the floor; their feet are there.

New experiments have demonstrated that traditional interior lighting may not have taken advantage of its potential effects on human behavior. Hallways and foyers were centrally lit so that the cones of light would cover the floor. People stand and see at a range of 4′8″ to 6′0″. Accordingly, it has been noticed that people will walk near the middle of centrally lighted corridors. They will stand near the middle of centrally lighted foyers. The closer they are to other people, the more likely they are to exhibit avoidance behaviors out of politeness and discomfort.

When the light source is oriented toward the walls in hallways and foyers, people will walk or stand closer to the wall. They are more likely to establish eye contact with others because of the increased distance. They are more likely to feel comfortable and safer. Recent research has demonstrated that there is a 30-percent reduction of noise in these well-lighted hallways and foyers.

Lighting clearly has an impact on people's perception of space. People need distance to feel safe from potential threats. The perception of distance is important, perhaps more important than the reality. Lighting can easily affect the perception of distance.

The easiest way to fully understand these concepts is to spend part of a day in an elevator. The fewer the people in the elevator, the further apart they will stand, but they are more likely to establish eye contact. As the elevator becomes more crowded, people will give each other social distance by practicing avoidance behaviors. They will look up or down but avoid eye contact, even though they are touching others due to crowding. Touching is legitimate and non-threatening when there is a crowd. However, watch what happens as the crowd departs the elevator: continued touching will be perceived as a threat, to the point that it becomes fear-producing enough to be considered an assault.

Lighting experts are thinking more than ever about how to use lighting to achieve behavioral affects.

Napoleon III

Napoleon III (1808–1873) introduced concepts that were later adopted by Hitler, Mussolini, and Franklin D. Roosevelt. Napoleon learned, as he ascended to power in 1853, that governments in financial crisis, fearing social unrest, spend money and build buildings. After all, only the government has money when there is a financial panic.

Napoleon III built roads and buildings. He proclaimed that cities needed broad boulevards so that people could enjoy the environment and commune with nature. His underlying purposes were to keep people busy thinking that all was well and to improve the military's ability to control the masses. In this latter regard, Napoleon had learned that a small number of people could barricade a narrow street, effectively neutralizing a large number of soldiers, who could not outflank the blockage. Broad boulevards were harder to barricade and more amenable to flanking maneuvers of troops. So, under the guise of urban renewal, Napoleon attempted to control the public by implementing a plan of street improvements.

Napoleon III did something else that, were it not for his perverse intent, would be the major objective of CPTED specialists: He authorized his chiefs of police to raze or demolish any building or habitat known to be the hideout of criminals. Baron Haussmann, the chief of police in Paris at the time, wrote in his memoirs that he delighted in his newfound authority to get rid of any building or structure that was unsightly merely by saying that criminals used it. Baron Haussmann was apparently very discriminating when it came to architecture, which must have been unsettling to many Parisians.

Hitler and Mussolini spent massive sums of money that were needed desperately by their constituents to prove that all was well within their governments. Following Napoleon's example, Mussolini and Hitler erected buildings and committed government funds to projects that would not have been supported by the private sector. Hitler initiated the Volkswagen car campaign to draw attention away from the excessive expenditures on the military that deprived consumers of badly needed money. Mussolini constructed buildings, including the ugly memorial to King Victorio Emmanuele in Rome, which looks like, and therefore is called, the "marble cake." Mussolini was effective in wiping out organized crime in Sicily by assigning the army to eliminate anyone who was connected remotely to the Mafia.

FDR had to adopt some of the same techniques out of necessity. Works Progress Administration (WPA) and Civilian Conservation Corps (CCC) employees built buildings all over the mall in Washington, DC, as well throughout the United States. These programs supplemented major public housing assistance projects that were supported under several domestic funding activities. Many large military family housing projects were funded as an indirect source of affordable housing as well as an incentive to join the armed services.

Some of the projects were clearly make-work in their orientation. There is still the shell of a bridge left in northeast Florida that was built by a CCC gang. Unfortunately, there is no water nearby, nor any reason for the bridge except for the future potential of a cross-state barge canal.

One thing leads to another in this world. Roads have to be used and buildings have to be inhabited. Bridges need traffic and ships have to be filled. Why? Because we have them! History has produced legacies for the present population that must not be taken for granted. Everything must be questioned because often what we are doing is justified for one purpose when the original reason was something different.

The issue here is to learn from real history, not from habit. Moreover, it is imperative to cut through the surface of official justifications for doing things so that we can understand the real reasons.

Contemporary Situations

Everyone who is in a competitive situation, especially those who are successful, uses any opportunity to his advantage. The people who play and manage major league baseball are not rocket scientists, but they record and map every pitch and every swing. Why? They want to know the tendencies of every player. It doesn't work every time for them, but it helps prove that random response is less valuable. Any edge is important.

The fast-food industry may be the most oriented to using the environment to control behavior. One major chain, which can be credited with the introduction of standard food products, pioneered most strategies in environmental manipulation. This corporation made the drive-through lane famous. It introduced the talking sign that has created stage fright and embarrassment for many a customer, although it increases impulse buying. The same chain introduced the two-window system, where you give up your money at one window and get your food at another. Customer participation is the implicit message in all of this chain's procedures.

This fast-food chain invites customers to place special orders, but then when you get to the second window, they tell you that you have to go sit in the "idiot" lane until your food is done. Had you ordered it "their way," you would have gotten your food immediately. Why do they put the "idiot" lane immediately in front of the second window? Is that to make it easier for the store employee to bring out your special order when it is finished cooking? Or is it possible that they want the people behind you to notice that you had to wait? Could it be that they want the person behind you to have to make a radical turn to get around you so that they will be reminded that it is the people with the special orders who mess everything up? Have you ever tried to balance your cold drink and your hamburger in one hand as you negotiated your way around some "idiot" who clearly must have placed a special order?

Most of the fast-food industry depends on customer participation to create at least the illusion of efficiency, which is supposed to contribute to low prices. Customers usually do not mind handing over their money first before getting their bag of food, which clearly prevents an unscrupulous customer from ruining things for everyone by running off without paying. The industry has found that customers are less likely to complain if a bag is placed next to the cash register while the money is being taken. The bag may even be empty as long as the customer believes that it is her bag.

Most parents teach their children to pick up after themselves. So does the fast-food industry. In the spirit of customer participation, it is expected that people will dispose of their leftovers and trash. Try leaving your tray next time and see how the other customers react. It will probably be the first time anyone looked at you or established eye contact. The fast-food industry has discovered that customers will generally avoid contact with others unless something unusual happens, whereas they are prone to stare and smile at other diners in traditional restaurants. Why? Because few people dress up to go out for fast food. Nor are they apt to use their best table manners, so they really want to avoid being seen by or seeing others, particularly people they know. The last thing anyone wants is to be seen wearing curlers or a stained sweatshirt while pigging out on a sloppy hamburger.

One major corporation recently hit on a brilliant strategy: They hire senior citizens to work in the customer areas, which is largely a cleaning and straightening job. Young people had traditionally performed these functions and were largely invisible to customers. But who can miss Grandma or Grandpa puttering around cleaning up? Grandma and Grandpa may even be a bit grumpy with someone who is messy or with a small group that is noisy or that leaves belongings in the aisles. People are less likely to be offended by an older person, so they will not lose face by submitting to the elders' control.

Most fast-food chains use a total environmental management concept that emphasizes stress. *Active colors are combined with cut-tempo music.* Employees are influenced to do everything quickly. Orders are repeated loudly, as though the food will really be custom made. Furnishings are designed for appearance and ease of cleaning, not for comfort. Trash receptacles and recycle bins are placed prominently to reinforce customer participation. The environment is designed to create the impression, if not the reality, that you got fed fast.

Employees wear matching uniforms. Some chains dress their new employees in different uniforms that identify them as trainees. This seems to elicit greater tolerance for their delays or mistakes. A customer would have to be a real jerk to complain about the service from someone who is just learning the job.

Food is generally well packaged, even if it is to be eaten on the property. This helps preserve the freshness, but it also keeps the customer from examining his purchase at the counter. The customer is less apt to complain about a mistake when he will have to get in line again or submit to the disapproval of other customers for butting in at the head of the line.

Food that is prepared already is arrayed in color-coded packages so that the customer can see what is immediately available. Once again, the customer is participating in the process that delivers fast food by being obliged to order what is ready. Customers also find themselves rushing to fast-food restaurants at odd hours in order to beat the crowd. Have you ever been in a discussion with fellow workers about where to go for lunch when one states that it is only 11:30 A.M. and you just have time to get to McDonalds? Why should we be in a hurry to get to a fast-food place? Because we know that we will get fed more quickly if we go at times other than breakfast, lunch, or dinner.

Finally, why do some chains refuse to use cueing lanes that are common in airports or banks? Why don't they use two outdoor signs so that you have time to organize your order before you get to the sign that talks? Why do the clerks call out for your order over the head of the customer in front of you who is trying to gather her stuff and get out of your way? Why do customers frantically scan the posted menus when everyone knows what a fast-food restaurant serves? The answer is stress. Customers under stress are more manageable, and they are more likely to buy impulsively.

Anyone who is in a competitive business will use any appropriate angle to get ahead. The environment is used to direct and control customer behavior for the sake of the business's objective: to deliver a quality service and make money. Other contemporary industries use the environment to their advantage. The convenience store industry is experimenting with new store designs and procedures. Gas stations have changed dramatically. The new kiosk gas station has several islands of pumps, convenient food items for sale, and a carwash. All of this is placed under a sea of light that is more welcoming and safer than the outside of traditional service stations.

5

USING THE ENVIRONMENT TO AFFECT BEHAVIOR

CHAPTER OUTLINE

Crime prevention through environmental design offers many methods to interfere with offenders stalking victims. Communities can locate women's washrooms away from telephones, light up suspicious areas, open up blind spots, and place legitimate businesses in areas formerly used for criminal approach. The point is to give offenders a smaller window of opportunity.[1]

—Marcus Felson

Human/Environment Relationships

Perhaps it was easier for ancient human beings to appreciate and respect their dependence on the environment. The environment provided sustenance and it provided challenges to survival. Humans had to adjust to their environment, for they were limited in the type and amount of changes they could make to it. Adaptation was the rule. Trial-and-error methods produced knowledge about clothing, fire, and the preservation of foods. When early humans learned that foods could be grown as well as found, the first step in using the environment to human advantage was made.

Humans eventually discovered that the environment could yield elements that were useful, but they had to be put in new combinations that were not inherent or endemic to nature. They learned to extract medicines and spices from plants and to extract and process metals for tools and for ornamentation. Somewhere along the line, early humans learned how to combine ingredients to cause chemical

[1]Marcus Felson, *Crime and Nature*, Sage Publications, 2006, p. 240.

reactions that produced alcohol. The final step for primitive human beings in the process of learning to control their environment was the harnessing of nature through water power and gravity. The wheel revolutionized human existence. Moreover, the discovery of humans' intellectual mastery over animals gave people greater power to manipulate the environment.

Most contemporary human responses to the environment are involuntary. They are either metabolic responses that are inborn or they are learned responses that seem to come naturally. Most responses are so automatic that they occur in our subconscious states. We don't have to think about most stimuli analytically to react to them. Our responses to the environment are similar from a pure survival standpoint, but our responses to other stimuli vary with our socialization and training.

An earlier chapter referred to the tendency for police to subconsciously scan openings—doors and windows. Illumination consultants scan ceilings.

Wallpaper advisors only look at walls. And floor specialists are always looking down. An engineer looks at structural cues. The architect looks at the appearance and functionality of a building. The fire chief looks at access. The normal user of a building, after her first encounter with it, only looks at where she is going. It is clear that we orient ourselves socially and vocationally to a range of subconscious and conscious responses to environmental cues.

Figure 5.1 presents a simple model of human/environment interactions that divides the basic reactional elements of humans into three

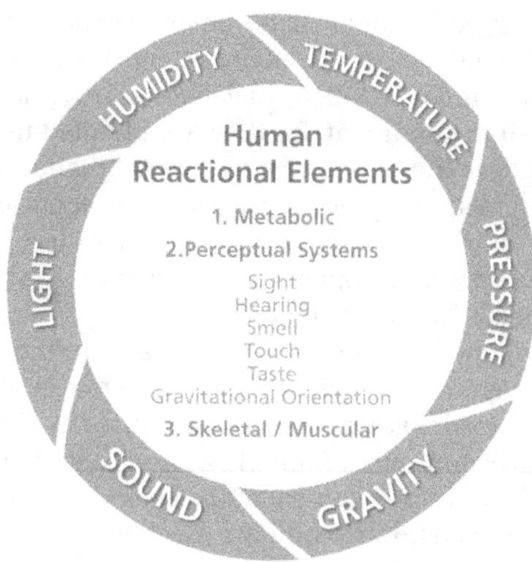

Figure 5.1 Human/environment relationships.

categories: metabolic, perceptual, and skeletal/muscular systems. The model identifies six elements of the environment that impinge on human beings: temperature, pressure, humidity, light, sound, and gravity.

Human metabolic mechanisms are mainly those that are biological. People are born with these mechanisms that scan the near environment. The near environment may be defined as that which we are touching or that which may be within reaching distance.

Temperature is a significant variable in affecting metabolic mechanisms. A controlled experiment would show that in a room full of people in which the temperature was changed radically in only half of the room, overall body temperature would not change significantly. Why? It's called *homeostasis*. The body automatically responds to a rise in temperature by opening the pores to emit moisture (sweat), which evaporates to create a cooling sensation of the skin. The veins expand and move closer to the surface of the skin to emit core heat. The mind automatically slows down certain body functions. The legs become uncrossed and the arms become unfolded.

This explains the paradox that occurs when there is a boating accident. The strong swimmer attempts to go for help. The weak or nonswimmer stays with the boat. Who survives? It's always the nonswimmer who automatically stays in a fetal position awaiting rescue. This natural reaction preserves core heat and allows the nonswimmer to survive. The swimmer turns up the internal motor and increases core heat: The body gets confused, the veins swell, the pores open, and the swimmer dies of hypothermia.

How may temperature be used to affect behavior? It is done all the time. Time and space relationships are important. A warm classroom is just about the worst possible environment for maintaining students' attention immediately after lunch. Once food reaches the stomach, the body transfers blood to the thoracic region to provide fuel for the muscular gyrations involved in digestion. Some of this blood comes from brain supplies, so the shortage of blood in the brain induces drowsiness and lack of concentration.

A hot room induces stress and anxiety. People will complete their business and leave for more comfortable surroundings. A cold room will also induce stress but in different ways. The use of temperature to control behavior is indisputable, but it must be used based on the uniqueness of the situation.

A police chief told the following story about the kitchen that had been placed in a new public safety building. Once the building was opened, what had been planned as an employee convenience became a hangout area. The chief of police would occasionally walk in and clear the area of employees who alleged that they were merely on break. The chief became the heavy in a growing management-and-labor conflict. With the advice of a CPTED specialist, the chief secretly arranged for a special damper to be placed in the air-conditioning ducts. The temperature rose 12 degrees in the kitchen, and no amount of tinkering with the thermostat helped. Eventually the employees wrote the kitchen off as a permanent problem, an aberration of the architectural design. The chief of police reports that now there are never more than three people in the kitchen, and there is usually only one person sitting. Where do you think that this chief of police and I met with one of his recalcitrant lieutenants who is in charge of a special project? You're right, the kitchen! Once the lieutenant had broken out into a sweat, the chief and I laid on the results of the evaluation of the lieutenant's project. It was amazing how quickly he responded positively to the proposed improvements.

Heat, light, temperature, pressure, sound, humidity, and gravitational effects may all be used to affect behavior. Each of these elements has already directed and channeled human reactions and growth in the natural environment. The question then becomes how to use these elements to enhance the achievement of human objectives.

Perceptual systems include the senses of sight, hearing, smell, touch, taste, and gravitational orientation. These are the human traits that are used to scan the middle and far environment. Most humans believe that the sense of sight is the strongest, but we actually rely on all our senses. Nearly everyone has observed the uncanny perceptual capabilities of a person who is either visually or hearing impaired. One wonders how that person is able to develop such instincts. But all humans, often without realizing it, very subtly use all their instincts continually.

One example that is used in CPTED training is to blindfold all the class members and drive them around town in a bus or van with the windows open. The students are asked if they think they can identify the area through which they have ridden. Most state initially that they do not think they can do so. But it doesn't take long for them to begin to pick things out as they concentrate on sorting their perceptions and bringing recognizable cues to the conscious state. The odor of bus exhausts and refracted sounds of traffic will suggest that they are downtown. The odors of dumpsters and cooking mingle with the voices of kids playing and balls bouncing to lead the class to the conclusion that they are in a housing area. The class finds that they are more likely to notice music and cooking aromas that are different from their own experience.

Some Russian research in the early 1980s found that newborn children have the same intellectual capacity as a mature adult. The difference is that they do not have the years of learning and the millions of bits of information that are compiled through life experiences that the adult uses to analyze environmental cues. The intellectual power is there, but its use has to await programming. A person raised in the country may have difficulty distinguishing among the sounds and smells of the inner city. Moreover, a nonresident is more likely to identify these cues than a resident, who has had time to become inured to her environmental condition. An understanding of these observations about behavior is important to the CPTED planner.

The visual sense collects information about what may be seen in the environment. This information is processed initially by the subconscious to determine its value. Everything that occurs physically within the line of sight of any human is captured visually, but it may not rise to the level of consciousness unless there is something significant enough about it that it stands out.

Each person's socialization and vocational training has established a set of variables that dictates the evaluation of visual scanning. Police officers notice things that other people fail to recognize. Customers and users of space respond to environmental cues and variables that may not be recognized by local residents or businesspeople who have become accustomed to that particular location. A builder or engineer may notice things that escape the conscious recognition of a property owner or security guard. Each person is attuned to a different visual perspective of the environment.

The auditory sense, hearing, is more powerful than most people imagine. Sounds are recorded by the ear and transferred to the brain for evaluation. Pressure changes are recorded by the ear and transferred as well.

The ears collect data about the environment that is processed by the subconscious. Significant data is passed upward to the level of conscious awareness for action. Other data is erased or stored in the subconscious. People are more likely to consciously "hear" music or other noise that is foreign to them and to be annoyed by it. The companies that specialize in background music purposely compose or recompose music so that it sounds familiar. Why? So that it will stay in the subconscious or subliminal state. Otherwise it would be noticeable and distracting rather than useful for suppressing extraneous or unwanted noise.

The olfactory sense, the ability to smell, is as powerful as the other senses. Smell is linked to taste, which is also linked to the visual sense. That is why chefs are so careful about the visual presentation of food as well as its taste and smell. Some of the smarter public housing designers have learned to use flowers and blossoming trees to serve as visual delimiters and to mask unpleasant odors.

Because smell defines many human functions, it may be important to maintain certain smells. Can you imagine a fish market that doesn't smell of fish? Can you imagine a popcorn vendor who sells canned popcorn? No way, because the interaction among sight, sound, and smell is critical to affecting behavior. A downtown mall in Louisville has problems leasing business locations that are near the exits. Why? Because restrooms are located near the entrances. The principle users of these restrooms are vagrants. The restroom entrances are near public telephones, which legitimize vagrant activities. The smell of urine is overpowering.

Real estate salespeople know the tricks of smell. Some homes or apartments have odors that are associated with water problems or animals. Mildew and backed-up drains really make a place seem less desirable. Pets can create a lot of problems through uncontrolled elimination of wastes and through the chemical excretions associated with territorial behavior. So, what does the wise realtor do with a "stinker"? The solution is to mask the odor or eliminate it. The latter usually costs too much, so masking is the normal response. Using freshly baked bread is an excellent strategy. The aroma not only masks other odors, it evokes powerful and pleasurable nesting responses.

A potential buyer may look at a house or apartment that has serious cosmetic problems. He will certainly be turned off and will comment that the place is in lousy condition. Add the smell of freshly baked bread and the prospective customer may say that the home really looks lived in or feels homey. He still may not want to buy it, but his overall impression will be different, more positive. He may appreciate the certain quality of the dwelling that caused the previous family to spend a lot of time there.

The smell of freshly baked bread could enhance the attractiveness of a renovated pedestrian mall or a strip shopping center, particularly where heavy pedestrian activity is expected. The developer or management company might want to offer lease incentives or loan guarantees to get bakeries to come into a project. It would also be desirable for the baker to be influenced to bake during business hours or early evening instead of the traditional middle of the night. Bakeries could be located temporarily to serve as inducements for pedestrian activity that in turn would increase other business prospects.

The tactile sense, touch, is more than what may be felt by the fingers. It is linked to the metabolic mechanisms as well as to the perceptual senses. Touch involves a complex set of sensors in the skin and muscles that give us the ability to perceive temperature, humidity, pressure, shape, texture, and weight of objects. Few people think of the sense that allows the individual to feel pressure, which may be something as slight as a breeze or a person walking behind them. The sensing of texture helps us discern the difference between yogurt and the side of a brick. It helps us to distinguish a slippery surface from one that has more traction.

Everyone has seen how people change their walking style when they encounter smooth, wet-appearing surfaces. They look down and take short, tentative steps. This would not be good for enhancing feelings of safety nor for encouraging people to establish eye contact. However, by making an area appear slippery, people can be kept from congregating there. A slippery or uneven surface may be used to direct the user's attention away from a private workspace or sensitive operation. Finally, have you ever noticed that the streets are always wet in automobile ads? It makes the car appear to move or to go faster. Besides, it looks better than dull, dry pavement.

Texture may have other important effects on behavior. The author recently surveyed a large high school. The walls in many of the high-capacity hallways, including the side walls of the auditorium, were cast in rough form concrete. The forms created extremely sharp ridges that were uniform throughout. The designer may have considered this to be aesthetically appealing and easier to construct. It may have been intended to reduce opportunities for vandalism, but it guaranteed people's avoidance of any proximity to the walls. The hallways were congested because everyone walked in the center. Fear of injury was intensified. All someone had to do to get hurt was to slip or be shoved against one of these walls.

Touch extends to interpersonal relationships, where it is also culturally defined. Anthropologists know that there are minimum and maximum spatial dimensions that are required for all human activities and relationships. Each function has its own set of needs. Distance between people tends to increase as the relationship becomes less personal. The men in certain Middle Eastern and Asian cultures hold hands when they walk or talk. The men in some other cultures place their arms around each other when they discuss business. South American men sit very close together for discussions. But don't mimic these behaviors with a North American male!

Touching is legitimate during certain times and in certain places. Otherwise, it can produce fear and result in avoidance behavior. Try observing behavior in elevators. Two people alone in an elevator will stand against opposite walls. They may nod politely and exchange pleasantries. As others enter at different floors, there is less eye contact and social exchange. By the time the elevator is full, everyone is either looking up or down to avoid eye contact, even though they are being touched on all sides. Friends will even drop their voices or stop talking altogether as the elevator becomes more crowded.

Interaction between the sexes on the elevator is even more interesting. A man and a woman who are strangers would not dare touch if they were alone. It would be fear producing and impolite. Yet, as the elevator fills up, it is socially legitimate for the man and woman to be pressed together, with little concern. They will move apart immediately as people exit. The same thing occurs on airplanes, buses, and in private cars. Think about it as you jam into your next car or elevator.

The gustatory sense, taste, is also important to our reaction to the environment. It is linked to smell. Remember when you couldn't taste anything the last time you had a cold? Taste is more complex than allowing us to differentiate among foods. We taste exhaust fumes as well as smell them. Our sense of taste contributes to metabolic mechanisms. The ability to sense temperature and humidity is supported by taste. Taste and touch are linked in the human perception of texture.

A human being's orientation to gravity, the proprioceptive sense, is linked to touching. This sense is the ability of the body to assess and interpret internal changes. The change or shift of muscle tension in various body parts indicates changing motion or elevation. Of course, this movement or shift of muscle tension is a direct response to gravitational changes. The human body is constantly monitoring and responding to space.

People do not like to stand on elevations. The human body is able to discern as little as one or two degrees of elevation change. How many times have you stood on someone's kitchen floor or back porch and felt depressions or low spots? Some instructors will report finding high spots in the front of lecture halls and standing on them throughout their presentations. Why? It is obviously a subconscious attempt to reinforce the student's attention. Humans prefer a steep staircase to a flight of stairs in which the risers are uneven. Many people are uncomfortable with heights. Do you remember when you were terrified to stand on an extended balcony but had no fear of one that was recessed?

Sympathetic reactions are good examples of how our other senses translate to our proprioceptive sense. Has your leg ever moved when you watched a high jumper or pole vaulter? Have you ever gotten dizzy or nauseated while watching a stunt film? Have you experienced a weird sensation of movement when a car next to yours backs up slowly at a stoplight? Why doesn't this sensation occur elsewhere? Answer: It is not legitimate to back up at stoplights, so your sense of movement is thrown off. Watch an audience at a circus when the tightrope walker loses her balance. The audience will sway with the walker.

Designers have used knowledge of these reactions to gravity to their advantage. Slight elevations have been planned in movement areas to prevent congestion and loitering. Elevated galleries may be used to raise the pedestrian height along the sides of a fortress-type convention center, to increase perceived visibility and reduce gathering behavior. Moving objects and uneven surfaces may deter lingering. The rough walls of the high school mentioned earlier may be desirable in park or other outdoor areas to discourage the use of the wall for leaning or sleeping. It certainly discourages graffiti and ball playing. The trick is to know what kind of behavior you desire and what type you want to suppress.

In conclusion, humans constantly react to the environment, both consciously and subconsciously. It is the task of the CPTED planner to always be mindful of these human/environment interactions and to practice bringing them to the level of conscious awareness. In this way they are an integral part of the application of CPTED concepts.

Use of Light and Color

The visual sense is the most comprehensive means of collecting information about the environment. It has been estimated that about 90 percent of all our information about the external world comes as a result of visual perceptions. However, our visual sense is so linked to the other senses that it is difficult to differentiate among them. For instance, when we say, "It looks like a carrot," or "It looks like sand," or "It looks OK to me," we are restating in visual terms what resulted from information that may have been captured by other senses. Smelling, touching, weighing, and tasting may have been involved in the data-gathering process.

Light and color are essential components of the environment. Light enables plants to grow. There would be no air to breathe or food to eat without light. Plants give off oxygen. The food we eat comes from plants or animals that eat plants. Light was essential in the development of natural fuels. Light from the sun heats the earth and illuminates human activities.

Humans have learned how to manufacture light for use at night or in places where there is no sunlight. Light is used as a therapy for depression. Light is used to produce biological changes. For instance, lights are left on in chicken coops to make the chickens think that it is daytime and so lay more eggs. Correctional researchers are now exploring the use of different lighting levels and colors on behavior in prisons.

Humans generally have a directional orientation to light. Its source is commonly from above. We are *cast in the most favorable light* when its source is above. We look awful when the source is below. We use a flashlight pointing up into our faces from the neck level to scare children at Halloween. Horror films and tragedies use lighting from low sources to enhance the sense of fear or foreboding. Conversely, comedies and upbeat musicals use highly placed light sources. We *highlight* our accomplishments and take a *dim view* of failures.

Light is a form of energy that can travel freely through space. The energy of light is referred to as *radiant energy*, which also includes infrared rays, ultraviolet rays, X-rays, and radio waves. Light is composed of colors that range from red to violet. These are the visible colors of light, whereas ultraviolet and infrared are invisible.

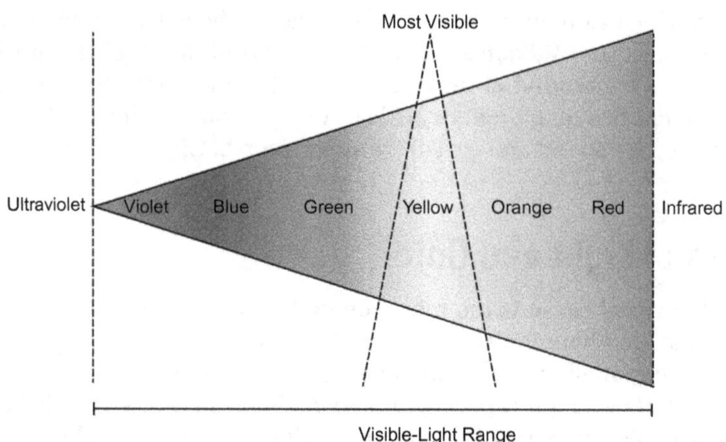

Figure 5.2 The visible light and color spectrum.

Light actually consists of energy that is emitted from excited (heated or phosphorescent) atoms. Excited atoms release and absorb energy in tiny bundles called *photons*. Light consists of streams of these photons. The different colors of light are made by photons with different energy levels. White light consists of a combination of all levels of photon energy. This is easily demonstrated by the use of a common prism, which disperses white light into all the different colors.

As shown in Figure 5.2, the visible spectrum of light is composed of the basic colors of red, orange, yellow, green, blue, and violet. Each has a different wavelength. The longest wavelength is red and the shortest is violet. Infrared has a longer wavelength than red. Ultraviolet has a shorter wavelength than violet. Both are invisible to the human eye.

Light affects human functions. Industry research has demonstrated that lighting levels have an impact on productivity and on the rate of accidents. Lighting levels must increase directly with the complexity of the job. Hence the expression, "Let's shed some light on the subject." Bright lights can have an adverse effect on less critical human activities. An expensive restaurant geared to the patron's desire for long, lingering meals would go under if lighting levels were intense. Accordingly, the restaurant owners place the ceiling in shadow and use table-lighting sources such as candles.

Acute depressions, which are suffered by most people at one time or another, are generally affected by light. Have you ever been depressed about a personal problem at work or home, possibly a medical concern, and found it hard to go to sleep? Many depressed people just want to go to bed and forget about their problems. But as soon as they get there, no matter how tired they are, sleep will not come. The person begins to shift positions. The more they shift, the higher the stress level goes. One's spouse or cohabitant gets grumpy about the disruptions, so the stressed person attempts to lie still. Then the anxiety level hits the ceiling. Sleep eventually comes, but it is disturbed.

Events are played out in dreams, repeatedly, in grotesque ways. The same speech or the same fouled-up athletic play is recycled over and over. Finally, as the clock approaches 4:30 to 5:30 A.M., the victim falls into deeper sleep, only to be awakened by the alarm at 6:30. One hint about the average range of time in which the individual falls asleep, 4:30 to 5:30 A.M., is that it is dependent on where the person lives within a given time zone. What begins to happen around 4:00 to 5:00 A.M.? The ambient light level begins to increase. The sun is coming up—it's a new day. Things always look better in the morning. Isn't it common for people to say, "Why don't you go home and sleep on the problem, because things will be better in the morning?"

It is an irony of human nature that when a person falls asleep watching television in the family room, someone will eventually wake the sleeper to inform him that he can't sleep there—it's time to go to bed. What was wrong with sleeping there? The problem is that by the time he complies with the urgent demands to come immediately to bed, he is wide awake and can't sleep! The underlying explanation for the behavior of the family-room sleepers is that for certain people it is easier to fall asleep with the television and lights on. It may be that they are lazy, or that they are prone to fall asleep in relaxing circumstances. It may be a subconscious method of dealing with stress and depression. The presence of light seems to be the key.

The next time you feel a little depressed and cannot go to sleep, go to the living room or den, turn on the television (a light source), and sit or lie in a comfortable position. Do not forget to warn your spouse or cohabitant, because he or she may come and mistakenly interrupt one of the best sleeps you've ever had. This is not a remedy for chronic or extremely acute depressions, but it may help you go to sleep. Hemingway's short story, "A Clean, Well-Lighted Place," was the writer's way of describing the need for light that is experienced by chronically depressed individuals. They will close the bar down and then sit in a well-lighted room awaiting dawn and the sleep that comes with it.

It is clear that light affects human behavior. Light may be used to attract people. The convenience-store industry has discovered that high lighting levels in stores, combined with more open space, increases sales. Too much or too little light will have different effects. It is now generally accepted that performance improves and fatigue levels drop in direct proportion to increasing levels of light, but this relates to the work or play environment. The important thing to remember is that each human function has an optimum lighting level. It becomes a question of deifining the human function and matching the level of light that is required to achieve optimum effects.

Color fills our world with beauty. Colors may be arranged in consonance to sooth and calm. Colors may be arranged in dissonance to produce stress and discomfort. Colors are used to describe moods. Some persons are said to be in *a blue mood.* Others are *in the pink.* Colors are associated with traditions. The Irish wear green on St. Patrick's Day for good luck. People in mourning for the death of loved ones wear black.

Colors also serve more functional purposes. Color serves as a form of communication. Red lights mean stop. Green lights mean go. Athletic teams wear opposing colors. Referees carry the dreaded yellow flags that signify penalties. The colors of some kinds of plant blossoms attract insects. Colorful fruits attract certain fruit-eating animals whose subsequent droppings spread fruit seeds for new plant growth.

Color is used as protection by many animals. Arctic hares turn white in winter as camouflage in their snowy environment. Similarly, fawns have white spots for protection. Chameleons change color to match the background in which they are hiding. Female birds develop mixed plumage of earth tones to protect their nests during the birthing season. The males retain their bright colors to serve as distractions for predators.

We do not really see colors. Our eyes merely pick up different wavelengths of electromagnetic energy, which is within the visible light spectrum. Color televisions produce thousands of tiny dots that glow in the primary colors of red, green, and blue. We see these dots in combinations that our brains interpret as different colors. The combination of blue, green, and red produces white light, which allows the television to show black-and-white pictures.

Colors can produce surprising effects. We have become so accustomed to these effects that we recognize them at the subconscious level. Cover half a sheet of white paper with another sheet of brightly colored paper. Stare at it for 30 seconds, then remove the sheet of colored paper. What happens? If you just conducted this demonstration, you will note that the half that was covered with the colored paper will appear lighter than the other half.

The eyes will produce an afterimage if we stare at a colored image for 30 seconds and then look at a white surface. This afterimage has the same shape but a different color. The afterimage of red will be green. The afterimage of green will be red. Blue areas become yellow, and yellow areas become blue. Black reverses with white. One common trick is to show an American flag with a yellow field and green stripes. What happens when you look at a white surface after staring at this yellow and green flag for 30 seconds?

Phantom colors also appear in areas that are really black and white. A flashing black-and-white pattern similar to the rolling of a television picture (in black and white) will produce phantom colors. Other colors appear lighter when displayed on a black background. Background colors will affect the perception of primary central color.

Colors affect behavior. Some behavioral responses are learned, such as responses to red lights and green lights. Blue police uniforms cause socialized responses that we tend to associate with authority. Some responses seem more natural, although one may become used to a color over time, thereby muting the effect. Red lights produce more activity within groups. People pass the time less well in red light. Red leads to an increase in blood pressure, respiration, and the frequency of eye blink. Blue has the opposite effect. It seems to suppress activity. Time seems to pass more calmly. Blood pressure, respiration, and eye blinks are lowered. Of course, there are mitigating factors.

A general principle says that the physical and psychological effects of light increase with wavelength and intensity. Thus, the *red-light district* of town effectively uses light as a communicator and as a behavioral stimulator. Red has the largest wavelength and violet has the smallest. It is interesting to note that visual perception is highest in the middle of the spectrum of visible light (color). The spectrum ranges from red to orange, yellow, green, blue, and violet. The middle, or yellow-green, bands have the most visibility. The reds and violets have the least.

So why aren't all police cars, ambulances, and fire trucks painted yellow-green? Some are, but many fire departments and police departments are staying with the traditional colors because of their communication value. We are taught to identify red fire trucks and red lights with emergency. Many police departments have switched to a combination of red and blue emergency lights. Each of these colors has different recognition levels depending on whether it is night or day. Color also helps us differentiate between a police car and fire vehicle. Traditional or cultural values will generally prevail over the predicted effect. However, this applies to a small number of situations.

Lighting has two purposes within the CPTED conceptual model: one is for the illumination of human activities and the other is for security. It is important for the CPTED planner, before spending extra money on security lighting, to think about using the behavioral effects of already existing lighting that is required for illuminating human activities to promote crime and loss prevention.

Lighting does make people feel safer, but most outdoor lighting has been installed with a confused set of objectives. Many streetlights are so high that they light only the street, not the sidewalk. Cars have lights; people do not! Lighting in many public, off-street garages is placed over the vehicle lanes, not where people are when they emerge from or attempt to get into their cars.

Illumination consultants emphasize planning for lighting to enhance natural opportunities for light that comes through windows. Lighting has to be planned for nighttime use as well. The primary measure or objective of planning for lighting is to place light fixtures in numbers and locations sufficient to provide complete coverage of the floor within a minimum number of footcandles or lumens of strength.

My own office has a centrally located bank of fluorescent lights. The cone of light does reach the total square footage of the floor, but I stand over six feet and sit at 54 inches. The illumination is fine for normal desk work, but it leaves the walls and bookshelves in shadow. This makes the office appear small and cramped to visitors, who are reacting to the office as it really appears. What psychological effect would occur if track lighting were installed to illuminate the walls? Would it matter as much to me as it would to a visitor in terms of comfort and perception?

The answer to these questions is that a change of lighting to better match the objectives of the space would be effective. Lighted walls or ones that reflect light, such as mirrored walls, make a room seem bigger. Pictures of certain types take the place of windows. Pictures give insight into imaginary places. However, the lighting strategy has to match the behavioral objectives of a space. No lighting engineer or consultant can design the ultimate lighting effects without explicit knowledge of the desired behavioral effects or objectives for that particular space.

Foyers and hallways have been traditionally lighted from the center of the ceiling. It was logical to assume that a centrally placed light would provide a cone width that would cover the floor. Some research that was conducted in Louisville, Kentucky, found that people who assembled in elevator waiting areas that were centrally lighted tended to stand in the center and avoid eye contact. When they were interviewed later, they felt that the lobby was uncomfortable and unsafe. The lighting in the same lobby was redesigned to illuminate the walls and leave the center of the room in shadow. People stood nearer to the walls and established eye contact. They felt that the room was very comfortable and safe. They even thought that the room was larger than its actual dimensions.

Hallways that are illuminated from the center of the ceiling are most likely to be perceived as crowded. People will walk toward the center and avoid eye contact. Once the illumination is diverted to the walls, people will walk closer to the wall and will be more likely to make eye contact with one another. They will walk faster, feel safer, and think that the hallways are wider. A fringe benefit is that there is a 30 percent reduction in noise, even though people are walking faster.

A number of factors are associated with this latter result, but it is clear that the walls help absorb some of the normal noise that is associated with people in motion.

Airports do a good job of promoting desirable behavioral effects through design. The tube-like pedestrian corridors that are used to move people from the landside to the airside terminals are generally enclosed, but the corridors above ground use a lot of glazing to increase visibility and natural lighting. In the walkways that are below ground or totally enclosed, the walls are covered with rented advertising space. These advertisements are generally required to be brightly colored and well lighted, not only to attract attention but to diminish the "dead" effect of the walls. Of course, a behaviorist will note that people walk closer to the walls, feel less cramped, walk faster, and feel safer.

The designers of the remodeled United Airlines terminal at Chicago's O'Hare Airport have gone a major step beyond other designers of underground pedestrian access ways. They have installed a sequential neon light system that appears to move with the pedestrian. The speed of the sequence is geared to a fast pace. The overall effect is enhanced by the use of background music that sounds like electronic wind chimes. The music seems to be synchronized with the moving light system. Subliminally below the effect of the light and sound is a woman's voice that continuously repeats the phrase, "Keep walking, keep walking." The walls use an intricate pattern of panels that are connected to matching overhangs. The panels seem to undulate along the passageway with the tempo of the light and music. One's first encounter is curiously but appreciatively bewildering. You are sure to tell others about it. However, some veteran travelers mock the subliminal message, "Keep walking, keep walking," as they sprint through the tube.

Private security directors and police detectives have long known the value of environmental effects on interrogations. The use of lighting, desk size, chair height, clothing color, and pregnant pauses have proven beneficial in eliciting information from uncooperative individuals. Psychologists use many techniques in the interviewing and counseling process. Police are now trained to use such diagnostic, as opposed to interrogatory, interviewing techniques when dealing with victims of crisis or abuse.

One of the most vexing uses of the environment is to position a visitor to one's office in direct or refracted sunlight. As an eyeglass wearer, I am made personally uncomfortable as a visitor to someone's office when I have to remove my glasses to see beyond the glare, only to find the host still sitting in an aura of light. My revenge is to move my chair to a more comfortable position, without asking permission. By invading the host's space, possibly moving beyond the side of the desk to the area behind it, out of the glare, I annoy my host by exposing this little bit of gamesmanship.

The following examples are just a sample of the kind of knowledge that is being gained through studies of the effects of color and light:

- Blue-green in operating rooms eliminates glare and helps physicians focus on the red and pink colors of the body. Yellow-green should be avoided, since the reflection on human flesh makes it appear sickly. Color variation is important to the frame of mind in both patients and staff.[2]
- Wearing black colors makes you look thinner and feel better.[3]
- Exposure to bright light helps overcome jet lag and reset circadian rhythms.[4]
- The deeper the density of a color, the more it inspires consumer trust. Bright orange and lime green should be avoided because they have negative connotations. Primary colors like red, blue, yellow, and green are generally well received by consumers.[5]
- Light may be used to cure winter depressions and the general blahs. Light has direct effects on learning and on treating affective disorders.[6]

These references to research on the use of light and color on human behavior are just the tip of the iceberg. A reference librarian at any public library can introduce the reader to an overwhelming volume of literature on the subject. Moreover, practically all libraries will offer an incredible array of literature on the use of architectural design and space management techniques to influence and manipulate behavior.

The problem is that researchers all have different standards for what they consider acceptable and pertinent research findings. The various professions tend to limit their reading and research to the topic areas that contain the name of their subject. A criminal justice specialist or academic criminologist will probably stick to that profession's journals and will look for the words *crime* or *crime prevention* in any list of references. The traffic engineer, on the other hand, will not be interested in a title with *crime prevention* in it. Likewise, the planner, developer, and architect look to the title for the determination of their interest. Paradoxically, experimental and industrial psychologists have developed a wealth of information over the years that could be used immediately in practical situations.

[2]Birren, F., "Color and Psychotherapy," *Journal of Interior Design*, Dec. 1983, 166.

[3]Malkin, N., "Nobody's Perfect," *Harper's Bazaar*, Jan. 1989, 90.

[4]Pool, R., "Illuminating Jet Lag," *Science*, June 1989, 1256; Czeisler, A., "Bright Light Induction of Strong Type or Resetting of Circadian Rhythm," *Science*, June 1989, 1238; Fackelmann, K., "A Light Touch Changes the Biological Clock," *Science News*, June 1989, 374.

[5]Tucker, J., "Psychology of Color," *Target Marketing*, June 1989, 40.

[6]Zimmer, D., "Light Fantastic." *World Press*, April 1987, 55; Graves, B., "Facility Planning: Shedding Light on Learning," *American School and University*, March 1985, 88; Pechter, K., "Heal Yourself with Light," *Prevention*, May 1984.

Feng Shui

Feng shui is the centuries-old Chinese art of promoting harmony in space. It has some mystical elements and many practical commonsense theories and observations about how people respond to space management and design. The mystical elements have served their purpose over time by developing a belief system about harmony in space that is near religious in nature. But each of these elements is expressed in fundamental concepts of environmental psychology in modern applications.

Feng shui is pronounced in many ways, depending on the dialect of Chinese or other Asian languages from which it is practiced. The common English pronunciation is similar to the sounds expressed by *fongue schway*. A growing interest in feng shui in North America and in Europe parallels the interest in CPTED. Moreover, studies of how people respond to space management and design are abundant in modern marketing research.

More than 150 books and manuals on the practice of feng shui have been produced over many centuries. Although there are some differences among them in definitions and use of terms, the fundamental concept of feng shui remains the same: the desire to promote harmony in space by emphasizing positive forces and minimizing or eliminating negative forces. Positive forces are often expressed as *ch'i*, and negative forces are referred to as *sha* or *negative ch'i*. Ch'i is the force that links humans with nature. Sha is ma-aligned, or bad, currents of energy that disrupt the environment.

Wind, water, light, and color are important elements in feng shui. They are observed by feng shui experts, called *geomancers*, in existing space to determine their effect, individually and in combination, on behavior. Environmental cues are established by how space is designed and used. These cues affect behavior in positive and negative ways. CPTED and feng shui are similar in observing that negative cues produce fear and avoidance behaviors on the part of normal or desired users of space. Positive cues produce desired responses and behaviors. Positive cues reinforce proprietary concern for space and territorial behavior.

The following are some of the many examples of feng shui and CPTED applications:

- Weaving pathways or roads are preferred over straight ones because they divert negative arrows of energy (sha) and they promote a wider field of vision for observation because of the need to maneuver.
- Offset glass-lined store entrances in malls and shopping centers deflect sha and increase visual access to identify the store and observe activities.
- Bay-type windows increase visual access to and from sidewalks and streets, promoting visual ease and harmony and thus increasing the perception of natural surveillance.

- Continuous sheer walls that serve as noise barriers along expressways tend to reflect negative energy and dominate the field of vision of drivers, thus producing tunnel vision and safety hazards.
- Sitting with one's back immediately in front of a window facilitates the absorption of negative energy, thus promoting discomfort and avoidance behavior of these spaces; it reduces the perception of natural surveillance.
- A teacher or boss whose desk or workstation faces students or workers reflects sha and creates conflict through their apparent inaccessibility and superior message. Instead, revealing one's side to the student, worker, or client produces ch'i, or positive energy, and a better team environment, which increases proprietary concern for space and territorial behaviors.
- Theater, meeting room, or classroom doors that open outward allow sha to escape from these spaces and promote easier egress for life-safety reasons.
- Sharp edges on buildings and corners in hallways project sha, thereby increasing anxiety and discomfort. Round or curving edges produce ch'i, resulting in increased comfort, wider fields of vision, and increased perception of surveillance.
- A bedroom door that opens immediately onto the head of the bed produces negative sha, which increases anxiety, thereby interrupting sleep. It also reduces the time for a person to identify and respond to an attacker.
- Landscaping that obscures windows and pedestrian approaches to buildings creates confusion and anxiety (sha); it also reduces natural surveillance.
- Enclosed elevators trap sha, or negative energy, which creates anxiety and avoidance behavior. A glass-backed elevator or one with mirrors on the back wall deflects sha and improves comfort. It also allows the potential user to see if anyone is inside and increases natural surveillance.
- Grid pattern streets facilitate the flow of sha, which facilitates speeding and ease of access for unwanted persons, which in turn increases anxiety and avoidance behavior for pedestrians and residents. Streetscape improvements can deflect sha and increase ch'i, thus slowing speeds, increasing drivers' field of vision, and enhancing the perception of safety.

It is clear that feng shui provides another tool for helping CPTED planners understand human and environment interactions. It also provides a better means for the CPTED planner to articulate environment and behavior concepts to the designers and users of space. For the CPTED practitioner, feng shui highlights that definition of space and interpretations of environmental cues have an important cultural dimension, which must not be discounted or ignored.

6

AESTHETICS, ENVIRONMENTAL CUES, AND TERRITORIAL BEHAVIOR: IMPLICATIONS FOR CPTED PLANNING

CHAPTER OUTLINE

Form Versus Function: The Battle with Aesthetics

Many people find it very difficult to resist the urge to mess with things. Nearly everyone has turned a screw one too many times and broken it off or made an extra cut on a piece of cloth that ruined it. In consumer goods, it seems that automobile manufacturers cannot resist the temptation to regularly change body styles. Men's ties get wider each year to a point, and then they start getting narrow again.

It is fundamental to human nature to go through cycles that start with an emphasis on function (e.g., getting the job done) and eventually end up focusing on form (e.g., how things appear). The form of things, or the aesthetic quality, tends to drive the thinking of consumers and designers alike. Once humans learn how to build something new or do something different, the initial attention to merely reaching the objective shifts with the confidence that comes with experience.

The history of the Ford Mustang automobile is a good example of the natural continuum in which function gives way to form or aesthetics. After World War II, the retooled auto industry had to go to mass production of inexpensive cars to recover from the loss of the demand for war material. Once the economy picked up and material became more available, competition caused the auto designers to add fins to the tails of cars and battering rams to the fronts. So much emphasis was placed on form that by 1962, function had been sacrificed. Then, in the second half of the 1964 model year, Ford introduced a sleek, efficiently designed car called the Mustang. It was an instant success and a trendsetter over the monstrous tail-finned vehicles of the late 1950s and early '60s. Throughout the '60s and into the '70s, planned obsolescence reduced many autos to failure within two to three years, and even Ford could not resist the temptation to change its design for the highly successful Mustang. The Mustang eventually failed as a product line in 1974 due to a number of changes Ford made to the design. The 1974 Ford Mustang barely resembled its 1964 predecessor.

Human activities seem to follow the continuum from an early emphasis on function to later preoccupation with form. Function gets overlooked, which generally results in catastrophic failure of the human activity. The "longhairs" of the 1960s became the "shorthairs" of the 1980s and '90s. The "crew-cut" crowd of the '60s now wears their hair long. The movie *Butterfield 8* was met with outright indignation by my hometown preacher when it was released in 1960. After years of waiting to see the movie, I was sorely disappointed in the content. Yet television soap operas in 1999 offered more explicit sexual and sensitive material than anything that could have been imagined even as recently as the early 1990s.

It must be that the changing world requires that people become gradually accustomed to change. Whatever the explanation, it is clear that nothing will ever remain the same except the predictability of change and human nature. Accordingly, it must be assumed that form, or aesthetics, will always outweigh function in any human endeavor.

CPTED concepts require the user to question everything. CPTED concepts require the user to relate design and use decisions to the objectives of space. But the CPTED planner must seek to achieve a balance between the necessity to meet the requirements of human functions and the need to fulfill the aesthetic demands. Otherwise, the human function may not meet its objectives.

Figure 6.1 presents a model of the conflict between function and form. The model presents form and function in reverse relationship. As the requirement for functionality increases, as in a military base, the tolerance for aesthetics or emphasis on form decreases. But at the other end of the spectrum, a tomb or mortuary has very little functional demand, so form is not only tolerated, it is demanded. Monuments and military bases, as human "activities," have clearly defined functional requirements, but the functional requirements of most human activities are not so obvious.

Most human activities fall within a few degrees plus or minus the center of the continuum. As their functional requirements become less clear, it is likely that form may win over function in the final design. Schools, houses, offices, shops, and major commercial centers are susceptible to the error of leaning too far toward aesthetics in design. It does not become a problem until the aesthetic demands alter the

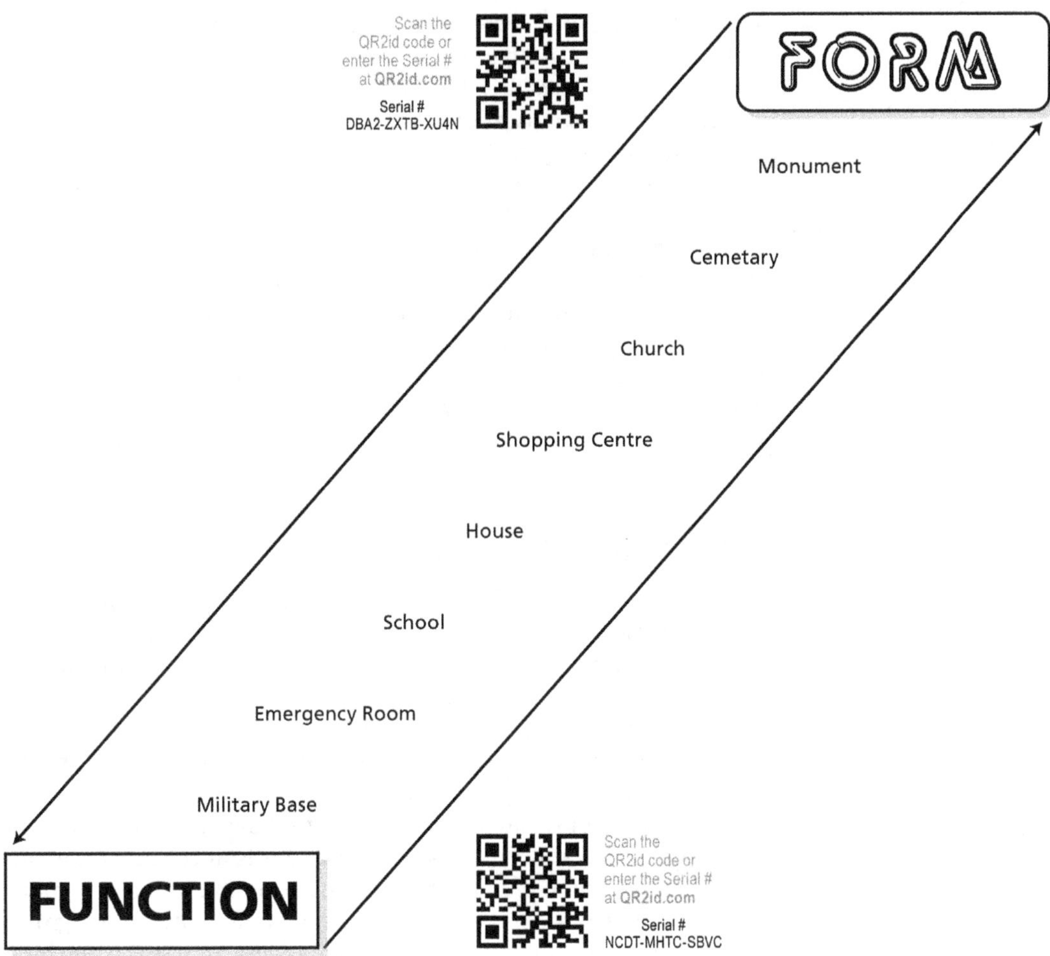

Figure 6.1 Function versus form.

human function. Designers in Louisville, Kentucky, forgot their objective of creating a pedestrian street when they installed cobblestones in place of paver tile or asphalt. People cannot walk easily on cobblestones. Jacksonville, Florida, designers forgot that 51 percent of our population wear high-heeled shoes at night when they specified that the new River Walk boardwalk site would use lumber strips that were separated, to allow pedestrians to see the water below. Downtown planners nearly everywhere forget to determine how the desired user of space will get to a location. Many buildings are designed to appeal to the pedestrian even though the ultimate user group has to arrive by car, park behind the building, and walk around to the front.

Perhaps the greatest service that a CPTED planner may provide is to question everything. It has been demonstrated that the CPTED approach works best when the planner is guided by the desire to make the human function work as the primary objective. This is not to say, however, that the CPTED approach is against aesthetics. Aesthetics are critical to human existence. Even the person who is most unmoved by aesthetics will not be indifferent to that aspect of design when it comes to marriages, christenings, bar mitzvahs, parades, burials, and other special events.

The best way for a person to use the CPTED approach is to (1) share the concepts and (2) ask questions. The most important thing is to ask, "What are you trying to do here, and how can we help you do it better?" The emphasis has to be on attaining the objectives of the human function, whatever it may be, instead of merely avoiding security problems. Human functions that work well have fewer security problems. Human functions that are failing experience more problems of security and loss, which exacerbate their demise.

Environmental Cues

Environmental cues have important effects on both normal and abnormal users of space. The cues that tell a normal user that she could be unsafe will usually have the opposite effect on the abnormal user, who will perceive the same cues as indications that he is at low risk of detection, thereby safe. Conversely, cues that tell a normal user of space that she is safe will increase the perception of risk for the abnormal user. He will feel unsafe.

Perhaps the only environmental cue that has the same effect on both normal and abnormal users of space is distance. The farther an individual is from a potential threat, the easier that threat is to manage. For instance, a person who has to encounter a drunk or a group of rowdy boys on a downtown sidewalk has very little space in which to squeeze by on the typical shrunken pedestrian space in a high-capacity street. Cars are whizzing by in high numbers and at high speeds. The net result is avoidance behavior. The pedestrian either refuses to come to that street or, if required to be there, chooses to avoid eye contact and hurry by the potential threat.

Distance is often a safety cue for the potential offender. The farther an offender or abnormal user is from a threat—in this case, a police officer or a determined landowner—the lower the value or impact of the threat. Distance is directly related to the magnitude of the number of excuses for improper behavior. For instance, "Coach, I didn't hear you yelling at me!"

"Officer, I thought you were waving Hi to me!" "I thought you were chasing someone else or you were after another car." These are typical excuses. Direct and close exposure to people in control of environments is anathema to the abnormal user.

CPTED planners can plan strategies to affect only the normal users of space, since they may be the primary objective of the human function. A shopping center or mall is a good example of human space that is oriented around attracting large numbers of desired (normal) users. An athletic facility or ocean beach is the same. Some other environments may influence the CPTED planner to emphasize behavioral affects on the abnormal (undesired) user. A public park may be oriented to attract normal (desired) users during daytime but strive to keep away abnormal (undesired) users at night. Strategies may be entirely oriented around the abnormal user because of the uniqueness of the area. For instance, managers of a reservoir or protected game area may need to eliminate all human usage. Owners of a warehouse, industrial zone, or riverfront docking area may specifically desire to exclude vagrants from using the location for any purpose.

It is easy to observe the various effects of the environment on behavior. The design of the environment exhibits cues that affect human behavior. The environment's management or how it is being used has direct effects on behavior. The way users react to the environment also sets off cues that affect others' perceptions of the space. A shopping center or mall is a great place to observe these human/environment interactions, especially late in the day or at night. People try to park next to other cars. They try to park within line of sight of their desired entrance. Once they exit their vehicles, they scurry toward the mall entrance, almost as though it were freezing cold. Their shoulders are rolled forward and they avoid eye contact with others by looking down at their feet. Anyone who converges on their path is given a wide berth and is viewed suspiciously.

This overt behavior pattern changes once the person reaches the entrance to the mall or shopping center. The shoulders roll back and the walking pattern changes from scurrying to strolling. Eye contact is established with others who are encountered nearby. Staring is permissible. People even report that they enjoy watching others to see what they are wearing and how they act. Try doing that in the parking lot and see the reaction it gets! These controlling or challenging cues say to others that someone is watching who feels safe and who will not tolerate any improper activity, but the avoidance behavior (cues) in the parking lot tends to reinforce the abnormal users' perception of safety or low risk.

Environmental cues in a residential area are important. Clean gutters and residents' staring behavior tell outsiders that they have been noticed. Holiday decorations make a clear statement that the residents are house-proud and competitive. Many euphemisms are used to describe this behavior, such as pride, cohesiveness, and community spirit. However, the underlying motivation is the basic nature of humans to be competitive, jealous, and envious—the real behavioral qualities that keep a neighborhood together.

Normal users of a space feel safer when they enter a neighborhood where the residents stare at them, thus acknowledging the visitor's presence. Abnormal users feel more exposed or at greater risk. Normal users feel unsafe in a neighborhood where people refuse to establish eye contact, where avoidance behavior is commonplace. Tightly curtained windows signify the withdrawal of concern by residents. Unkempt lawns and sidewalks indicate a retreat from the street. Conversely, the loosely curtained window and manicured, or at least cared for, sidewalk and adjacent planting strip convey a cue that says, "We own this."

Residents and nonresidents of a space act differently and respond differently to environmental cues. Residents become inured to the gradually changing environment. Nonresidents see it as it is. A shabby restaurant or convenience store may be popular among residents because they identify with the owners and have a proprietary concern for the continuity of the establishment. Resident customers or clients are loyal to their favorite store, even if the prices are not competitive. Why? Humans are social animals and need familiarity as comfort against daily stresses and pressures. Therefore, it is easy to become accustomed to environmental conditions that may be repugnant to outsiders.

Nonresidents of a space see places as they are. Environmental cues jump out at them as they enter a new area. Accordingly, their attitudes are affected by that first impression. This differentiation of the resident from the nonresident is crucial to the CPTED planner. Environmental cues will either make or break a project that has failed to identify and define the target user group. Successful projects must also continuously assess their user group to ensure that design and space management procedures are consistent with the potentially changing behavioral patterns.

Environmental cues are observed continuously by all humans and they are reacted to in the decision-making process that directly affects the productive use of space and the related quality of life in places that work and that are achieving the aims of the human function. Territorial behavior is linked directly to environmental cues because the cues are manifestations of proprietary concern and ownership.

Territorial Behavior

Cave dwellers cleared areas in front of their cave to mark their private space. Now the first thing a person does when moving into an office or apartment is to put their "stuff" up. Travelers always unpack their bags and hang up their clothes once they check into a hotel room, before they do anything else. This not only helps to hang out the wrinkles, it personalizes the room. Each traveler has his or her own habit in this regard. As a regular traveler, I have observed a wide range of idiosyncrasies among associates. Some will place all of their belongings in either the closet or the drawers; others will stack everything in neat little piles on the spare bed. Most business travelers will leave as much as possible of their clothing in the suitcase but will produce an elaborate display of business materials and working papers.

Territorial behavior is characteristic of all human, even all animal, existence. Humans establish hierarchies of territories, or turf, that range from private to semiprivate to semipublic to public space. Humans in particular have a need to establish both temporary and permanent ownership of space. That a person's home is his castle is a universally recognized concept and legal tradition. Experts in crisis intervention know that even the most minor offense that involves an intrusion into one's abode is a major stress-producing event for the residents. Police are trained to be sensitive to an individual's concerns and resultant fears about even minor burglaries. It is common knowledge that the meekest person is fiercely protective of the home front.

Humans and animals mark their turf. People put up signs of ownership, pictures in rooms and flowers or other landscaping outdoors. Animals allocate turf naturally based on the number of animals, the food supply, and the terrain. South American llamas establish territories in perfect squares. Common squirrels allocate yard space and fight whenever another squirrel ventures into an established space. Dogs defend their turf vigorously, even when they are outsized. Interestingly, other animals tend to acknowledge turf identities and respond accordingly. Human beings mark their turf using fences, signs, and plain border definition. The common law requires that turf or property be identified as a prerequisite to the defense of property rights.

Everyone encounters turf identity and recognition problems daily. A person goes through many transitional turf states from the time he or she arises and goes to work until returning home. The homemaker encounters a daily interaction with turf issues. Child supervision and lawn maintenance are part of the process of marking turf. Admonitions to children, such as, "Don't leave our yard," or "Don't walk through the neighbor's yard," reinforce turf identity. Hanging out laundry is a simple reinforcement of turf that is generally taken for granted. Where the family automobile is parked is a more direct establishment of turf. This is why the broad, undifferentiated parking areas in many apartment or public housing complexes are anathema to successful housing management. Accordingly, one of the better ways to establish harmony in a garden apartment complex is to arrange the parking areas as cul-de-sacs so that parking spaces seem to belong naturally to certain housing groups.

Turf identification, behavioral responses, and environmental cues are linked. For example, on moving to Louisville in 1985, I went to the downtown area to photograph the convention center, which had nearly destroyed the commercial activities around it even though it was originally intended to revitalize them. Parking on the east side of the center, I stepped across the street to take a panoramic shot of the building. However, as I attempted to step onto the sidewalk, I encountered three young men who were passing along in front of a series of porn shops. The orange- and green-haired youngsters wore chains and leather jackets and were prominently displaying (and playing) a boom box. Without stopping to think, I did an about-face and went back across the street to study the roofline of the building. Of course, I neatly concealed my expensive camera as well. What had I done?

I had not only conceded turf to these young men, but through my overt avoidance behavior I had also reinforced their territorial behavior. What would have happened if these same young fellows had visited the NCPI campus and actually had the audacity to walk down one of the hallways when I was teaching a class? It is easy to surmise that the reaction would have been different. The young men would have been immediately challenged and the boom box would have been turned off. The class members would have then assisted them in finding the main entrance to the campus. Why would my reaction to the young men have been so radically different just because of the difference in location? Obviously, I would feel safer with a classroom full of police and security officers. Moreover, I would be defending my own turf and therefore would automatically put fight before flight or put challenging behavior before avoidance behavior in responding to the situation.

It would have been ludicrous for me to have challenged the young men on the downtown street. First, I had no right of ownership. Second, I could have been beaten up for my trouble. Any challenge would have been just too much of a threat to the macho identity of the youngsters. They would have been compelled to demonstrate their ownership or territorial prerogatives; otherwise they would have lost the stability or foundation for coping within their environment. This sense of retention or loss of fundamental control is crucial to the existence of users of a space. Fear is a strong and dangerous motivator of human-response mechanisms.

Territorial behavior is demonstrated through both design and use responses. Any area that is well defined by borders and signs says to the user that it is controlled, that it is owned. Permanent ownership of space is defined by law, by deed, by occupation, by acknowledgment, and by design. Temporary ownership of space, such as one's seat at a meeting, is defined by occupancy and by signs. Signs of temporary ownership include marking the space by leaving a personal item (e.g., briefcase, jacket, or notebook) to signify that the space has been claimed. A newspaper or magazine will not suffice in the claiming of temporary space, because these items are not personal enough in nature. Sometimes other forms of physical signs are appropriate. A chair that leans up against a banquet room table says that someone went to some effort to signify claim. The chair did not get there by itself.

The physical definition of ownership sets the stage for the user's enforcement of territorial prerogatives. For example, if someone moved your jacket and briefcase from a seat at a meeting while you were off to get a cup of coffee, you would be within your rights to actively challenge the individual on your return. An active challenge would be something like this:

"Excuse me, but I think you took my seat." The language is polite, but the message is clear that the person violated another's space. A more direct and challenging approach might be: "Obviously you knew that someone had already claimed this seat when you moved my stuff!" Both of these challenges are formally polite but are clearly stated as an indictment.

Consider the opposite situation wherein an individual approaches another who is already sitting in a desired spot. "Excuse me, but would you mind terribly doing me this awfully important favor by letting me have your seat?" First, how can someone "mind terribly" doing an "awfully important" favor? Certainly, this is a phrase or expression, but it also says that one has to "mind" a lot to refuse the "awful" inconvenience of moving to a less desirable spot, especially after going to the trouble of getting there early to claim a choice seat. Of course, the person who already owns the seat is put on the spot by having to refuse the request. However, anyone who is involved in marketing knows that guilt is the strongest tool in making sales. People are affected by their perception that they owe something to the salesperson who took the time to help them look at or try out a product. Accordingly, a passive challenge may be as powerful as an active challenge. It depends on the situation.

Users of space respond to challenges based on their perception of the situation. Environmental cues that indicate extended or intensive territorial concern convey the sense of safety for the normal user and risk for the abnormal user. Challenging behavior on the part of the normal or desired users of space enhance design features that signify ownership. These behaviors reinforce territorial markers. I have experimented with this phenomenon in a variety of neighborhoods.

Once, while driving through a residential area in Minneapolis, I stopped along the curb in an older neighborhood. The gutter was clean and the homes were well maintained. Flowers and little fences were prominent on the edges of lawns. Some residents had even placed flowers in the planting strip between the curb and sidewalk. As I emerged from my car, an elderly man who was watering his lawn began to demonstrate staring behavior by edging over toward the car and moving his head about in exaggerated motions, with a perplexed expression on his face. What was he communicating? Why couldn't he simply have waited until I approached him to let him know what I was doing before he challenged me? The answer is that he felt very secure on this street and naturally exhibited intense proprietary concern for what was happening on his turf.

As I jumped about to avoid being doused by the spray of water from the hose that the man was holding, I responded to his question about my intended business by asking for the correct house of a person who he knew lived four doors down the block. The older man pointed this out and then repeated it in very emphatic terms as I began to walk down the street.

"I said, young man, that the Smiths live down there!" What was he trying to communicate? I realized that he was indicating that if I was going to the Smiths that I had better move my car in front of their house and not leave it parked on the curb in front of his house.

In another neighborhood, which was clearly run-down and poorly maintained, I was neither challenged nor stared at, even as I began taking photos. The few people who were outside disappeared. There were no flowers in the planting strips and there was very little border definition of individual yards. Front porches were largely bare of any furnishings. Many of the homes had fenced-in back yards that obscured visual access. What was the message emanating from the design and use behavior in this neighborhood? Had these people turned their backs to the street? Had they surrendered their territorial imperatives? What reaction would this environment trigger in an abnormal or undesired user? Would that person feel safe, at low risk of challenge?

While conducting a CPTED training program in Trenton, New Jersey, I assigned a 10-block section of a residential area to one of the class teams for their site assessment project. The area was composed of small, tightly packed row homes that came all the way to the sidewalk. It was easy to see major differences in territorial concern as we walked along the street. On one end we observed that the windows on each house were tightly curtained. There were no flower boxes hanging below the windows, and the front stoops were not upgraded. They were also poorly maintained. No chairs or benches were in front of the homes, and the sidewalk was uneven and considerably littered and dirty.

Farther down the street, awnings placed over front doors and windows became more numerous. Windows were loosely curtained.

Stoops were upgraded. The farther one went, the more the street changed. Flower boxes were hung beneath windows and placed next to the sidewalks. Chairs and benches were prominently placed in front of homes. At the very end of this section of homes, flower boxes had been placed along the curb, and the sidewalk had been replaced in many areas with decorative brick.

What were these environmental cues saying to both the normal and abnormal users of this street? Had the folks at one end turned their backs to the street? Had they surrendered their sidewalk? What were the residents at the other end saying to passersby? The team that was assigned to conduct a site assessment found out very quickly: Some boys attempted to sell them drugs at one end of the street and the Trenton Police stopped them at the other end in response to a neighbor's call about some suspicious-acting people who were walking around looking at houses. Is it hard to guess which end was the one where the drug sellers were and which the one where the police confronted them?

Temporary custody of space is nearly as important as permanent ownership. The next time you are in a checkout line at a drugstore or supermarket, watch the territorial behavior that goes on. Airplane ticket lines, fast-food restaurants, and banks share the same phenomena. What happens when someone steps out of line to look at a display or to pick up another product? There is a tendency for the people behind to move forward, to assume the other person's space. They are very reluctant to step back when the person returns, as though this is their way of indicating their displeasure.

Drivers are even worse about the moving custody of space. I watched a driver actually speed up, nearly causing a collision, when an oncoming driver made a turn across his path. What was in the mind of the aggrieved driver? Was he trying to punish the other one for preempting his space and creating a dangerous situation? Wasn't he making the situation worse? Yet this happens every day on the street. My study of assaults in Fairfax County, Virginia, found that more than 10 percent of all reported assaults occurred as a direct result of disputes between drivers. It is very common for drivers to aim their vehicle at an oncoming car that is going the wrong direction down a one-way street. How many times have you waited at night until an oncoming car was right on you to switch on your high beams to let them know that they had failed to switch theirs off? This must be the natural way to scold another driver who endangers one's safety through their lack of attention: by increasing the danger to both.

Temporary custody of space has some interesting, if not funny, implications. For years, I have routinely moved people's stuff around during the first break of a CPTED lecture or presentation. It is simply a great way to involve the audience in understanding territorial behavior. This practice ended in a near-calamitous situation when I was giving a presentation of safe neighborhoods to a group of senior citizens.

I called a break to let the folks get a cup of coffee or tea. Immediately, without thinking, I moved a few purses and jackets. Within minutes there were a number of groups arguing openly until I shouted for quiet to admit, rather smartly, that it was all a joke to show them about territorial behavior. Most people laughed until the crowd parted to reveal an elderly gentleman who was shaking his finger in my direction, shouting that it was no joke, that he had already called another old guy a jerk for moving his stuff. The man was really upset.

Proprietary regard for space has proven throughout history to be a motivating force. The convenience-store industry is finding that the employee who is busy throughout the store is more likely to protect it than the one who spends most of his time behind the counter. When the industry converted to lower shelves and wider aisles, the employees complained that they would have to restock more often. They wanted to put everything out as it was delivered, instead of storing some products first until the smaller shelf systems were depleted. After all, why stack things twice when you can put it all out on high shelves in the beginning. Yet in restocking more frequently, employees are busier, time passes more quickly, and losses are lower in the new stores. This is a powerful example of the impact of management of space on increasing and extending proprietary concern, which then affects profit and losses. The employee who regularly services and stocks an area of a store is going to notice more things and act more protective than one who only occasionally goes to that area.

Oldham and Fried's article, "Employee Reactions to Workspace Characteristics,"[1] reported that employees were most likely to withdraw from offices and experience dissatisfaction when the following conditions were present:

- The workspace was rated as dark.
- Few enclosures surrounded employee work areas.
- Employees were seated close to each other.
- Many employees occupied the work area.

It seems to be axiomatic that people will take care of space and assets in which they have a proprietary concern. Perhaps there is a lesson here for increasing productivity and reducing loss. Common experience is replete with examples. For instance, take-home police cars cost less to operate than pool cars. Carpenters and machinists have always been required to buy their own tools. They take better care of them that way. Likewise, a homeowner who physically

[1] Oldham, L., and Fried, G., "Employee Reactions to Workspace Characteristics," *Journal of Applied Statistics*, Feb. 1987, 176.

participates in the care of common areas is more apt to pay attention to what transpires there.

The better a place is defined regarding ownership, the more likely a nonresident or visitor is to be conspicuous. Another near standard that is emerging from CPTED experience is the objective of minimizing unassigned space. Multiple-purpose space may best be assigned to the most prevalent user group, with the provision that others can use it when necessary. Hallways, foyers, and stair systems are generally unassigned, despite the fact that the interior spaces that they adjoin are claimed. It is common for interior decorators to recommend that uniform color and furnishings be used in these areas, which further detaches them from any perceived ownership.

It is a given that humans behave territorially. All humans move transitionally each day from private to semiprivate to semipublic to public space and back again. It is an inexorable process that will never change. The CPTED planner needs only to bring these observations to the conscious level in order to share these behavioral concepts with people who are making decisions about human space and to ask the questions that no one else thought to ask.

Visual Bubbles, Landscape, and Art

Human beings are born with natural responses to certain environmental stimuli. Other responses are learned within the context of culture, education, training, and experience. Tests with newborn humans and animals reveal that they inherit natural responses to visual stimuli. For instance, when newborns are shown a film from the perspective of someone approaching the edge of a cliff, the subjects will automatically react when they think they are going over the side. Visual stimuli are some of the most important to humans, but by no means are they mutually exclusive of other forms of perception.

Perhaps the best means of understanding the impact of visual space is to use a camera as an analogy. Cameras are designed to simulate functions of the human eye. The lens admits light that is reflected from objects. The light energy has been altered by objects, which allows the images to be represented on the film. Similarly, the retina, or back of the eye, absorbs the light energy and interprets the various wavelengths into three-dimensional shapes. This is where the similarity to the camera ends, because the field or width of vision and depth or distance of vision of a camera may be adjusted. Conversely, the human eye records the environment with a fixed field of vision and depth perception.

Humans establish "visual bubbles" that vary in depth, height, and width according to territorial definition and geography. A visual bubble may be defined as that space in which a person consciously recognizes things within the environment. Most environmental cues are dealt with subconsciously, outside of the visual bubble, unless something unusual happens to bring one of these elements to the level of consciousness. For instance, an opaque fence in a person's back yard will establish the outer limit of a visual bubble. Symbolic fences may create the same effect of psychologically obscuring what is happening on the other side, or outside the visual bubble. Thus, an offender who thinks that a solid fence provides concealment unknowingly has the added benefit of the fact that neighbors or passersby are probably not looking anyway.

Why is this idea important to a study of CPTED? The answer is that the visual sense scans the middle and far environment to collect information for immediate survival and protection. Environmental cues are assessed by all the human perceptual senses. But the visual sense provides information about hazards, finding one's way, identity of objects in the environment, and what attracts the perceiver. There is a whole field of study dedicated to the perception of art, sculpture, advertising, fashion, landscape design, and safety. For instance, highway safety is almost totally linked to visual perception. Traffic engineers know that certain locations have a high volume of accidents. Other locations seem to induce excessive speeds. Noise attenuation barriers along the side of expressways are known to create tunnel vision in drivers, leading to accidents.

The following are some examples of the importance of planning for visual space in CPTED:

- Downtown pedestrian malls and regional retail malls quite often use landscape elements and sitting areas to push customers closer to businesses on the theory that they will be more likely to make a purchase if they are within the zone of influence of the business. But the customers' field of vision is dominated by individual elements of the store and is prevented from identifying the store itself. This results in hostility and avoidance behavior that can lower sales and create the perception of lack of safety, particularly when the customer has a limited number of choices for maneuvering.
- One-way streets with off-street parking and synchronized traffic signals surely speed up the flow of vehicles and diminish the disruption of continuous speeds. But this ease actually reduces drivers' field of vision to a narrow visual bubble, which results in higher speeds, more hazards, and little notice or surveillance of surrounding land uses and activities.
- The height of ceilings in hallways and meeting rooms has a direct relationship to attentiveness and movement; low ceilings suppress behavior and high ceilings tend to stimulate activity and attention.

- Transitional landscaping on curving portions of walking and bike trails increases the depth of vision and provides the user of this space with more information and choices regarding safety hazards or criminal threats.
- Wider porches in front of convenience stores help give customers more choices to avoid potential contact with nuisance persons, thus increasing sales to, for instance, adult customers who would avoid the store if they had to encounter juveniles.
- Towers and spires on buildings located on corners or intersections help people find their way and relieve anxiety about distances and identification of places.
- Noise barriers along expressways can contribute to an increase in accidents by creating tunnel vision for drivers when the barriers are constructed of sheer walls and opaque materials.
- Opaque enclosures of trash receptacles and loading docks will dominate the field of vision of passersby. Conversely, transparent fencing material used in screening of trash receptacles and loading docks will cause these areas to fall into the visual background, which is precisely what the designer intends.
- Hostile landscaping can reduce maintenance costs and prevent graffiti and unwanted entry to properties.
- Landscaping helps identify borders between public and private space. It also helps reinforce the definition of desired behaviors by defining movement areas.
- Art and sculpture are powerful tools in promoting territorial behavior and proprietary concern for space. They attract attention to spaces and help people find their way. One of the greatest values of street art is how it contributes to triangulation, which helps people psychologically connect places, thus increasing perceptions of territoriality and control.

7

CRIME AND LOSS PREVENTION

CHAPTER OUTLINE

Introduction

The challenge of crime to society changes with the advance of civilization, particularly as technology continues to improve. Advancing technology brings greater opportunity and human comforts. But it also introduces new opportunities and temptations for human greed.

In the preface to the original printing of *Oliver Twist*, Dickens described 19th-century criminals in London:

> *I had read of thieves by scores—seductive fellows, amiable, faultless in dress, plump in pocket, choice in horseflesh, bold, great at song and fit companions for the bravest … But I had never met with the miserable reality. It appeared to me that to draw a knot of associates in crime as they really do exist; to paint them in all their deformity, in all their wretchedness, in all the squalid poverty of their lives; to show them as they are. It appeared to me that to do this would be to attempt something which was greatly needed, and which would be a service to society.*

Dickens wrote this defense in the preface to his book after intense public criticism of his audacity in openly describing criminal conditions in England. The so-called good society was shocked that

Dickens would publicly describe the actual conditions of crime, but his work served to reinforce the notion that criminal behavior is limited solely to the lower classes of society. Although Dickens's works forced the upper classes to acknowledge the existence of criminal conditions, this sentiment prevailed into the 20th century. Societal and scientific concepts of crime are related to the antisocial behavior of bad people or career criminals. It is still popular in some areas of society to associate criminal behavior with the poor physical and social conditions of the impoverished segments of our population, whereas psychological explanations of offending are preferred by others. However, many social scientists persist in identifying the origins of criminal behavior with lack of opportunity and improper education.

Some attempts have been made to legitimize criminal behavior as the only means of existence for individuals who would otherwise be law-abiding citizens if only they were given the chance in life that is enjoyed by the middle and upper classes. A small number of individuals who are loosely associated with an ideology labeled *radical criminology* believe that crime is caused by the military-industrial establishment through its denial of opportunity to all but the upper classes. The popular musical stage show and subsequent film *West Side Story* implanted this notion, at least in American society, by characterizing delinquent behavior as the product of a disadvantaged environment. Unfortunately, much of contemporary theory about criminal behavior and rehabilitation focuses on what may be a limited view of human behavior. The many diverse sociological, psychological, and biological theories of criminal behavior do not explain the known, but officially unacknowledged, realm of criminal behavior that relates to dishonesty, cheating, and breach of duty that may be pervasive in all societies, at all levels of class and social position. The problems of white-collar crime, organized crime, insurance fraud, financial fraud, and evasion of duty (e.g., tax cheating) may actually be greater than ordinary crime in terms of overall social, economic, and political effect. Studies of individual honesty reveal the surprising fact that a great proportion of our society may be prone to dishonesty.

Dr. W. Steve Albrecht of Brigham Young University's School of Business conducted numerous studies of white-collar crime. In a the film about the subject, *Red Flags*, Dr. Albrecht cites the results of studies of honesty among the general public that reveal the following:

- Thirty percent of the public will steal or be dishonest on a regular basis.
- Thirty percent of the public will steal or be dishonest depending on the situation (and risk).
- Forty percent of the public will never steal or be dishonest, regardless of the situation.

Where does the definition of criminal behavior start and stop? Should we continue to limit our concerns to the individuals who are responsible for the reported crime rate and those arrested for ordinary crimes? Is it desirable to uncover the true extent of criminal behavior and fraud in our society and its impact on our lives? Is it worth the risk?

Crime

Crime is so common to human existence that it is taken for granted. That is, everyone knows what it is, so it needs no definition. But does the general public *really* know what crime is? Do legislative and governmental bodies know?

Few people have a clear idea of the true nature and scope of crime and criminal behavior. The following definition of crime from *Webster's New Collegiate Dictionary* provides some insights into a broader understanding of the problem. According to Webster's, crime is "an act or commission of an act that is forbidden or the omission of a duty that is commanded by a public law and that makes the offender liable to punishment by that law." This definition provides a broad description of crime that includes behavior that is *prohibited* as well as behavior or acts that are required by law.

What are the level and importance of crime to society?

A report on world crime trends in James Q. Wilson's *Crime and Human Nature* presented a clear distinction between proportions of crime in developing countries versus developed countries. *Developing* countries experience a more even breakdown between crimes against people (43 percent) and against property (49 percent). *Developed* countries experience a higher proportion of crimes against property (82 percent) than crimes against people (10 percent). However, drug-related crimes do not vary proportionally between developing and developed countries.

These observations of more than a decade ago would seem to have credence as we progress well into the 21st century.

US Burglaries Overview

- In 2010, there were an estimated 2,159,878 burglaries in the United States—a decrease of 2.0 percent compared with 2009 data.
- Burglaries increased 2.0 percent in 2010 compared to the 2001 figures.
- Burglaries accounted for 23.8 percent of the estimated number of property crimes committed in 2010.

- Of all burglaries, 60.5 percent involved forcible entry, 33.2 percent were unlawful entries (without force), and the remainder (6.3 percent) were forcible entry attempts.
- Victims of burglary offenses suffered an estimated $4.6 billion in lost property in 2010; overall, the average dollar loss per burglary offense was $2,119.
- Burglaries of residential properties accounted for 73.9 percent of all burglary offenses.[1]

The crime figures for the United States do not provide a true picture of crime because, somewhat obviously, unreported crime and minor crimes are not included in official reports. US statistics on reported crime revealed a level of nearly 15 million serious crimes in 2010. These serious crimes include murder, rape, robbery, aggravated assault, burglary, larceny, theft, and motor vehicle theft.

Retail business operators traditionally have a much better understanding of the impact of crime and dishonesty, particularly in terms of the impact on the costs of consumer goods. But even astute businesspeople may not be aware of the true magnitude of the effect of crime and dishonesty on their own business liability.

Levels of Crime

Many decisions about what to do about crime are based on the levels of crimes or security incidents that are reported to authorities. Knowledge of offenders is limited to those people who are caught and either the offenses they were caught committing or the ones that they are willing to divulge to authorities.

There are four levels of crime that must be considered in understanding the impact of crime in our communities and in making rational judgments about public responses:

1. *Reported crime* is measured by the FBI Uniform Crime Reports and by security incident reports. Over 21 million major crimes were reported in 2008, with the rate of solving crimes hovering around 20 percent. Most are crimes against property, but they still produce fear of crime.
2. *Unreported crime* is measured by the National Crime Surveys. These surveys reveal that only 35 percent of all individual victimizations are reported to law enforcement agencies. The remainder are not reported for a number of reasons. These crimes include everything from the most minor offenses to the most serious. The results of this annual survey demonstrate that law enforcement's

[1] *Crime in the United States*, 2010, US Department of Justice, Federal Bureau of Investigation, released Sept. 2011.

overall success rate is approximately 7 percent when unreported crimes are added into the base.

3. *Unacknowledged crime* is another large category of crime that is committed against individuals and organizations. These crimes are measured, albeit poorly, by "shrinkage" data that is maintained in accounting and inventory control systems. The levels of loss are enormous. A commonly accepted level of shrinkage in property inventories is 10 percent. That is, about 10 percent of all products and goods disappear from inventories. Shoplifting and employee theft dominate these areas. The ratio of employee theft to shoplifting runs at 7:1 to 5:1, depending on the product line. The value of reported and unreported crime amounts to about $37 billion annually. Unacknowledged crime costs the public another $100–200 billion.
4. *Undetected losses* are those that have yet to be discovered. Theft of time and illegal loans against insurance policies that are not authorized by insurees are examples of a nearly unlimited list of crimes. The losses in this category drive total loss levels in all four categories up to about $650 billion annually. The impact on the US public is staggering. These losses drive the cost of consumer products (e.g., health insurance, auto insurance, consumer products) so high that they become unattainable. Most individuals are aware of reported crime. Few are aware of the actual extended level of crime that includes unreported victimizations as well as unacknowledged or undetected losses. Victimization surveys in many countries reveal that many offenses are never reported, for a variety of reasons. Here are some general facts about the problem:
   - The US Internal Revenue Service estimates annual losses of US $100 billion due to income-tax cheating.
   - The Hallcrest Report on private security in the United States, published in 1990, estimated that "theft of time" cost US industry nearly $125 billion each year.
   - Fraud and abuse of the insurance system account for a range of 10–20 percent of premiums paid throughout the world, which translates into an annual loss of US $48–96 per person in Europe and $110–220 per person in the United States. The cost of crime and dishonesty to business, especially to the retailer, has many direct and indirect effects. Direct losses may be measured in terms of "shrinkage" and apparent business decline. Indirect losses may be measured in terms of reduced productivity, increased overhead, employee absenteeism, and neglect-related capital costs for repair and replacement of equipment and buildings.

The costs of customer and employee victimization may be added on to the total. Positive community image and marketing opportunities suffer.

Finally, declining business success reduces the local tax base, resulting in the further decline of public services and loss of confidence in government. Accordingly, business areas that begin to decline lose their "clean, well-lighted" image, producing a negative impression on potential business investors.

Admittedly, some of these shocking trends in crime losses and dishonesty may be unique to the US culture. Nevertheless, it must be assumed that some level of unreported or undetected economic crime transcends all nations and societies. Some important conclusions may be drawn from these findings:

- Most crime statistics are limited to reported crimes without counting the higher levels of unreported, unacknowledged, or undetected crime.
- Public policy and public attitudes about crime, crime control, and criminal behavior continue to be limited to the popular notions about violent crimes and common offenses against property.
- The potential impact of true crime levels on the economy and the quality of life may be much more negative than imagined.
- The continued acceptance of dishonesty and cheating among the general public and the government serves only to legitimize this behavior for future generations, thus guaranteeing the continuing existence of public corruption, personal dishonesty, and high crime levels.
- Contemporary social, psychological, and biological theories of crime and criminal behavior do not explain the pervasiveness of economic crime throughout all levels of society and culture.

Explanations of Crime

Criminologists have attempted for years to develop explanations of crime and delinquency. Theories have been created to explain the origin of criminal behavior. Other theories have been used to identify approaches to treatment or rehabilitation. None has proven successful in providing a comprehensive understanding of crime and delinquency. Accordingly, public policy has been guided by a succession of philosophies about the causes of crime. Most of the philosophies can be organized and summarized around five categories: legal, social, psychological, biological, and political.

Legal theorists have argued for many years that the decision to commit crime is rational. That is, the offender weighs the circumstances and makes a decision to commit an offense based on his or her perception of the amount to be gained versus the risk of punishment. This belief has its basis in the so-called *pleasure-pain principle.*

Crime control under this model is oriented around certainty of punishment and making the punishment fit the crime.

Social theorists believe that criminal behavior is related to and is the result of social conditions. Criminologists and the criminal justice system have spent countless amounts of time and resources attempting to validate social explanations of crime. Many of these theories hover around some compelling arguments that social conditions, such as lack of opportunity, improper associations, and poor environmental conditions, cause people to commit crime. Social theories helped bring about urban reform and contemporary public housing programs. The now defunct Model Cities and Planned Variations programs were massive experiments in social engineering. Social theories seem to possess the greatest appeal as explanations of crime for public policymakers, although interest has waned with the failure of these programs.

Psychological theorists prefer to explain crime in individual terms, whereas the sociologist focuses on group dynamics and segments of the population. The psychologist searches for explanations associated with individual choices to commit crime or with mental pathologies that result in dysfunctional behavior. Learning theories have emanated from this area of research and hold some promise for treating and controlling certain behaviors.

Biological explanations of criminal behavior range from the bizarre to some that are scientifically valid. Nineteenth- and early 20th-century researchers attempted to prove relationships between body types and criminal behavior. These included everything from degrees of musculature to the numbers and locations of "bumps" on the head. Some contemporary biological researchers have established relationships between chemical deficiencies and behavior. Others have demonstrated hereditary relationships between violent fathers and their offspring, hence offering somewhat scary support for what was thought to be the archaic belief in "bad blood."

Political theorists skip the behavioral explanations. They believe that crime and criminal behavior are natural societal reactions to oppressive capitalistic government. The so-called military-industrial establishment is at fault. These radical criminologists espouse a Marxist view that says that society is wasting its time attempting to treat criminal behavior. Anarchy and violent overthrow of the system are the preferred methods of crime prevention. Some other political theories are based in a belief that class or power conflict, the clash between the "haves" and "have not's," is the cause of criminal behavior. Research findings are dismal, at least if one is looking for evidence to validate a pet theory. Some weak evidence still exists for a few social theories. Stronger evidence is available to support learning theories, which are subsumed under the psychological umbrella. Only rhetorical support exists for most of the political theories. Hundreds of years of experience with the legal theories that form the basis of our criminal justice system provided no answers to the causes of crime. However, it is clear from the research that although we know how to control behavior through legal restraints and supervision, we do not know how to treat misbehavior or how to prevent what causes it in the first place.

Criminologists and public policymakers have failed to acknowledge and deal with this total level of criminal behavior and loss. Public policy continues to be based on "common" crime that is committed by people who, because of their environmental limitations, are confined largely to the lower socioeconomic segments of our population. Self-reporting studies and common knowledge reveal that criminal behavior occurs at all levels of society, possibly at the same rate. The only differences are the type of offenses and the payoff.

Implications for Public Action

First, it is clear that programs must be founded in fact. Information must be used to enhance cooperative efforts. Facts must replace unsubstantiated beliefs in determining program approaches. Second, popular theories of criminal behavior have to be viewed in terms of the failure of social, psychological, and biological theories to explain the broad range of criminal activity throughout all levels of our society. This means that what we do know has to be used while we await further information from science. Supervision, control, interagency cooperation, and environmental management are known capabilities.

Finally, the statistics about crime and victimization in public housing must be considered the tip of the iceberg in terms of a real understanding of the problem. This also means that the relationship between developmental activities and the contiguous neighborhood has to be defined and taken into account in planning. Uncontrolled criminal activity in public areas, especially housing, affects the quality of life in the projects. It affects the perceptions and the subsequent development of attitudes and behavior of the children who grow up in these places. It affects the neighborhood. Can a healthy neighborhood absorb a public housing project and make it part of its social fabric? Can a project reach out to a troubled neighborhood and become the focal point for neighborhood development? These questions must and can be answered in a well-controlled and fundamentally CPTED neighborhood project. Young people experience problems that go beyond traditional concepts of crime and victimization. Young people under 24 years of age account for about

51 percent of all arrests. Young people under the age of 18 account for 17 percent of all arrests and about 40 percent of all arrests for serious property crimes.

Some more startling facts include these:

- People under age 18 are the most highly victimized segment of our population.
- People under age 18 are the least likely segment of our population to report a criminal victimization.
- People under age 18 are seven times more likely to be victimized by another young person than by an adult.
- Suburban youth experience a school dropout rate of 25 percent and urban youth a dropout rate of 35 percent.
- Child molestation and abuse are immeasurable, but it is estimated that 1,100 children died as a result of neglect in 1986.
- Drug and alcohol use are common for elementary, middle, and high school students—7 percent of eighth-grade students used marijuana by grade six; 62 percent of eighth-grade students who reported having tried cocaine said that they tried it first in seventh grade.
- High school seniors reported (1986) having used drugs in 57 percent of all interview responses.
- Thirty-five percent of all boys age 0–18 will be arrested at least once; 18–21 percent of these young men will become career offenders.[2]
- Young people under age 18 represent only 27 percent of the US population. Yet this same age group is commonly more than 50 percent of the population of public housing projects. Habitual offender programs have estimated that a disproportionate number (per capita) of officially identified habitual juvenile offenders reside in public housing, in contrast to other housing forms.

Contemporary Crime Prevention and Interagency Concepts

There has been a proliferation of crime prevention, delinquency control, and community organization projects and programs that have been pushed and sold throughout the past 30 years. Many of these programs were based on a number of compelling social theories that did not pan out in the implementation stage. Accordingly, local units of government, criminal justice agencies, and public

[2]Wolfgang, Marvin E., "Delinquency in Two Birth Cohorts," *American Behavioral Scientist*, 1983, 37(1), 75–86.

housing authorities are worn out with many of the tried-and-failed program approaches and philosophies.

Fortunately, two areas of crime prevention and control have continued to surface positively in evaluations and in common experience. These are interagency program approaches and CPTED. This does not mean that other programs have not been successful but rather that these two areas present greater opportunities for success than others.

Moreover, these concepts provide an organizational and environmental basis for the use of other, more socially oriented programs, giving them a better chance of successful implementation.

There is a growing belief among mental health and youth development professionals that young people who grow up in large, undifferentiated environments fail to learn respect for property and property values. It is believed that these children will have greater difficulties controlling their behavior as they mature. Likewise, children who grow up in large undifferentiated environments, with little or sporadic supervision and control, will also experience more difficulties. The CPTED emphasis on promoting territorial behavior and natural approaches to behavioral control fit well into these emerging child development concepts. The emphasis on interagency cooperation and collaboration enhances these strategies.

Criminal Justice: A Misperceived Concept

Many people in the public and private sectors have a limited viewpoint of law enforcement and security operations. A highly placed official in a major oil company recently told the author that he thought the security people were there to screen employees and provide protection against terrorist attacks. Many criminologists, criminal justice practitioners, and security administrators suffer from the same delusion. "Catching thieves" is the most visible and popular role for law enforcement and security operations. Crime fighting is synonymous with images of the cartoon "hound-dog detective" who always gets his man. McGruff "taking a bite out a crime" is a symbolic reference to the traditional watchdog who catches crooks by the seat of their pants. Catching "bad guys" seems to be the focal point of most law enforcement and security programs, yet it is the one thing that we fail to do most of the time!

There is clearly a misplaced emphasis on apprehension. In practice, we solve only about 20 percent of all serious crimes.[3] The National Crime Surveys have found that only about 38 percent of all

[3] Federal Bureau of Investigation, *FBI Uniform Crime Reports*, Washington, DC: US Department of Justice.

victimizations are reported to authorities. Children are victimized more often than any other age group.

Habitual juvenile offenders account for a disproportionate share of all crime committed by young people. We know all of this, but it doesn't seem to have much impact on our overall public policies and priorities. NCPI's definition of crime prevention provides some insight into a new focal point for law enforcement and security programs: "The anticipation, recognition, and appraisal of a crime risk, and the initiation of some action to remove or to reduce it" may seem an awkward way of saying it, but it says to me, "If it ain't apprehension, it's gotta be crime prevention."

The crime-related aspects of law enforcement and security include at least six major functions. It is useful to examine each element individually to see how it relates to crime prevention:

1. *Crime prevention* in this limited context is that process of eliminating or reducing the opportunity to commit an offense or the denial of access to crime targets.
2. *Detection* is the critical process of monitoring the activities and functions of the community to gather intelligence about the activities and associations of known offenders and to identify and discover criminal activity that would have gone unnoticed. This process is fundamental to crime prevention and crime control. You can't prevent it if you don't know about it!
3. *Suppression* is the act or method of restraining or controlling the activities of would-be or known offenders. A simple example of suppression is the monitoring and intense supervision of habitual juvenile offenders. Another example is the practice of active warrant service, particularly for repeat adult offenders. The objective of these community control strategies is to prevent crime.
4. *Investigation* is the follow-up procedure for examining a criminal incident with the objective of solving the crime and resolving the problem. Contemporary case management systems are limited to solving the crime and arresting the offender, instead of the traditional practice of following up on an offense to resolve the situation, prevent it from happening again, or to bring the offender to justice. Contemporary case management systems focus on solvability factors that are valid for no more than the 20 percent of all serious crimes that are solved, thus overlooking effective case resolution for the 80 percent of crimes that will not be solved. Case resolution and victim follow-up are good crime prevention.
5. *Apprehension* is the first step in the application of legal sanctions to accused offenders. Traditional police values called for the use of prevention and suppression of crime, using the arrest-and-prosecutive process only where punishment was required. That is, apprehension and prosecution were traditionally viewed as a final

resort, not the primary solution, when other methods of crime control failed.

6. *Prosecution* is the official presentation of fact to the court with the intent of denying an individual's basic right of freedom because of criminal activity. The courts are used where other social controls fail. Crime prevention can be enhanced by providing special support for the prosecution of habitual offenders who have proven themselves to be career offenders.

Offenders do not have to be locked up to be incapacitated. All that has to be done is to effectively control them, either through close supervision or residential treatment programs. The effective control of repeat offenders is good crime prevention. Prosecution programs can assist in crime prevention. However, crime prevention may now be perceived as something that special-unit people do to divert the public from the basic ineffectiveness of law enforcement and security programs. As long as this continues, crime prevention will still be relegated to a gadget orientation. An objective study of any law enforcement or security operation will reveal that the primary requirement for crime-related services is prevention, in its broadest sense. Each of us must ask the following three questions before we continue in our present activities or allow our organizations to proceed within the limited understanding of the role of crime prevention:

1. What is the requirement for our services?
2. How do we spend our time and resources?
3. What are the results?

Crime prevention and security personnel can help their organizations develop department-wide crime-prevention programs. These programs may include the integration of covert intelligence-gathering activities aimed at property crime with a joint public and private information-sharing and suppression effort. Expanded case management systems designed for 100-percent follow-up using a range of resolution methods may be initiated, along with improved patrol productivity programs such as Directed Patrol. Interagency programs may be developed to increase the monitoring and supervision of troubled, problem, and delinquent youth. In essence, crime prevention needs to become more visible and assertive and accept its integral role in the functions of prevention, detection, suppression, investigation, apprehension, and prosecution.

Productivity Tools for the Crime- and Loss-Prevention Specialist

Do you, as a loss- or crime-prevention specialist, desire to expand or improve your program? Do you wish that the rest of your organization would take your program seriously? Do you feel at times that what you are doing is "pyramiding"? That is, does it seem that the harder you work, the more work there is? If your answer is yes to these questions, you are probably suffering from an acute case of "special-unit-itis." Some symptoms of this malady are:

- Feeling like a mushroom, being kept in the dark and fed "organizational waste"
- Feeling that when everything else fails, they give it to *you* to fix
- Representing the organization in situations where it's clear the audience is going to shoot the messenger
- Feeling that everyone in your organization is either brain-dead or conspiring to screw up anything that relates to your job so that you will have to take it over to make sure that it is done well
- Laboring under the assumption that your devotion to carrying the organization will lead to an improved life as a consultant or "icon" of crime prevention in the year 2013.

Do you recognize these symptoms? If so, you are probably terminally ill with the admirable but quixotic trait of being a professional crime- or loss-prevention officer. Bless you, your reward will come in the end! The crime- and loss-prevention field is faced with the need to move past the developmental years of establishing the technology of our profession to the integration of prevention concepts into the way we run our organizations and our communities.

As a full-time police intern in 1968, I had the unique opportunity to experience firsthand a number of major shifts in public and law enforcement technology. The need to control the actions of personnel resulted in the practice of having special units or functions run interference while the rest of the department remained at the station. This worked so well that many chiefs and sheriffs embraced it through the late 1960s to the 2000s.

Unfortunately, the special units diverted attention away from the growing lack of productivity of the bulk of the organization—the operations division. It was simply easier to manage special units for special problems than it was to achieve compliance behavior or improved performance from the rest of the organization. The public and private sectors have suffered from this shift in organizational thinking. Stringent security procedures impede private-sector productivity and labor relations. High-volume, hands-on services in the public sector are still being delivered by specialists who are outnumbered 7:1 by operations personnel. Specialists achieve productivity levels of 85–92 percent, whereas operations personnel function at 10–40 percent. Yet a time and task analysis reveals that crime-prevention services are pervasive. That is, the potential volume is such that only the operations division of a law enforcement agency or the worker division of a company can actually deliver crime- or loss-prevention services.

There is nothing wrong with the specialist functions. The absurd debate in the early 1970s about generalist versus specialist functions missed the point that both are required. However, the specialist functions need to manage and coordinate services rather than deliver them. The concept and role definition of program management has emerged from the realization that humans will take the path of least resistance. As long as a special unit is ready and willing to take on a problem, why bother! It is easy to repress personal responsibility by reinforcing the escape route of "hold the scene and wait for the smart guys." The adoption of a program management system will help eliminate or lessen the effects of the special-unit-versus-operations conflict.

The special-unit style of management usually undergoes four phases:

1. A unit or assignment is created to respond to a problem or a public policy decision. The staff members are hand-picked and quickly develop their program. High connections and considerable influence are enjoyed.
2. The normal turnover, promotion, or burnout of staff results in the assignment of people who are less controversial or charismatic. This is done to bring the unit into line and heal some internal breaches.
3. Cutback management forces the reduction of resources in all special units and peripheral programs. Token positions are retained and unit responsibility is curtailed, usually under the guise of reorganization.
4. The unit or function disappears quietly after a key staff member retires or resigns.

Contemporary administrators must develop a more functional viewpoint of the organization. City- or market-wide service needs demand organizational approaches that produce volume. The source of major productivity potential has to be where the greatest investment in resources is placed.

Finally, the competence of the organization is the major factor in developing citizen satisfaction and consumer support.

Consider the following example. Twelve crime-prevention officers are going to try to conduct surveys of 180,000 households so that the homeowners may receive a discount on their insurance. How long will this task take? Each officer will have to survey 15,000 homes. At a normal pace, the job will be complete in 10 to 15 years. What do you think the city manager will have to say about this estimate? How long would it take the patrol division, even though they would be limited to previously uncommitted time? Clearly, the key to productivity is to match resources with demand. Thus, the program management role of the special unit becomes paramount.

Program management may be defined as an approach to improved organizational effectiveness that identifies the importance of fixing responsibility for coordinating each major activity at a single point. These activities are either top priorities of the organization or are, most often, requirements for service that cross-cut unit lines. The concept behind program management is that the major functions or service need areas are identified formally as programs. Special units or individuals may then be assigned to plan, manage, and monitor the organization's performance in carrying out the goals and objectives of the program area.

The mission of a special unit changes significantly when it assumes a program management function. Time has to be allocated properly among the following functions:

- Planning, managing, and monitoring the program
- Delivering the highly complex or unique services that require specialist attention
- Conducting internal and external liaison and problem-solving services

The temptation to take on large caseloads must be avoided. Clear guidelines and procedures must be developed to assure that work is distributed properly, according to the volume and substantive requirements of the program. The program management unit has to be perceived by line personnel as being in a collaborative role instead of an evaluative one. Experience has shown that clear goals, objectives, and performance reporting are the keys to successful implementation of program management.

Even a person whose position in the organization is not very powerful can try some or all of these strategies:

- Develop a long-term program plan for crime and loss prevention.
- Conduct an analysis of present productivity levels of your operations personnel and identify alternatives that will save or recover time.
- Present a comparative analysis of the value of a new program that increases and improves crime- and loss-prevention services versus the existing approaches.
- Find an alter ego in your organization and enlist this person's support.
- Change the way you personally do business. Stop trying to carry the whole load.
- Practice delayed gratification: Each day, do something for the future of your program instead of working in one more speech.

It is the author's contention that the crime- and loss-prevention specialist should promote his role in the CPTED process. Participation in the local or organizational review process of the design and use of the environment we build may lead to greater productivity and reduced losses.

Following these steps will definitely bring the mushroom out of the dark and help redefine crime and loss prevention as a program management function rather than a technical services specialty.

Crime Versus Loss Prevention

The use of the terms *crime prevention* and *loss prevention* seem redundant to many people. Criminologists and criminal justice specialists do not perceive the difference between the concepts of crime prevention and loss prevention.

The general public probably does not distinguish between these terms, either. Moreover, there is considerable controversy among social scientists and criminologists about the definition of crime prevention.

Some criminologists have attempted to develop classifications of definitions of crime prevention. The following are common descriptions that differentiate approaches to crime prevention:

1. *Punitive approaches* are based on legal assumptions that crime may be controlled or prevented through punishment that fits the crime. The theory is that criminals will not commit a crime if they will receive one more unit of pain than the amount of pleasure or value derived from a criminal act. This concept depends on the creation of a system whereby it is apparent that a criminal will be apprehended and punished for committing a crime. This is a classical criminal justice model that relies on the perception that an offense will be detected and punishment will be swift.
2. *Mechanical approaches* are defined as measures that are taken to deny the opportunity for an offender to commit a crime. These methods depend on the denial of access to vulnerable properties or individuals. They also include the use of natural strategies to increase the perception of surveillance and access control, to ward off the potential offender.
3. *Corrective approaches* are aimed at eliminating the motives for committing crime. These concepts are usually associated with focusing attention on the so-called social, economic, and political causes of crime. It has always been socially desirable to advocate attention to the root causes of crime.

Other criminologists have reversed the order of these typologies of crime prevention by referring to primary, secondary, and tertiary approaches. *Primary approaches* are concerned with creating barriers or obstacles to criminal activities (i.e., mechanical). *Secondary approaches* emphasize the implementation of a criminal justice and crime-control system that guarantees the likelihood of detection, apprehension, and punishment (i.e., punitive). *Tertiary approaches* focus on dealing with the cause of criminal behavior and the treatment or rehabilitation of offenders (i.e., corrective).

It is clear from both of these approaches to defining crime prevention that the corrective and the related tertiary approaches are the most socially desirable. But time has run out on attempts to control and successfully treat criminal behavior. Many of the theories relating to causes of crime and treatment have failed to explain the wide range of criminal behavior and dishonesty that occurs in our communities and within our institutions.

The NCPI has adopted the following definition of crime prevention:

> *Crime prevention is the anticipation, recognition and appraisal of a crime risk and the initiation of some action to remove or reduce it.*

This may seem like an awkward definition. It may even seem to be limited to the primary or mechanical approaches, which might not seem to be socially desirable. After all, these approaches seem to deal only with creating barriers to criminal activity, without addressing the root causes. Yet this definition acknowledges the uneven and incomplete understanding of the causes of criminal behavior, the knowledge that crime and dishonesty is pervasive throughout all socioeconomic levels and that people are motivated by a hierarchy of needs that starts with individual security.

Many people believe that the real priority is to deal with the popular root causes of crime, the so-called social, economic, and political causes. Some have criticized block clubs and community organization approaches as means of adult repression of young people. Self-help methods (e.g., personal safety practices and the use of locks and residential alarm systems) have been stigmatized by evaluators as dealing with the symptoms but not with the causes. This criticism fails to take into account the self-centered nature of human behavior. Behavior change starts with the individual, then moves to the near group before it emerges as a collective societal reaction. It is difficult to conceive of getting the citizens of a community or the employees of an organization to devote their attention to global change or to demanding broad social, economic, and political metamorphosis until they progress through a continuum of steps ranging from self to family to neighborhood to community.

A person is not going to worry about changing the attitude of "city hall" until he feels safe in moving from his home to his car or source of transportation to work. A person is not going to worry about the economic status of the world until she feels secure in paying the rent and covering the basic costs of sending her kids to school. A person is not going to be anxious about the neighborhood until he knows that the house is safe and the immediate neighbors are trustworthy.

A basic principle of medical treatment is to control and stabilize a situation before attempting treatment. It is basic to emergencies that the situation must be controlled before it can be resolved. An offender must be placed under the control of society before he can be rehabilitated. Even an automobile that is in disrepair must be diagnosed before repairs can be accomplished. It is clear that steps cannot be skipped in dealing with human activities. The world will not change until people change and then set about changing their community, once their hierarchy of needs is met.

It is self-evident that most people will not be able to effect global change, especially when and until we can protect ourselves and our property. Accordingly, it makes the most sense to focus on the punitive and mechanical approaches to controlling crime while we continue to support the corrective or tertiary approaches to finding solutions to the causes of criminal behavior and its treatment. Control of behavior must precede its treatment in any case.

The term *loss prevention* is broader than crime prevention because it includes a wider range of behavior than that which is defined legally as criminal. Loss may be defined as the removal or taking of an object or asset of value. Loss may be due to crime, poor productivity, incompetence, inefficiency, or lack of management attention. Loss may result from poor employee morale or lack of motivation to complete a work task or to use resources properly. The loss of value may be financially measured, or it may be assessed in emotional terms. The improper use and management of talent may also become a loss category. Loss occurs on a broader scale through natural causes, such as storms or earthquakes.

Loss and loss prevention are directly related to the achievement of human functions and objectives. This concept is more important to the practical use of CPTED methods than to dealing merely with losses due to criminal behavior. There is a fine line that separates pure criminal behavior from the proper care of and responsibility for the expenditure and use of resources.

NCPI recasts its definition of crime prevention into the following one for loss prevention:

> *Loss prevention is the anticipation, recognition, and appraisal of a risk of loss and the initiation of some action to reduce it (the loss).*

The cost of prevention, although sometimes higher than the loss itself, is legitimate because of the secondary and tertiary costs. It is better to prevent the opportunity for employees to steal than it is to arrest employees for stealing. It is preferable to prevent a loss or a crime from occurring than to handle it after the fact. Crime and loss result in higher costs for goods and services. They result in inconvenience and, at times, the removal of a valued or needed service. The pain, suffering, and denial that result from reactions to loss affect everyone.

Medical bills are higher. Unnecessary and painful medical procedures result from doctors who are hesitant to incur liability because of the abuse of the insurance system and the related decisions of the courts and juries, which often approve unconscionable settlements of claims.

Two Types of Risk

Crime, and especially loss prevention, depends on the concept of risk management. Most individuals and organizations encounter two types of risk: pure and dynamic. *Pure risk* is the potential for loss of value, with no possibility of gain. The risk is total. *Dynamic risk* is more like gambling in that one is willing to chance the loss of money or resources for a potential profit or gain. A purchaser of a lottery ticket is willing to lose the cost of the ticket price in exchange for the potential winning value. A store owner risks the cost of rent, salaries of employees, and the purchase of goods to make a profit. A police department attempts to project or predict areas where it will get the most value out of the investment of officer time.

The acknowledgment of risk and the management of risk are inherent to management of resources. The most successful managers assume that risk management is a primary element of success. Poor managers assume that risk is a threat to survival. Unfortunately, many of these poor managers continue to thrive in bureaucracies.

Risk Management

The international standard ISO 31000 provides detailed guidance in the area of managing risk. However, in broad terms, there are five options available to those responsible for managing risks: risk avoidance, risk reduction, risk spreading, risk transfer, and risk retention.

Risk avoidance is the process of limiting or eliminating opportunities for loss. This is accomplished by reducing the number of activities or exposures to loss. It is also accomplished by the complete alteration or cessation of human activities and functions that are vulnerable to risk. This is a negative approach that is justified only through cost-benefit analysis that indicates a greater potential loss than gain through the continuance of an activity.

Risk reduction occurs through what is commonly referred to as *procedural security*. Loss possibilities are offset through dramatic alterations of the process of accounting for or controlling human functions. Checks and balances are implemented to increase the likelihood of exposure or to reduce the opportunity for someone to steal or to break the law.

Risk spreading is the diversion of resources and assets for the purpose of lowering loss exposure. Distance, location, and time are used to create the spreading of assets. Barriers are also included in this concept of risk management. Security engineering and physical security approaches are inherent in the spreading and denial of access.

Risk transfer is the fundamental aspect of insurance. A large group of individuals share a common risk, such as a property or casualty loss. Health insurance is a direct form of risk transfer.

Risk retention is the conscious acceptance of the potential for loss. Potential losses are not necessarily covered by insurance nor by other means of security. The owner or individual simply assumes the possibility of a loss.

Risk management is inherent in the operation of any business. It is also inherent in the operation of a community or neighborhood. Without acknowledging it, most people assume the risk of criminal victimization. But they are less likely to continue to assume that risk once they have been victimized. Fear and concern about crime usually relate to a part of one's community that is distant, a place where one is not likely to go. Avoidance behavior ensues, thus perpetuating the perception that a particular place is unsafe.

Conclusions

Criminologists and public policymakers have perpetuated a limited definition and understanding of crime and criminal behavior. Many myths about the causes of crime exist because they are socially desirable. However, criminal behavior is pervasive throughout all levels of society, although it is popular to focus on common crime and common criminals.

The concept of loss adds to the magnitude of crime and criminal behavior. It also adds to the reality that conventional reactive approaches to crime and loss are failing. CPTED concepts integrate productivity and profit with security and loss prevention. Profit to a neighborhood is quality of life. A happy neighborhood does not tolerate or experience crime and loss problems. A well-run business has fewer losses. A good school has higher achievement levels and a lower incidence of disruptive behavior and criminal incidents.

A downtown or shopping center that is successful in attracting customers makes greater profits and has fewer losses.

Attention to crime and loss prevention will produce payoffs. Crime and loss prevention are inherent to human functions and activities, not just something that police or security people do.

8

EXAMPLES OF CPTED STRATEGIES AND APPLICATIONS

CHAPTER OUTLINE

CPTED Strategies

CPTED strategies have emerged from history and from contemporary crime prevention experiments. Most of the strategies are self-evident. That is, the reader will probably think, "I knew that!" The strategies and examples contained in this chapter are basic. Their applications are unlimited.

CPTED concepts have been and are being used in public housing projects. Schools and university properties are using CPTED applications that were initially pioneered in the Broward County, Florida, school CPTED program that was funded by the federal government. (Appendix A contains a matrix summary of these concepts.) The list of potential CPTED applications is practically endless. It would be difficult to find any human function that is not amenable to the use of CPTED concepts. It is merely a matter of looking at the environment from a different perspective, questioning everything, and learning the language of the various professions involved in making decisions about our communities. *Learning the language* means being able to communicate with others and to understand their objectives. This is the principal reason that CPTED planners are trained to share concepts and ask questions that no one else would think to ask.

CPTED planners are trained to reprogram their thinking from focusing solely on security and crime prevention to emphasizing the objectives of the agency or organization that they are trying to help. It is important to remember a CPTED motto, "What are you trying to do here, and how can we help you do it better?" If you are meeting your objectives, the potential for crime and loss will be reduced. It is an axiom that human functions that are achieving their objectives will experience fewer crimes and losses. Crime and loss are byproducts of human functions that are not working.

The following are the nine major CPTED strategies that can be used in any number of combinations:

1. *Provide clear border definition of controlled space.* It is a common-law requirement that space must be defined to preserve property rights. Boundaries may be identified physically or symbolically. Fences, shrubbery, or signs are acceptable border definitions. The underlying principle is that a "reasonable individual" must be able to recognize that he is transitioning from public to private space. Similarly, the arrangements of furniture and color definition are means of identifying interior spaces. Plaques and pictures

on walls in hallways help define ownership and are powerful environmental cues that affect the behavior and predispositions of owners, normal users, and abnormal users alike.

2. *Provide clearly marked transitional zones.* It is important to provide clearly marked transitional zones moving from public to semipublic to semiprivate to private space. As transitional definition increases, the range of excuses for improper behavior is reduced. The user must be made to acknowledge movement into controlled space.
3. *Relocation of gathering areas.* It is appropriate to formally designate gathering or congregating areas in locations with good natural surveillance and access control. Gathering areas on campuses may be placed in positions that are out of the view of undesired users, to decrease the magnetic (attraction) effect.
4. *Place safe activities in unsafe locations.* Within reason, this strategy may be used to overcome problems on school campuses, parks, offices, or institutional settings. Safe activities serve as magnets for normal users who exhibit challenging or controlling behaviors (e.g., staring) that tell other normal users that they are safe and that tell abnormal users that they are at greater risk of scrutiny or intervention. Some caution must be used to assure that a safe activity is not being placed in an unreasonable position that cannot be defended.
5. *Place unsafe activities in safe locations.* The positioning of vulnerable activities near windows of occupied space or within tightly controlled areas will help overcome risk and make the users of these areas feel safer.
6. *Redesignate the use of space to provide natural barriers.* Conflicting activities may be separated by distance, natural terrain, or other functions to avoid fear-producing conflict. For instance, the sounds emanating from a basketball court may be disruptive and fear producing for a senior citizen or toddler gathering/play area. The threat does not have to be real to create the perception of risk for the normal or desired user.
7. *Improve scheduling of space.* It has generally been found that the effective and productive use of space reduces risk and the perception of risk for normal users. Conversely, abnormal users feel at greater risk of surveillance and intervention in their activities. Well-thought-out temporal and spatial relationships improve profit and productivity while increasing the control of behavior.
8. *Redesign or revamp space to increase the perception of natural surveillance.* The perception of surveillance is more powerful than its reality. Hidden cameras do little to make normal users feel safer and, therefore, act safer when they are unaware of the presence of these devices. Likewise, abnormal users do not feel at greater risk

of detection when they are oblivious to surveillance potentials. Windows, clear lines of sight, and other natural techniques are often as effective as the use of mechanical or organized methods (e.g., security guards).

9. *Overcome distance and isolation.* Improved communications and design efficiencies increase the perception of natural surveillance and control. School administrators have learned to carry portable radios to improve their productivity as well as create the perception of immediate access to help. Restroom locations and entry designs may be planned to increase convenience and reduce the cost of construction and maintenance.

CPTED Applications

There are many examples of CPTED applications. Those that follow are intended to stimulate readers to think of adaptations to their own environmental settings. Each situation is unique, requiring its own individual application of CPTED concepts. No two environmental settings are exactly the same, even though they might serve the same function. Accordingly, readers, now hopefully CPTED users, will have to use the strategies that make the most sense in each different location.

Objectives for Commercial Environments

1. *Access controls.* Provide secure barriers to prevent unauthorized access to buildings, grounds, and/or restricted interior areas.
2. *Surveillance through physical design.* Improve opportunities for surveillance by physical design mechanisms that serve to increase the risk of detection for offenders, enable evasive actions by potential victims, and facilitate intervention by police.
3. *Mechanical surveillance devices.* Provide businesses with security devices to detect and signal illegal entry attempts.
4. *Design and construction.* Design, build, and/or repair buildings and building sites to enhance security and improve quality.
5. *Land use.* Establish policies to prevent ill-advised land and building uses that have negative impact.
6. *Owner/management action.* Encourage owners and management to implement safeguards to make businesses and commercial property less vulnerable to crime.
7. *User protection.* Implement safeguards to make shoppers less vulnerable to crime.
8. *Social interaction.* Encourage interaction among businesspeople, users, and residents of commercial neighborhoods to foster social cohesion and control.

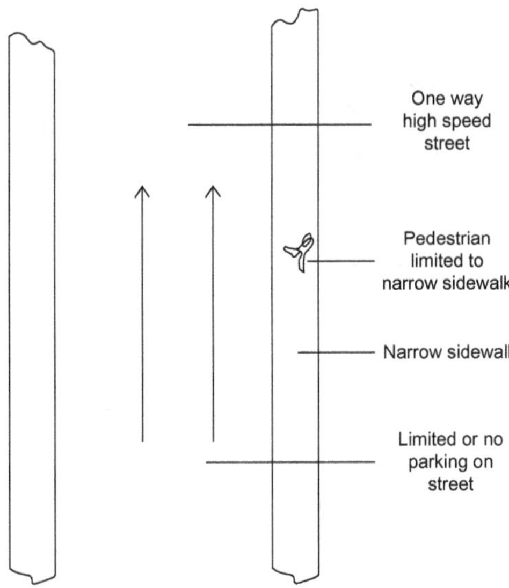

Figure 8.1

9. *Private security services.* Determine necessary and appropriate services to enhance commercial security.
10. *Police services.* Improve police services to efficiently and effectively respond to crime problems and to enhance citizen cooperation in reporting crime.
11. *Police/community relations.* Improve police/community relations to involve citizens in cooperative efforts with police to prevent and report crime.
12. *Community awareness.* Create community crime-prevention awareness to aid in combating crime in commercial areas.
13. *Territorial identity.* Differentiate private areas from public spaces to discourage trespass by potential offenders.
14. *Neighborhood image.* Develop a positive image of commercial areas to encourage user and investor confidence and increase the economic vitality of those areas.

Downtown Streets and Pedestrian Areas

Downtown Streets

Poor design and use (Figures 8.1 and 8.2):

1. The growing dominance of vehicles over pedestrians resulted in off-street parking, one-way streets, synchronized traffic signals, and shrunken sidewalks to accommodate cars and trucks.

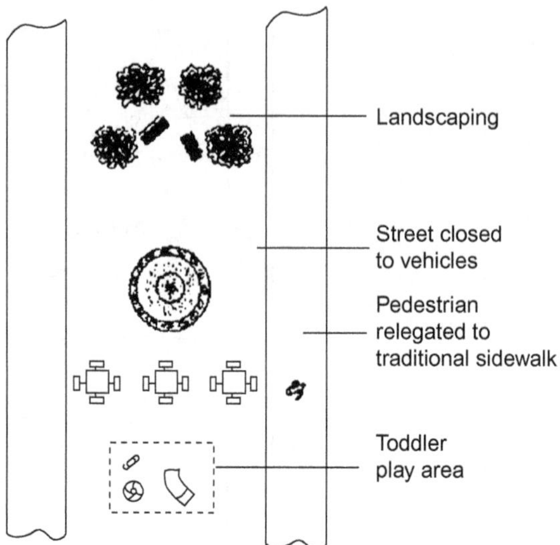

Figure 8.2

2. Pedestrian-oriented businesses have failed or chased buyers to the shopping centers and malls. As businesses moved, there was less pedestrian activity, which forced even more businesses out.
3. Narrow pedestrian footpaths increased conflict and fear between vagrants and other abnormal users of space. Normal users avoided these streets, thereby reinforcing the decline of business and normal downtown activities.
4. Downtown streets became "no man's land" at night and on weekends.
5. Pedestrian malls were created to replace the vehicle with people, but most failed because the designers lost track of their Three Ds. Aesthetics cement objects in the place of people.
6. Many of the cement objects—amenities and landscaping—attracted abnormal users. Litter and bird droppings made outdoor sitting areas undesirable for normal users.
7. Normal users feel threatened and unsafe in these areas. Abnormal users feel safe and at low risk of intervention. Authorities are obliged to surrender these areas to vagrants because of special interest group pressure and the lack of any consistent normal use of the area.

Good design and use (Figures 8.3 and 8.4):

1. One option is to purposely decrease the vehicle capacity of the street by reestablishing on-street parking, wide sidewalks,

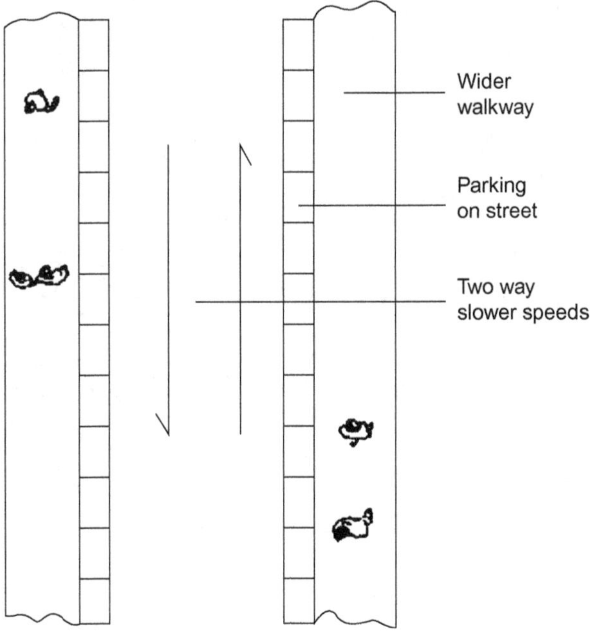

Figure 8.3

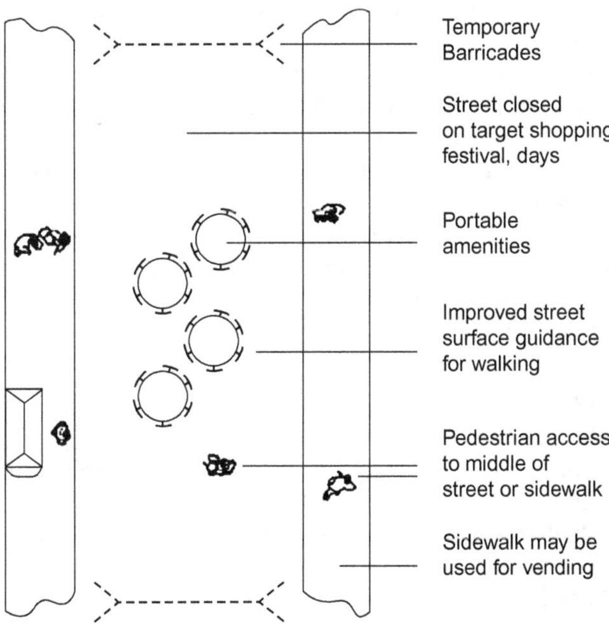

Figure 8.4

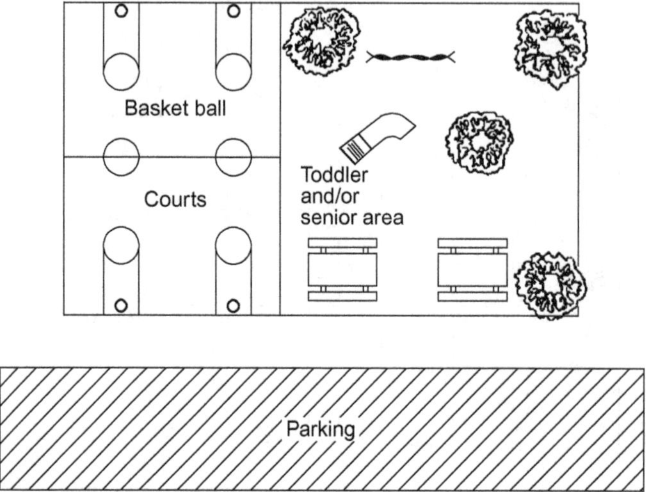

Figure 8.5

two-way streets, and nonsynchronous traffic signals. These changes should reroute commuter and other through traffic.

2. Higher pedestrian capacity will limit vehicular access to those with terminal objectives on the block (e.g., residents or purposeful shoppers).
3. Another option is to schedule the street for temporary closings on target shopping days and festival times. Portable amenities may be used and stored when not in use. Businesses may be granted variances of local codes to use vendor carts and other ways to extend business activities into the street.
4. The planned increase of normal users will make them feel safer and exhibit controlling and challenging behaviors, much as they do in indoor shopping malls.
5. Abnormal users will feel at greater risk.

Barriers to Conflict

Poor design (Figure 8.5):

1. A toddler and/or senior recreation area is immediately contiguous to a conflicting activity of basketball.
2. Basketball activity involves aggressive behavior and noise, which is annoying and threatening to senior citizens and parents with small children.
3. The athletic activity may serve as a magnet for abnormal users of space.

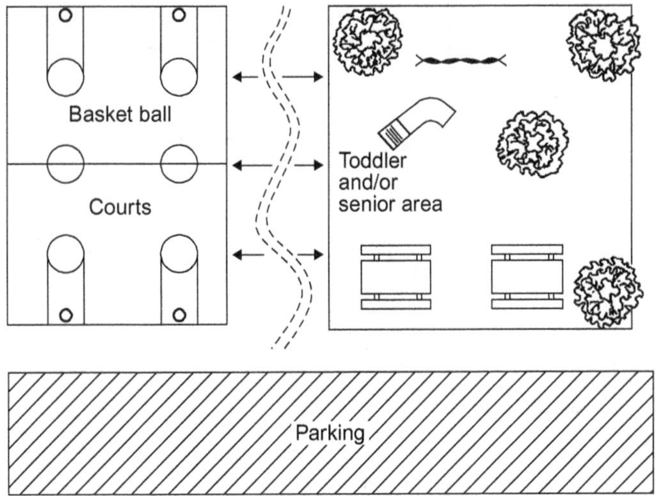

Figure 8.6

4. The designated athletic activity may legitimize certain offensive behaviors, such as swearing and physical abuse, which threatens normal users and passersby.

Good design (Figure 8.6):

1. A natural barrier of distance, elevation, or a parking lot may be used to avoid conflict.
2. Any natural barrier will reduce the propensity for the undesirable or abnormal users to preempt the contiguous spaces.
3. Abnormal users will feel at greater risk when there is a clear barrier through which they have to pass.

Outdoor Sitting Areas

Poor design and use (Figure 8.7):

1. Sitting walls have replaced the traditional benches and picnic tables in open spaces, but they are easy to hide behind and serve as a barrier to effective surveillance.
2. Elevation drops and terraced sitting areas reduce perceived opportunities for natural surveillance, which makes abnormal users feel safer in colonizing or preempting these spaces.
3. Tourists and office workers who would like to eat lunch in these areas or take an evening stroll will be afraid to go there if vagrants are already there or have left signs of their regular use (e.g., litter, graffiti, human waste).
4. Litter and waste present odor problems and may attract scavengers. If it looks and smells bad, it must *be* bad, which defeats the purpose of an outdoor sitting area.

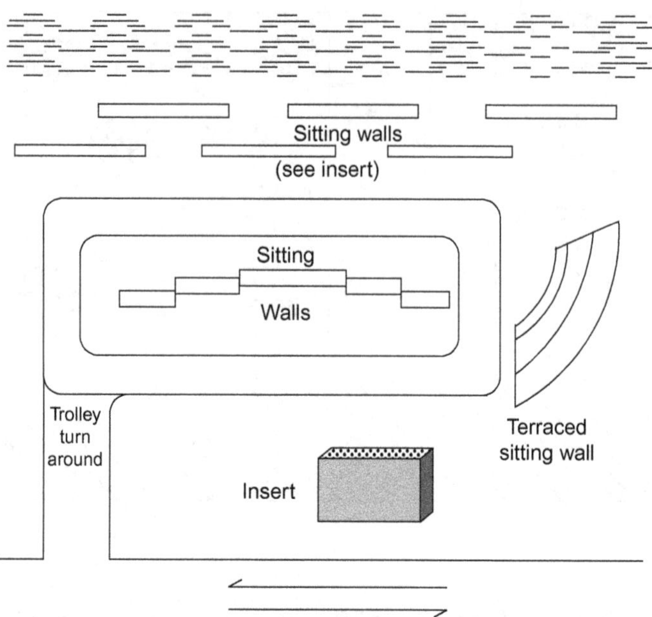

Figure 8.7

Good design and use (Figure 8.8):

1. Sitting rails may be used in place of more expensive walls. This will increase natural surveillance and prevent improper use while still meeting the functional and aesthetic demands of the open space.
2. Terraced sitting or staging areas should be oriented so that they are clearly visible from the street.
3. Open spaces can be made to work with CPTED concepts while reducing overall construction costs. Normal users will feel better about coming to these areas and they will displace abnormal users.

Plazas

Poor design and use (Figure 8.9):

1. A typical plaza in a rehabilitated business area meets all the local code requirements for landscaping and aesthetics but at the cost of reducing the usable square footage.
2. Aesthetics or form outweighed function in the selection of cobblestones to use in replacing the street paving. These stones are difficult to walk on, especially for women in high-heeled shoes and for the elderly.

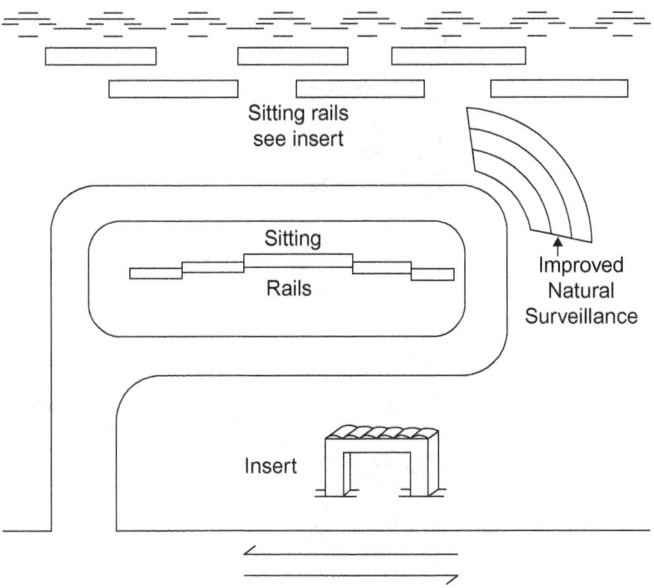

Figure 8.8

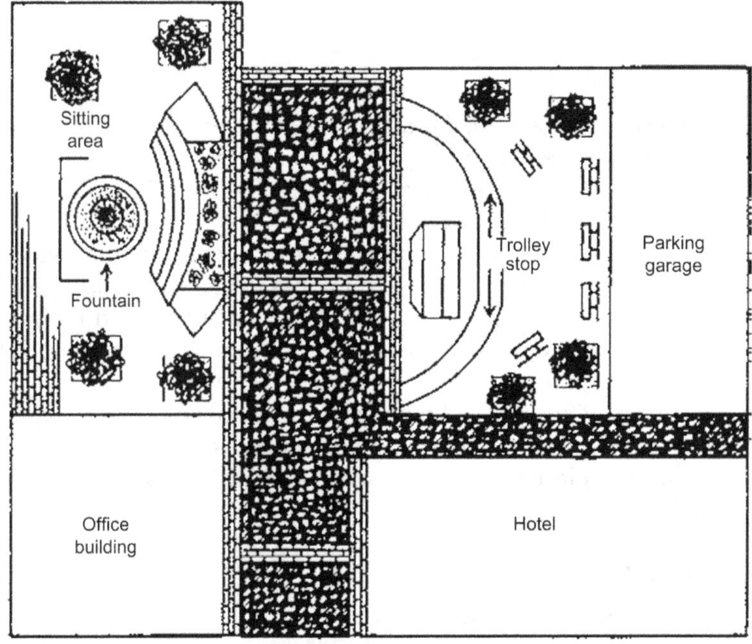

Figure 8.9

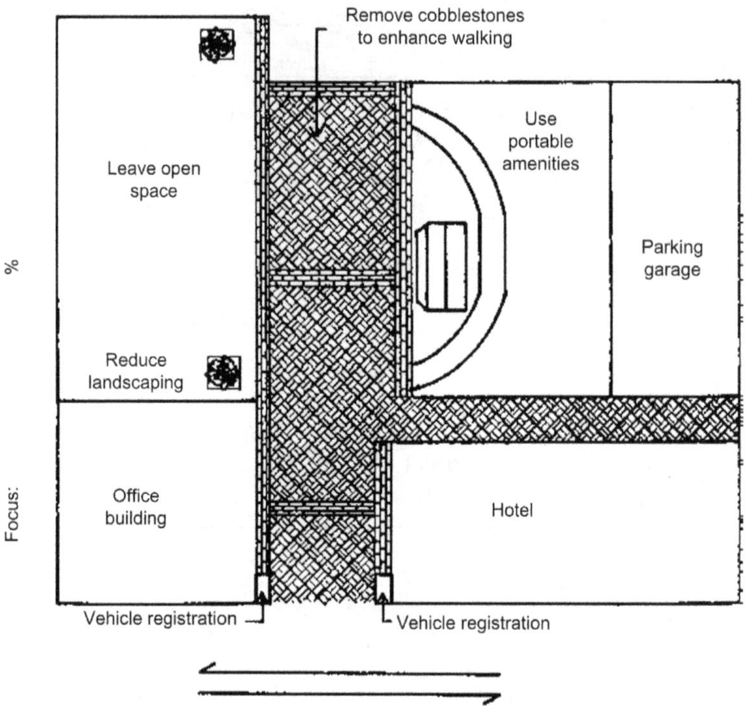

Figure 8.10

3. Benches, tables, and the fountain area may easily be colonized by vagrants or serve as bombing targets for pigeons.
4. Normal users will feel at risk and abnormal users will feel safe.

Good design and use (Figure 8.10):

1. Compromises must be made between form and function. Paver tiles may be used in place of cobblestones to make walking easier.
2. Portable amenities and landscaping may be substituted for permanent furnishings to increase flexibility in planning outdoor events.
3. Vehicles may be allowed limited and restricted access to facilitate a wide range of uses and to allow police patrols.
4. A well-used plaza will attract normal users and make people feel safe.

Pedestrian Malls

Poor design and use (Figure 8.11):

1. The present design and traffic-flow pattern reduce parking opportunities.

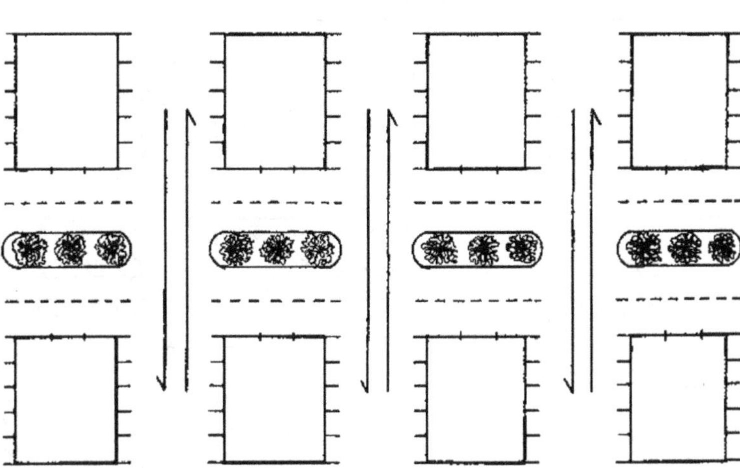

Figure 8.11

2. The pedestrian area and upgraded median are excellent, but is all this space needed everyday? Will it be used regularly, or will it be used mostly on holidays and weekend shopping days?
3. This design plan would be a problem for senior-citizen shoppers who may have to park some distance away. Parallel parking is also a problem for the senior-citizen shopper.

Good design and use (Figure 8.12):

1. Traffic flows may be controlled to allow for angle parking, to recover needed parking that is close to shops.
2. Vehicular speed may be radically controlled to reduce pedestrian conflict.
3. Barricades may be used to close off vehicular access during certain periods of high pedestrian activity or low-use periods. The design is flexible, allowing a variety of use patterns based on commercial and promotional planning.

Good design and use (Figure 8.13):

1. Traffic flows may be controlled to allow for angle parking, to increase available spots and frontal access to business.
2. Vehicular speed may be radically controlled to reduce conflict with pedestrians.
3. Barricades may be used to close off vehicular access during certain periods of high pedestrian activity or low-use periods.
4. Barricades may be used permanently or temporarily to control through access of vehicles.

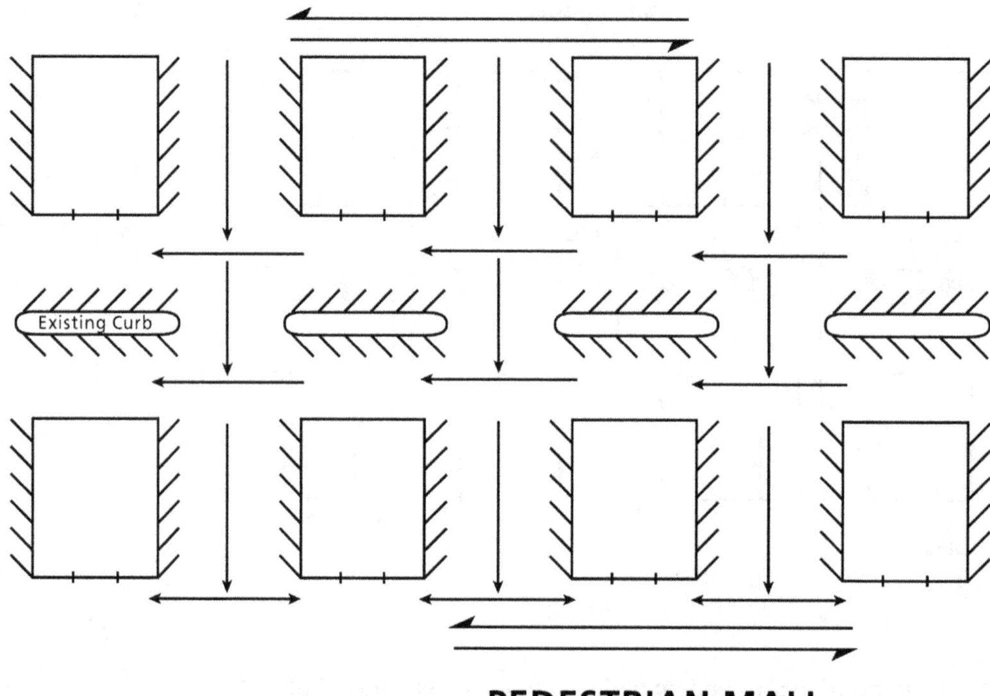

Figure 8.12

Parking Lots and Structures

Parking Lots

Poor design and use (Figure 8.14):

1. A typical lot layout on the ground level or each level of an off-street garage. Late arrivals get the less desirable spots, which are generally located in unobserved places. Early arrivals take the best, safest spots, but they are the first to leave, and at the safest times when an attendant may still be there.
2. The last in are the last out, generally when the lot is deserted.
3. This situation has been overlooked for years, with the assumption that the early arriver should naturally get the advantage. This is not a valid assumption where customers or employees are legitimately shopping later hours or scheduled for late shifts. Fear, higher victimization, and liability problems arise.

Good design and use (Figure 8.15):

1. Barriers are used to divert parking activity to create safe locations for late arrivals.

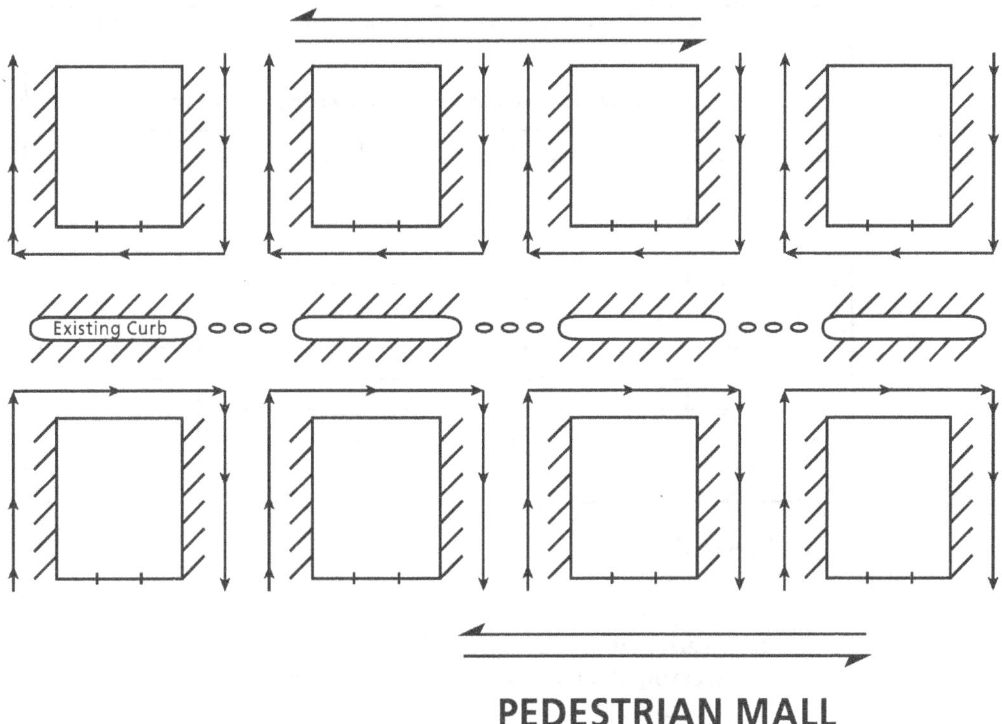

Figure 8.13

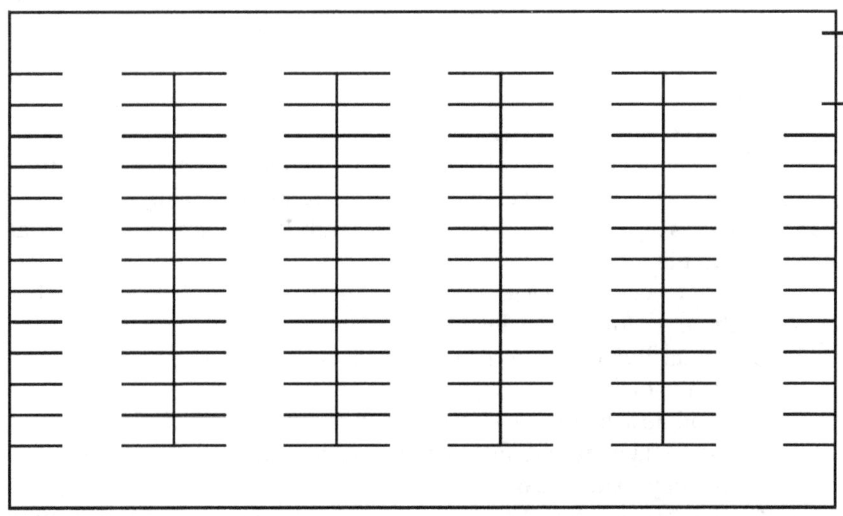

Figure 8.14

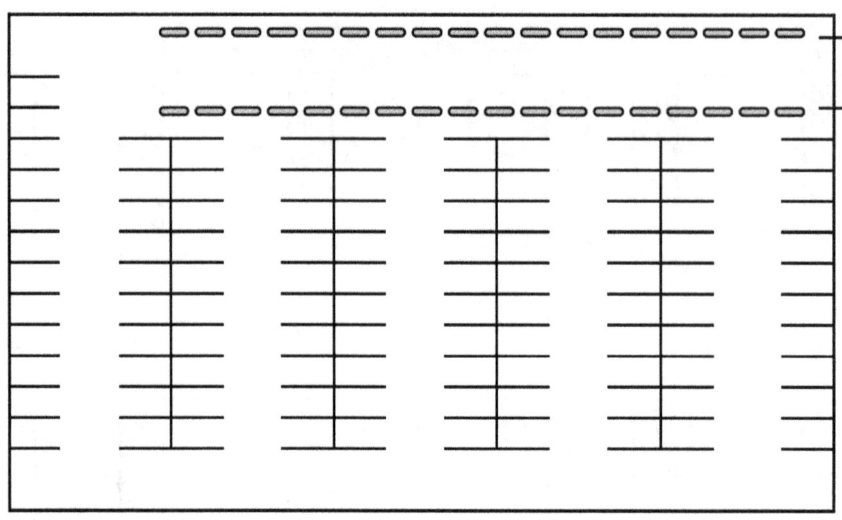

Figure 8.15

2. A variety of plans may be used, depending on a parking needs assessment. Floors may be alternately closed. Aisles may be partially opened.
3. Some balance between the legitimate needs of early arrivals and late arrivals should be achieved.
4. Physical barriers (e.g., cones or barricades) are less upsetting to users than attendants or guards who are directing flow past what are perceived as choice spots. However, guards or attendants are useful to serve in a rule enforcement or reinforcement function.

Parking Lot Access

Poor design and use (Figure 8.16):

1. The parking attendant's location prevents this person from providing natural surveillance over the employee parking area.
2. Landscaping may serve as an additional barrier to natural surveillance.
3. Employees will feel less safe and abnormal users will perceive that there is a low risk of detection.
4. A guard would have to be employed to protect employees and their vehicles.

Good design and use (Figure 8.17):

1. The parking attendant's location is naturally in a position to control all parking areas.
2. Employees will feel safer and abnormal users will know that they will risk detection.

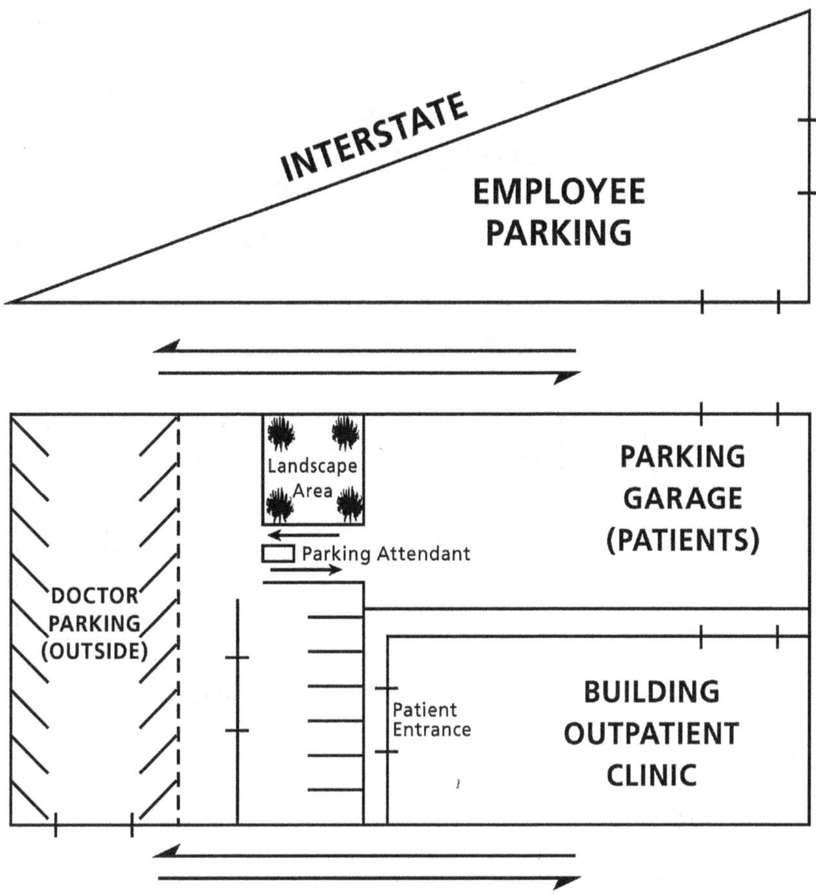

Figure 8.16

3. This design would free the guard for patrolling activities elsewhere.

Parking Structures

Poor design and use (Figure 8.18):

1. Ground levels of parking garages are underused and create a fortress effect on the pedestrian as well as on contiguous land uses.
2. Reinforced concrete retaining walls are commonly used and reduce surveillance opportunities. This creates the perception of lack of safety for the normal user and low risk for abnormal users.
3. Retaining walls do more to hide automobiles than to assure safety. Designers and local planners are often confused regarding the purpose of such walls.

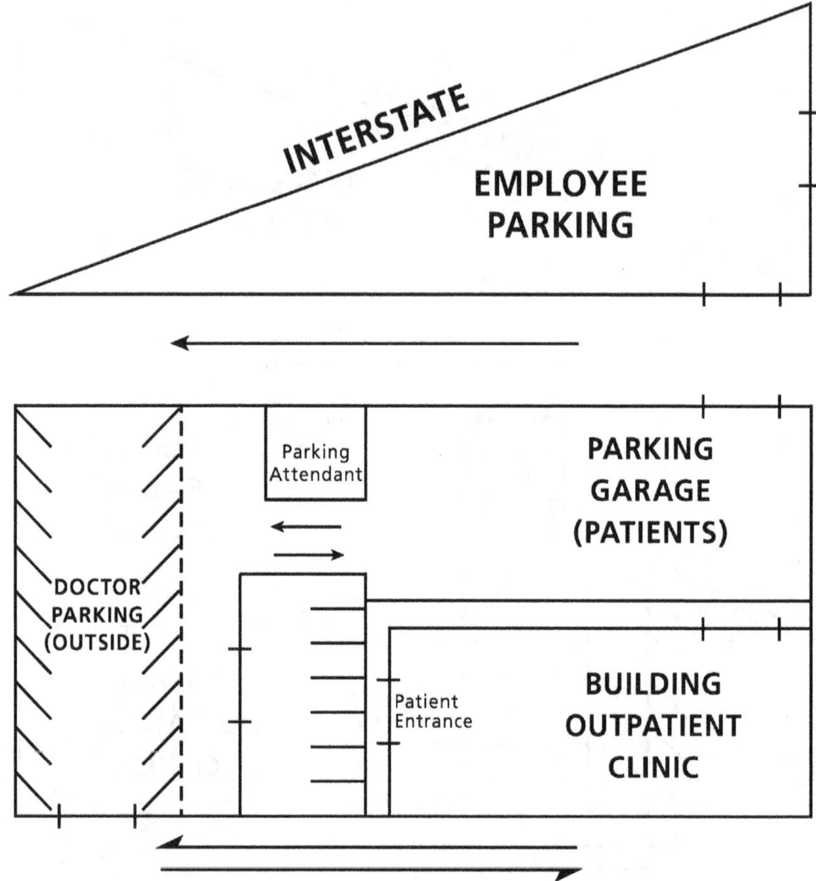

Figure 8.17

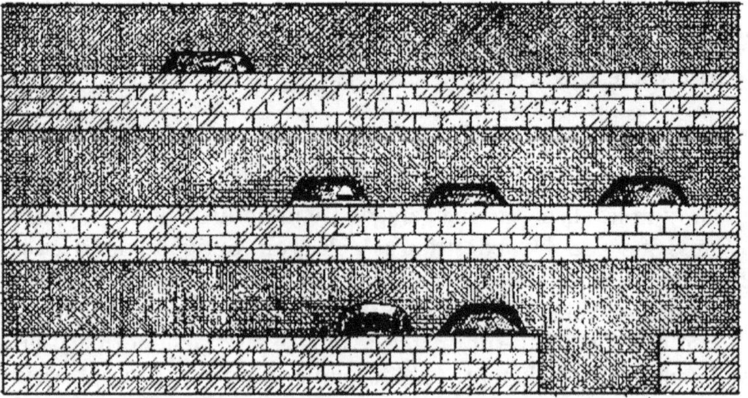

Figure 8.18

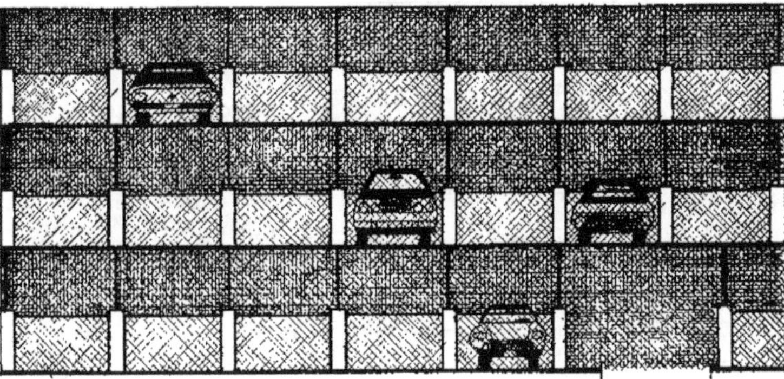

Figure 8.19

4. Lighting inside parking structures is generally located over the driving lanes instead of illuminating the parking spots, where people are outside their cars and most vulnerable. Cars have their own lights; people do not!

Good design and use (Figure 8.19):

1. Ground spaces should be dedicated to pedestrian-oriented businesses and activities, leaving the airspace for the car. This set-up will increase business revenues and enhance the perception of natural surveillance and access control for the garage and adjoining street space.
2. Retaining walls should be replaced with stretched cable of railings that allow for maximum surveillance and illumination. This will produce a considerable cost savings and improve perceptions of safety for normal users. Designers may even improve on the aesthetics over the concrete walls.
3. Reflective paint or materials should be used inside, and all pedestrian areas should be illuminated to increase feelings of safety.

Office and Industrial Systems

Office Access

Poor design and use (Figure 8.20):

A. Elevators go from below ground to working floors so that people have access to all floors.

B. Main entrance from which people could go directly to elevators without registering.

C. Side entrance that allows no surveillance by receptionist or guard and that allows access to the elevators.

D. Guard/receptionist booth that is not centrally located but is positioned so the person stationed there cannot see who enters or exits.

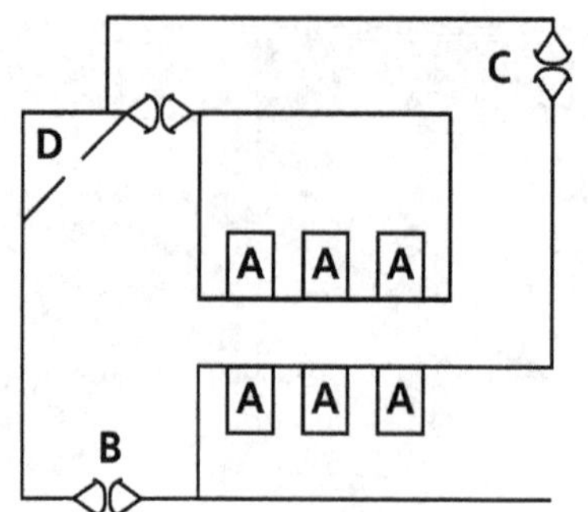

Figure 8.20

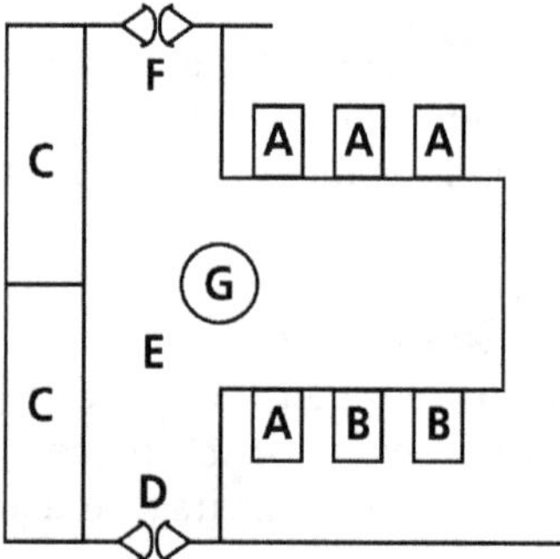

Figure 8.21

Good design and use (Figure 8.21):

A. Elevators serving lobby and floors above.
B. Separate elevators serving lobby and floor below.
C. Restrooms that are visible from the entrances.
D. Main entrance.
E. Main floor corridor that is visible from main entrance.
F. Controlled access/egress door.
G. Security/receptionist station to screen entrances.

Office Building Site Plan and Parking

Poor design and use (Figure 8.22):

A. Parking is undifferentiated by time of day and day of week.
B. Through access and nighttime use are poorly defined and unclear.
C. Cars parked anywhere are not subject to scrutiny by security, law enforcement officials, or building management.

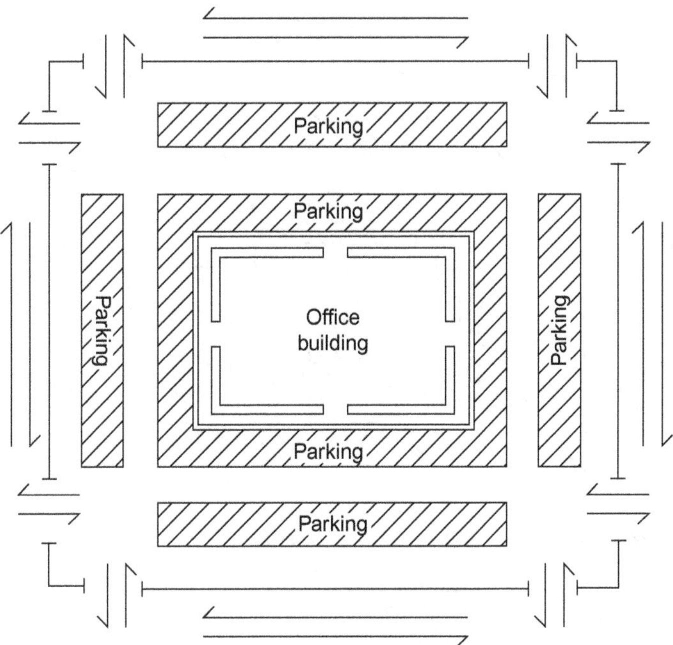

Figure 8.22

Good design and use (Figure 8.23):

A. Parking is zoned (numbers 1-5) and clearly identified by allowable spatial and temporal uses.
B. Improper parking is more subject to notice and scrutiny by local law enforcement officials and security officers.
C. Zones may be closed depending on need.

Shipping and Receiving and Vehicle Access

Poor design (Figure 8.24):

1. Confused and deep internal access for external vehicles.
2. Easy mix of external vehicles with those of employees.
3. Multiple access from facilities to employees' vehicles.
4. Shipping and receiving in same location legitimizes people coming and going with boxes.
5. Guard or full-time monitor required to screen access and packages.
6. Wide range of excuses for improper behavior, thus increasing pressure on guards or shipping/receiving clerks.

Good design (Figure 8.25):

1. Parking segregated from external delivery or vendor vehicle access to property.
2. All employee/visitor parking clearly visible from buildings.

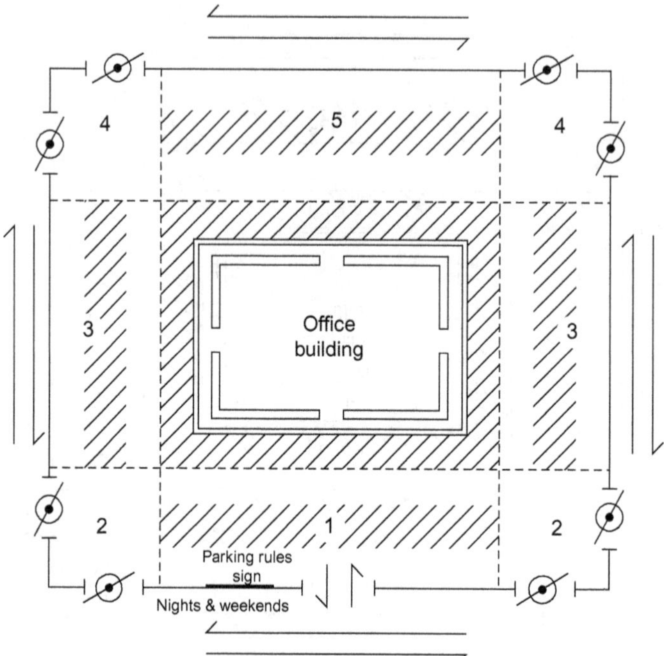

Figure 8.23

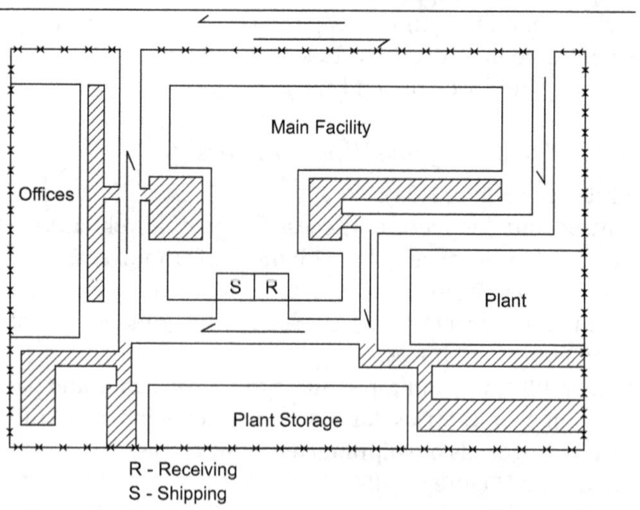

Figure 8.24

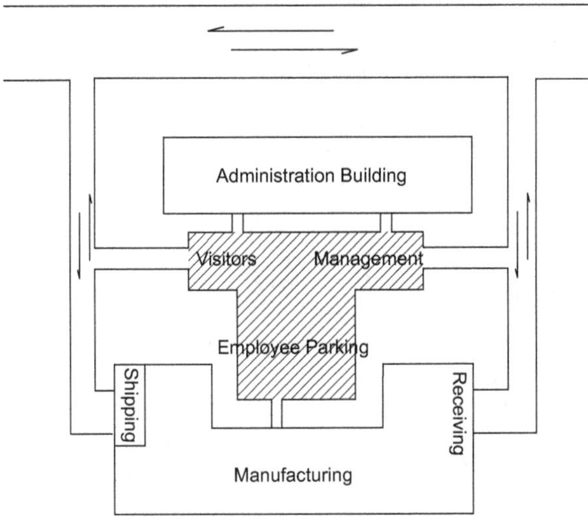

Figure 8.25

3. Shipping and receiving separated by distance, which reduces range of excuses.
4. Legitimate behavior narrowly defined by location.
5. Transitional definition of movement is clear from opportunities for signage and rule enhancement in purchase/shipping orders and policies.

Plant Design

Poor design (Figure 8.26):

1. Confusing vehicular internal access.
2. Too much access for external vehicles to building entrances, which may easily promote collusion between employees and vendors or subcontractors.
3. Shipping/receiving located in same site, which may encourage abuses.
4. Extended locations of employee parking and strict access control through security negatively affect morale and subsequent labor negotiations.
5. Receptionist position (in office) provides little natural access control and surveillance.
6. Perimeter security fencing encloses a large area, which increases cost and vulnerability.

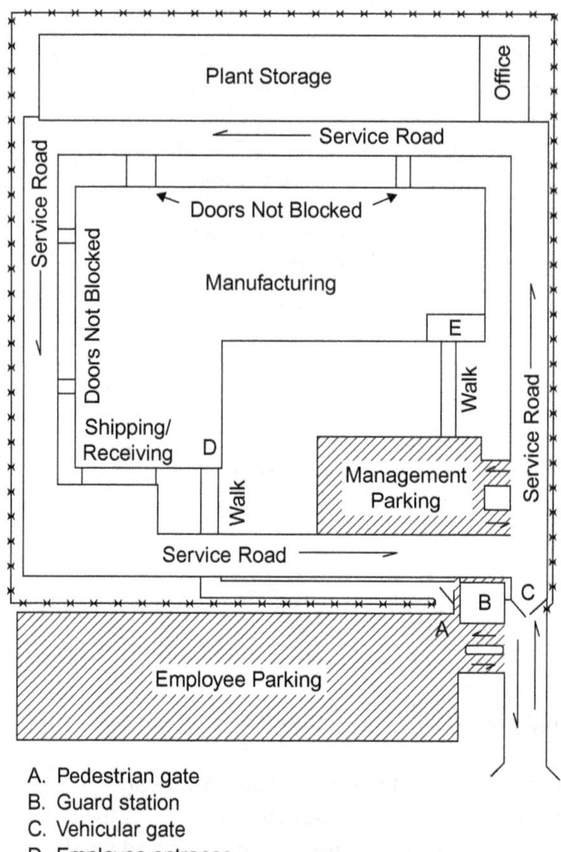

Figure 8.26

Good design (Figure 8.27):

1. Campus site plan emphasizes openness and natural distance to increase an intruder's perception of risk of surveillance.
2. Convenient employee parking in front of building increases perception of surveillance of employees from the building while decreasing the negative effect of isolated parking on morale.
3. Segregated shipping/receiving may reduce opportunities for theft.
4. Guard post may be partially staffed or eliminated altogether by replacing it with a receptionist or other natural (nonorganized) function to provide the perception of natural access control and surveillance.
5. Reduced magnitude and cost of perimeter security.

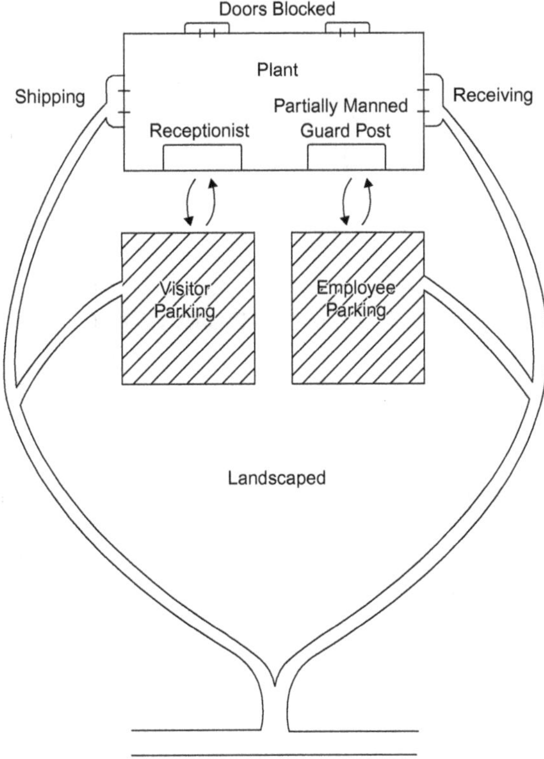

Figure 8.27

6. Employee parking is protected by distance from public street access and by direct line of sight from the reception areas.
7. Site development and building costs should be reduced. Internal space footage requirements should also be reduced.

Hallways and Restrooms

Hallways

Poor design and use (Figure 8.28):

1. Most hallways in schools, hospitals, and offices are left undifferentiated. They do not identify what is on the other side of the wall or who owns it.
2. Hallway uses become confused by the placement of lockers and furniture. Hallways are for movement, not for gathering behavior.
3. Tenants or people who are assigned internal spaces or work areas will actively control their spaces but will assume little proprietary regard for the adjoining hallways or corridors.

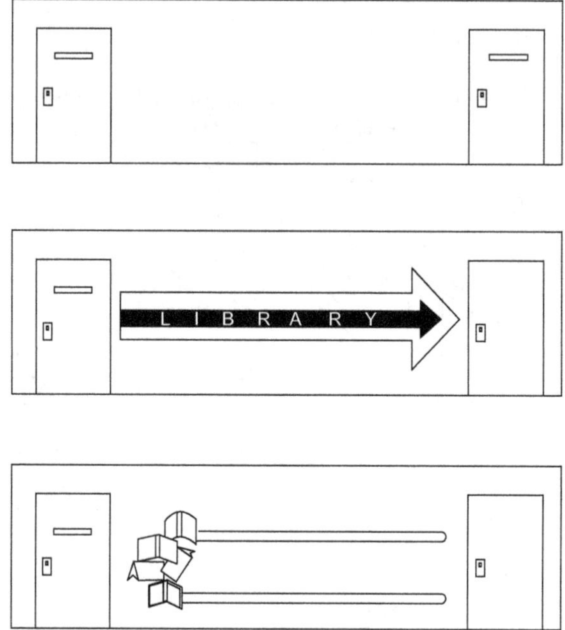

Figure 8.28

4. Hallways usually carry the definition of extremely public space, even though extremely private space is only inches away.
5. Some new buildings prohibit any decoration or encroachment by tenants into hallway systems as part of an interior-decorating plan.
6. Multiple-purpose classrooms or meeting spaces suffer from lack of ownership.
7. Normal users demonstrate avoidance behavior in these undifferentiated spaces, which makes abnormal users feel safer and in control.

Good design and use:

1. Hallways may be assigned to the tenant of the adjoining internal space. Users should be influenced to mark their turf, to identify their boundaries.
2. Boundaries and turf cues should be extended to consume unassigned or undifferentiated spaces.
3. The legitimate uses of hallways and corridors need to be reinforced through policies and signs.
4. Graphics may be used to promote movement and to indicate direction.

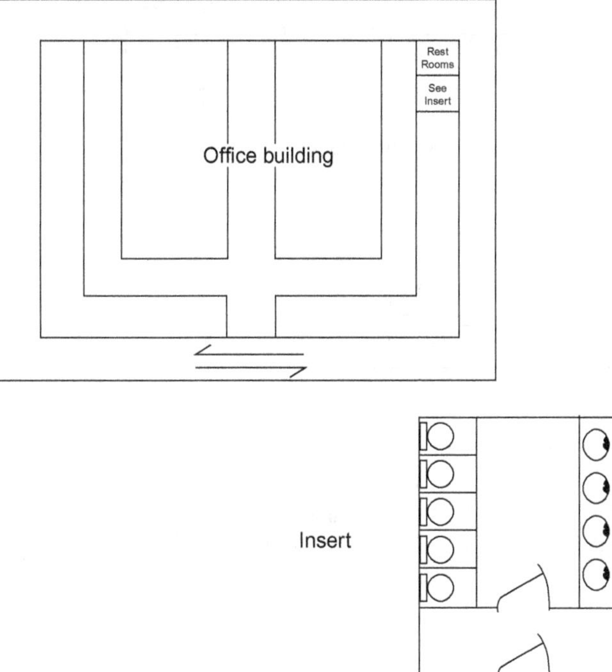

Figure 8.29

5. Floor coverings and colors may be used to identify public versus private spaces.
6. Normal users recognize and honor others' turf or ownership cues. Normal users feel safer in these areas and exhibit challenging and controlling behaviors. Abnormal users respond to these cues by avoiding these areas or with avoidance behaviors when they are in the vicinity.

Restroom Location and Entrance Design

Poor design and use (Figure 8.29):

1. Restrooms are traditionally isolated by location as a cultural sensitivity and for economic reasons.
2. Public restrooms are common sites for illegal and illicit activity.
3. Many children are afraid to use the restroom at school.
4. Malls and shopping centers have tended to hide restrooms as a means of reducing demand for this nonrevenue-bearing facility.
5. The lack of convenient and clean restrooms clearly reduces the average time per visit to most stores and businesses, thereby reducing sales.

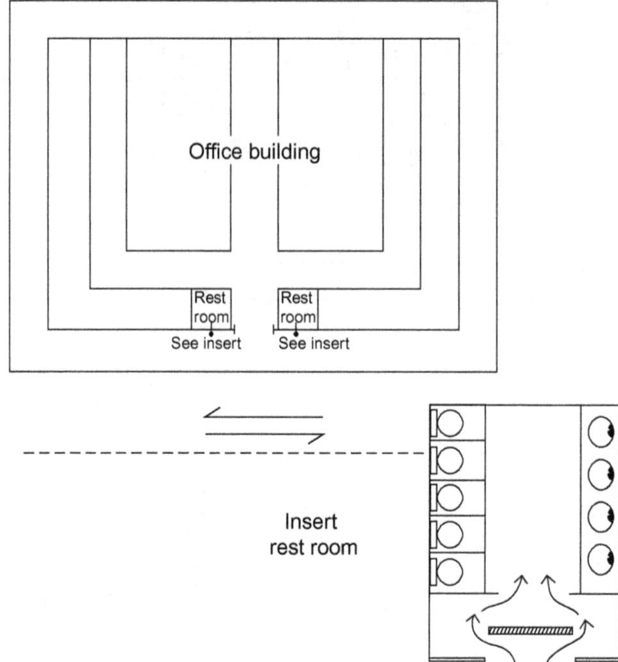

Figure 8.30

6. Isolated locations and double-door entry systems present unsafe cues to normal users and safe cues to abnormal users.
7. Double-door entry systems produce a warning sound and transitional time that is an advantage to abnormal users.
8. A normal user or guard must move inside the second door swing to figure out what is going on in a restroom.

Good design and use (Figure 8.30):

1. Restrooms should bc located in the most convenient and accessible places to increase use, which increases the perception of safety.
2. A maze-type entry system or doors placed in a locked-open position will increase convenience and safety.
3. Normal users may determine who is in the restroom by glancing around the privacy screen or wall.
4. Abnormal users will feel at greater risk of detection.
5. Customer (or student) convenience and safety should contribute to the attainment of the objectives of the restroom space.

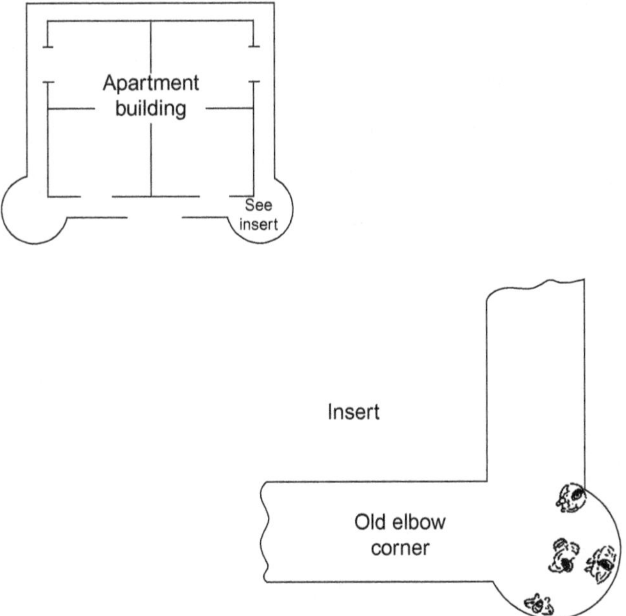

Figure 8.31

Informal Gathering Areas

Poor design (Figure 8.31):

1. Hallways and corners in schools, office buildings, malls, and apartments attract small groups of abnormal users who preempt this space and promote conflict.
2. Normal users avoid these areas, which reinforces the perception of risk.
3. Congestion is often created elsewhere because of the avoidance behavior of normal users.
4. The avoidance behavior reinforces the perception of safety and turf ownership of the abnormal users.

Good design (Figure 8.32):

1. A safe activity may be located in the poorly used space to displace the unsafe use.
2. A safe activity will serve as a magnet for normal users, who will be attracted to the area.
3. The safe activity and normal user behavior will create and intensify the perception of risk for the abnormal user.
4. Space utilization and productivity will go up in most cases.

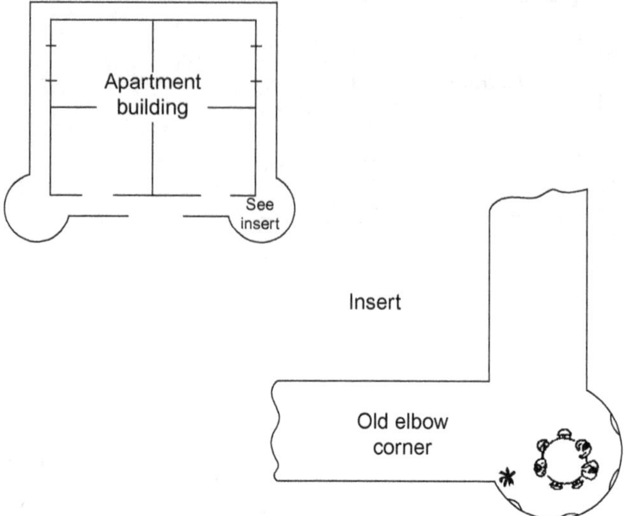

Figure 8.32

Malls and Shopping Centers

Shopping Mall Parking

Poor design (Figure 8.33):

1. Parking is 360-degree and undifferentiated.
2. Safety hazards persist because of uncontrolled access to all lanes.
3. Undesirable nighttime activities occur.
4. Transition from public to private space is undefined.

Good design (Figure 8.34):

1. Parking is enclaved in relation to business entrances.
2. Lateral access by vehicles is severely restricted.
3. Aesthetic design opportunities are enhanced to screen ugly parking lots.
4. Extreme transitional definition exists, thereby reducing escape opportunities.
5. Parking areas may be closed with barricades at various times of the day.

Mall Design

Poor design and use (Figure 8.35):

1. Malls have traditionally been designed in a fortress style, which turns its back on the parking areas.
2. Many dead walls on the least-used sides or backsides of malls prevent opportunities for advertising and limit natural surveillance.

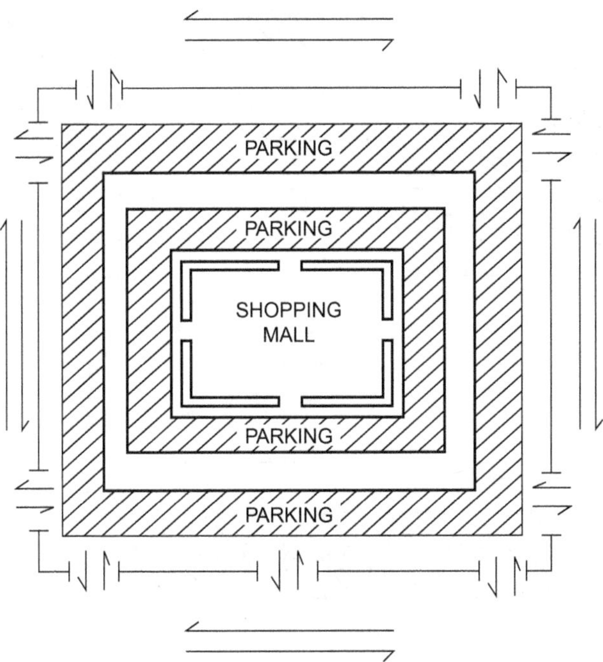

Figure 8.33

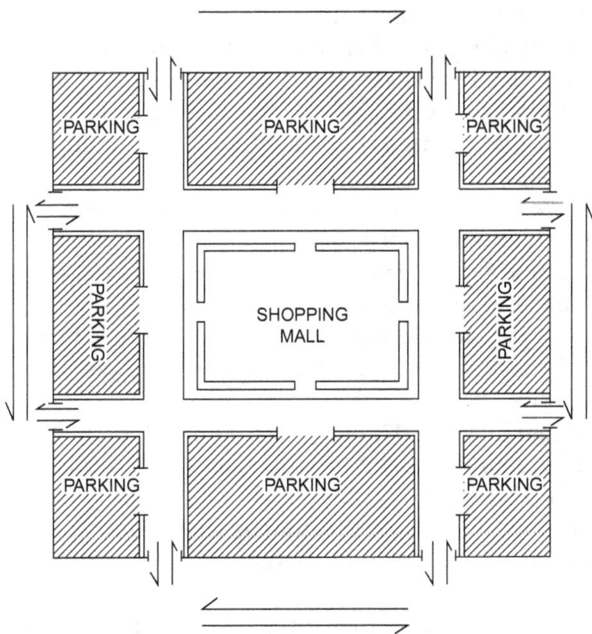

Figure 8.34

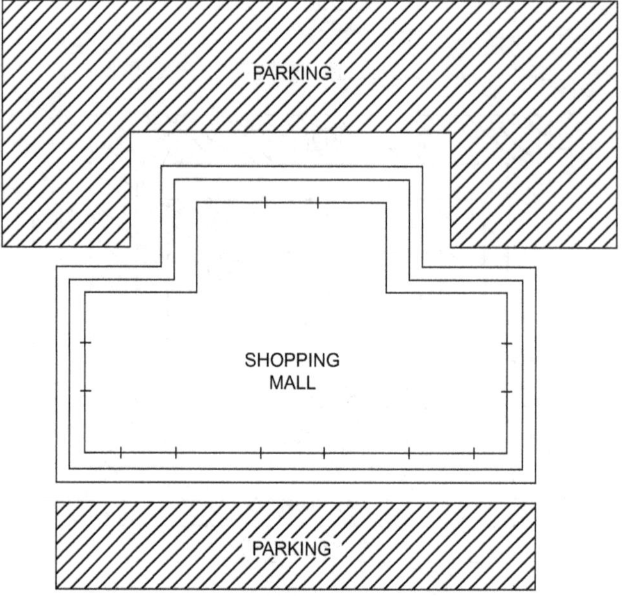

Figure 8.35

3. Designers tend to reflect their perceptions of an area in their designs. Buildings in isolated areas will end up fortress-like in form. The dead walls serve as a barrier to surveillance from or to the building, despite the fact that many people are inside the building, separated by a 16-inch wall from the parking area.

Good design and use (Figure 8.36)

1. Display cases may be attached to dead walls to market products and to reduce the negative effect of the fortress designs.
2. Active displays with lighting and mannequins will attract attention and create the impression of natural surveillance.
3. False windows and lighting panels may also break up the monotony of the fortress designs and reinforce the impression of natural surveillance.

Poor design (Figure 8.37):

1. Shopping center parking is contiguous to a major conflicting activity of a play area.
2. The location of the basketball hoops legitimizes the presence of young people in and near the parking area, to chase balls and for informal gathering.
3. Normal users feel that their property and their persons are at greater risk.

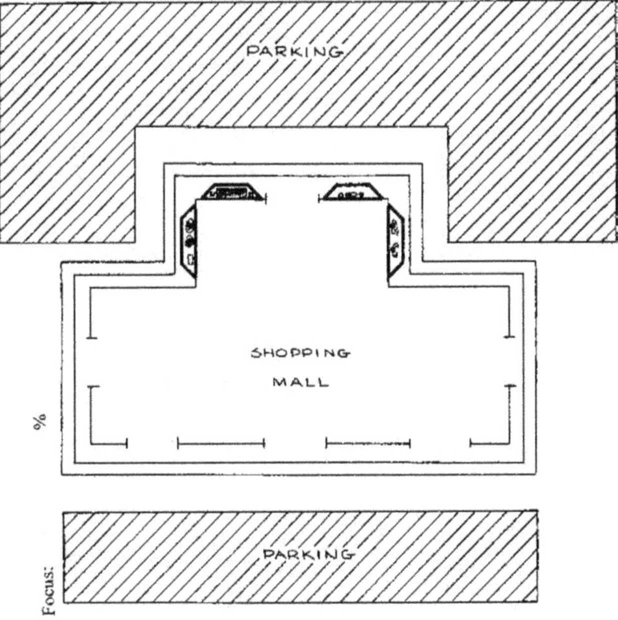

Figure 8.36

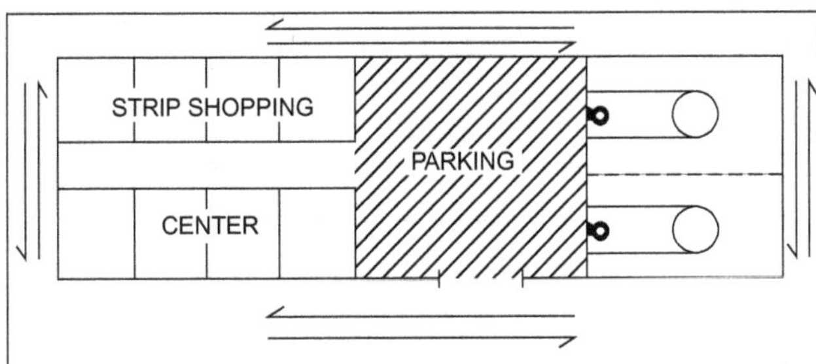

Figure 8.37

4. Abnormal users feel safer.
5. Even legitimate use of the play area is perceived negatively by others.

Good design (Figure 8.38):

1. Distance may be used as a natural barrier to conflicting activities.
2. The natural barrier of distance reduces the range of excuses for being in the wrong place.
3. Abnormal users will feel at greater risk of scrutiny and detection.

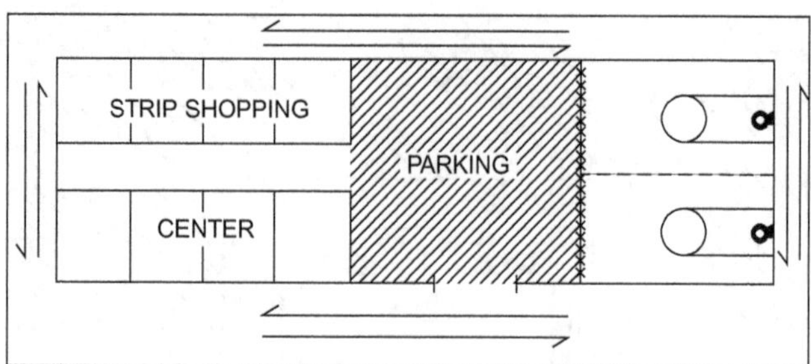

Figure 8.38

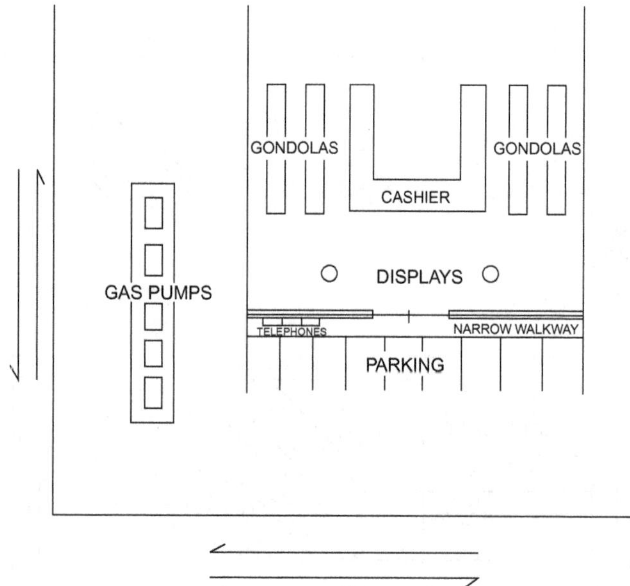

Figure 8.39

Convenience Stores and Branch Banks

Convenience Stores: Traditional Design

Poor design and use (Figure 8.39):

1. Gas pumps were installed after original site planning, so most were placed wherever there was an open area. This often resulted in a site placement that is not surveillable from the cashier location in the building. Some stores have installed windows that affect cashier location and surveillance.

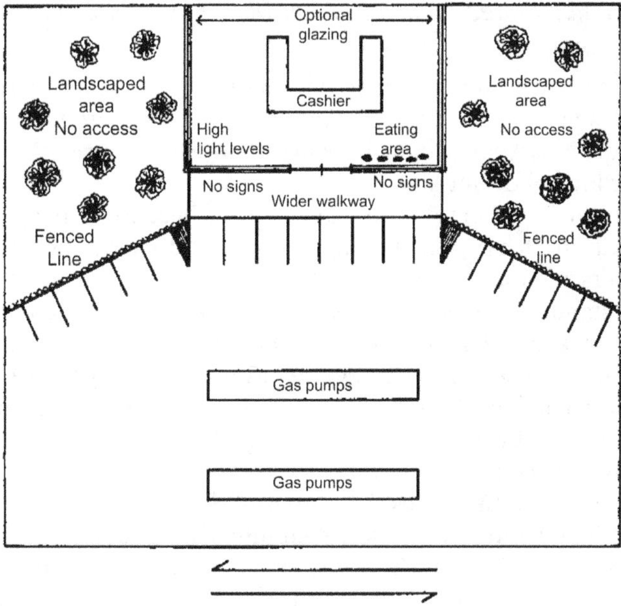

Figure 8.40

2. Parking is traditionally in front, but walkways are generally too narrow for customers to avoid close contact with young people or construction workers who legitimately hang out in these areas.
3. Telephones are often placed too close to the store entrance. Young people hang out in these areas, as do some undesirables, which turns off normal adult customers. Robbers like to stand at a pay phone as a cover for casing a store.
4. Although the research is conflicting, the centrally located cashier station does result in the cashier having her back to customers when only one clerk is on duty. A frontal or rear location of a central cashier station would be preferable.
5. It is common for stores to obscure the front windows with signage and to orient gondolas and shelves perpendicular to the front of the store. Signage prevents customers and police from looking into or out of the store. Improper gondola and shelf orientation prevents clerks from observing customers. Likewise, abnormal users feel safer in stores where gondolas and shelf systems eliminate natural surveillance.

Good design and use (Figure 8.40):

1. Parking in front is always more convenient and safer.
2. Most stores use ample amounts of glazing in the front, which improves both natural and perceived surveillance.

Convenience Stores: Locations Near Dense Commercial or Housing Sites

1. Convenience stores located in these sites experience robberies associated with access from the rear of the store to the front. Escape is easy around the back of the store into dense commercial building or housing sites.
2. Customers are afraid to use these stores because of hanging-out activity by local residents and undesirable users, such as drug dealers and unruly young people.
3. The standard *modus operandi* is for a perpetrator to come from behind a convenience store to the front and rob the cashier. Escape is so easy that stakeout teams of police may not catch the robber that they observe committing the offense, because the person may easily melt into the buildings that are contiguous to and behind the convenience store.
4. A fenced line that takes the corner of the building diagonally to the property line will reduce or eliminate the robberies that come from behind the store. The fence increases the offender's perception of exposure, even though the fence does not provide a continuous enclosure of the property.

Convenience Stores: Hexagon Shaped

Poor design and use:

1. Double-entry systems make customer control difficult.
2. Eating areas may attract people who hang out.
3. The design will work only on corner lots.

Good design and use (Figure 8.41)

1. Telephone location and interior management may reduce customer conflict between juveniles and construction workers and adult buyers.
2. Well-lighted gasoline areas will serve as a sea of light, attracting customers.
3. Eating areas in the front of the store will attract adult customers who may find it inconvenient to eat hot foods in their vehicles. Small seat and table designs will keep people from lingering or hanging out.
4. Marketing studies have demonstrated that impulse customers prefer a store that has other customers, which means that they have to see those customers in order to be attracted.
5. Segregation of customer groups is achieved by the hexagonal design, which makes these groups less threatening to each other.

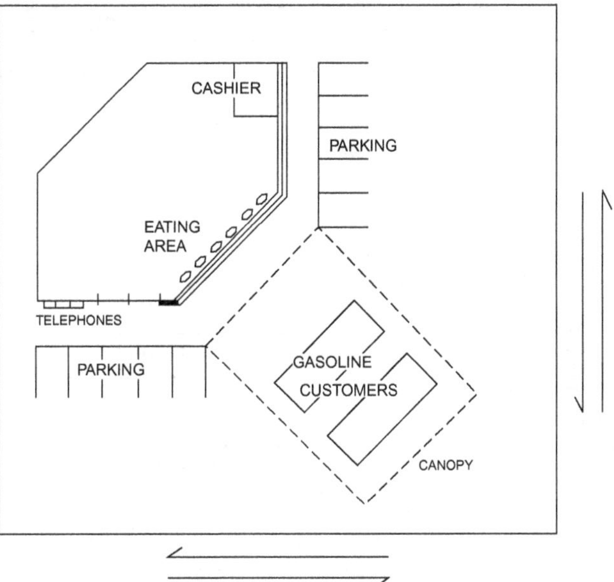

Figure 8.41

Convenience Stores: Fan Shaped

Poor design and use:

1. Some stores do not have continuous glazing across the front.
2. Fan designs are ineffective when they are in midblock locations.

Good design and use (Figure 8.42):

1. Clear view for cashier of all parking and gas pump areas.
2. Corner locations allow for effective vehicle access and excellent surveillance and control.
3. Elevated store and cashier locations increase control and customer confidence in safety.
4. Site efficiency in terms of cost benefit is high.

Convenience Stores: Kiosk Shaped

Good design and use (Figure 8.43):

1. Store oriented to gas sales.
2. Three-hundred-degree surveillance for cashier.
3. Late-night robbery control through use of bank teller window.
4. Welcoming environment includes high light levels and bright colors.

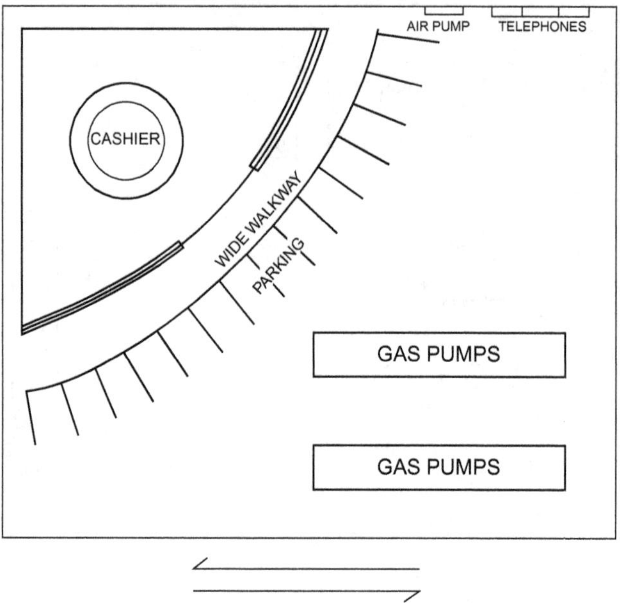

Figure 8.42

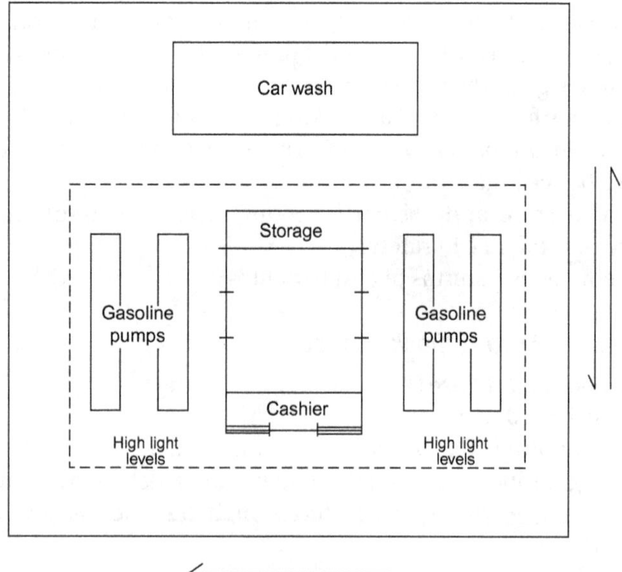

Figure 8.43

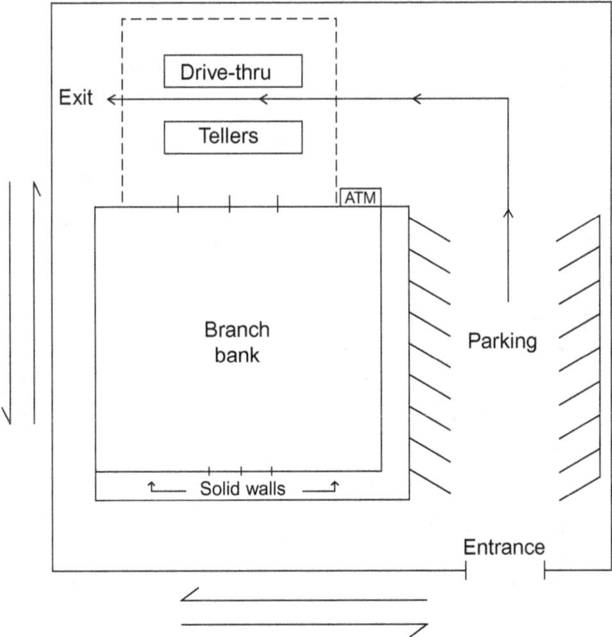

Figure 8.44

5. Newer site plans place the car wash to the side instead of the back of the property.
6. Employee compliance with security procedures makes the kiosk store one of the most safe and defensible.

Branch Banks

Poor design and use (Figure 8.44):

1. Most branch banks were designed as mini-fortresses reflecting the architect's perception that people would have more confidence that their money was safe.
2. Corner lots were the most desired to allow for customer drive-through on the side and back. Engineers desired this set-up to reduce the hazard of vehicles slowing down on the public street to enter a parking area that was visible from the street. Planners desired parking on the side or in back to hide vehicles. Planners had concluded by the mid- to late 1950s that cars were ugly and asphalt parking lots were uglier, so they promoted local codes requiring that buildings be placed on the front lot line so that parking could be hidden behind the structure.

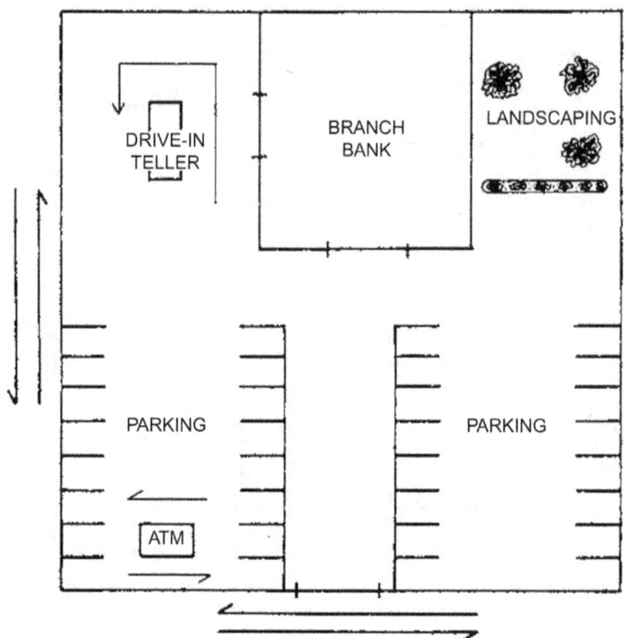

Figure 8.45

3. Automatic teller machines (ATMs) were originally located adjacent to the secure teller area so that they could be serviced easily, but the traditional design and flow plan caused the secure teller areas to be in the back of the bank, so ATMs ended up being placed in areas with little or no natural surveillance.
4. Customers have to park on the side or in back of the bank and then come around on foot to the front or side doors. This is inconvenient and increases their perceived exposure to robbers.
5. Studies have shown that robbers prefer the fortress-type branch bank because they feel that they are less exposed to surveillance from the outside. The fortress design was based on an assumption that went unchallenged for over 30 years.

Good design and use (Figure 8.45):

1. Bank placed on the rear lot line, allowing customer parking and access from the front.
2. ATM located in area with the greatest natural surveillance and independent from the building. Customers prefer to be able to drive up to the ATM and remain in or close to their vehicle for safety and convenience.
3. Parking should be in front where it is most visible. A curb lane should be used to bring vehicles deep into the property prior to

allowing them to disburse into the parking area. This will reduce the concern about traffic hazards by increasing the exit speed of the vehicles.
4. The curb laning of vehicle access will serve as a transitional process that forces the user to acknowledge movement from public to semipublic to private space.
5. The building design should emphasize a maximum of glazing to increase the perception of natural surveillance and openness from and to the structure.
6. Abnormal users will feel a greater risk because of the improved natural surveillance and access.

Objectives for Residential Environments

1. *Access control.* Provide secure barriers to prevent unauthorized access to building grounds, buildings, and/or restricted building interior areas.
2. *Surveillance through physical design.* Improve opportunities for surveillance by physical design mechanisms that serve to increase the risk of detection for offenders, enable evasive actions by potential victims, and facilitate intervention by police.
3. *Mechanical surveillance devices.* Provide residences with security devices to detect and signal illegal entry attempts.
4. *Design and construction.* Design, build, and/or repair residences and residential sites to enhance security and improve quality.
5. *Land use.* Establish policies to prevent ill-advised land and building uses that have negative impact.
6. *Resident action.* Encourage residents to implement safeguards on their own to make homes less vulnerable to crime.
7. *Social interaction.* Encourage interaction by residents to foster social cohesion and control.
8. *Private security services.* Determine appropriate paid professional and/or volunteer citizen services to enhance residential security needs.
9. *Police services.* Improve police services to provide efficiency and effectiveness.
10. *Police/community relations.* Improve police/community relations to involve citizens in cooperative efforts with police to prevent and report crime.
11. *Community awareness.* Create neighborhood/community crime-prevention awareness to aid in combating crime in residential areas.
12. *Territorial identity.* Differentiate private areas from public spaces to discourage trespass by potential offenders.

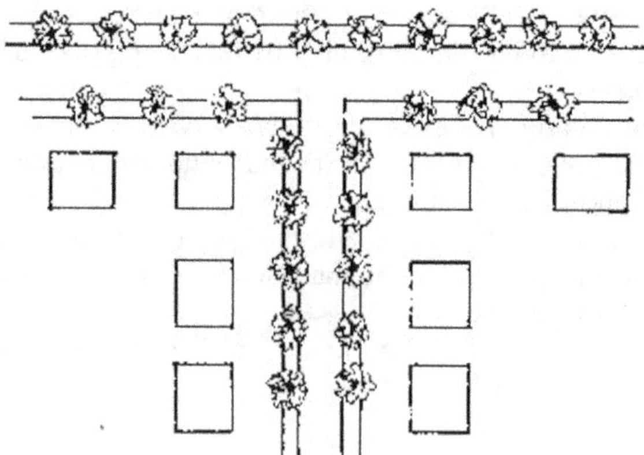

Figure 8.46

13. *Neighborhood image.* Develop positive neighborhood image to encourage residents and investor confidence and increase the economic vitality of the area.

Residential Streets

Figure 8.46:

1. Street is quiet with a small amount of through traffic.
2. Residents recognize neighbors' cars and stare at nonresidents who may be passing through or stopping.
3. Gutters are clean and front yards are well maintained, which indicates extended territorial concern. Front porches have furniture and other signs of use.

Figure 8.47:

1. A proposed land-use change involves the building of a new neighborhood school, which is generally socially desirable.
2. The school generates increased pedestrian and vehicular activity. Nonresident cars will park in front of homes, taking up what had previously been viewed as the proprietary space of residents.
3. Property value growth and retention will fall. Residents will subconsciously turn their backs to the street and alter their patterns of property use.
4. Residents' controlling or challenging behaviors (e.g., staring and verbal challenges) will diminish.

Figure 8.48:

1. The neighborhood school is changed to an expanded school that loses its neighborhood identity. Users have very little attachment or concern for the neighborhood.

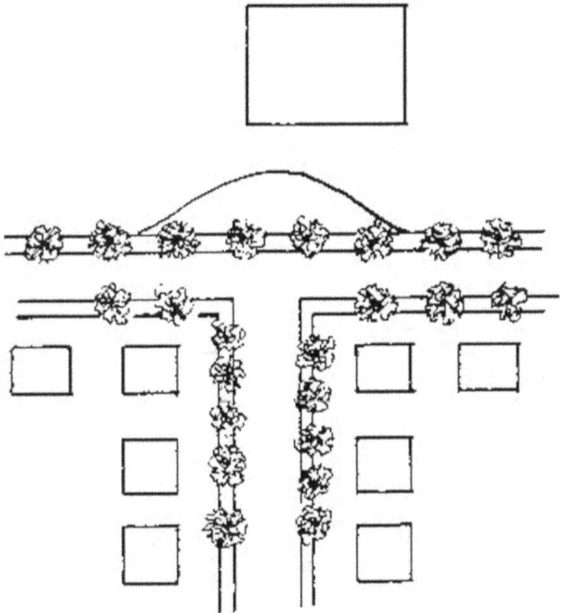

Figure 8.47

Figure 8.48

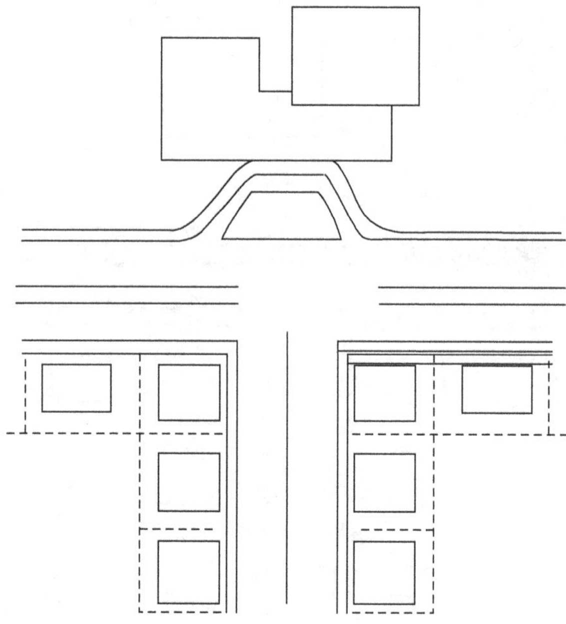

Figure 8.49

2. Traffic increases and more parking activity occurs in the neighborhood. Property values drop and long-term or original residents move out.
3. New residents accept the changed conditions and exhibit few signs of extended territorial identity and concern.

Figure 8.49:

1. The expanded school is further developed to regional status.
2. Streets have already been upgraded from residential and subcollector status to the next higher level of traffic flow. Street capacity improvements have resulted in the increase of on-street parking and the removal of trees. Sidewalks and front yards are pushed closer to the dwelling units.
3. The neighborhood is already susceptible to a zoning change request and the possibility of the development of transient housing, which may be disguised as low-income or scattered-site publicly supported housing.
4. Any major land-use change will contribute to higher demands for public services, increased housing turnover, and a growing crime rate.

Figure 8.50:

1. The encroachment of marginal business and/or transient housing will ultimately be replaced by high-density commercial or

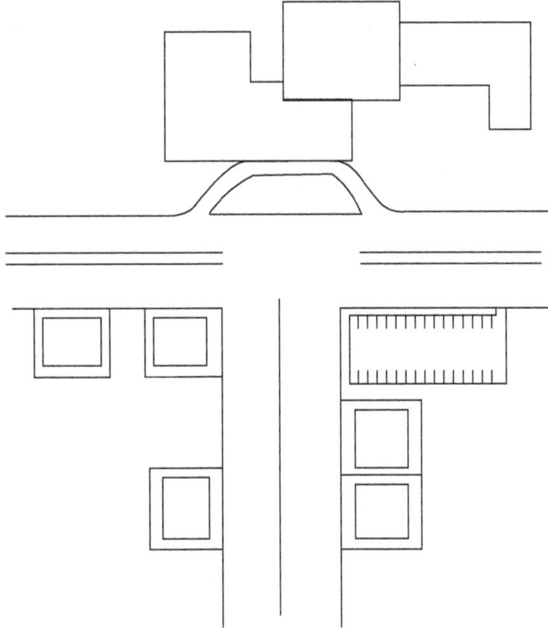

Figure 8.50

industrial activities, which will be the only viable land uses once the original site has deteriorated.

2. Vacant or abandoned lots will be used in the interim for overflow parking and unauthorized drug dealing or recreational use. The area will be perceived as dangerous or undesirable for residential uses. Normal users will avoid the area, and abnormal users will feel that they have lower risk of detection or intervention.
3. Some unscrupulous developers will use this process as a means of controlling large parcels of land for long-term development while capitalizing on the long-term plans through the short-term investment in transient housing or marginal commercial activities—both of which help to progressively reduce the property value.

Figure 8.51:

1. Access to the new school may be isolated from the contiguous residential streets. School property vehicular access may be planned for an alternative location that may be connected to an existing high-capacity commercially or industrially oriented street.
2. Pedestrian flow through the residential area will still increase, but vehicular and parking activity will be diverted.

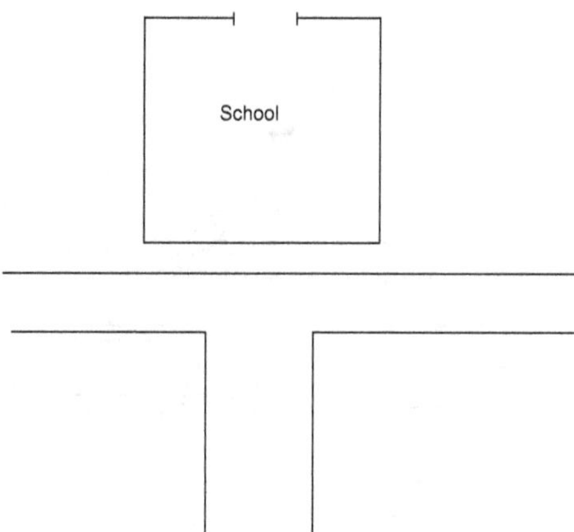

Figure 8.51

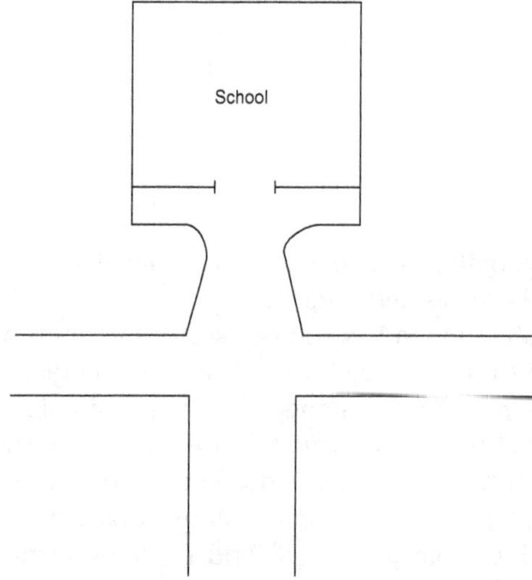

Figure 8.52

Figure 8.52:

1. An alternative strategy to the conflict created by the new school would be to create a major set-back to allow for a transition lane and temporary waiting lane for buses and parents who may be awaiting student pickup.
2. Traffic-control devices or procedures may be used to direct and divert vehicles from the residential area.

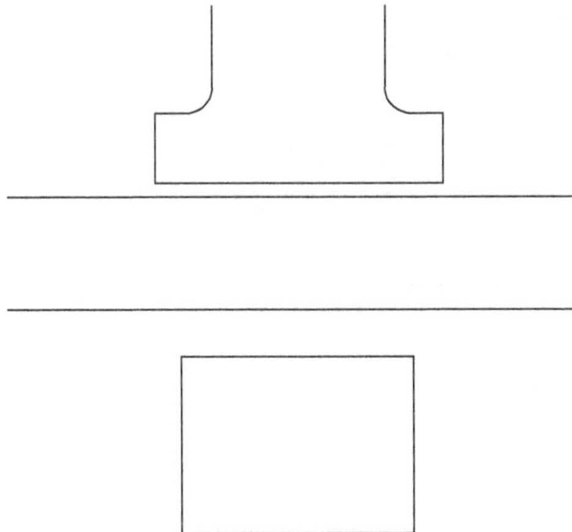

Figure 8.53

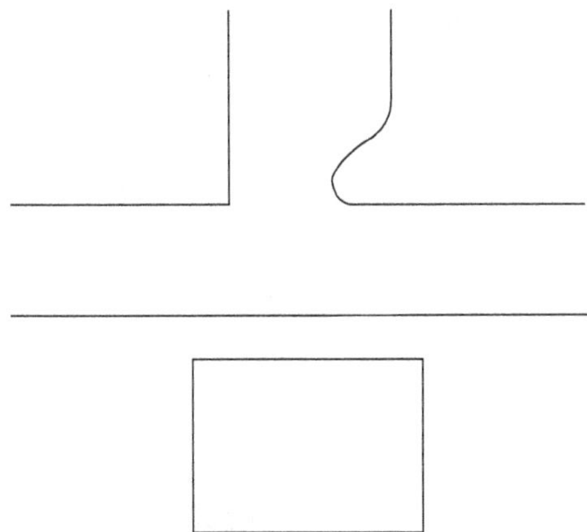

Figure 8.54

Figure 8.53:

1. A partial "choker" may be used to divert right-turn traffic from the affected neighborhood.

Figure 8.54:

1. The street affected by the traffic associated with the school may be permanently diverted by closing the street with a cul-de-sac or turnaround *T*.
2. Emergency vehicle access may be enhanced through the use of drive-over plantings or knockdown gates. Malleable steel pins or links may be used in latching devices or chains to make it easy for emergency vehicles to push open the barriers.

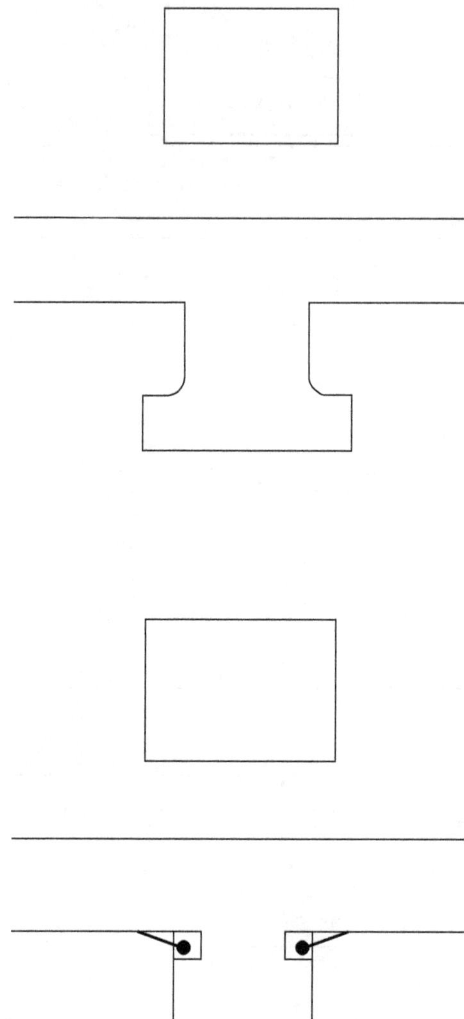

Figure 8.55

Figure 8.56

Figure 8.55:

1. The street affected by the traffic associated with the school may be closed in the middle, thus creating a dead end. The middle street closing may use a turnaround ball or a *T* to facilitate emergency and public service vehicle access.

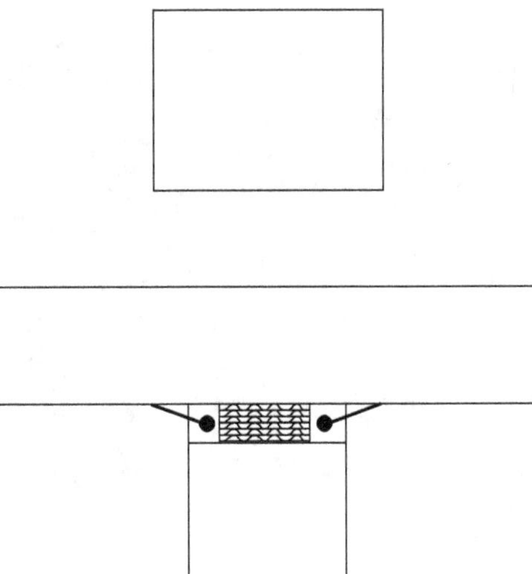

Figure 8.57

Figure 8.56:

1. The street affected by the traffic associated with the school may be choked off by the installation of entrance narrowing devices, walls, and columns.
2. The entrance definition may be physical or symbolic. Columns and entrance definition may he installed without encroaching on the roadway in situations where the street entrance is too dangerous for a choking effort or where other factors are involved, such as resident preferences.

Figure 8.57:

1. The street affected by the traffic associated with the school may be choked off with entrance definition devices.
2. The pedestrian walkway may also be upgraded through the installation of paver tiles or by raising the crosswalk by three inches to serve as a modified speed hump that warns drivers that they are entering a private area.

Residential Development: Curvilinear Streets

Figure 8.58:

1. Conventional curvilinear plans minimize unassigned space, which extends territorial concern.
2. Children are more likely to be observed and controlled by residents.
3. Some bleed-through traffic may occur if drivers become aware that they may avoid the northwest major intersection.

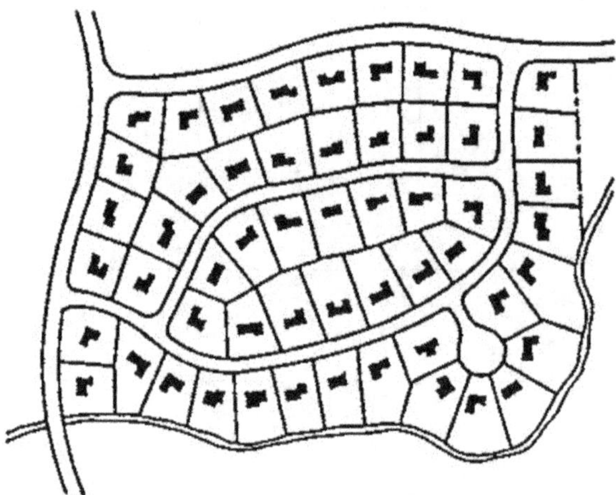

Figure 8.58

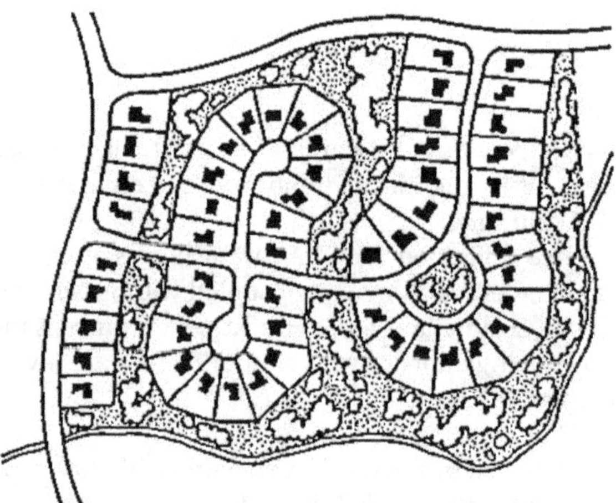

Figure 8.59

Figure 8.59:

1. Today cluster curvilinear streets are more appealing because of amenities and green areas, which are marketed heavily by developers. Many local planning regulations require these features in planned unit developments.
2. The increase in unassigned areas may result in residents' reduced proprietary concern. Unassigned areas may be aesthetically appealing, but residents will feel little attachment and may psychologically turn their backs on activities occurring there.

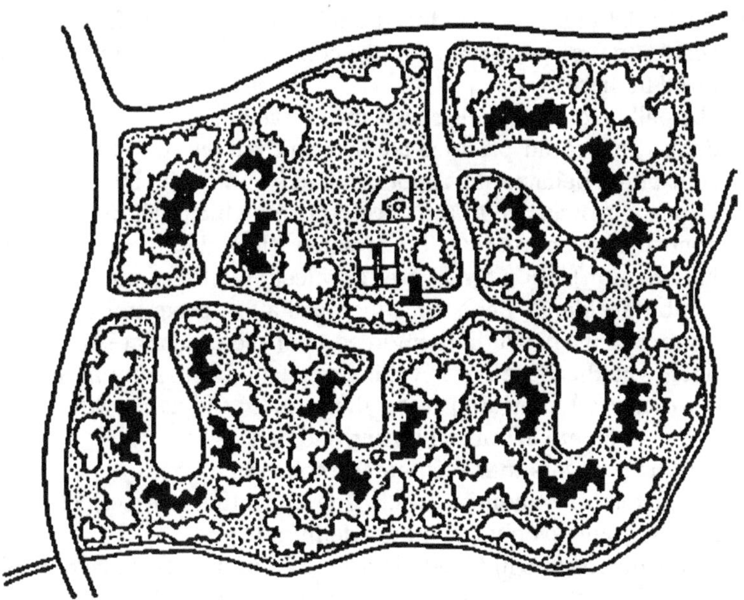

Figure 8.60

3. Deed restrictions or covenants are often very strict in terms of what residents may do in the open areas. This further reduces territorial concern.
4. Young people often go unsupervised in the open or green areas. There is some evidence in public housing, as well as in planned developments (cluster concept), that children growing up in undifferentiated environments fail to learn respect for property rights, which negatively affects their values and behavior.
5. CPTED planners may recommend that open areas be assigned to contiguous clusters of homes. Landscaping or other physical changes may be used to establish border definition.
6. Residents may be provided with financial and other inducements to participate in the maintenance of the open or green areas. This participation will increase their proprietary concern for the previously unassigned space.

Figure 8.60:

1. A townhouse cluster design is economically viable. Open spaces and amenities are important attractions to buyers.
2. This townhouse development creates an excessive amount of unassigned space that is often protected by strict deed restrictions or covenants.

3. Territorial concern is reduced and abnormal users feel safer in accessing the open areas. Young people are less likely to be scrutinized in these areas.
4. The ball field and tennis courts may serve as a magnet to nonresidents. This could produce conflict and reduce the likelihood of controlling behavior by residents. Use by nonresidents will legitimize their presence in the development, which will increase the abnormal users' perception of safety (low risk of detection or intervention). The normal user may feel threatened and therefore exhibit avoidance behavior, which will affect other normal users. Abnormal users will be reinforced by these cues that say that no one owns this space or is willing to challenge the improper use. Normal users may stop using these areas altogether, which has been a problem in public housing and parks.
5. CPTED planners may recommend the assignment of open areas to clusters of buildings. Landscape and other physical changes may be made to enhance border definition.
6. Residents may be induced to participate in maintenance of these areas through financial or other inducements. This will extend proprietary concern for these areas.
7. CPTED planners may recommend the addition of one or two buildings on the north side of the development to provide a natural barrier to potentially conflicting activities. This should appeal to the developer as a profitable move that will produce the added benefits of increased perceptions of safety. CPTED planners may recommend the closure of the internal street in the middle, or at one end, to eliminate through traffic. This may help eliminate or reduce the probability of drive-by drug sales.

Residential Streets: Options for Private Use

Figure 8.61:

1. Each end of the block is choked off. One end uses a closure of the incoming lane (ingress). The other end closes the outgoing lane (egress).
2. Play areas are installed to thrust activities more into previously public areas to increase visual and physical attention.
3. A combination of straight-in and parallel parking is used.

Figure 8.62:

1. Additional crosswalks are added to break the street into four quadrants. This will increase the definition of the pedestrian space in the street.
2. Crosswalks should be legally designated under local ordinances to create pedestrian right-of-way.
3. Crosswalks may be raised two to three inches to reinforce drivers' perception of transition.

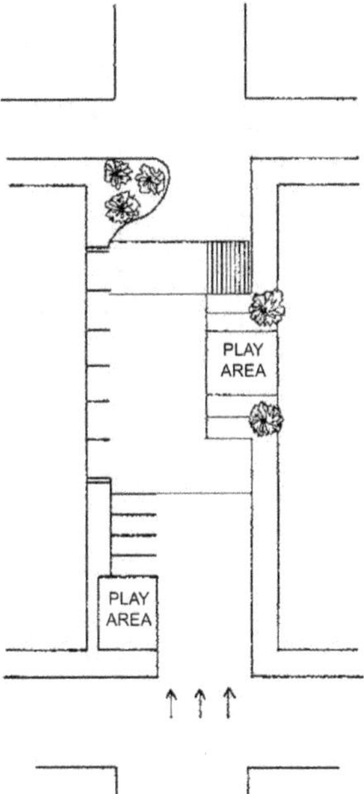

Figure 8.61

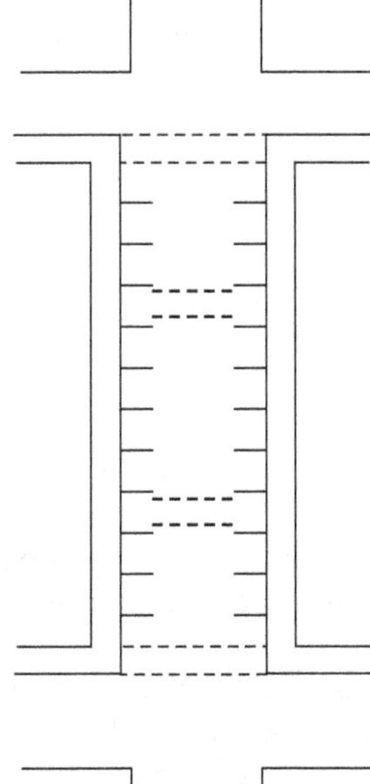

Figure 8.62

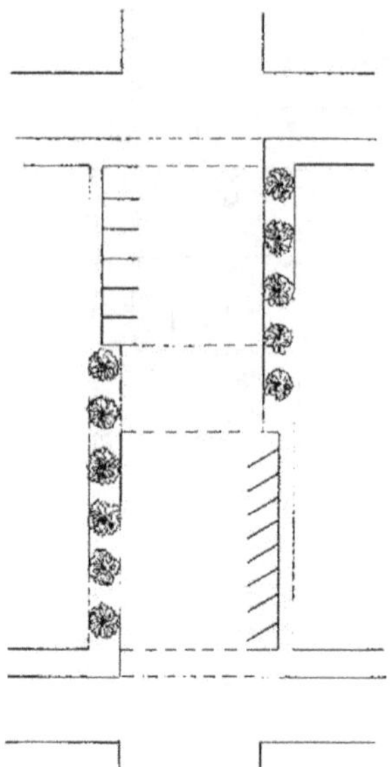

Figure 8.63

Figure 8.63:

1. A combination of parking styles—parallel and straight-in—may be introduced to create space for more landscaping. This combination of landscaping and parking will narrow the entrance (ingress and egress).
2. Crosswalks should be upgraded to enhance transitional definitions.
3. A middle block or central area should be defined with texture change to be used for occasional block activities. Entrances should be choked off or closed with barricades during planned block parties or functions.

Figure 8.64:

1. One end of the street may be closed by installing a play area with safety barriers.
2. Parking arrangements may be alternated between angle and parallel to create more parking and to narrow the street.

Figure 8.65:

1. Entrances may be choked to slow down traffic.
2. A block gathering area may be installed to create a place for parties and other functions. These areas will also further the perception of the block as private.

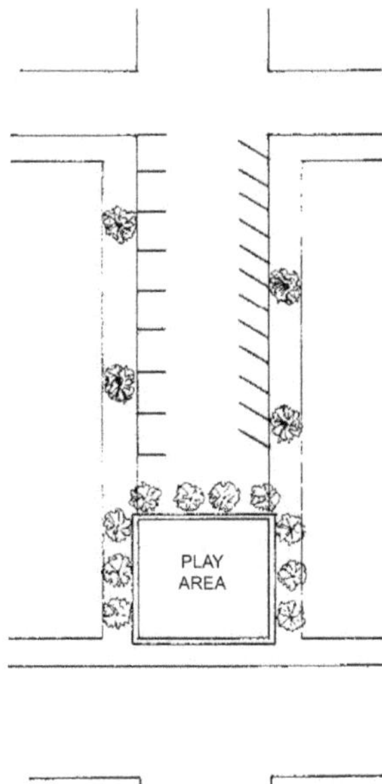

Figure 8.64

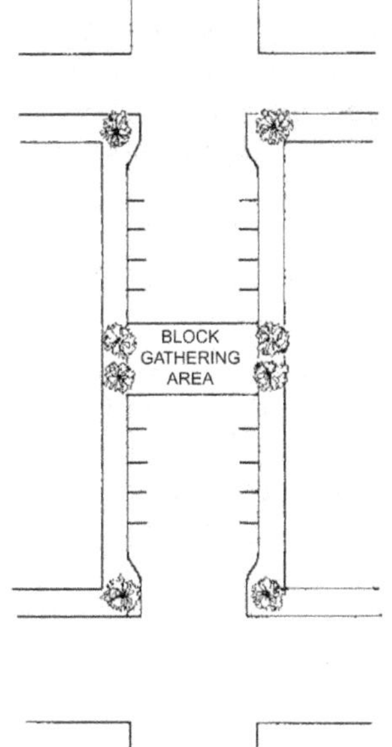

Figure 8.65

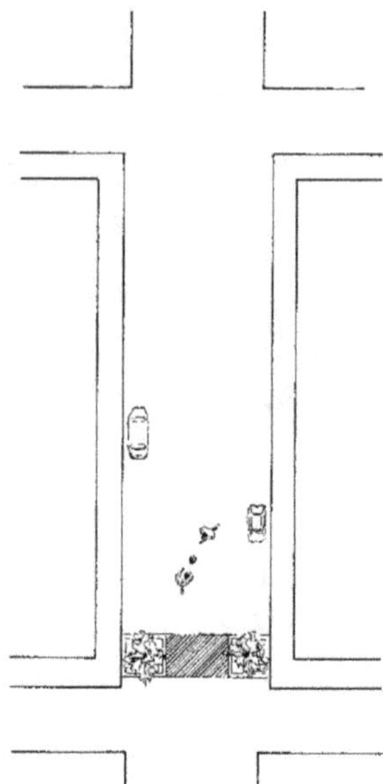

Figure 8.66

Figure 8.66:

1. A simple closing will create a cul-de-sac effect that will eliminate through traffic.
2. A drive-over (for emergency vehicles) area may be created by reducing the elevation of the center of the planter. Replaceable flowers or bushes may be used to increase the perception of closure in the drive-over area. Another option is to use knockdown bollards.

Figure 8.67:

1. Landscaping improvements may be installed to make the street more appealing for pedestrian activity.
2. An additional crosswalk may be installed in the middle of the block to enhance pedestrian convenience and to slow down traffic.
3. Crosswalks should be legally designated under city ordinance. They may also be raised two to three inches to reinforce drivers' perception of transition.

Residential Streets: Recovery of Grid Systems

Figure 8.68:

1. Boundary control is established by creating cul-de-sacs in the middle of most access streets.
2. Access is limited to two points that connect with internal streets.

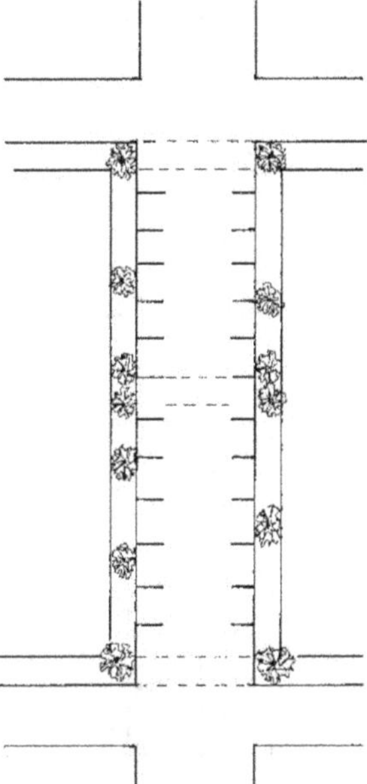

Figure 8.67

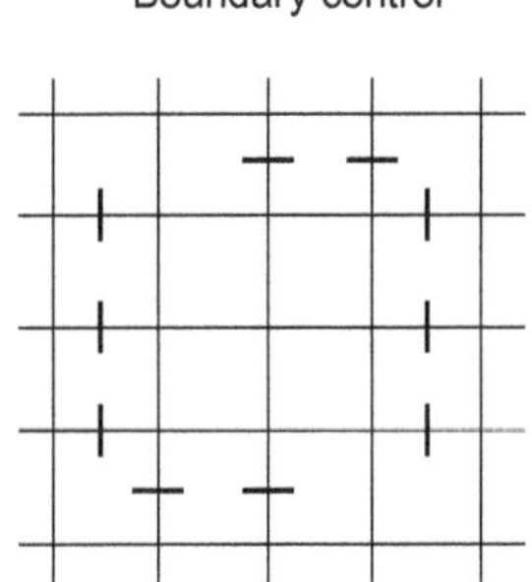

Figure 8.68

Figure 8.69:

1. Internal controls are established by installing a system of diagonal diverters to loop traffic in and out.
2. Through traffic is denied. The diverter angles should be based on resident input and an analysis of access needs.

Figure 8.70:

1. One-way traffic flows are established to reduce through access.
2. Speed controls should be used to reduce pedestrian and vehicle conflict that may result from higher speeds on the one-way system.

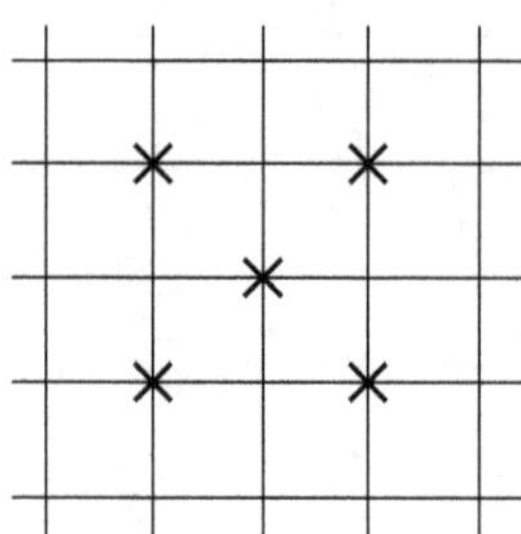

Figure 8.69

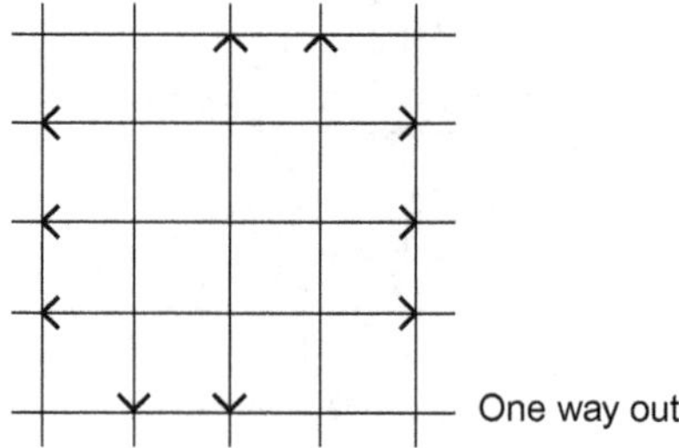

Figure 8.70

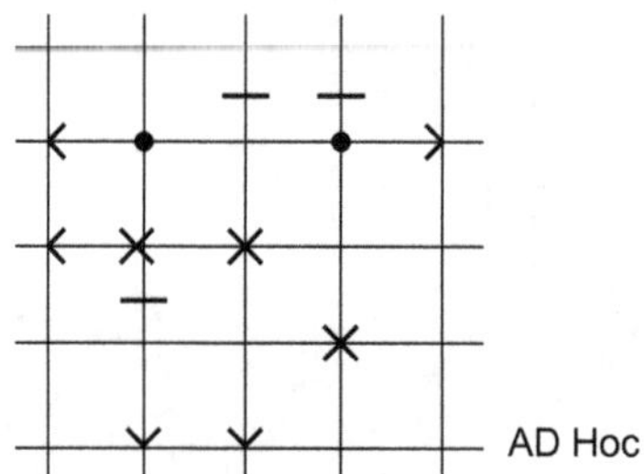

Figure 8.71

3. Parking plans may be altered to include alternating combinations of angle parking and street landscaping.
   Figure 8.71:
1. An *ad hoc* plan of cul-de-sacs, diagonal diverters, and one-way flows make the streets more private.
2. This approach provides some flexibility for long-term planning.

9

CPTED IMPLEMENTATION PROGRAM PLANNING

CHAPTER OUTLINE

Planning is a process of self-examination, confronting difficult choices, and establishing priorities. Planning addresses the following questions:

- Where are we now?
- Where do we want to be?
- How do we get there?
- How do we measure progress?

The principal reason that community activities and programs have failed in the past is that they were never implemented or they take too long to be implemented. This may seem overly simplistic, but there are volumes of research literature that describe the failure of attempts to implement new social and community-based concepts in terms of the lack of cooperation and planning. Most of these activities consumed many local resources and time but failed to deliver any services or achieve any objectives. Excuses range from "Well, it's not in the budget" to "It has to go out for bid, then it can be placed in the budget."

New activities or programs start with great expectations and excitement. This leads to a second phase, which is a period of concern. Things do not seem to be happening the way they were planned. Eventually it becomes clear that the plans have broken down and there is much embarrassment. A hunt for the guilty is immediately carried out to forestall criticism from the community or from those who would have been served by the new activity. Even after the guilty are identified as the key players and decision makers responsible for the plan's failure, there is a tendency to punish the innocent. This is done by declaring that the program or concept is not feasible or that the recipients of the services abused the privilege. Accordingly, the services will have to be denied to everyone.

Among the reasons that new programs or services are not implemented are the following:

- *Inadequate problem assessment.* Everyone thinks that they know what the problem is, so there is the tendency to skip this step.
- *Undiagnosed organizational needs and capabilities.* There is the assumption that the organizations and individuals involved have the skills and resources to take on new activities.
- *Solutions that do not fit the problems.* This is the tendency to have untried, trendy, or favorite solutions looking for problems to address.

One of the best ways to overcome these problems is to conduct a community self-assessment that incorporates the information that is collected as part of the analysis process. The self-assessment process must involve the community, public policymakers, and the key staff from public and private agencies that will be required to coordinate services and activities. The main objectives of the community self-assessment are to:

- Identify the strengths and weaknesses of the present community responses to crime and safety problems
- Compile a community resource inventory
- Identify organizational capabilities that must be developed or enhanced

There are a number of important reasons for going through the self-assessment process prior to making any plans or commitments to programs or activities:

- *Authority.* The self-assessment establishes the credibility and objectivity of the interagency committee's findings and recommendations for action. It substitutes facts for beliefs in dealing with issues and problems that are usually politically and socially sensitive. How can this process be criticized when it is members of the community or organization who are publicly identifying strengths, weaknesses, and needs for responding to crime and safety problems?
- *Liability.* In general you can be sued for anything. However, assume there was an assault on your property last night. The very

next day, lawyers and expert witnesses are watching and taking pictures of your maintenance company cutting back bushes and tree limbs. Plus you had a consultant or the local police officer conduct an assessment of your property and you did nothing till the day after the assault.

- *Budget.* It is extremely difficult to increase budgets or to add new items to existing budgets for programs and activities that are not yet proven or guaranteed to be successful. Financial resources are easily developed when there is an overwhelming demand or public support for a new program or activity. The self-assessment helps legitimize the need for the commitment of resources by demonstrating that an exhaustive effort was made to identify the needs of the community.
- *Scope of activities.* The self-assessment helps increase confidence and credibility in the plan of action, which in turn helps remove restraints to the range of activities that are undertaken. Caution is usually associated with fear of failure and results in weak or ineffectual commitments to getting the job done. Programs fail because they are never implemented sufficiently to prove their worth.
- *Discovery.* The systematic and unbiased approach to "turning over all the stones" usually provides startling revelations about assets and capabilities that already exist in the community. It is common for the interagency steering committee to discover that there are more local resources than there is need, that the real problem is lack of coordination. Additionally, it is common to discover that there is more community support than assumed by elected officials or by self-proclaimed community leaders.

The self-assessment process may be compared to the medical model of identifying problems and solutions. This is a process of diagnosis, prognosis, and prescriptive action:

- *Diagnosis (Dx).* The process of taking a series of measurements and observations about community or organization needs, agency activities, and results. The observations are made in terms of the elements and key components of the CPTED concept.
- *Prognosis (Px).* The development of an overall understanding of the health, the strengths, and the needs of the community or organization in terms of crime and safety-related problems and current responses.
- *Prescriptive (Rx).* The specific actions that are required to meet the goals and objectives established during the prognostic stage of the self-assessment and planning process.

The medical model provides insights into the phenomenon of why programs fail. Too often in social and community programs, problems are defined in the language of solutions. Popular solutions do not always fit the problem. Popular programs treat the symptoms instead of eliminating the problems that produce the symptoms. Another metaphorical analogy from the medical field that may be applied to social programs is "The operation was a success, but the patient died!" The self-assessment process is one sure means of ensuring that the plan of action is reasonable and appropriate.

The medical model translates into three basic steps required to be completed in planning:

1. *Normative.* Is the process devoted to providing answers to the question, "What should we be doing and why?" The information that is developed during the *diagnostic* step is used to help answer these questions. It is important to set aside discussions about solutions to avoid missing some obvious discovery opportunities.
2. *Strategic.* Is the process associated with developing answers to the question, "What can we do and how?" These questions help us examine alternatives and ensure that final decisions are based on good *prognostic* information.
3. *Operational.* Is the process directed toward answering the question, "What will we do and when?" Building on the answers to the questions in the previous two steps, the *prescriptive* step outlines specific action to be taken.

The most important tasks to be completed in the planning process can be listed as follows:

- Collect data and survey existing conditions (Dx)
- Analyze data and identify all opportunities and limitations (Dx)
- Formulate goals and objectives (Px)
- Generate alternative concepts (Px)
- Develop each concept into a workable solution (Px)
- Evaluate alternative solutions (Px)
- Translate solutions into policies, plans, guidelines, and programs (Rx)

Implementation

CPTED Task Force

The interagency or organizational steering committee that was set up to conduct the self-assessment and develop the plan of action will have to provide leadership and oversight for the implementation process. The committee or council will need to be composed of chief executives of the key agencies, community representatives, and staff from the agencies involved. The same mix is required for an organization-level committee. It is recommended that the interagency be divided into at least two groups: policy level and staff.

The participants at the policy level should meet regularly to approve plans and activities that are developed by the members of the staff group. The policy group must have the authority to appoint people to workgroups to complete tasks that are required for implementing the program. Workgroups should be used to carry out discrete tasks as well as to provide ongoing planning, coordination, and evaluation. 

The most important activities and tasks of the steering committee are to:

- Conduct and periodically update the self-assessment of crime problems and needs in the community or organization
- Identify goals and objectives for improvement
- Publish the community or organization self-assessment report
- Designate working groups and responsibilities for the implementation of the planned improvements
- Provide oversight to implementation activities and develop remedial action as necessary

Program Management

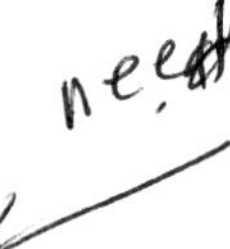

It is clear that there will be many activities and tasks involved in the implementation of a CPTED program. The interagency or intraorganizational nature of the program will make coordination even more difficult. Accordingly, an individual program manager or program management committee should be appointed to provide the ongoing coordination, scheduling, and monitoring of activities. Several people who possess good management skills and who are placed in high-level staff positions in the key agencies may serve in a program management workgroup that is authorized by the policy-level steering committee.

The program management function includes the following requirements: 

- System design and planning
- Coordination
- Training
- Assistance
- Monitoring
- Management of the process
- Handling highly complex or unique tasks that may not be delegated

Meetings

Meetings should be conducted on a regular basis so that participants can plan their schedules around meeting times. An agenda should be prepared for each meeting containing distinct tasks and expectations for results or outcomes of the meeting. One strategy for maintaining attendance and interest in the meetings is to establish a rotating position of chairperson, who is responsible for planning and running the meeting. This rotating position could be filled by the various interagency members in turn, which will help ensure that everyone participates and understands the importance of coordination. Don't forget to document progress achieved for the next meeting.

Planning for Change

Many people hate change. Yet going forward in the 21st century we will see many changes, because change is everywhere. The security industry and law enforcement are changing. Not every manager is a visionary, but visionaries can be developed through communication and empowerment. Such managers aren't developed overnight. Change takes time. Are you ready for future changes?

First and foremost in planning for change is the need to *control expectations*. This is necessary to ensure that support will be there for the program when it is needed. It is important to avoid the creation of unrealistic goals or timetables for action. It is equally important for the interagency steering committee to establish and stick to a reasonable schedule of activities.

Another important admonition in planning for change is the need to avoid the tendency to seek out "canned goods" or "instant recipes." It is easy to skip the dull drudgery of developing a program from scratch by going elsewhere and lifting out someone else's program. This can spell disaster because outside programs may not be adaptable. Moreover, the adoption of a "canned program" will leave participants with very little understanding of the intricacies and nuances of the program operation. This knowledge is critical when it comes time to fix problems.

Program planners have a tendency to feel the need to either rush the planning process or to go too slowly. Some people might feel the need to rush through planning in order to get the program or services in place. This can result in much embarrassment and failure when it is discovered that the wrong solutions or methods are being used. Conversely, a planning committee that equates length of time with good planning may never get the job done and could lose community support in the meantime. Therefore, it is recommended that both pitfalls be avoided by adopting a *development strategy* that balances the importance of careful planning with early experimentation and testing of new concepts or methods. Instead of rushing to get to final form or never getting there, it can be made clear that the program is still in the developmental process, and that includes learning about and revising the services and procedures as they are implemented.

This strategy will improve the cooperation and collaboration needed from the people who will carry out or receive the new services.

Finally, one of the primary impediments to planning for change is the issue of *evaluation*. Evaluation can be a trap if it is done poorly or if it is connected to some unrealistic anticipated outcomes. Evaluation that is conducted by outsiders may appear to be more objective, but it does little to assist the program planners in remedial improvements. Program planners lose a lot of time educating the outside evaluators about the project activities and services. Evaluation that is conducted internally provides direct feedback to program planners and administrators. Accordingly, evaluation should be considered a tool for program planning and monitoring. Outcomes will still be measured and objectivity may be assessed through any interested outside parties' audits of project data.

Mission Statements, Goals, Objectives, and the Process

Mission statements are used to define the scope of responsibility for and interest in a program or service. The mission statement stakes the claim or territory of the program. It also provides all concerned individuals with a formal reminder of the purpose of the program. *Goals* are more specific statements used to identify program components or intended areas of accomplishment. *Objectives* are the steps or milestones that must be reached in attaining an individual goal. The use of these terms furnishes a hierarchy for planners and managers to use in determining the priorities and interrelationships of program activity.

The importance of having well-defined objectives cannot be overstated. To the extent that objectives are not established or are poorly defined, the project will suffer from incomplete planning, uncertain execution, and difficulty in evaluating progress. Following are several requirements for setting objectives:

- *Measurable.* Objectives should be phrased in concrete, measurable terms so that their achievement at project completion can be demonstrated.
- *Related to time.* Progress toward the achievement of objectives is difficult to assess unless there is an understanding of when the full objective will be reached.
- *Related to cost.* Objectives must clearly relate to project costs and expenditures so that activities may be assessed or evaluated in terms of return on investment.

Goals and objectives should be reassessed periodically to ensure that they still reflect the wishes and needs of the community. Changes in the political climate and the funding process or those brought on by internal project assessment may require some changes in the focus of the program. However, some caution should be used in making changes that are inconsistent with the original mission statement.

Time and Task Planning

Many excellent tools for time management and task planning are available in manuals or computer programs. Spreadsheets may be used to plan activities as well as expenditures. A variety of charts may be used to develop an understanding of program activities. Some of these techniques incorporate dependency networks and critical-path analysis to assist in task planning and setting priorities.

Agreements

Some communities have rushed into interagency agreements and discovered that everything needed to be changed after the program was planned. Others have found that agency heads were very hesitant to sign an agreement because they were not clear about the commitments they were making. The best approach is to commit to a process that incorporates two agreements. First is the *agreement to agree* that commits the participants and agencies solely to the community self-assessment process. There is the expectation that this agreement will ultimately lead to a plan of action and a final interagency agreement to implement the plan of action. The second, or *formal interagency agreement,* may be signed long after the program has commenced and the partners are sure what their commitments entail.

Evaluation and Monitoring

Evaluation is defined as a process of making judgments about the worth of something. In the present context, evaluation involves a systematic examination of project activities and the impact of these activities on the objectives of the project. Evaluation efforts are directed at the documentation of changes or improvements and at a determination of the extent to which those effects may be attributed to project implementation.

Evaluation can be of assistance to administrators and project staff by providing feedback on the efficacy of the project (or specific project activities), thus guiding decisions related to project management. Evaluation also can serve as a vehicle for technology transfer, documenting techniques that were successfully employed within a project.

The involvement of staff in the evaluation process is critical, because project staff members are the ones who are most knowledgeable about project operations. The project manager will, in most cases, be responsible for planning and managing the evaluation efforts.

Summary of Evaluation Steps

The following are the steps that should be followed in the evaluation process:

- Define goals and objectives of the project.
- Define evaluation criteria appropriate to the goals.
- Identify and define target population.
- Identify important project variables (e.g., how does the project work, and what makes it work?).
- Choose the appropriate evaluation design(s).
- Identify data sources and data points appropriate to evaluation criteria, target population, and design.
- Consult with staff concerning data and collection procedures.
- Collect data.
- Analyze data.
- Formulate conclusions.
- Present recommendations for change.

Types of Evaluation

There are several types of evaluation that are relevant to the CPTED program. Formative, program monitoring, process, impact, or intensive evaluation can all be used effectively in the program. These approaches can be summarized as follows:

- *Formative evaluation.* This is used to develop and pretest concepts during the planning process. Meta-evaluations are conducted to help construct strategies that may be part of an overall program.
- *Program monitoring evaluation.* Here the focus is on measuring change. It is the least expensive of evaluations, but it can provide decision makers with important information regarding the progress of each project.
- *Process evaluation.* This evaluation type is concerned with the operations of the various project components that account for the success of a project. A relatively simple evaluation process would provide a well-documented description of the project activities, specification of the project recipients, identification of the time period involved, definition of the project locale, and discussion of intended and unintended effects.
- *Impact (or intensive) evaluation.* This evaluation type allows the evaluator to draw conclusions about the causal relationship between project activities and various impact measures. An

impact evaluation requires a research design that allows the evaluator to make comparisons between the effects of the presence and absence of program activities.

Evaluation Design

Evaluation designs vary in terms of the degree to which they allow project effects to be isolated and separated from factors outside the operation and control of the project. Four evaluation designs are outlined here. This list is only one topology of design and is not meant to be inclusive:

- *Pretest/posttest design before and after comparison.* This design consists primarily of a comparison of data collected on evaluation criteria prior to project initiation with data collected at project conclusion. This design is the simplest and least expensive. However, it does not allow causal linkages to be drawn between observed changes and project implementation (i.e., it does not rule out the possibility that outside factors effected the change).
- *Pretest/posttest with a comparison group.* Through the use of a comparison group, this design allows greater confidence that observed changes are in fact due to the program and not to outside factors. Obviously, similarity between the comparison and target groups is critical to the evaluation results.
- *Controlled experimentation with random assignment of available population to target and comparison group.* This is the most sophisticated and expensive of the designs. It compares preselected, similar groups, some within the population of target groups served and some within the comparison group. The critical aspect of the design is the random assignment of participants to the groups prior to program implementation.
- *Time series.* This design compares data collected after project initiation with estimates of what the data would be if trends from past years were to continue.

Evaluation Objectives

A final issue in the evaluation of programs relates to how objectives are set for the program. These objectives in turn become the focal point for the evaluation. Externally produced objectives will always evoke a conservative response on the part of program planners. Outside evaluators will negotiate with program planners to produce a set of objectives that are often easily measurable but that may not be as valuable as those that are harder to measure. Internally produced evaluations, on the other hand, may be accused of being biased, but this depends on the motivations for the evaluation.

The program planner who defines objectives for the purpose of guiding the activities of the project will set higher standards than when the objectives are used to make external judgments of achievement. Accordingly, the development of objectives must be conducted in the context of program planners wanting to determine whether they accomplished their desired results. Evaluations must be developed according to accepted standards, but the effort must be an integral component of program development and implementation, something that is a proprietary concern of the program specialists.

Evaluation is an essential component of program development, implementation, and management. It is an ongoing management tool that is central to the process of communication. The creators and staff of programs must be integrally involved in the evaluation process. Moreover, the method must suit the program and its process.

10

CPTED TRAINING OUTLINE

CHAPTER OUTLINE

Goals

The goals of this module on CPTED are to alter and expand the participants' perception of their immediate physical environment. By altering the perception of the physical environment, participants will be more capable of understanding the direct relationship of the environment to human behavior and to crime. An increase in this basic understanding should result in the increased likelihood of the individual to confidently question or challenge decisions that affect her immediate environment—particularly those that may have a direct bearing on the safety of the individual, her family, and her neighborhood.

An understanding of the direct relationship of the environment—its design and management—to human behavior is a prerequisite to increasing the success of citizens' efforts in crime prevention. It is the key to effective community organization, because it gives citizens power to protect and control their physical environment and quality of life. However, CPTED is not the total or exclusive answer for a community seeking to eliminate or reduce environmental obstacles to social, cultural, or managerial control.

Learning Objectives

CPTED does not require an extensive technical background or understanding. But to be effective as a community strategy, basic CPTED concepts must be understood by as many people as possible, even if that understanding is in layperson's terms. Otherwise, true public policy setting will remain in the hands of technocrats and politicians.

The following learning objectives should be considered as the absolute minimum for successful completion of this module:

1. The participant should be able to recall the meaning of the acronym CPTED: Crime Prevention Through Environmental Design.

2. The participant should recognize the underlying premise of CPTED and recall the two underlined words in the definition as key CPTED descriptors. The CPTED premise is "that the proper design and effective use of the built environment can lead to a reduction in the incidence and fear of crime—and to an increase in the quality of life."
3. The participant should be able to recognize and define (in a brief one-sentence definition or example) the three basic CPTED strategies of natural access control, natural surveillance, and territorial reinforcement.
4. The participant should be able to distinguish (by definition or example) among the organized, mechanical, and natural crime prevention strategy classifications.
5. The participant should be able to recall the reference to the CPTED approach to space assessment and list the components:
   - Reference 3-D concept:
     - Components Designation
     - Definition
     - Design
   - The "Three-D" approach to space assessment provides a single guide in determining how the space is designed and used:
     - All individual space has some designated purpose.
     - All individual space has social, cultural, legal, or physical definitions that prescribe the desired acceptable behaviors.
     - All individual space is designed to support and control the desired behaviors.
6. The participant should be able to demonstrate his new awareness and understanding of CPTED concepts by providing a descriptive example of a good and a bad CPTED setting in at least one of the following types of locations:
   - A residential neighborhood that is near a major street intersection
   - A neighborhood park
   - Neighborhood schools
   - Public parking lots
   - A public housing area
   - An industrial/commercial center
7. The participant should be able to describe the functions and location of the following types of information:
   - Crime analysis data and law enforcement data will provide police reports and trends, crime patterns, and the *modus operandi* (MO)
   - Demographic, city planning, census bureau, and nature of the population

- Land use by city planning, zoning, engineering: Describe the physical allocations and use of land
- Observation: Go out into the neighborhood, see what is happening, where, when. why, how, and by whom
- Resident or user interviews, people's perceptions, conduct security assessment/audit
- Coordination and communication among police, security, planners, architects, and engineers

8. How law enforcement and security can best use CPTED:
- Law enforcement organizing neighborhoods and businesses through neighborhood watch, business watch, community-oriented policing, conducting security surveys
- Community and business organizing as well as church groups

9. Optimizing CPTED:
- Communications and social media
- Security, architects, planners, engineers, and community
- Evaluation and maintenance
- Develop a state-of-the-art program
- Reduce liability and improve the quality of life within the community

10. The participant should be able to draw a simple map of her residential or business neighborhood showing:
- Street layout
- Land use
- Pedestrian and vehicular usage
- Crime (or fear) problem areas
- Current boundaries of geographic, ethnic, or neighborhood identities

These learning objectives represent the minimum that is required to develop efficiency and skill in the use of CPTED concepts. Meeting these objectives would be a clear indication of the ability to perceive the relationship of the environment to human behavior—particularly criminal behavior. It should not be expected that any sort of brief overview presentation (e.g., one lasting 30 minutes) is sufficient for individuals to fully understand the concepts of CPTED. A longer period of a combined seminar and workshop, preferably with a field trip or exercise, is best. However, some change in individuals' appreciation of the human/environment interaction can be expected even after a relatively short, nonparticipatory session. Finally, participants should gain an understanding of the various types of CPTED strategies for both schools and residential properties.

11

OBJECTIVES FOR A SCHOOL ENVIRONMENT

CHAPTER OUTLINE

Introduction

CPTED concepts have been and are being used in Schools and university properties are using CPTED applications that were initially pioneered in the Broward County, Florida, school CPTED program that was funded by the federal government. The list of potential CPTED applications is practically endless. It would be difficult to find any human function that is not amenable to the use of CPTED concepts. It is merely a matter of looking at the environment from a different perspective, questioning everything, and learning the language of the various professions involved in making decisions about our communities. Learning the language means being able to communicate with others and to understand their objectives. This is the principal reason that CPTED planners are trained to share concepts and ask questions that no one else would think to ask. CPTED planners are trained to reprogram their thinking from focusing solely on security and crime prevention to emphasizing the objectives of the agency or organization that they are trying to help. It is important to remember a CPTED motto, "What are you trying to do here, and how can we help you do it better?" If you are meeting your objectives, the potential for crime and loss will be reduced. It is an axiom that human functions that are achieving their objectives will experience fewer crimes and losses. Crime and loss are by products of human functions that are not working. The following are the 11 major CPTED strategies that can be used in any number of combinations:

1. *Access control.* Provide secure barriers to prevent unauthorized access to school grounds, schools, or restricted interior areas, using a variety of access card readers and cards.
2. *Surveillance through physical design.* Improve opportunities for surveillance by physical design mechanisms that serve to increase the risk of detection for offenders. CCTV is being used more and more in schools as well as on buses.
3. *Mechanical surveillance devices.* Provide schools with security devices to detect and signal unauthorized entry attempts.
4. *Congestion control.* Reduce or eliminate causes of congestion that contribute to student confrontations.
5. *Psychological deterrents.* Provide psychological deterrents to theft and vandalism.
6. *User monitoring.* Implement staff and student security measures at vulnerable areas.
7. *Emergency procedures.* Provide teachers with means to handle emergency situations as well as lock-down procedures.
8. *User awareness.* Initiate programs to promote student awareness of security risks and countermeasures.
9. *User motivation.* Encourage social interaction, social cohesion, and school pride by promoting extracurricular activities, providing amenities, and upgrading the visual quality of the school.
10. *Territorial identity.* Highlight the functional identities of different areas throughout the school to increase territorial identity and reduce confusion.
11. *Community involvement.* Promote public awareness and involvement with school faculty and student achievements and activities.

School Campus Control

Poor design (Figure 11.1):

1. Informal gathering areas are preempted by groups of students who often promote conflict.
2. Isolated areas are used by students who want to smoke or to engage in unauthorized or illicit behavior.
3. Interlopers or trespassers seek out out-of-sight areas to contact students for drug sales or other improper activities.
4. These areas are very difficult to monitor and control.
5. Most authorities attempt to maintain surveillance of these areas in an attempt to control behavior.

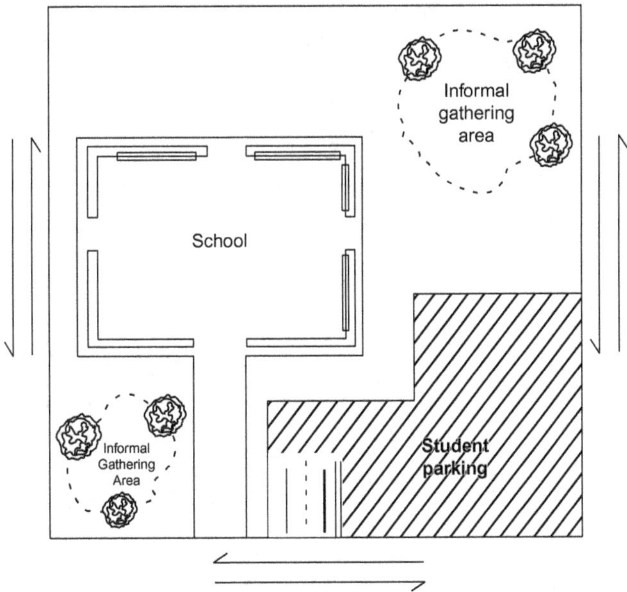

Figure 11.1

Good design (Figure 11.2):

1. By designating formal gathering areas, all other areas become off limits.
2. Anyone observed in spaces that are not designated as formal gathering areas will be automatically subject to scrutiny.
3. Abnormal users will feel at greater risk and will have few excuses for being in the wrong places.
4. Teachers and administrators assume greater challenging powers by the clear spatial definition.
5. Provide schools with mechanical surveillance security devices to detect and signal unauthorized entry attempts.
6. Reduce or eliminate causes of congestion that contribute to student confrontations.
7. Provide psychological deterrents to theft and vandalism.
8. Implement staff and student security-monitoring measures at vulnerable areas.
9. Provide teachers with procedures and means to handle emergency situations.
10. Initiate programs to promote student awareness of security risks and countermeasures.
11. Encourage social interaction, social cohesion, and school pride by promoting extracurricular activities, providing amenities, and upgrading the visual quality of the school.

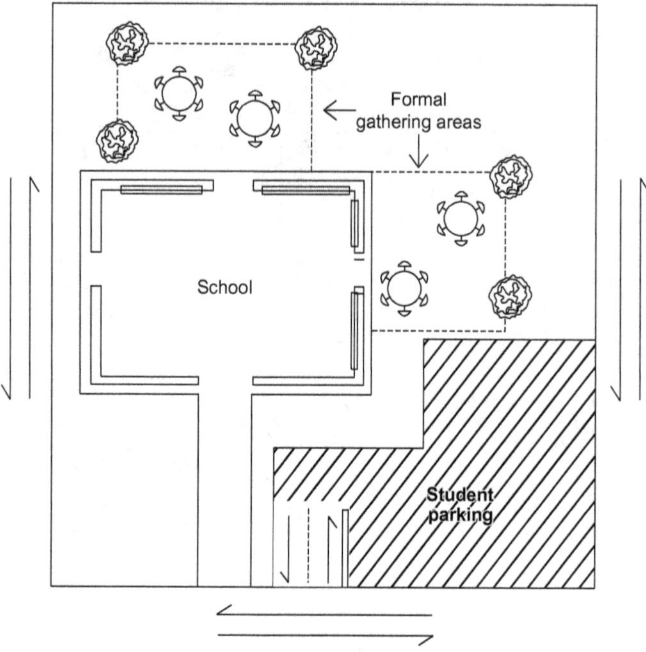

Figure 11.2

12. Highlight the functional identities of different areas throughout the school to increase territorial identity and reduce confusion.
13. Promote public awareness and community involvement with school faculty and student achievements and activities.

High-School Parking Lots

Poor design (Figure 11.3):

1. Multiple access points increase the perception that the parking area is public and provide many escape routes for potential offenders.
2. The location on the periphery of the site reduces any clear transitional definition of movement from public to private space, thus allowing an abnormal user to feel safe or at low risk of confrontation.
3. The openness of the lot increases the range of excuses for improper use.

Good design (Figure 11.4):

1. Use of barricades to close off unsupervised entrances during low-use times controls access and reinforces the perception that the parking area is private.

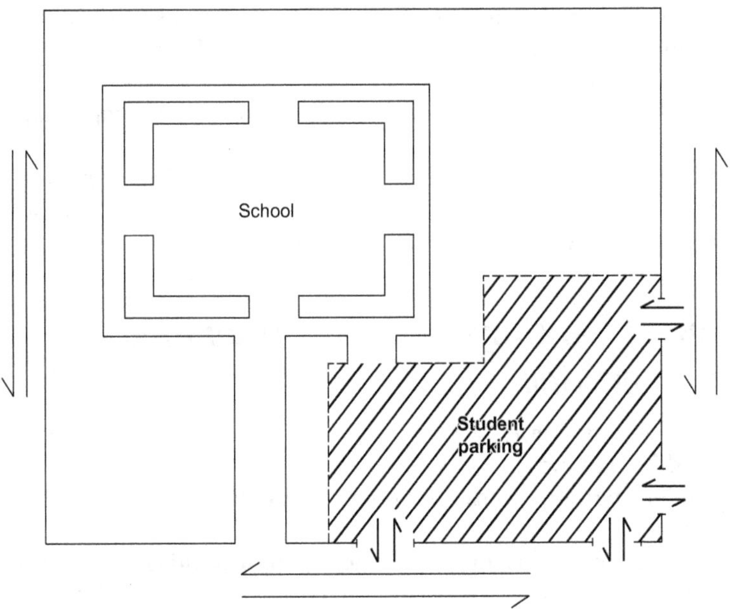

Figure 11.3

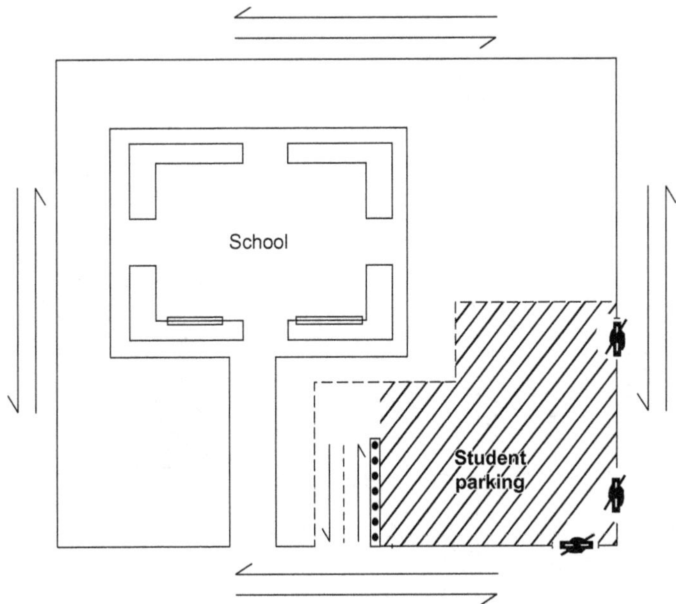

Figure 11.4

2. The curb lane in the open entrance forces the user to transition from public to semipublic to private space, with a radical turn into the parking area.
3. The symbolic isolation creates the perception that escape may be easily blocked.
4. Violation of the barricade and traffic-control devices draws attention to the abnormal user and establishes probable cause sufficient to stop the individual for questioning.

Student Parking and Driver Education Relationships

Poor design (Figure 11.5):

1. Student parking is an unsafe activity.
2. Student parking on the periphery of the campus is in an unsafe location.
3. The isolated location has few opportunities for natural surveillance.

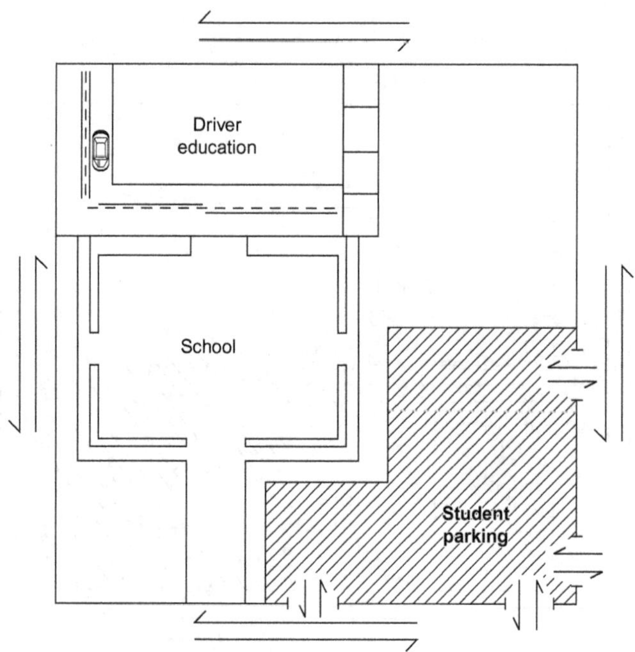

Figure 11.5

4. Poor transitional definition creates the perception of safety for abnormal users and risk for normal users.

Good design (Figure 11.6):

1. Driver education is a safe activity, monitored by responsible teachers and students.
2. The switch of driver education with student parking in an existing location provides a natural opportunity to put a safe activity in an unsafe location and an unsafe activity in a safe location.
3. The new location for student parking (in this hypothetical example) is in the direct line of sight from office windows.

Courtyards and Corridors

Poor design and use (Figure 11.7):

1. Many site planners or users of space fail to adequately define the intended purpose and uses of courtyards.
2. Uses could be aesthetics, thermal support of the building, or gathering areas. Each use presents different requirements and space management plans and policies.

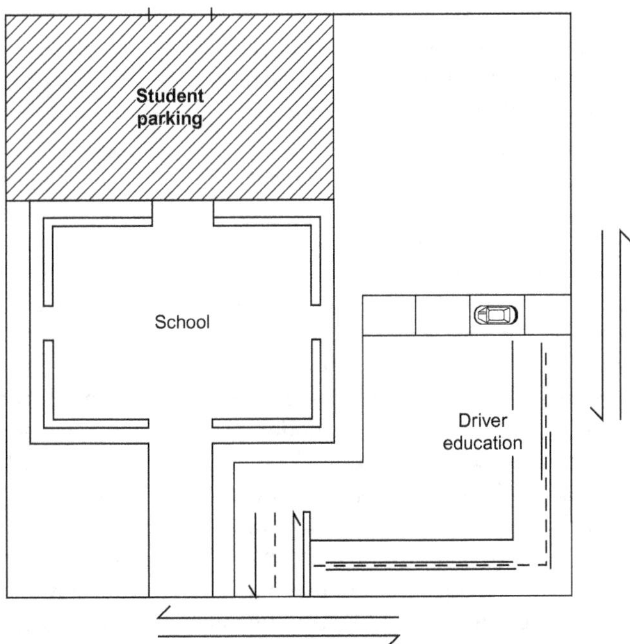

Figure 11.6

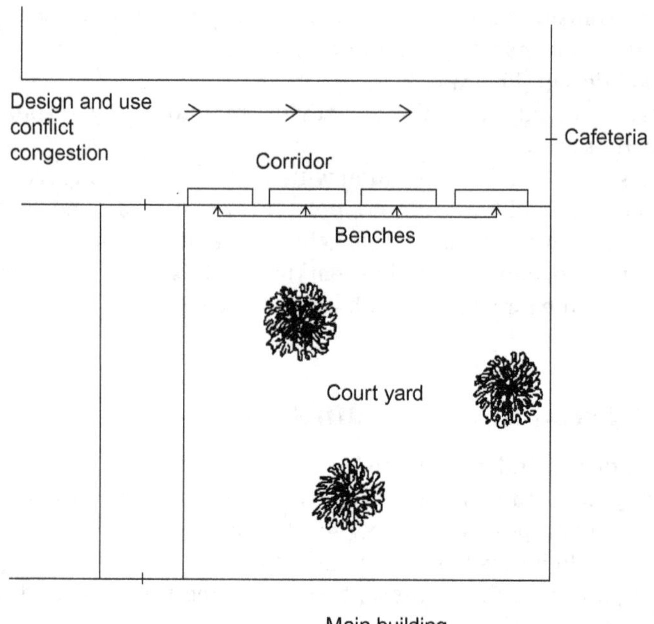

Figure 11.7

3. Corridor and courtyard confusion is exacerbated by the installation of benches and other furnishings along the corridors.
4. Benches are sometimes used as barriers to access to courtyards, with the mistaken idea of protecting the grass from encroachment by students or pedestrians.
5. Corridor/courtyard conflict often leads to congestion, noise, and personal conflict.
6. Groups of students or others will often colonize, or preempt, spaces creating further conflict and fear.
7. Normal users will avoid using these areas. Abnormal users feel safer and at low risk of detection or intervention.

Good design and use (Figure 11.8):

1. The intended purpose and uses of the courtyards and adjoining corridors are clearly defined in policy and in the physical design.
2. Furnishings for courtyards that are intended for gathering behavior may be designed to break up group size or provide only minimal comfort, to shorten the staying time.
3. Portable amenities may be used more effectively than permanent ones, depending on intended use patterns. Accordingly, physical support is provided only when the specific behavior is desired.
4. Normal users will feel safer moving through these areas. Abnormal users will be more subject to control and will find it more difficult to preempt these spaces.

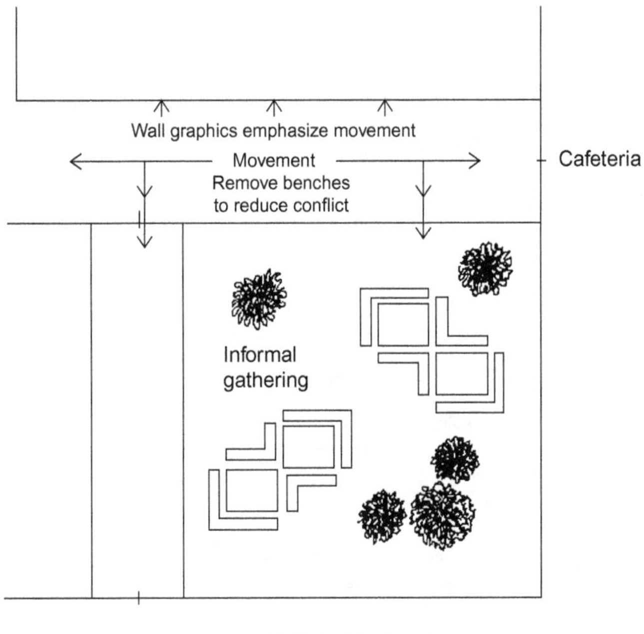

Figure 11.8

School Lunchtime Hallway Use

Poor design and use (Figure 11.9):

1. The same hallway is used for coming and going.
2. Conflict occurs as groups attempt to go to the cafeteria while others attempt to return to class.
3. The arrival of the first group and the departure of the second are the most controlled because there is no other group moving at the same time. All students are supposed to be going in the same direction, so the hall monitors and administrators are perceived to be more powerful. There is a limited range of excuses for improper behavior.
4. Hall monitors lose control because of the coming and going after the first group eats.
5. It takes longer to get groups (subsequent to the first) through the lunch line due to the conflict and congestion.
6. Most classroom and locker thefts occur during the lunch period in school systems.

Good design and use (Figure 11.10):

1. Ingress and egress to the cafeteria may be separated spatially and temporally to define movement relationships.
2. Each group will arrive faster, with fewer stragglers.
3. Abnormal users of space will feel at greater risk of detection.

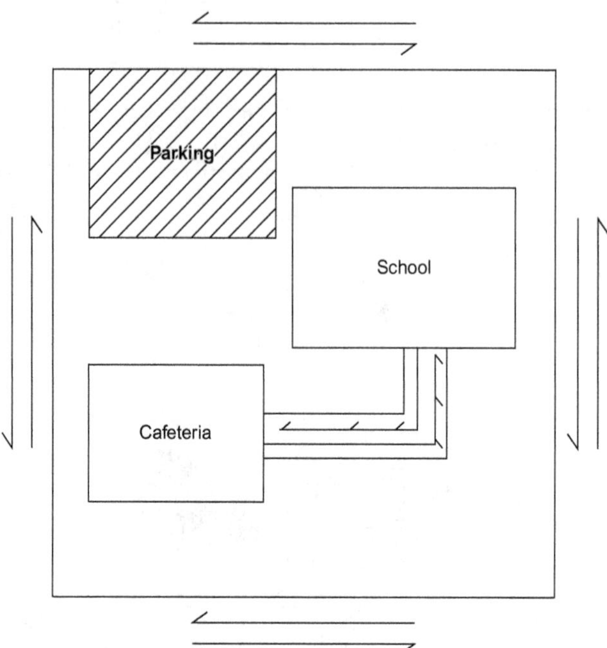

Figure 11.9

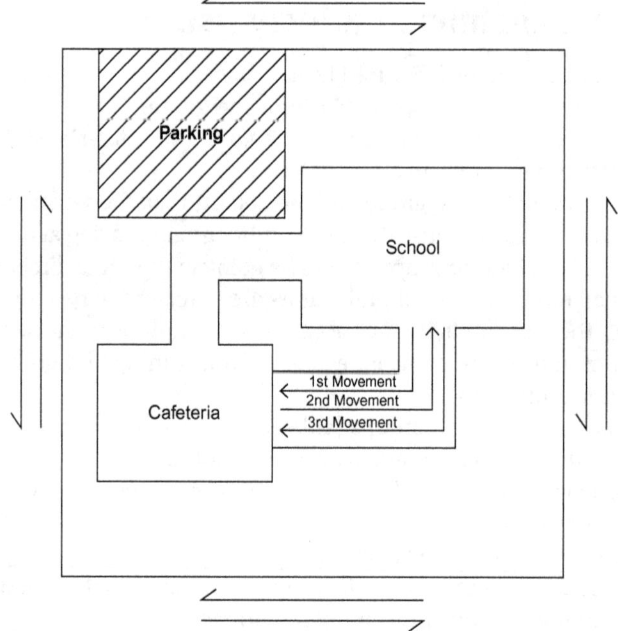

Figure 11.10

4. A time, or temporal, separation of movements to and from the classroom area will require the addition of at least five minutes for each shift. This time may be taken from that allotted for eating, since each group will arrive faster and, therefore, be fed faster.

Safe Activities in Unsafe Locations

Poor design (Figure 11.11):

1. Many noncurricular activities at schools (e.g., military recruiting, college orientation, picture and ring sales, club functions) are assigned to locations in the office, cafeteria, or gymnasium.
2. Office, cafeteria, and gymnasium areas provide poor design support for these noncurricular activities.
3. These noncurricular activities often impede the normal operations of the functions of the existing space.

Good design (Figure 11.12):

1. Problem areas on school campuses are well known and easy to map.
2. Problem areas shift with changing groups and trends of supervision.

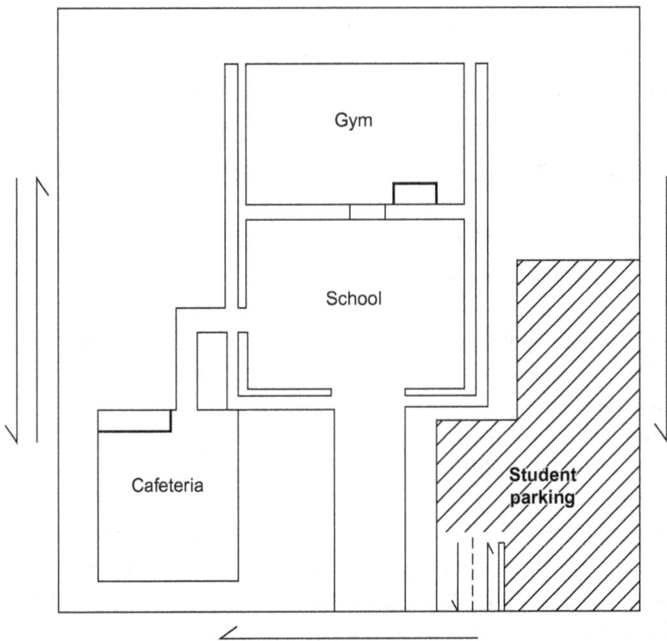

Figure 11.11

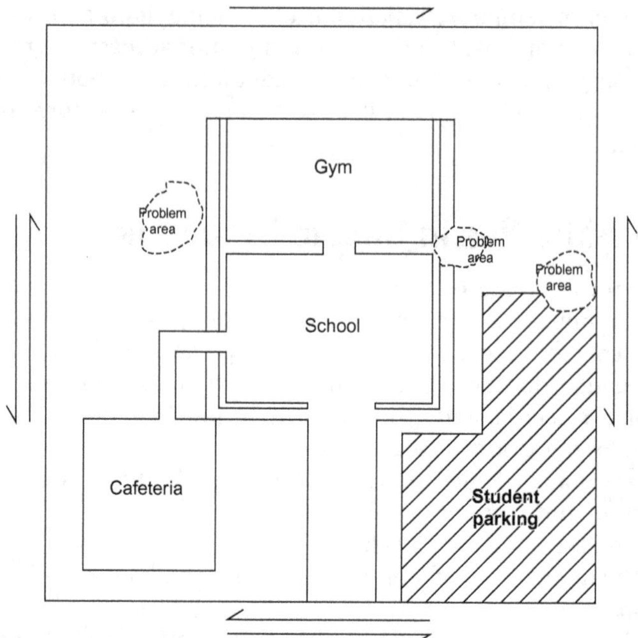

Figure 11.12

3. Safe activities may be placed reasonably in many problem areas to attract normal users and displace abnormal or undesirable activity.
4. Normal users will feel safer and abnormal users will feel at greater risk or unsafe.

Convention Center and Stadium

Convention Center

Poor design and use (Figure 11.13):

1. Many convention centers are placed purposefully in deteriorated areas to stimulate renewal. They are financed largely by public tax dollars or publicly backed bonds, since normal investors will not take the risk.
2. Convention centers have suffered from fortress designs, which must reflect the designer's negative perception of the location as well as the unique logistics requirements of convention activities.
3. Parking and pedestrian access are impeded by the fortress designs and by the deteriorated condition of surrounding areas.
4. Local codes often require parking to be placed behind structures and obscured by landscaping.

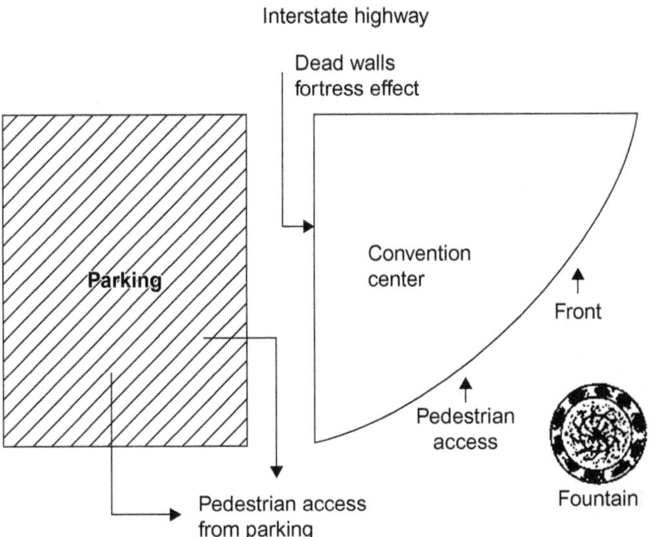

Figure 11.13

5. Local codes generally require the creation of plazas and open sitting areas. Developers are influenced to install fountains to enhance the aesthetics of an open area, but experience has shown that fountains and amenities in open areas attract vagrants, especially if they have already become established as the indigenous population.
6. Convention centers and their related parking structures usually are not designed to contain a variety of pedestrian-oriented businesses at the ground level, which would attract people all day and on weekends.

Good design and use (Figures 11.14 and 11.15):

1. Change local codes to allow parking in front of convention centers, where it is safer.
2. Delay installation of permanent amenities and fountains until the intended user population has clearly taken control of the site.
3. Thrust the convention center and parking structures into the airspace above, and place businesses and nightclubs at the ground level to increase year-round and evening activity. This will improve business and increase the number of normal users, who will feel and act safer.
4. Consider altering the exterior and use patterns of existing sites by adding galleries to offset fortress effects and increase both real and perceived surveillance opportunities. Galleries may be used to increase outdoor activities for exhibits and vendors, thus putting safe activities in what had been perceived as unsafe locations.

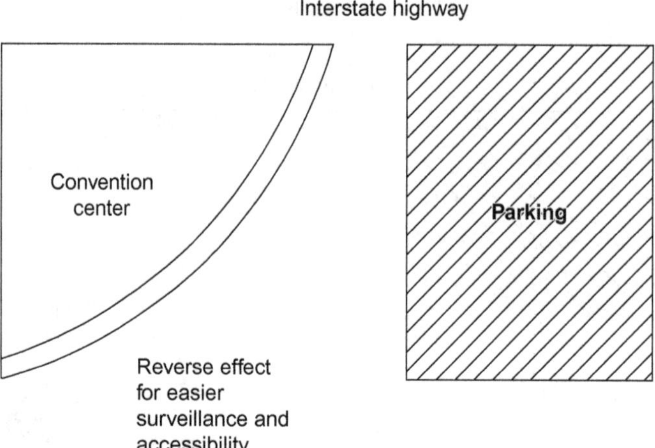

Figure 11.14

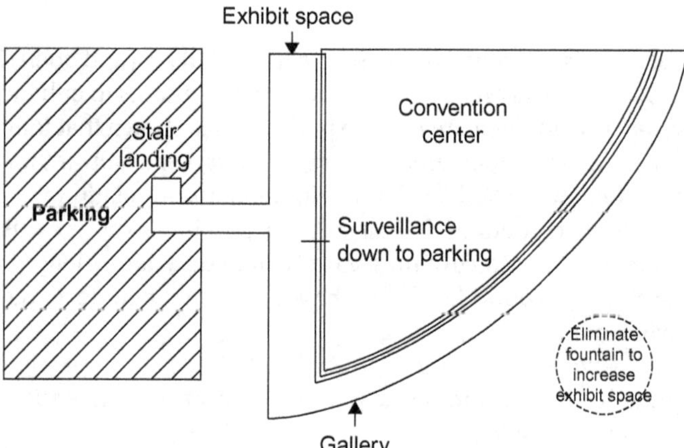

Figure 11.15

Stadium Entrance and Ticket Control

Poor design and use (Figure 11.16):

1. Traditional designs provide no transition from undifferentiated parking and informal gathering areas to the entrance and ticket-control functions.
2. Groups of students and others tend to congregate in front of entrance locations, which produces fear and concern for adults and young people who want to enter the stadium.

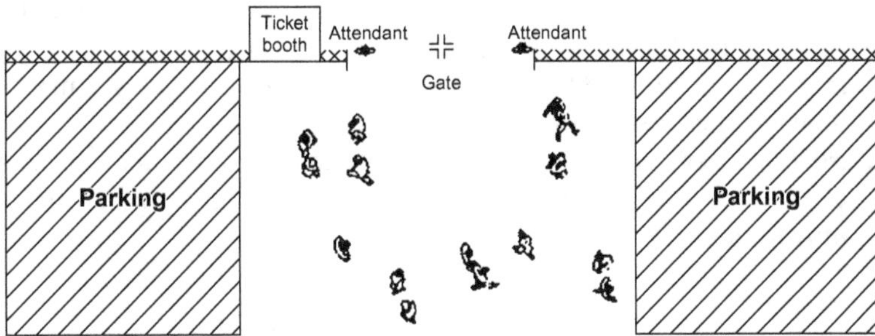

Figure 11.16

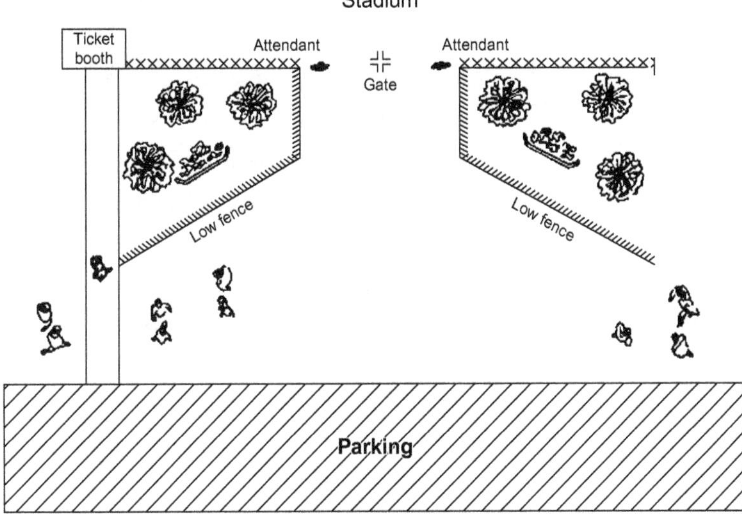

Figure 11.17

3. Ticket booth personnel and gate attendants cannot see over the groups of bystanders.
4. Normal users feel the lack of control and avoid these areas or pass through them quickly, thus reinforcing the control by abnormal users.

Good design and use (Figure 11.17):

1. A funnel design forces informal gathering behavior farther out into the parking area.
2. Gathering behavior is more difficult deeper into the parking area because of the perceived pedestrian/vehicular conflict.

3. Gate attendants have greater line of sight control of the parking lot and pedestrian areas.
4. The range of excuses for different behaviors narrows with the width of the funnel as one approaches the gate. Attendants have more power to exert their influence over people seeking entry as they are channeled into the funnel.
5. Normal users feel safer as they approach the entrance because of the narrow definition of behavior deep into the funnel—movement only.

PART 2

12

TACKLING CRIME AND FEAR OF CRIME THROUGH URBAN PLANNING AND ARCHITECTURAL DESIGN

Paul van Soomeren
DSP-Groep, Amsterdam/Rotterdam, The Netherlands

CHAPTER OUTLINE

Urbanization and Crime

Big cities all around the world are becoming more and more attractive to people from rural areas and abroad because of their financial power and economic opportunities, cultural wealth and places of interest (culture, tourism), job opportunities that offer a standard of living many people strive for, or simply for the lifestyle they promise (Burdett and Sudjic, 2010 and 2011; Florida, 2008; Landry, 2000 and 2006).

To quote former United Nations Secretary-General Kofi Annan: "The world has entered the Urban Millennium." But this urbanization also carries underlying risks that must be recognized: coping with new citizens and offering the required numbers of quality and affordable housing options as well as a variety of job opportunities and amenities for sports, art, culture, and recreation. This is a demanding challenge for local authorities. If this process fails in major cities, it is often due to a lack of social coherence and formal or informal social networks.

In the end, the quality of life decreases. Last but not least, big cities offer numerous criminal opportunities to those who come looking for illegal activities.

These and other problems faced by major cities worldwide are closely related to the developments we've just mentioned as well as the political, economic, and social transitions of modern societies that have been taking place in recent years. Urban attractiveness—especially of major urban areas—has been accompanied not only by a rise in crime rates and safety problems but also by an increase in feelings of insecurity due to fear of crime by many inhabitants, which consequently led to a reduction in the quality of life and may cause a destabilization of urban societies. Furthermore, a growing risk of terrorist activity in the wake of the September 11, 2001, attacks in the United States has created more insecurity, particularly in major cities with important and highly symbolic targets.

Although it is not possible to compare big cities in several parts of the world without bearing in mind their geographical, political, or cultural differences, some common trends and developments can be observed worldwide.

Fast Growth

The attractiveness of big cities causes a drift from rural areas to urban ones. Legal and illegal immigrants from abroad are attracted by economic possibilities. Political and administrative management capabilities must keep pace and create proper administrative responses and strategic plans. Otherwise, overpopulation, disorder, higher crime rates, and uncontrolled growth of problematic areas may arise.

Children and youths are the most vulnerable groups. These groups in particular have a high potential for being adversely affected by these problems.

Integration

Although major cities are a better labor market compared to rural areas, the creation of jobs may not be in step with demand, thus causing high unemployment rates. As a result, enforced idleness and poverty may lead to illegal activities. Young males in general—and unemployed young males in particular—are at high risk. The nationwide French riots in November 2005 in the *banlieues* showed that unsuccessful integration of this group can destabilize urban society (Duclos, 2006; Manière de Voir, 2006; check also the collective *aclefeu*).

Uncontrolled influx often leads to an erosion of existing neighborhoods, and a rise in crime (especially involving young males) may follow these developments: theft and burglary, use and trading of alcohol and drugs, violence, vandalism, and a general increase in antisocial behavior (incivilities) of all kinds: pub brawls, littering, insulting behavior, aggressive begging, disputes between neighbors, and the like.

Criminal Opportunities

Big cities not only attract offenders and petty crime, they also attract traditional organized-crime groups and well-organized economic criminals. There are numerous opportunities for these people to carry out their criminal activities and hide in the urban environment (Felson, 2002). They use the city as both as a crime scene and an area of retreat.

These developments can be recognized in urban areas all over the world, especially in larger cities. They have a major impact on the quality of people's lives and often lead to (sometimes exaggerated) feelings of insecurity or fear of crime. Regardless of whether fear is based on facts or not, it may damage urban societies and trigger problematic reactions. The issues of crime, security and the quality of life in urban areas, and the adoption of measures designed to tackle feelings of insecurity, crime, and the underlying problems have thus become key concerns to all institutions concerned with security, crime prevention, and social policy.

Safety and Security as Serious Problems

Safety and security are thus serious problems in any big city in the world, and among the risks, crime ranks high: serious crime as well as petty crime, arson resulting in small or devastating fires, terrorism … this list of crime incidents is long and will have to be shortened, defined, and tailored to fit the local situation in any city.

In this respect, crime is a phenomenon that somewhat resembles the famous dragon with several heads. There are more than 25 distinguishable types of crime (see also: *European Sourcebook of Crime and Criminal Justice Statistics 2003*, Appendix 1).

Besides crime there is also the fear of crime. This is a different phenomenon.

This chapter focuses on the types of crime concentrated in urban environments and with an opportunistic nature—in short, crimes that might be reduced by urban planning and building design (these crimes are indicated in **bold** in Table 12.1).

Crime has serious consequences for the social fabric of a society as well as for the economic welfare and development of a country. Crime will influence the level of fear and well-being of citizens, and crime may endanger the image of a country or city. In short, crime is harmful to a society. It is therefore essential in any country to tackle crime using the regular repressive actions taken by the police.

Table 12.1 Types of Crime.

Domestic violence	Assault	Robbery
Violence (semi) public areas/assault	Kidnapping	Traffic crimes
Fraud	Graffiti	Theft (motor)cycles
Shoplifting	Theft	Sexual offenses
Burglary	Homicide	Workplace crimes
Corruption	Car theft	Arson
Vandalism	Pickpocketing	Bribery
Drug trafficking	Threat	Environmental crimes
Pickpocketing	Extortion	Blackmail
Terrorism	Drugs	Robbery

From Old School to More Sophisticated Approaches

Tackling crime is a job that has to be done. The European Urban Charter asserts the basic right for citizens of European towns to "a secure and safe town free, as far as possible, from crime, delinquency, and aggression." This basic right to a safe community has been enshrined in many national and local crime-reduction programs all over Europe (see, e.g., DOE, 1994; DETR, 1999; and van Soomeren and Woldendorp, 1996).

But crime and crime prevention are too important to be left to police action only. Research and experience from all over the world show that it is important to tackle crime with an integrated endeavor that focuses on reactive crime approaches as well as social approaches and new and sophisticated crime-prevention techniques such as biometric approaches, CPTED, intelligent closed-circuit television (CCTV), urban safety communication, and so on. What is needed is an approach that combines several branches and institutes of government and private business in a coordinated and well-orchestrated manner. Crime is no longer just a matter for police. The new crime-prevention approaches focus on partnership and lots of other institutions, governmental as well as private business (see Figure 12.1).

The final declaration of an international conference organized by the Council of Europe's Congress of Local and Regional Authorities of Europe (CLRAE; 1997) stated:

> *... that crime, fear of crime and urban insecurity in Europe are major problems affecting the public (...) and that finding satisfactory solutions for them is one of the main keys to civic peace and stability.*

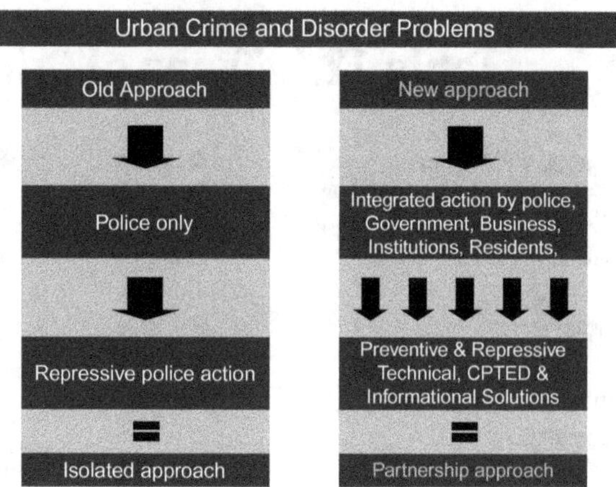

Figure 12.1 Old and new urban crime approaches.

And the first recommendation from this conference was:

> ... *that local and regional authorities in Europe develop integrated crime reduction action plans, with continuing public involvement, in which crime reduction is included as a policy in all aspects of the responsibilities of local authorities. Such a plan should define the nature and type of crime to be tackled, objectives, timetable, proposals for action and be based on a wide ranging up-to-date survey of statistics and diagnosis of crime.*

In this respect, CLRAE also stressed that it is important to "promote collaboration between the police and professional designers and ensure that police officers are specially trained to advise on the relationship between crime and the built environment."

The UN guidelines on crime prevention (UN, 1995) also stress the importance of well-planned crime-prevention strategies to prevent crime and victimization while also promoting the safety of communities and contributing to the sustainable development of countries. Effective, responsible crime prevention enhances the quality of life of all citizens. It has long-term benefits in terms of reducing the costs associated with the formal criminal justice system as well as other social costs that result from crime. Crime prevention offers opportunities for a humane and more cost-effective approach to the problems of crime.

Preventive strategies have to be accompanied by effective repressive action as an important part of the local and national policy. All involved agencies have to act efficiently, and the foundation should be up-to-date information and data (a knowledge-based approach). Modern surveillance techniques such as CCTV and automatic number-plate recognition (ANPR) have to be implemented in a city-wide system that is able to react quickly and adequately to safety threats and disturbances (Gill, 2003, on CCTV; Flight and Van Egmond, 2011, on ANPR). Other modern techniques such as GPS, biometric approaches, tracking and tracing, and intelligent design may also be used. Furthermore, social and economic "techniques" and approaches are needed to tackle crime as well. Social media will definitely play a vital role in decades to come. New crime patterns and even new crimes will result from the "virtualization of society," but also completely new approaches in crime prevention will appear.

Thus, successful safety strategies for major cities are complex and require coordinated cooperation of many institutions and people over a sufficient period of time to analyze the situation, find the necessary answers, and implement the proper solutions. Three basic principles for creating urban safety strategies are:

- Integrated approach
- Quality management
- Early intervention and planning

Integrated Approach

The police are important players from a repressive perspective, and potentially from a preventive perspective, but a safety strategy has to approach all relevant players and responsible institutions with links to safety issues. This means that all agencies concerned with urban, social, and economic policies have to be part of an integrated concept, that is, education, health, urban planning/housing, economic development, employment agencies, immigration, poverty, and other municipal agencies have to join forces to create an integrated strategy. This also implies the integration of the private sector, that is, local business, nongovernmental organizations, or interested citizens and groups of citizens.

Quality Management

All activities in an urban safety strategy must be well funded to achieve the desired impact. A sustainable effect demands a mix of temporary action and long-lasting, coordinated effort from all participants (Colquhoun, 2004). Proper evaluation, starting before and continuing during and after the implementation of the crime-prevention scheme or safety plan, ensures that success is measurable and corrections can be made to achieve maximum effect. In implementing crime-prevention policies, projects, or schemes, it is important to describe beforehand the existing context, the planned intervention (broken down into mechanisms to be fired), and the foreseen outcome. In their

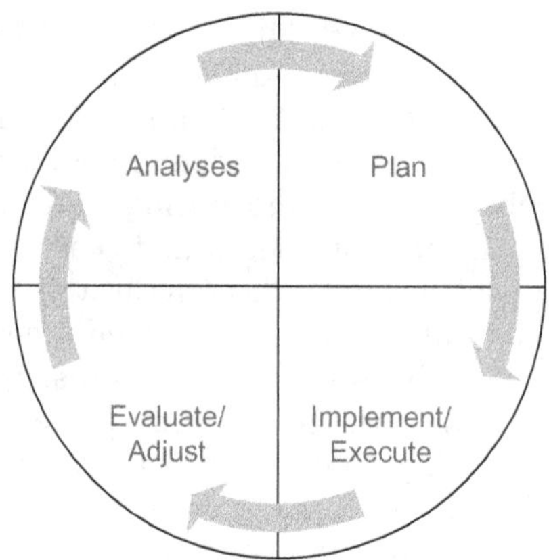

Figure 12.2 Quality management in crime prevention (as introduced in the European standard ENV 14383-2).

book *Realistic Evaluation,* Pawson and Tilley (1997) refer to CMOs—a combination of a specific *context,* a *mechanism,* and an *outcome* or effect. This way the evaluation of a policy, project, or scheme may be used to learn what works and what does not work. A strategy we once coined as *evalu-learning* (van Soomeren and Wever, 2005). Note that in this approach every intervention—every CMO—is specific for that situation.

Any strategy that targets problems associated with crime also has to be dynamic, assessed, and upgraded on an ongoing basis using a "plan, do, check, act" policy circle, adopted in quality management approaches such as ISO 9000. Either the UN Guidelines or European Standards of TC325, such as ENV 14383-2/TR 14383-2 (see also Benbouzid, 2011, Chapter 5), which are also based on a quality-circle approach, may be used for crime prevention (Figure 12.2).

Early Intervention and Planning

Crime prevention and safety management are more effective and successful when applied in early stages. Hence, children and young people should be a primary target group for preventive measures. Investing in youth is a much more promising strategy than targeting prevention at adults. The same principle applies to technical prevention, such as target hardening, CCTV, or CPTED implementation. The maximum preventive effect can be achieved only when it is integrated into the early stages of urban planning. The concept of prevention therefore has to be communicated thoroughly to all partners from government and the private sector to make sure that prevention is implemented during the planning stage of every major urban development.

CPTED/DOC in Europe: Policies and Concepts

To tackle crime and the fear of crime, we should no longer look only at the police and justice system but also turn to new approaches that focus on urban planning (cities, public space), architectural design (buildings, streets), building components and product/industrial design. The Justice and Home Affairs Council of the European Union (meeting in March 2001) reached the same conclusion when they came to a political agreement on the conclusion of the EU experts' conference Towards a Knowledge-Based Strategy to Prevent Crime (Sundsvall, Sweden, 2001):

> *Crime Prevention Through Environmental Design, or Designing Out Crime (CPTED/DOC), has proven to be a useful, effective, very concrete and feasible strategy to prevent crime and feelings of insecurity, integrated in a multidisciplinary approach. Best practices regarding CPTED/DOC should be collected, evaluated and made accessible for stakeholders. This process should utilize a common framework of concepts and processes, and transferable principles should be identified.*

This EU conference also underlined: "as regards prevention of the fear of crime, that the fear of crime should be viewed and treated as a social problem in its own right."

Again in 2011, the Council of the European Union (Brussels, March 24, 2011) acknowledged that:

> *Crime Prevention Through Environmental Design (CPTED) is a proactive crime prevention philosophy based on the theory that proper design and effective use of the built environment can lead to a reduction in crime and the fear of crime, as well as an improvement in the quality of life for the community, and that it aims to reduce or even remove the opportunity for crime to occur in an environment and promote positive interaction with the space by legitimate users.*

The EU council then considered that:

> *... there are a number of obstacles that have been identified in relation to the development of CPTED, such as the lack of knowledge, resistance to change, perception of panacea, cost, lack of legislative and practical support, economic influences; while there are a number of advantages to introducing CPTED, such as reduction of crime and fear of crime, improvement in the quality of life for the community, it is not possible to adopt only one solution to all problems (criminality, fear of crime, antisocial behavior etc.), but accepting the principles of CPTED is an important first step in that direction; the responsibility for reducing crime and the fear of crime should be shared between the police, local authorities, local businesses, the voluntary sector and the local community; training*

> *and information on the CPTED principles should be provided to everyone involved in the urban planning process to ensure that all participants are aware of their roles and responsibilities in relation to preventing crime and reducing feelings of insecurity within the community.*

And last but not least, the EU council invited all European member states to:

> *... build upon the knowledge and experience gathered on the subject of CPTED... make available information on the CPTED principles for use in the education, training and continuing professional development of those involved in the urban planning process and the design of buildings ...*

These statements and recommendations are based on assumptions regarding the interrelationships between the physical environment and human behavior. It is obvious that the results of urban planning and architecture do influence the choice of conduct and choice of routes of all people (young/old, woman/man, potential offender/potential victim). Quoting Winston Churchill rather loosely, we may say: We shape our buildings, streets, squares, public spaces, and amenities, and thereafter they shape us.

Hence, urban planning, architecture, and design also have an impact on crime and the fear of crime by influencing the conduct and attitudes of, for example, offenders; formal guardians such as police; informal guardians such as residents who carry out surveillance of an environment; potential victims (and/or targets) of crime, or victims of the fear of crime.

Examples

A great number of experiments have shown that particular types of crime can be reduced by modifying the opportunity for crime in the built environment and without leading to the displacement of crime (Hesseling, 1994).

Moving the nighttime tavern crowd away from vacant storefronts after closing time will inevitably reduce the number of incidents of burglary and vandalism of those stores. Controlling the access into, as well as the natural lines of vision through, underground parking areas will increase the opportunity for offenders to be seen and caught. This in turn will reduce the number of assaults and car crimes in those parking areas. The list of examples of successful opportunity-reduction measures goes on.

There are numerous examples of housing projects where bad design has contributed to the general decay and decline of urban areas. Badly designed housing estates have been rebuilt with thought and consideration to diminishing criminal opportunity. There are many cases of residents, who had previously feared for their safety, wanting to return to an estate following its refurbishment. New estates and housing projects are now incorporating good crime-prevention features at the design stage. In addition, researchers have identified reductions in crime following, for example, the introduction of design changes in large municipal housing estates.

Another building category that is benefiting from good planning ideas is the shopping center. The location of the center, car parks, and transport infrastructure are all being incorporated into the design stage in order to accommodate good design features. Supermarkets are also adopting designing-out crime measures to reduce both internal theft and crime committed by customers.

There is also overwhelming evidence concerning fear and the built environment, e.g., pedestrian subways, lack of surveillance, and, in particular, the level of lighting and dark streets. Similar parallels can be drawn with regard to vandalism. When questioned, offenders (and victims) of burglary, car theft, and rape/assault have all mentioned environmental/design factors (Cornish and Clarke, 1986). Research findings show that the feelings of insecurity victims experience are clearly related to the very same features of a place that attract offenders to commit a crime. No wonder more and more local and regional authorities in Europe are now insisting on planning applications showing proof that the principles of crime prevention and fear reduction by urban planning and building design have been adopted. The European CPTED Standard might help local authorities in this respect (ENV 14383-2; or the Korean standard KS A 8800); all they need to say to planners and architects is, "Apply that standard!" Furthermore, nowadays there is more than enough knowledge on all available CPTED sources (Michael, Saville, and Warren, 2012), theories, and possible actions and schemes (Cozens, 2005).

A Common Framework of Concepts

Building a "common framework of concepts," as the EU expert asked for in 2001 (Sündsvall, Sweden), already has a long history in CPTED/DOC theory. We may in fact distinguish *three* concepts (see Figure 12.3):

1. *The physical environment.* Buildings, streets, houses, components, products, and so on. Design, from the smallest chair to the city as a whole.
2. *Crime.* Criminal offences that really happened: a burglary, an act of vandalism, a robbery, etc. (refer to Table 12.1).
3. Fear of crime or (more generally) feelings of insecurity.

These three concepts are interrelated, but their relationships with one another are certainly not straightforward. Take, for example, the relationship between crime and feelings of insecurity or fear of crime.

Figure 12.3 One theme, three concepts.

Research has shown this relationship to be a dynamic and sophisticated one. Not necessarily all people who live in a high-crime area feel insecure. Some do, some don't. People experience fear differently, according to their age, lifestyle, gender, level of social contact within the community, perception of neighborhood decline or rehabilitation, socioeconomic or cultural background, and personal experience as a victim of crime. (See also Bourke, 2005, for the cultural aspects of fear.)

There are even examples of crime-ridden neighborhoods where most residents still feel fairly safe. Crime is, of course, only one of the things responsible for causing feelings of insecurity. Its influence can be counteracted by other factors. Preventing crime (or bringing crime rates down) does not necessarily mean that feelings of insecurity will temper as well. This is a warning one should bear in mind when discussing this subject in more depth.

The relationship between the physical environment and feelings of insecurity is a tricky one as well. Some environments are perceived as secure but are in fact not safe at all. Research has repeatedly shown that city centers are unsafe. Nearly all types of crime flourish in city centers: violence (Ramsay, 1982), burglary (Clarke and Hope, 1984; Pease, 1992), theft and street attacks (Poyner, 1981 and 1983), and vandalism (Van Dijk and Soomeren, 1980 and 1982). Modern techniques of compiling indexes and maps on crime and fear of crime show comparable results (see Figures 12.4 and 12.5).

Yet people often find busy and vibrant city centers or shopping centers safe and secure. Reasonably safe and harmless areas or neighborhoods are often perceived as unsafe. People can mistakenly interpret certain signs. A crowded street full of people shopping happily and drinking coffee and beer in or outside pubs may be wrongly seen as security or safety, because the offenders can't be seen. They are, as

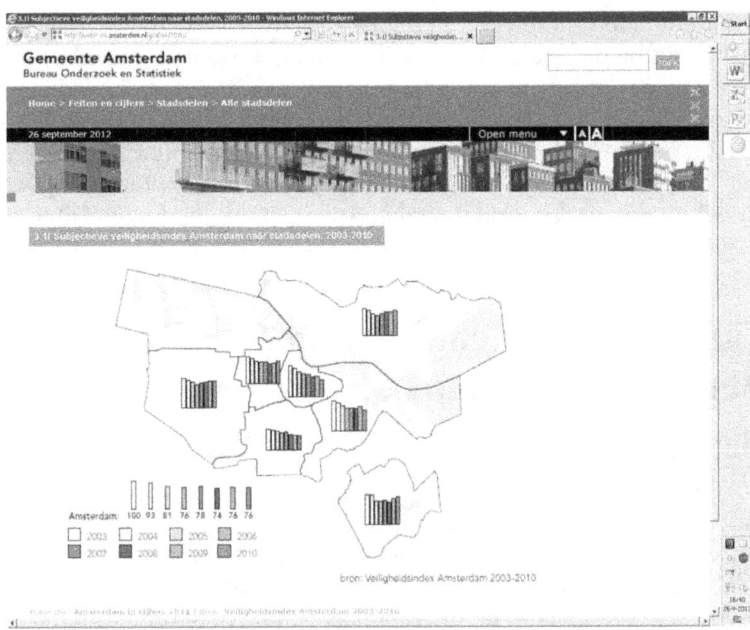

Figure 12.4 Amsterdam index for crime, 2003–2010. Source: Veiligheidsindex, Bureau Onderzoek en Statistiek, Amsterdam (www.os.amsterdam.nl).

Figure 12.5 Amsterdam index for fear of crime, 2003–2010. Source: Veiligheidsindex, Bureau Onderzoek en Statistiek, Amsterdam (www.os.amsterdam.nl).

it were, "hidden" in the crowd. A lonely street, littered and vandalized, may again be mistakenly seen as insecure, but when all offenders are drinking beer in the city center (or burgling other people's homes in faraway, well-to-do neighborhoods), this may in fact be quite a safe street.

In a nutshell, what is summarized here is the scientific debate that followed the publication of Jane Jacobs' book *The Death and Life of Great American Cities* and the related work of Elisabeth Wood (1961). In the next section, we elaborate on the discussion.

Theory: From Offender to Situation; From Reaction to Prevention

Nature and Nurture

The traditional explanations for crime fall into the category of the nature-versus-nurture debate. Those who support the *nature theory* stress the importance of our biology and heredity and state that this is how people become criminal. People are affected by diet, body chemistry, and genetic hardwiring, just as birds are programmed to migrate south and fish to return to the same rivers. These are the factors that create a propensity to misbehave.

On the other hand, there is the *nurture theory*. According to the ideas of this theory, it is our upbringing and education that determine our behavior. Our family and our friends influence us to, or not to, commit crime. We can still hear our parents warning us about learning bad behavior or hanging out with the wrong kids. We see children abused by their parents, who then themselves become parental abusers. These are the stories of the nurture theory.

Nature and nurture explanations still exist. Nurture explanations are *personality theories*. Nature explanations are called *environment theories*. Together with a third approach, *opportunity theory*, they constitute the major streams of thought that have been created to explain and prevent crime. However, what policymakers needed (and still need) is not so much a scientific explanation of crime but a method for tackling crime that makes it more manageable. This need for feasible methods for policymakers led criminologists to search for alternatives to the personality and environment theories related to crime and criminals. As a result, opportunity theory emerged in the 1960s and 1970s.[1]

Opportunity theory stresses the importance of four cornerstones: offender-situation-victim-guardians. The theory states that a criminal

[1] We should add that the concept of opportunity had already appeared in 19th-century criminological publications. Until the first half of the 20th century, however, it was not considered very relevant. Opportunity as a useful concept for crime prevention was elaborated upon around 1920 by researchers of the Chicago School (see CLRAE, 1987).

offence will take place only if the first three factors are present and the last factor (guardians) is not present. Hence, this opportunity approach focuses on the situation in which an offender meets—or seeks—an "undefended" victim, whether a person to assault, a bank to rob, or a house to burgle. In this approach the focus is shifted from a reactive point of view—taking action after a crime has occurred—to a more proactive stand: taking action before a crime occurs and thus preventing the offence.

CPTED, DOC, and DAC

One of the most productive areas in which the opportunity approach has proved its worth is in urban planning and building design. In Canada and the United States, this has come to be known as crime prevention through environmental design, or CPTED (pronounced *sep-ted*). In Europe the concept is called designing-out crime, or DOC (Clarke and Mayhew, 1980) or design against crime, or DAC (Davey, 2005).

C. Ray Jeffery and Other Basics (Health, Fire, and Traffic)

The term CPTED was coined by C. Ray Jeffery, who published a book in 1971 arguing that sociologists and criminologists had considerably overstated the social causes of crime and neglected both biological and environmental determinants. Jeffery suggested that crime prevention ought to be focused on factors related to the biology of crime and especially to reducing the environmental opportunities for crime.

According to Clarke (2001), Jeffery's book:

> *... met with either indifference or considerable hostility from criminologists, who were particularly offended by the biological arguments. The book contained few prescriptions for reducing opportunities, but his followers, in particular, Tim Crowe (1991), have now developed a comprehensive set of guidelines to reducing opportunities for crime in the built environment, intended to guide police, town planners and architects. These guidelines have been promulgated in hundreds of training sessions given by Crowe and others throughout the United States.*

It is worth mentioning here that since the end of the 1990s, guidelines have also been issued in Europe. One example is the set of European Standards issued by the European Committee for Standardization (CEN) technical committee 325 (TC325), such as the European standard ENV 14383-2 on the prevention of crime and the fear of crime by urban planning and building design and the standards and technical guidelines that follow this standard. The process of how these standards emerged in a social, cultural, and criminological diverse Europe is analyzed and described by Bebbouzib (2011). There are now also standards on, for example, "dwellings," "shops," and "offices." Standards on "schools," "public transport," and "ram raiding" are being developed. National guidelines are also useful; like the UK Secured by Design, the Dutch Police Label Safe/Secure Housing and the Safety and Security Effect Assessment (*VeiligheidsEffectRapportage*; see, e.g., *Crime Opportunity Profiling of Streets [COPS],* Chapter 3, or guidelines in the form of checklists [Voort and Wegen, 1990]). Danish guidelines (DS 470) relating to violence and vandalism are also relevant here.

The CPTED theory is based on the simple idea that crime is partly a result of the opportunities presented by the physical environment (see also Kube, 1982, and www.e-doca.eu). If this is the case, it should be possible to alter the physical environment so that crime is less likely to occur.

This idea resembles a view on the history of **healthcare**. The latter stresses the importance of the environmental ameliorations that have significantly changed the heath situation and life expectancy in Western countries in the last few centuries. The enormous progress in people's health situations can only partly be attributed to better medical practices. It was mainly caused by engineers (clean water, better sewage systems), technicians, city maintenance institutes, architects, and urban planners.

The idea behind CPTED also resembles the approach taken to prevent the devastating potential of **fires** from causing damage. From the 16th century onward, it was (next to the increasing professionalism of fire brigades and their instruments) urban planning, architecture, and engineering that did the trick.

Traffic safety is yet another example. Reductions in the number of people killed and wounded in traffic-related incidents have been brought about mainly as a result of technical solutions (airbags, safer cars), urban planning, and engineering/road design (traffic flow, roundabouts, speed bumps/sleeping policeman, road closures, and more recently the concept of shared space).

To learn more about the roots of CPTED and DOC, let us now turn to the grand old men and ladies who built the foundation of this theory.

Jane Jacobs

Jane Jacobs (1961) focused on the places where crime is committed and the physical characteristics of those places.

The essential part of Jacobs' theory is simple. As Jacobs put it: City streets are unsafe because they are deserted. This problem can be solved by giving streets three main qualities:

- A clear demarcation between public and private space.
- There must be eyes on the streets—the eyes of residents and the eyes of people who are just passing by.
- Buildings must be oriented toward the street.

Streets must be used continuously, both to add to the number of effective eyes and to induce people in buildings to watch the streets.

For Jacobs, crime prevention and natural surveillance are more or less the same. That is why she placed high hopes on night shops, restaurants, pubs, bars, and the like. Amenities such as these draw people onto the streets. Residents then like to watch the busy and crowded street, and natural surveillance (or informal control) results. Crime does not get a chance.

At this point Jacobs' theory fails from the point of view of crime prevention.

Several research findings show pubs, bars, and (night) restaurants to be particular trouble spots (Ramsay, 1982). As mentioned earlier, the same goes for busy city centers. In her line of reasoning, Jacobs clearly overlooked two other lines of thought that hold as well (see Figure 12.6; see also Mawby, 1977, and Skogan and Maxfield, 1981).

Furthermore, Jacobs seems not only to overestimate the influence of natural surveillance on offenders; she also overestimates the influence the physical environment has on human behavior. Creating better *opportunities* for natural surveillance (or informal control) does not automatically result in real effective control.

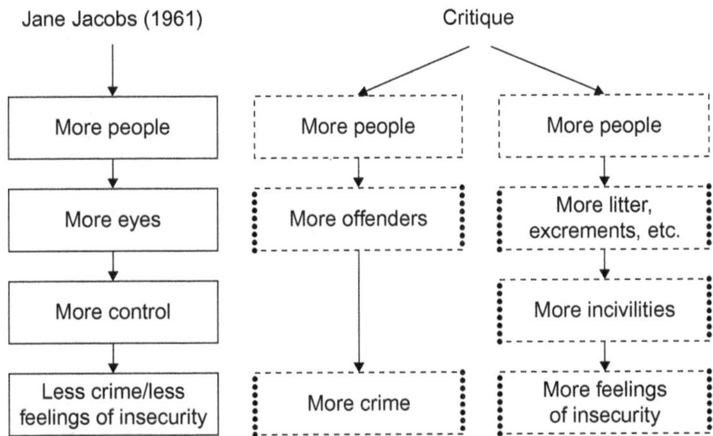

Figure 12.6 Jane Jacobs (1961).

Oscar Newman

The second approach to fall under CPTED is the *defensible space* theory by the architect Oscar Newman (see Figure 12.7). Newman published his book independently and at about the same time as Jeffery (1972).

In his book *Defensible Space* (1972), Newman, like Jacobs, held the view that crime was allowed to flourish because housing design prevented residents from exercising informal control over their environment (see also: Newman, 1973). Informal control, Newman argued, arises mainly from natural surveillance, coupled with a feeling of territoriality deep within the resident's soul: "*see* what's happening there . . . stop those blokes from violating *my* environment!"

Newman put much of the blame for the high crime rates of public housing estates on their layout and design. He holds the view that architectural and town planning characteristics of buildings or building complexes have a direct influence on the nature and extent of local crime:

> *Our work over the past two years, concentrating on ... the spatial organization of our inner urban residential areas, has led us to conclude that the form of the static components of our living environment is, in and of itself, a factor which significantly affects crime rates. (Newman, 1973)*

Newman's central concept, referred to as defensible space, includes four different design elements: territorial definition, visibility/surveillance, stigmatization, and adjacent areas. These four elements

Figure 12.7 Territoriality reinforced by visibility.

contribute both individually and in concert to the creation of a secure environment (Newman, 1972 and 1973).

Territorial Definition

With the use of real or symbolic barriers, a particular residential environment can be subdivided into zones that are more manageable for the residents, stimulating residents to adopt proprietary or territorial attitudes, i.e., "This is my area, my territory." A key point here is the transition from private space (easily manageable) to public space (difficult to manage).

Visibility/Surveillance

Residents must be able to survey what is happening in and around public spaces inside and outside the building. This is one of the conditions for territorial definition.

Stigmatization

Proper use of materials, good architectural design, and last but not least, good structural planning can prevent residents of a particular building or complex from being seen as vulnerable and/or from being stigmatized, both of which can lead to a feeling of isolation.

Adjacent Areas

The security of adjoining areas is partly determined by the "strategic geographical location of intensively used communal facilities."

Newman proves his theory in two ways. First, he carries out an analysis of crime in 133 public housing complexes in New York City using figures obtained from the New York City Housing Authority Police Department. For a number of offenses, these figures show exactly where offenses are committed in and around a housing complex.

The elevator was proven to be the most dangerous location within the building, followed (at some distance) by the hall and the lobby, with the stairway in fourth place (mainly fire escapes at the rear of the building).

Newman pins a second piece of evidence to his theory, however, by comparing two adjacent housing complexes. One of them, says Newman, has many good defensible-space features; the other one does not. Crime is minimal in the "good" complex, whereas it is high in the "bad" complex. According to Newman, these differences cannot be dismissed because of differences in the characteristics of residents in the two complexes (also see: Newman, 1975, and Newman and Franck, 1980).

Newman was fiercely criticized on methodological grounds and for failing to consider the social origins of informal control and the origins of crime. In spite of this criticism, Newman's ideas became very popular in the States. A whole generation of defensible-space followers emerged. Several CPTED projects were implemented and evaluated in the 1970s. Discussion, criticism, trial and error in those projects, and new research (also by Newman himself; see, for example, Newman and Franck, 1980) resulted in a reformulation of the defensible-space theory. Newman's theory became less physically deterministic. In his new defensible-space theory (Newman, 1979), he stressed the importance of social agents. Newman placed his hopes on, as he called it, "communities of interest"—small clusters of residents sharing more or less the same lifestyle, age and family cycle. Architecture and urban planning come in to play when Newman says that one should build houses or apartments for such communities of interest. Hence, town planning can create social cohesion in this.

In retrospect, Clarke (2001) argues that:

> *... Newman, and some other enlightened architects such as Richard Gardiner (1978), put forward a wide range of detailed design suggestions to change these conditions and make housing safer. The purpose of Newman's suggestions was to encourage natural territorial behaviour on the part of residents by enabling them to give surveillance to the public spaces around their individual residence. His thesis was savagely criticized by criminologists and other social scientists, who accused him of "environmental determinism" and of making simplistic extrapolations to human behavior from the territorial behavior of animals. Nevertheless, Newman has had an enormous impact on the design of public housing in many parts of the world. The wholesale abandonment of tower block buildings for public housing owes much to his arguments about their criminogenic potential. In recent years, the federal government in the United States has once again begun to pay attention to Newman (Cisneros, 1995), commissioning him to publish a restatement and defense of his views (Newman, 1996).*

The theories of Jacobs and Newman are both of great importance and they have brought the discussion to new frontiers. However, Jacobs and Newman built their theories on quicksand comprised of the magic concept of natural surveillance, or informal control. Their theoretical constructions stress the importance of creating better physical *possibilities* for informal control. But creating those possibilities does not actually result in effective control being exercised, because:

- Residents have to make *use* of the possibilities given (which they often do not or do not want to do).
- Offenders have to perceive control and they must not be able to "escape" it (for example, by hiding).

In short, Jacobs and Newman forgot that it takes two to tango: not only community life, surveillance, or control but *also* offenders who are shifting from criminal to noncriminal behavior. Jacobs' and Newman's theories deal with the community angle and will be most useful if one wants to reduce feelings of insecurity or fear of crime. If one wants to prevent real crime, however, the most important piece of the puzzle is still missing: the offender (see Figure 12.8).

Theories linking offenders and the physical environment they live and operate in have a long history, starting with the work of the Chicago School.

The Chicago School

Shaw and McKay (Shaw, 1929; Shaw and McKay, 1931, and 1969) mapped the residences of known juvenile delinquents in Chicago (and some other U.S. cities). They borrowed the zonal model of urban form (developed by Burgess and Park) and showed that the rate of delinquent residences was highest in the concentric zone adjacent to the central business district. The rate declined with increasing distance outward.

Borrowing yet another component of the Chicago School theory, Shaw and McKay also showed that within specific "natural areas," a high delinquency rate (number of delinquents living in an area) coexisted with other social problems such as poverty, broken families, and disease. This high delinquency rate persisted until the mid-1960s (Shaw and McKay, 1969). In these slum areas (the zone of transition), the traditional organizations and institutions (schools, churches, family) had lost their power to teach people respectable (i.e., noncriminal) behavior. Social control was reduced and social disorganization won the day.

Figure 12.8 Never forget the offender.

Youths living in such neighborhoods were taught the (criminal) job by the older boy living next door. In this way a neighborhood constantly "produced" new generations of criminals. The Chicago School focused on offenders, but the main interest of people like Shaw and McKay concentrated on the neighborhood level.

The Geographical or Spatial School

In the 1970s, offender-based research started to focus on the rational, spatial, and environmental choices made by offenders. Pioneering work was published and edited by Paul and Patricia Brantingham (1975, 1980, and 1981), who studied the spatial patterns of burglary and formulated a *spatial choice theory* that is very useful for property crimes. One of the striking things about criminals, they argued, is that most of them behave like ordinary people most of the time. And they like to operate near their home base, as was shown by Rhodes and Conly (1981).

Criminals do not like to work too close to their home base because they fear they will be recognized by neighbors. The results of these offender preferences are shown in Figure 12.9. However, offenders are, again, like most people, mobile. They travel to school, work, shops, and entertainment and recreation locations (see Figures 12.10 and 12.11). They develop an action space—a mental map or 'awareness space,' the parts of the city they have knowledge about (see also Carter and Hill, 1979; Chainey and Ratcliffe, 2005). Researchers, urban planners, and architects can play with this thought and develop models at a macro level (urban planning, transportation) and at a micro level (architecture).

This type of geographical modeling was later developed into sophisticated computer models using geographical information

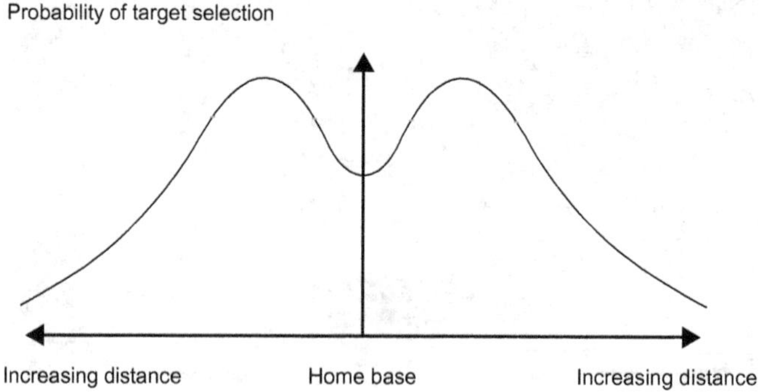

Figure 12.9 Search area for individual offender (cross-section view).

systems (GIS), as can be seen in books on GIS and crime mapping, such as Chainey and Ratcliffe (2005) and Ratcliffe (2012).

Another useful lesson from the Brantinghams is the idea of offenders being quite rational people, making decisions (choices) in steps: "Should I enter this neighborhood, this street? How risky will it be entering this estate? Will I be seen while burgling this house?"

Barbara Brown and Irwin Altman (1981) built a conceptual model based on these ideas. The choice-making process of a burglar consists of a step-by-step judgment of environmental cues. Table 12.2 (based on Brown and Altman) summarizes these cues for four different levels (neighborhood, street, site, and house).

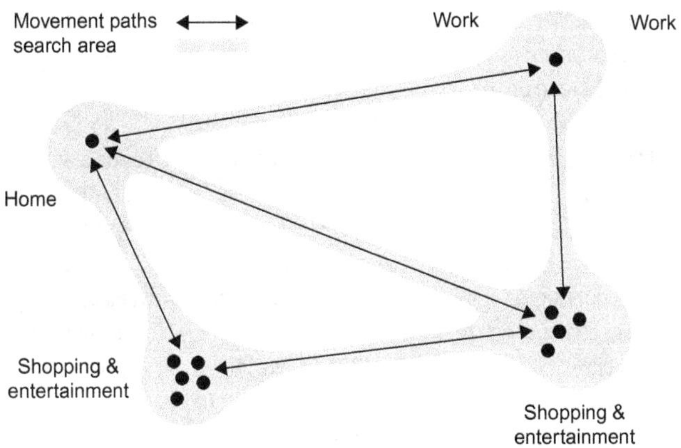

Figure 12.10 Complex search area for individual offender.

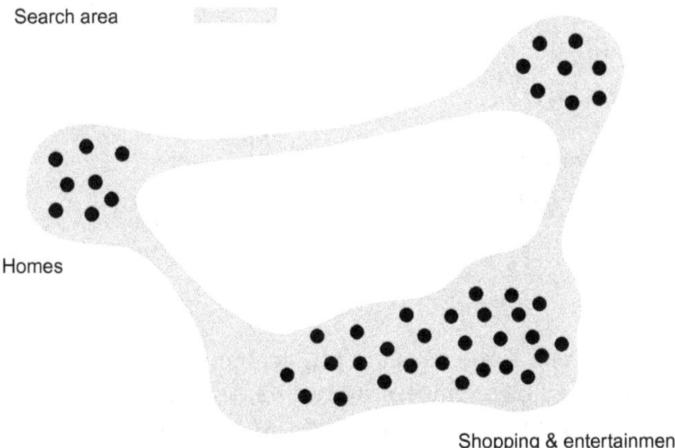

Figure 12.11 Complex search area for clusters of offenders.

Table 12.2 A burglar's Vulnerability Factors Associated with Neighborhood, Street, Site, and House.

Factor	Neighborhood	Street	Site	House
Detectability	See: Street	Design: Winding vs. narrow Distance: Street to house Lighting: Windows, door positions relative to street	Shrubs, trees, walls, fences blocking burglar Burglar seeing into house (door and window positions) Auditory cues, dogs barking	General visibility by neighbors or others Windows positioned to see returning occupants once inside
Actual barriers	River, canal, railway	Locked gates, fences, guards	Locked gates, fences, guards; is opening large enough to carry away goods?	Locks, alarm system; is opening large enough to carry away goods?
Symbolic barriers	Parks, shrubs, trees, roads (routing!)	Welcome signs Neighborhood watch signs Distinctive vegetation for streets	Distinctive personalizing items in yard: mailboxes, flower gardens, marking of entryway from street	Nameplate, signs on door (neighborhood watch)
Traces	Signs of lack of control, e.g., litter, graffiti	Cars parked on street Mail, newspapers,in box or on street	Equipment indicating interrupted activity: lawn mower, toys Sprinklers (working) Appropriateness of lighting	Hearing TVs, radios, voices, telephones Lights Cooking odors
Social climate	See: Street	Reactions by others, staring, questioning, ignoring, looking	See: Street	See: Street

(Based on Brown and Altman, 1981.)

As you can see, some cues are physical in nature and can be well or badly designed by engineers, architects, and planners. Street lighting, for example, proves of vital interest to crime prevention and reducing the fear of crime (Painter, 1996; Farrington and Welsh, 2002). Or, take improvements in the layout, design, density, and materials of housing and its related surrounding space. This theme was explored in the EU project COPS (see COPS, BRE, 2005). Quite a lot of the cues shown in Table 12.2 are of a social nature.

The perspective that criminal behavior is a result of rational choices and decisions made by offenders appears to provide the most immediate payoff for those crime-control efforts aimed at reducing criminal opportunity (Clarke and Cornish, 1985). This perspective was, as previously mentioned, developed following the Chicago School tradition and the publications of Paul and Patricia Brantingham. However, this perspective was turned into useful crime-control policy by writers on the subject of *situational crime prevention* (for an overview, see Clarke and Mayhew, 1980, or Heal and Laycock, 1986). Situational crime prevention was developed by the British government's criminological research department in the mid-1970s (Mayhew et al., 1976; Clarke and Mayhew, 1980; Clarke, 1997). The situational approach is principally not concerned with architectural design and the built environment, nor is it particularly focused on predatory offences such as robbery or burglary. Rather, it is a more general approach to reducing opportunities for any type of crime occurring in any type of setting. The situational approach stresses the importance of developing specific crime-prevention strategies. The container has to be opened in order to show the various types of crime one has to analyze and prevent: vandalism, burglary, violence, and so on. These types of crime have to be analyzed by crime experts using a situational approach. They should study, for example, burglars and burglary in one part of the city to learn about the social and physical conditions that may prevent burglars from burgling. These conditions can then be implemented by town planners, architects, social workers, or municipal institutions and/or laid down in building codes and regulations.

Recent economic-criminological research shows that this long-term strategy works. Ben Vollaard and Jan van Ours showed in their research the effect of a change in the Dutch building regulations implemented around 2000 (Vollaard and Van Ours, 2011). The change made burglary-resistant doors and windows obligatory in newly built dwellings. After a few years the crime-preventive effect of this change was impressive (see Figures 12.12 and 12.13, taken from a presentation held in 2011 in Rotterdam by Professor Jan van Dijk).

Also of interest here is a comparison using data from the International Crime Victim Survey which makes it possible to compare a country like the Netherlands, changing its building code and investing in burglary prevention, with a country like Denmark, which is not changing its building code and not investing that much in burglary prevention. In the Netherlands the overall victim percentage for burglary is now less than 1 percent (0.8 percent = a 0.5-percent

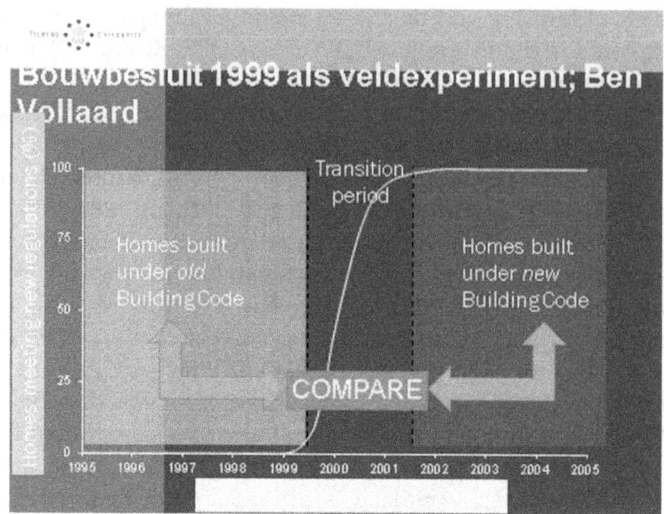

Figure 12.12

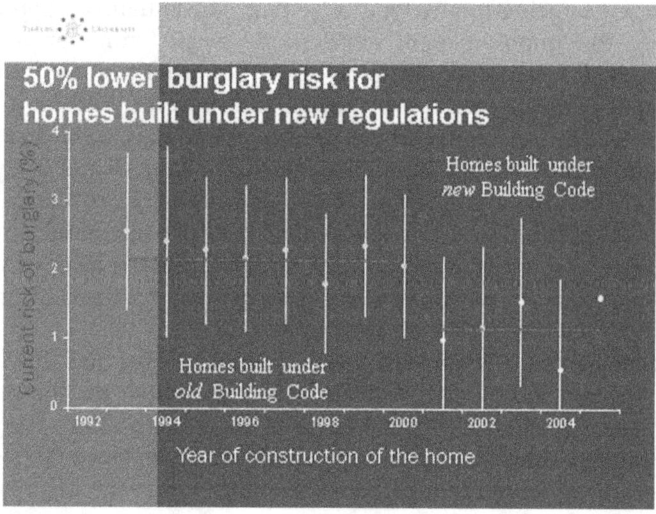

Figure 12.13

decrease between 2004 and 2010), and in Denmark it is 3.6 percent (an increase of 0.9 percent between 2004 and 2010).

Lessons

Some of the outcomes of crime prevention are impressive, but still the ideas and theories reviewed in this section do not give a clear-cut

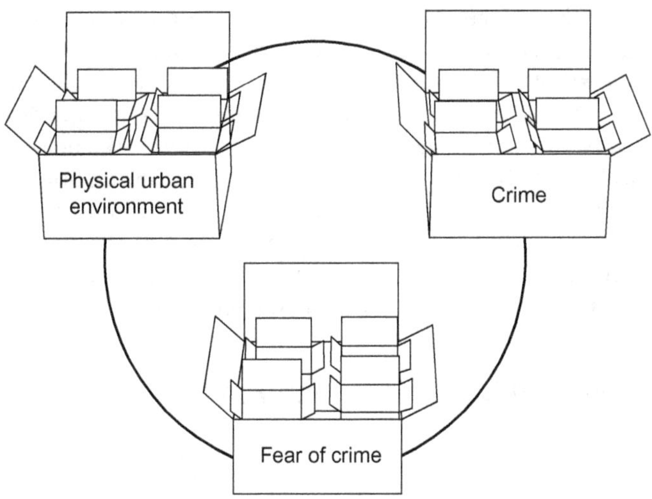

Figure 12.14 Container concepts.

answer to the question of how to prevent crime or feelings of insecurity through environmental design.

First, two different perspectives can be clearly distinguished: The Jacobs/Newman theory is aimed at *residents*, the environmental influence on residents' fear of crime, and their ability to exercise control. The most useful application is not crime itself but instead social cohesion and feelings of insecurity/the fear of crime. This perspective is complemented by *offender*-based theories that support analysis of the decision-making processes of criminals.

Second, it is clear that the main concepts that are discussed here are, in fact, *container concepts* (see Figure 12.14). The container called **crime** is a box full of various types of offences, each needing its own specific approach.

The **physical urban environment** is a "container concept," too. It contains a *social* environment (filled with thousands of residents, employees, police officers, and offenders) and a *physical* environment consisting of houses, streets, public buildings, and, last but not least, products like mobile phones, laptop computers, cars, bikes, and so on.

The **fear of crime** (or feeling insecure) is clearly a black box, too. This box contains striking differences in age, gender, lifestyle groups, and more (Vanderveen, 2006).

An important lesson thus may be that universal solutions for reducing (fear of) crime by changing the physical urban environment are unlikely to work. The building codes and standardization probably are the only exception here.

What is always needed first is an analysis of the various problems associated with crime in a specific environment (the context), followed by an analysis of the responses to these problems in a specific environment (the planned interventions and mechanism to be fired). Both analyses must be specific to the area and the type of crime, i.e., no sweeping theoretical generalizations and no multiuser blueprints on how to complete the job of environmental crime prevention—just grassroots solutions for specific crime problems. Crime prevention must be viewed as a multiagent process and not a set of standard tricks. This brings us to the more practical problem of research and implementation.

Research and Implementation Problems

Research

The physical environment certainly influences both crime and the fear of crime or feelings of insecurity. However, its influence may not necessarily be the same for every environment. In Jacobs' work we are confronted with this dilemma: pubs, restaurants, and night shops may promote community life and reduce feelings of insecurity, but all too often these amenities cause the crime figures in a neighborhood to rise. Offender-based theories and residents/control-based theories are thus not interchangeable. The perspective taken by a researcher will influence the answers he can give. The best way to proceed is to incorporate *both* theories and perspectives. A further problem is that research is often based on shaky ground because of unreliable crime (or offender) data. Nevertheless, crime is the work of humans. Buildings do not commit crime. An offense takes place only if there is a potential offender who is motivated (not predestined!) and physically able to commit that offense and who is not restrained by social thresholds or guardians (see Figure 12.15).

The physical environment mostly plays a secondary role. The physical environment is at best a prerequisite for *informal control* (natural surveillance) or a way to help prevent (by physical or symbolic means) offenders from entering a neighborhood, housing estate, building, corridor, or apartment.

Implementation

Implementing responses to crime is a subject that is all too often overlooked. Many problems can arise: unwillingness of institutions, bureaucracy, lack of communication and coordination, lack of knowledge. The outcome of this process is that the best (or even good) responses to crime are seldom implemented. Steering the process of implementation is probably even more difficult than formulating responses (or crime-prevention measures). To overcome these

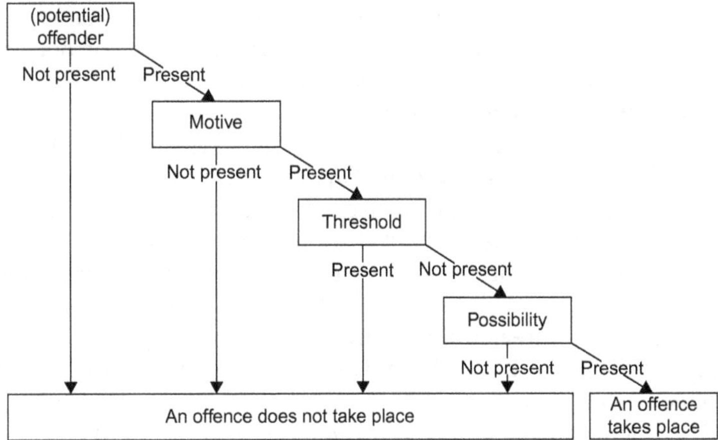

Figure 12.15

problems, one can at best try to improve communication, coordination, and the transfer of knowledge. Practical instruments, building codes, regulations, standards, and schemes such as Secured by Design, the Dutch Police Label Safe and Secure Housing, and the European standard (CEN, TC325, ENV 14383-2) help overcome these implementation problems. Also important is the exchange of knowledge and experience among practitioners, researchers, and specialists. Special networks like the International CPTED Association and chapters such as the European Designing Out Crime Association (www.e-doca.eu) are important exchange and transfer tools. The same goes for CPTED training and courses given everywhere around the globe.

The Fear of Crime

The phrase *fear of crime* usually refers to the fear of personally becoming a victim of particular types of crime, e.g., a question in a victim survey that asks respondents how likely they think it is that they will be burgled (or what have you) in the coming year. Another type of question often posed in a victim survey to measure vulnerability toward street crime and feelings of insecurity in relation to the urban environment is: How safe do you feel walking alone in your home area after dark? Do you feel very safe, fairly safe, a bit unsafe, or very unsafe? (see also the International Crime Victim Surveys questionnaire). Answers to this question have typically been shown to paint a different picture of fear of crime from questions that, for instance, ask about perceptions of risk (Vanderveen, 2006). In response to the question of *street safety*, women and the elderly typically emerge as the most fearful. This may be because the prospect of being out after dark evokes anxiety about a greater range of mishaps (e.g., accidents as well as crime) for some people.

Why do people feel insecure being in public and semipublic spaces? The degree of fear and the kind of crimes a person is afraid of differ significantly depending on gender and age. Women, the elderly, and disabled people are more likely to fear crime. They fear for their personal safety and are afraid of street violence and, in particular, sexual assault. It is far more terrifying to be confronted with crimes like rape, which threaten a person's integrity and dignity, than with the loss of material goods. For this reason women are usually more affected by this feeling than men.

Frightening or fearful places are not necessarily places where actual crimes occur. Nevertheless, fear influences the way people behave with regard to public spaces. In particular, women and the elderly are more likely to use avoidance strategies that keep them away from problematic areas and situations. They tend to restrict their own activities because of the fear of crime. This behavior has effects on neighborhoods and may even lead to economic decay.

Studies of public areas where sexual assaults have occurred show that the type and characteristics of fearful places—for example, poor lightning and the presence of hiding places—correlate with the occurrence of crime.

Starting in the Netherlands (RPD, 1985; Hajonides, 1987) and followed by Austria and later Canada (Wekerle and Whitzman, 1992), a rather unique line of "research" has been developed: inventory studies of locations experienced as "fear-provoking." This research was initiated by the women's movement. The objective is practical: to improve perceived and actual safety.

This research is done in an extremely practical way: A group of women check several places in the city or neighborhood. They often do this twice for each place: at daytime and after dark. Nowadays they are often accompanied by a few politicians, police officers, lighting experts, urban planners, and city maintenance experts. Plans for amelioration are sometimes made on the spot; research, action, and coordination are unified during these public (crime) audits.

The following is a summary of the factors most mentioned:

- *The presence or absence of people* in the area (passersby, users, or residents).
- *The status or function of the area,* which determines the involvement of the people present. For example, is it a public area or is it a demarcated community space?
- *Visibility.* Can residents and passersby see what is happening in public and semipublic spaces?

- *Possibility for surveillance.* Can users themselves survey the space properly (lighting, obstacles, unexpected corners, etc.) and can they get their bearings properly in the area?
- *Management and maintenance.* A badly maintained, impoverished environment is a sign that nobody feels responsible for the area or what happens in it.
- *The degree of diversity.* Large mono-functional areas (industrial estates, office complexes) are deserted for the greater part of the day and night, i.e., no social control. There is also no surveillance on isolated secondary roads.

Not all of these features need be present at one time.

Selm (1985) found that women avoid locations because of the **presence** of particular people. Some locations are used by fear-provoking people, such as drug users, or which have a fear-provoking function, such as prostitution. The latter puts into perspective the much-lauded theory of guaranteeing safety with the presence of people.

This study also examined whether the women's perceptions were justified: Are the fear-provoking locations indicated by them also the locations where fear-provoking things happen? A comparison of data from their survey with police data from the locations where sexual offences took place (Loef, 1985) and research data from Germany (Gensch and Zimmer, 1980) and the Netherlands (Flight and van Soomeren, 2004) showed that the **type** of location that women point to as generating fear corresponds with the type of location where rapes and sexual assaults actually take place.[2]

Three Factors Characterizing "Frightening" Places

Three main factors can be distinguished as characterizing an "unsafe or fear-generating location": fear-generating functions, vandalism and bad maintenance, and problematic urban design.

Fear-Generating Functions

Crimes against an individual are more likely to occur in locations with fear-generating features, such as prostitution or drug abuse, or in locations with certain types of entertainment or activities that attract people who generate fear in others.

Urban planning and design must aim to avoid such mono-functional areas. This can be achieved by mixing, for example, dwellings, entertainment, and shopping. Social control can be improved

[2]According to this German study, only 30 percent of rapes took place outside the home, whereas it is known that many rapes (42 percent) are carried out by people known to the victims (Metz and Rijpkema, 1979). This data makes one wonder whether women would do better to fear people they know at home rather than strangers on the street.

in this way, and the "generators of fear" can become less dominant. If such an "entertainment" area already exists, it is important to offer alternative routes for pedestrians. These routes must be busy, well lit, and easy to survey.

Vandalism and Bad Maintenance

The importance of regular maintenance and cleanliness cannot be emphasized enough. Such efforts must be coordinated and continuous. Litter and graffiti must be removed quickly, and repairs must be carried out in such a way that original materials are matched. It is vital that the public realm does not lose its character through neglect, becoming alienating to citizens and visitors and giving encouragement to potential offenders because they feel no one cares (Parker, 2000).

The idea that graffiti spraying and other forms of petty crime and incivilities promote further bad behavior has now been tested experimentally. Researchers at the University of Groningen (the Netherlands) deliberately created such settings as part of a series of controlled experiments designed to discover whether signs of vandalism, litter, and low-level law breaking could change the way people behave. They found that they could, by a lot—doubling the number of people who are prepared to litter and steal. This finding also proved that the Broken Windows Theory (Wilson and Kelling, 1982) was correct.

The Dutch researchers selected several urban locations that they then arranged in two different ways and at different times. In one condition—the control—the place was maintained in an orderly way. It was kept free from graffiti, litter, and rubbish. In the other condition—the experiment—exactly the same environment was arranged in a way where it looked like nobody monitored it or cared about it: Windows were broken, there was graffiti on the walls and litter all around. The researchers then secretly monitored the locations to observe whether people behaved differently when the environment was disordered. The results supported the theory. Their conclusion, published in the journal *Science* (Keizer et al., 2008), was that "one example of disorder, like graffiti or littering, can indeed encourage another, like stealing."

The first experiment was conducted in an alley that is frequently used to park bicycles. As in all of their experiments, the researchers created two conditions: one of order and the other of disorder. In the former, the walls of the alley were freshly painted; in the latter, they were tagged with graffiti. In both states a large sign prohibiting graffiti was put up so that it would not be missed by anyone who came to collect a bicycle. Researchers then attached a flyer promoting a nonexistent sports shop to all the bikes' handlebars. This flyer needed to be removed before a bicycle could be ridden. When owners returned, their behavior was secretly observed. There were no rubbish bins in the alley, so a cyclist had three choices. He could (1) take the flyer with him, (2) hang it on another bicycle (which the researchers counted as littering), or (3) throw it to the ground. When the alley contained graffiti, 69 percent of the riders littered, compared with 33 percent who littered when the walls were clean.

The other experiments were carried out in a similar way. In one, a temporary fence was used to close off a shortcut to a car park, except for a narrow gap. Two signs were erected, one telling people there was no throughway and the other saying that bicycles must not be left locked to the fence. In the "order" condition (with four bicycles parked nearby but not locked to the fence), 27 percent of people were prepared to trespass by stepping through the gap, whereas in the "disorder" condition (four bikes locked to the fence, in violation of the sign), 82 percent took the shortcut.

The most dramatic result, though, was the experiment that showed a doubling in the number of people who were prepared to steal in a condition of disorder. In this case an envelope with a €5 (US$6) note inside (and the note clearly visible through the address window) was left sticking out of a mailbox. In a condition of order, 13 percent of those passing took the envelope (instead of leaving it or pushing it into the box). But if the mailbox was covered in graffiti, 27 percent took the envelope. Even if the mailbox had no graffiti on it but the area around it was littered with paper, orange peel, cigarette butts, and empty cans, 25 percent still took the envelope.

In sum, these controlled experiments show that degraded surroundings can degrade behavior. The cleanliness and state of repair of a place obviously affect our attitudes and feelings. But locations that are neglected or badly maintained also give an impression of danger because a lack of occupancy can indicate a socially disorganized neighborhood. A sense of ownership or territoriality is often considered vital in making a place feel safer. If residents feel that the area beyond their doors does not belong to them, they will not feel responsible for its maintenance. As a result of this research, urban design should adopt measures to increase people's sense of territoriality.

Problematic Urban Design

This is the third factor that characterizes an unsafe or fear-provoking location. Several issues may cause or increase fear of crime in public areas: lack of surveillance, isolation, and lack of alternate routes.

Lack of Surveillance

A lack of surveillance caused by poor lighting or by the presence of nooks and crannies that could act as potential hiding spots makes people feel insecure. Passing along or through such areas can be a frightening experience because people have little control over the situation (Painter and Farrington, 1997).

The visual or real borders that separate areas owned by different actors or stakeholders should not become barriers to lines of sight between buildings and public spaces. Such a situation could cause a decrease in social control, which may increase crime and fear of crime. Awareness of the environment and the ability to see and understand what is happening are important in ensuring a feeling of control in any given situation (Parker, 1997a, 1997b; Poyner, 1997). The fear of crime can therefore be reduced by good lighting, clear lines of sight, and the elimination of hiding places for offenders (ILE, 1999). To improve the personal safety of potential victims, a potential offender and his/her facial features should be identifiable from a distance of at least 4 meters.

Isolation: Lack of Visibility by Others

Some locations—such as industrial estates, large office complexes, public transport stations, shopping centers, and city parks as well as multistory parking garages, underpasses, or semipublic areas within dwellings and blocks of high-rise buildings—are quiet and isolated during particular times of the day or night. The situation may be improved if these locations are populated or at least watched over by residents. The diversity of functions in a neighborhood is thus an important factor in avoiding huge mono-functional and isolated areas for which visibility by other humans is impossible to provide day and night.

Windows of dwellings that face public areas are found to have a strong reassuring effect on most people because they seemingly provide access to help, should it be needed. Major thoroughfares for pedestrians, as well as entrance areas to blocks of apartment buildings, should therefore be visible from dwellings, public buildings, cars, and so on. For the same reason, rooms or infrastructure designated for communal use in residential buildings should not be situated in the basement or in isolated parts of the building.

If social control is impossible to impose, quiet and semipublic areas (e.g., city parks, railway stations, pedestrian underpasses, bicycle sheds, storage spaces) may be closed off during certain times of the day. At the very least, the option to close these spaces should be provided. The general idea is, of course, to get these paths, routes, and spaces populated and well surveyed.

Lack of Orientation and Alternative Routes

Knowing where you are and which way to turn contributes to a feeling of security. In situations of personal danger, it is important to find the fastest and shortest way out. Good signposting is very important, especially in areas with poor visibility, to reassure people they can find an escape route if necessary. Alternative routes that avoid potential entrapment spots should also be provided for remote pedestrian routes and routes that pass through fear-generating area.

Tackling Crime and the Fear of Crime by Urban Planning and Architectural Design: Examples and Instruments

In Europe, as we have seen, CPTED-like crime-prevention approaches are also known as the *situational approach, designing-out crime* (DOC), or to stress the more social and organizational aspects of the approach, the *reduction of crime and the fear of crime by city maintenance, urban planning and architectural design* or the Situational Crime Reduction in Partnership Theory, also known as SCRIPT (van Soomeren, 2001).

Generally speaking, the European version of CPTED by whatever name is certainly strongly focused on social and organizational issues as well as the physical environment, but for the purpose of this chapter we will use the term CPTED.

In this section we look at a few examples of CPTED approaches as implemented in European countries:

1. Crime and the fear of crime in high-rise estates
2. Police labels to implement crime prevention, such as Secured by Design (UK) and the Police Label Safe/Secure Housing (1998, the Netherlands)
3. European standardization

Crime, the Fear of Crime, and Incivilities in High-Rise Estates

Many high-rise housing estates worldwide were built in the 1960s and '70s and were predominantly used as social or public housing. In most Western countries (Asia seems to be an exception here), these estates have run into serious trouble. Crime—in particular, the fear of crime and incivilities—soon began to hamper the Corbusier look-alike architectural structures and town planning. These estates were built as a kind of "poor man's Utopia" by idealistic architects. Examples can be found in all European countries, and most of the former Utopias have become crime-ridden nightmares (van Soomeren, 1995; in the UK, Hough and Mayhew, 1982)

From the 1980s and 1990s onward, many of these estates were either completely demolished or fundamentally redeveloped. What went wrong with the initial structures can be impressionistically sketched by looking at the work of Alice Coleman, *Utopia on Trial* (1985). In her book, Coleman launches a fierce attack on post-war blocks of apartment buildings (the alleged Utopias). Coleman does this in the shape of a court case (fictional, of course), complete with indictment, furnishing of proof, defendants, cross-examinations, and a guilty verdict. She bases her case on an extensive research study in three areas of London: two inner-city areas and one suburb. She includes more than 100,000 apartments and more than 4,000 single-family dwellings in her extremely detailed analysis. She compares the design of the apartment buildings with the design of "unplanned" pre-war single-family dwellings according to six indicators of social malaise, which she terms *incivilities*: litter, graffiti, vandal damage, children in care (!), urine, and feces. She did not research crime.

Coleman's "guilty" architectural features are very similar to those listed by Oscar Newman and are mainly put down to the large scale of the buildings (the number of apartments per block, the height of buildings, the number of blocks per complex) and accessibility (number of apartments per entrance, number of internal connecting gangways between blocks, number of sides from which the block is accessible, etc.). Coleman's message reads as follows: The more large scale and accessible a building, the more incivilities there will be.

Coleman doesn't stop there. In her book she includes a large number of social and sociodemographic variables. These include population structure, poverty, unemployment, concentration of problem households, selective migration, and the presence or absence of formal control. She concludes, however, that these factors do not explain—or, rather, do not sufficiently explain—the "social malaise." There is, however, one exception to this rule: Child density was found to influence the degree of social malaise in the complexes examined: "... High child densities are important and can mask the effect of design" (Coleman, 1985).

Coleman not only criticizes; she also indicates corrective or preventative measures that could be taken. The essence of her saving message is "Small is beautiful." Not large-scale buildings but small, not-too-accessible units. What she favors most are detached or semi-detached houses (1920s/1930s-type homes) with small, fenced-in front gardens and large back yards that border the back yards of their neighbors. As far as objections about the cost in terms of space and money are concerned, Coleman dismisses them as myths. She claims that the real grounds for building huge high-rise apartment buildings are neither financial nor spatial but instead are due to the caprices of architects and planners.

A Multibillion Nightmare

Based loosely on the ideas of Oscar Newman and Alice Coleman, tens of thousands of dwellings and thousands of estates have been demolished. With these being relatively new apartments, the costs ran—still run! —into billions of Euros. The dreams of several architects, planners, and engineers obviously became crime-ridden nightmares in which fear and incivilities ruled.

Police Initiatives: Secured by Design and Dutch Police Label Safe Housing

Secured by Design (UK)

In 1989 the police in the United Kingdom introduced Secured by Design (SBD), a scheme that is nowadays operated by most police forces in England and Wales (www.securedbydesign.com). This scheme was a huge success right from the start.

At this time, every British police force has trained specialists known as architectural liaison officers (ALOs), or, as they are known in London, crime-prevention design advisors (CPDAs). An insight into their role and skills can be found in a manual published by the Home Office (1997). In this manual, the police acknowledge that the physical environment can have a significant influence on criminal behavior, because the criminal relies on opportunity, anonymity, easy access, and quick escape routes.

The ALO police officers are essential for the implementation of the Secured by Design scheme. SBD is aimed at actively encouraging the adoption of improved security measures. Developments that have followed police guidance can receive approval and gain entitlement to use an official logo or label as an accolade and for promotion in sales literature. The police award the SBD label to new dwellings or housing estates that possess good crime-preventative and fear-reducing features. This police certificate obviously gives recipients a marketing advantage when it comes to selling or renting these houses.

The UK Secured by Design scheme has been evaluated by the Building Research Establishment (BRE). Pascoe (1992, 1993a, 1993b) recommends:

> *... returning to greater flexibility, shown by some of the designers, at the creation of the scheme. We suggest that this and other studies have identified the situational cues that an offender uses in his decision making. It is now possible to construct a risk model combining different patterns of cues to give an actual risk value for burglary for each specific building type, location and lay-out.*

By criticizing the fixed format of SBD and showing the great importance of the offender perspective, Tim Pascoe was actually promoting an approach taken in the Netherlands.

The Dutch Police Label Secured Housing

This program was introduced nationwide in 1996. The objective was, and is, to reduce crime (mainly burglary, car-related crime, theft, vandalism, and nuisance crime) and the fear of crime through environmental design, architectural measures, and target hardening.

Both the British and Dutch labels are aimed at activating and supporting the client (from private investor and owner to housing association). In the end it has to be the client who demands safety and security measures from architects and urban planners. SBD and the Dutch label help formulate these demands in a more clear and controllable fashion. In this respect, a police label is only a means to improve communication between clients and architects/planners.

The Dutch program borrowed Alexander's pattern language (Alexander, Ishikawa, and Silverstein, 1997) and focuses more on urban planning and landscaping. The offenders' perspective (Burik et al., 1991; Korthals Altes and van Soomeren, 1989) is another cornerstone of this scheme.

The language of the architectural world was chosen to develop the guidelines for crime prevention and fear reduction. The mission was to develop guidelines for new and existing houses as well as for new and existing environments on all spatial/geographical scale levels (district planning, building layout, building design, building components).

Altogether, two manuals were produced: one for new neighborhoods and one for existing neighborhoods, each containing about 50 requirements (see: Police Label Safe/Secure Housing and first prototype version, Korthals Altes and Woldendorp, 1994). Each of the 50 requirements has to be checked (okay = 1 point; not okay = 0 points), and in the end a fixed minimum number of points must be scored in order to acquire the police label. The manual makes use of a very strict page format. Each requirement is dealt with on a separate page.

The Extensive Manual for the Dutch Police Label

To compile the guidelines for the Secured Housing Label Manual, 55 patterns of design elements that could have possible crime-preventative and fear-reducing effects were derived from Alexander's work. Crime and the fear of crime are not isolated acts or feelings. Instead they can be seen as processes, a result of a series of spatial patterns. For the sake of analogy with the planning process, and following Alexander's example, the 55 patterns summarized in the manual were arranged from large to small scale levels (macro to micro). The approach taken in the manual can be likened to a parachute jump: In the beginning one has a good overall view of the area, and later on more and more details are revealed. In the manual, patterns are distinguished at several levels:

- Urban planning and design (size of the district, density, height and scale, access to the district by car and bicycle, etc.)
- Public areas (public lighting, open-air parking, private garages, playing facilities, tunnels and subways, bus stops, rear passages, including neighborhood management, maintenance, supervision, etc.)
- Layout (back yards, rear paths, etc.)
- Buildings (estates, semidetached houses, layout of single-family terraced houses, inner grounds, enclosed squares, etc.)
- Dwellings (orientation of living rooms, low roofs, main entrances, target hardening, etc.)

While parachute jumping, the ALOs can use the Secured Housing Label Manual as an automatic safety device that forces them to open their parachutes at the earliest moment possible. Acting too late—e.g., only checking target hardening of the houses—makes it impossible to gather enough points to award the Secured Housing Label, because in descending through the five levels and 55 patterns, each pattern has to be checked (okay = 1 point; not okay = 0 points). Once landed on the ground, a minimum number of points need to have been scored. In the manual every pattern adopts a very strict page format.

The Police Label for "New Estates"

When housing project developers or housing associations apply for Police Label Secured Housing, their building project and its environment must meet certain requirements. The label may be used only after the police have granted their permission. This permission cannot be given for a part of the project; it is all or nothing, an integral approach.

ALOs are, of course, not designers; they are not supposed to make plans, but they have to check housing against the patterns summarized in the manual. Therefore, these police officers have to be trained to be flexible in their thinking. Backed by the rigid structure of the manual, ALOs can negotiate with architects, planners, and builders. Together they will find enough flexibility in the manual. This flexibility is generated by:

- A combination of an objective (what) stated in rather broad terms and the concrete elaboration (how) that is presented for each of the 55 patterns. When there is doubt on one of the elaborated guidelines, it is always possible to return to the objective and find an alternative solution.
- A system of basic points and points that can provide compensation to enable the total score threshold to be attained.
- The relationship between different patterns/pages that is indicated in the manual, thus opening the door to yet another way of compensating for weaknesses in a plan or project.

A Police Label for Existing Environments

Based on experience with the label for new estates, a second label along the same lines was published for existing houses and neighborhoods. This label enables police officers to structure negotiations on safety and security with the various players involved in the maintenance of existing houses/dwellings, estates, environments, and neighborhoods (see Figure 12.16).

Because crime prevention in environments that already exist involves more players with vested interests, it was decided to break up the label for existing housing into three different certificates: level, certificate player, or stakeholder.

- Dwelling: Home ownership or renting a dwelling
- Complex/estate: Housing association, group of owners
- Environment/neighborhood: Local authorities

Hence, for each scale level, the most appropriate or potentially motivated player is given the opportunity to apply for a certificate. The police award the Police Label Secured Housing in an existing area when 60 percent of all dwellings and 60 percent of all complexes in a neighborhood obtain all three certificates.

A New Period and a Critical Note

Together with the Dutch Police Force, the owner of the intellectual property of the police label, the Ministry of the Interior/Home Office, decided that this label was sufficiently developed for use by the local

Figure 12.16 ____ Source: Armando Jongejan.

authorities. A few of the requirements had already found their way to the obligatory building codes and regulations (burglary-resistant doors, windows, lighting, etc.).

The national government decided that the local authorities are the natural players in the building world and they have to work together with the ALOs. But was this the right decision? Is this the right way to develop the quality of the Dutch Police Label Secured Housing? To take this product away from the Dutch police as a neutral player in the world of builders and project developers is arguable (see also: Jongejan, 2007; Jongejan and Woldendorp, 2012). In the Netherlands, more than 400 local authorities are responsible for developing new estates. Developing quality, accessibility, and standards for the creation a safe and secured environment is a big challenge for the Dutch local authorities and the National Centre for Crime Prevention and Safety. A change is certainly necessary. The answers will become apparent in a few years' time (see also: www.politiekeurmerk.nl).

Evaluation of SBD and the Dutch Police Label

Evaluations of the UK and Dutch schemes show very good results so far. Burglary drops sharply when this scheme is implemented in a new or existing environment (Nauta, 2004, shows a drop of about 80 percent in the risk of burglary!). Other opportunistic crimes such as theft, vandalism, and street violence also seem to go down after implementation of these schemes. In addition, the fear of crime is significantly reduced by the use of the police-label schemes (López and Veenstra, 2010).

However, seeing these types of labels as a good and finished product is probably the biggest threat to them. After their nationwide introduction, these labels were clearly successful and effective, but after a few decades their effect may very well begin to wane due to changes in crime patterns, perceptions, and the working methods of offenders, not to mention the changes in planning, architecture, and building that will take place. Hence, like every product, crime-prevention initiatives such as SBD or the Dutch Police Label also have to follow a normal life cycle (Berry and Carter, 1992).

When the effects of an initiative have bottomed out, management will have to make a reasoned decision to extend the life of their product by measures such as relaunching, providing additional resources, or re-innovation of the scheme. In the Netherlands the National Center for Crime Prevention and Safety (CCV) did so and asked for new research into burglaries, including interviewing burglars (Handel and van Soomeren, 2009) and the effect of the label (Lopez and Veenstra, 2010).

However, it would have been even wiser to define the label and manual right from the start as a process instead of a finished product. Essentially this process consists of structured negotiations between crime-prevention specialists and architects/planners that are aimed at combining the best knowledge and efforts from both expert worlds in order to prevent crime and to reduce fear. In this respect, it is useful to keep the roots of, for example, the Dutch label and its manual in mind:

- Research on environmental crime prevention
- Site-specific and building type-specific crime analysis
- Incorporation of the offenders' perspectives and working methods (police "prevention interviews" of offenders; see Burik, 1991; Handel and van Soomeren, 2009).

Crime analyses and interviews with offenders must be seen as an essential part to keep labels like SBD and the Dutch label up to date in a changing (criminal) environment. Hence, the big challenge is not only to "sell" more and more labels but also to develop a system—a continual research process—by which systemized police knowledge of the risks of crime and the perceptions and working methods of offenders is used to constantly adapt the labeling scheme. Part of this system should be a careful and constant evaluation of the risks encountered by labeled and nonlabeled houses, neighborhoods, and environments.

There are serious doubts as to whether the Dutch are still on the right track. By taking the scheme away from the police, one of the main success factors of the scheme was taken away, too. Whether the Dutch local authorities and the Centre for Crime Prevention and Safety will be able to devote enough energy and expertise to develop and maintain the system in the long run is questionable. On the other hand, this change from the police to local authorities is an experiment in itself and thus worth following.

European Standard on Designing Out Crime

An interesting initiative at the European level is the European standard on crime reduction by urban planning and building design (CEN, TC325, ENV 14383-2, TR 14383-2, and more standards).

Why Standardization?

Voluntary agreement among countries, institutes, and people as to what a product or process is, what it should look like, and what it should do or accomplish is important. For this purpose, standards are a key component of the united European market. But of course the idea of standardization can also be used within one multiagency group, because standardization facilitates communication between different participants or stakeholders working in a single process or implementing a project (e.g., crime prevention). Standards thus facilitate cooperation and collaboration, making processes more transparent. Following a standard is something people as well as organizations do on a purely voluntary basis: "Compliance is not compulsory."

In the mid-1990s it was decided to try and draft a general standard—in part, a process standard. This standard had to focus on the options available to local and regional authorities, urban planners, architects, and building engineers to reduce crime and the fear of crime together with the police, security firms, insurers, and residents.

A European Standard for the Reduction of Crime and the Fear of Crime by Urban Planning and Building Design: TC325

The Comité Europeen de Normalisation (CEN) is the official body that oversees the development of new standards. Looking from a distance, the process appears to be rather easy. All one has to do is write a short text—say, 20 pages—in which is explained how one "shall" reduce crime and the fear of crime by urban planning and building design. However, this work takes years and years because 100-percent consensus and agreement from all European countries and all European stakeholder organizations (police, architects, planners, security, and insurance) is essential. As we have already mentioned, a standard is a voluntary agreement.

Political agreement is reached in an official committee (a Technical Committee, or TC) set up for the purpose of making a standard. Expert Working Groups do the real work. In January 1996 the Technical Committee 325 of CEN (TC325) held its first meeting in Denmark. The scope of TC325 is:

> *Preparation of European standards on building design and urban planning to provide performance requirements for the prevention of crime in residential areas at new and existing housing, including local shops, in order to ensure safety and comfort and to minimise fear of violence. Standards on building products and security devices are excluded.*

It was decided to organize the work in Working Groups, and these WGs have so far produced the following standards:

- EN 14383-1: Terminology
- ENV 14383-2: Urban planning (later on converted in TR 14383-2)
- CEN-TS 14383-3: Dwellings

- CEN-TS 14383-4: Shops and offices
- CEN-TR 14383-5: Petrol stations (work in progress)
- CEN-TR 14383-6: Schools (work in progress)
- CEN-TR 14383-7: Facilities for public transportation, such as stations, stops, etc (work in progress)
- CEN-WD 14383-8: Measures to prevent ram raiding by cars (work in progress)

Standard on Urban Planning and Crime Reduction

As an example, we will concentrate here on the standard formulated by WG 2 of CEN TC325 on Urban Planning. (For an in-depth analysis of the consensus-forming process and its devastating effects in France, see also: Bibel Benbouzid's theses, 2011.)

The aim of WG 2 is to provide those engaged in urban planning and environmental crime prevention, as well as all stakeholders such as authorities and residents, with advice, guidance, and checklists on the effective multiagency action needed to minimize the risk of crime and the fear of crime. It is important to note that the text of the European standard for crime prevention by urban planning must be used in a concrete situation—for example, a new building plan on the outskirts of Paris, a plan for the renovation of an old harbor site in Amsterdam, or a plan for a city center in Seoul.

Introductory Questions: Where, What, and Who?

Although there may be a variety of players involved, in theory the approach is always simple. It starts with answering three questions:

- *Where?* Identify the exact location of the area and the type of area.
- *What?* Identify the crime problems that occur in this existing area or the problems that may occur in this new area in the future.
- *Who?* Identify the stakeholders involved in defining the problem and implementing the measures to prevent and reduce problems associated with crime.

When these three questions have been answered, three important issues remain to be solved:

- What guidelines can be given for CPTED strategies, measures, and actions that are necessary and feasible to make an area more safe and secure? The standard identifies several guidelines for the measures and actions that may be taken.
- How will these CPTED strategies, measures, and actions be implemented and executed?
- What will the cooperation process in which all stakeholders participate look like?

Process

The central idea of this European standard is that a group of stakeholders (police, planners, authorities, developers, residents) should look together at a concrete plan for building or refurbishment in, say, London, Madrid, Amsterdam, or Berlin. The stakeholders will then discuss the risk of crime and a list of strategies. A project team, working team, or working group is the platform for this discussion. A definitive set of strategies and concrete measures will be chosen according to space, time, budget, and personal preferences; the definitive measures will be recommended by the working group to an authority responsible for taking the final decision.

The standard presents a stepwise method to help and support an effective and efficient process of implementation, execution, and evaluation. This part of the standard is based on the international standards relating to quality management (ISO 9000 series; refer back to Figure 12.1).

A flowchart is presented showing essential steps, such as creating a general mission statement for a plan or project by the responsible authorities. These authorities have to initiate a process aimed at preventing crime and the fear of crime in a new or existing environment.

If not already in existence, a multidisciplinary working group that includes representatives of the stakeholder organizations involved in this particular design and planning process will be established. The working group will follow a procedure that includes six well-defined steps:

Step 1: Analyze. Analyze the present or future crime-preventative and fear-reducing performance of the environment specified in the mission statement.

Step 2: Objectives. The working group shall define more precisely the objectives being pursued and the time by which they should be attained (project plan, milestones).

Step 3: Plan. The working group shall draft a plan containing the following: a proposal of what is likely to happen in the near future if *no* measures are taken to prevent crime and/or the fear of crime; strategies that will probably be most effective to achieve the safety and security objectives formulated in step 2; and measures and actions to be taken, including costs and anticipated effects. The working group shall present the plan to the responsible body of authorities and all stakeholders.

Step 4: Decision by (local or regional) authorities.

Step 5: Action and implementation;

Step 6: Checking and corrective action. In case problems associated with crime and/or the fear of crime occur at an unacceptable level, authorities decide on corrective action, such as taking additional crime-prevention measures or further refurbishment of the area.

In short, this standard on the reduction of crime and the fear of crime by urban planning presents the user with:

- Ideas on how to tackle and prevent crime by urban planning.
- A procedure on how to organize the CPTED process in the best possible way. Once again, such a standard is *not* a law; it is not obligatory to use the standard. But if a group of stakeholders or local/regional authorities are in charge of a building project, they can agree on using this standard. From that moment on, the standard becomes a voluntary code that is followed by all stakeholders in the project.

Conclusion

Crime and the fear of crime are serious problems in the modern world. New approaches to reduce and prevent crime and the fear of crime (feelings of insecurity) have been developed in recent decades. One of those approaches is based on the experience that particular types of crime, such as burglary, car crime, street violence, vandalism, arson, and theft, as well as the fear of crime can be reduced by modifying the opportunity for crime in the built environment. This approach goes by the name of crime prevention through environmental design (CPTED) or designing-out crime (DOC).

In the beginning, the CPTED/DOC approach was hampered by some serious teething problems. Three valuable lessons (do's and don'ts) have been learnt from these teething problems:

- The first lesson was that some authors lost track of the human—the social—factor. By placing too much emphasis on the physical environment, these authors forgot the offender and victim. A more secure and safer city is the result of a safety policy that aims at the physical *and* the social environment (see also: Saville and Cleveland, 1998).
- The second lesson was that some practitioners focused completely on urban planning and building design, forgetting that every newly built neighborhood, public area, or building needs good maintenance. Without maintenance, every plan and design will deteriorate and eventually will be destroyed.
- A third lesson was that in the beginning, every group of crime-prevention practitioners was too eager to win the battle all on their own. It took some time before crime prevention was seen as the joint responsibility of different sectors of society, therefore needing a broad-based partnership of public authorities,

politicians, the private and voluntary sectors, police, residents, urban planners, architects, and the maintenance sector.

All these teething problems have since been overcome, resulting in what is often called the *second generation* of designing-out crime. Today CPTED/DOC is a real, effective, and mature crime-prevention policy.

In this chapter we have looked at the theoretical cornerstones of this approach, and we have seen examples of approaches that are trying to incorporate CPTED theory and practice into the everyday policy making of local, regional, and national bodies involved with pursuing the basic right for every citizen, as formulated in the European Urban Charter: to live in "a secure and safe town free, as far as possible, from crime, delinquency and aggression."

From the examples presented in this chapter we may learn valuable and practical lessons. One example—crime, fear of crime, and incivilities in **high-rise estates**—showed that CPTED in this case is part of a "billion-Euro initiative" to demolish and rebuild or renovate these estates.

These crime-related problems can clearly not be solved by one or only a few separate players, whether the police, the local authorities, housing associations, residents, or architects and planners. A partnership approach is thus a prerequisite for effective action.

The same goes for approaches to reduce the **fear of crime** and **feelings of insecurity**. Even though the relationship between the fear of crime and the real risk of crime is sometimes not consistent or is even missing, fear constitutes a social problem in its own right because it reduces the quality of urban life (residents who are afraid to go out, who avoid certain places, etc.). European approaches have shown that factors such as the presence or absence of people, the function of an area, visibility and surveillance, diversity, and city management and maintenance are important influences on fear. Physical and technical measures have a big impact, and in this respect one may even argue that the fear of crime is not a police issue but more an issue for architects, planners, city management, and the press. Again, a partnership approach is needed to bring down the levels of fear.

This **partnership approach** is fully incorporated in new schemes and initiatives such as the Secured by Design Label (UK), the Police Label Secured Housing (the Netherlands), and the European Standard for the reduction of crime and the fear of crime by urban planning and building design (CEN TC325). These labeling and standardization approaches are clearly beyond the simple CPTED approach of just target hardening. The European police labels and the European standard are complete packages containing technical, physical, social, and organizational measures to reduce crime and the fear of crime. We believe that this is clearly the way to go.

These examples show that CPTED and DOC are successful and effective approaches to reducing crime and the fear of crime. However, CPTED and DOC focus primarily on *physical measures*. European experiences (see the examples on high-rise buildings and the fear of crime) show that physical measures must be linked to *social measures*. Last but certainly not least, a further important element is *organizing and structuring the partnership process of reduction or prevention of crime*. The police labels and the European standard provide examples of structuring negotiation and implementation processes.

Hence, the most effective approach must be founded on three elements:

- *Physical approaches* such as CPTED and DOC focus on architecture, urban planning, target hardening, etc.
- *Social approaches* focus on victims, offenders, guardians, city management and maintenance, etc.
- *Organizational approaches* focus on structuring the partnership process of implementing measures.

We previously described this approach as *SCRIPT*: Situational Crime Reduction in Partnership Theory.

The challenge is, therefore, to convince national, local, and regional authorities that CPTED/DOC is an important option. Crime can be reduced by urban planning, architecture, design, and management. To be able to use this approach, authorities must know what to do—the ingredients, measures, and best practices. And last but not least, authorities must know *how* to do it—the implementation and the process.

Best practices, knowledge, and experiences will have to be disseminated in each country throughout Europe and even worldwide. A good structure for this exchange exists in the form of a worldwide organization and network specializing in CPTED: The International CPTED Association (ICA; www.cpted.net), which has separate chapters in continents and countries such as Latin America (www.cpted.cl), the UK Designing Out Crime Association (www.doca.org.uk), and the European Designing Out Crime Association, or E-DOCA (www.e-doca.eu).

About the Author

Paul van Soomeren is executive director of DSP-groep (www.DSP-groep.nl), a research and consultancy bureau based in Amsterdam, the Netherlands, specializing in urban challenges such as crime prevention, CPTED, health and safety, youth, welfare, and culture.

Mr. Soomeren (born 1952) studied social geography and, subsequently, urban and regional planning at the University of Amsterdam. He worked at the Ministry of Justice and Ministry of Interior Affairs

(National Crime Prevention Institute) for three years before going on to found the DSP-groep in 1984.

DSP-groep currently has a total of 60 staff members, all of whom have worked in government, private institutions, universities, or commercial organizations. DSP-groep is an independent research and consultancy firm specializing in urban planning and design, crime prevention, education, sports/leisure, art and culture, and social management. It carries out assignments for local and national government, European institutions, nonprofit organizations, and private companies.

Mr. Soomeren is director of the board of the International CPTED Association (ICA) and the European Designing Out Crime Association (www.E-DOCA.eu) and a visiting professor at the University of Salford's Adelphi Research Institute (UK).

References

Alexander, C., Ishikawa, S., Silverstein, M., 1977. A Pattern Language. Oxford University Press, New York, NY, USA.

Berry, G., Carter, M., 1992. Assessing Crime Prevention Initiatives: The First Steps. Home Office, Crime Prevention Unit, London, UK.

Benbouzid, B., 2011. La prevention situationelle (genese et developpement d'une science pratique 1965–2005), Thèse de doctorat de géographie, d'aménagement et d'urbanisme, Université Lumière Lyon 2, Ecole Nationale des Travaux Publics de l'Etat, Lyon, France.

Bottoms, A.E., Xantos, P., 1981. Housing policy and crime in the British public sector. In: Brantingham, P.J., Brantingham, P.L. (Eds.), Environmental Criminology. Sage, Beverly Hills, CA, USA.

Bottoms, A. E., 1987. Environmental criminology and its relevance for crime prevention. In: Junger-Tas, J., Rutting, A., Wilzing, J. (eds.) Crime Control in Local Communities in Europe (the Cranfield Conference 1987). Lochem, the Netherlands.

Bourke, J., 2005. Fear (A Cultural History). Virago Press, London, UK.

Brantingham, P.J., Brantingham, P.L. (Eds.), 1981. Environmental Criminology. Sage, Beverly Hills, CA, USA.

Brantingham, P. J., and Brantingham, P. L., 1980. Residential burglary and urban form. In: Criminology Review Yearbook, originally: Urban Studies, 12 (3), Oct. 1975, pp. 475–486.

Brantingham, P.J., Brantingham, P.L., 1975. The spatial patterning of Burglary. Harv. J. 14 (2).

Brown, B.B., Altman, I., 1981. Territoriality and residential crime: a conceptual framework. In: Brantingham, P.J., Brantingham, P.L. (Eds.), Environmental Criminology. Sage, Beverly Hills, CA, USA.

Burdett, R., Sudjic, D., 2010. The Endless City. Phaidon Press, London, UK.

Burdett, R., Sudjic, D., 2011. Living in the Endless City. Phaidon Press, London, UK.

Burik, A. van, van Overbeeke, R., van Soomeren, P., 1991. Modus operandi woninginbraak: eindrapportage daderonderzoek, Van Dijk, Van Soomeren en Partners/DSP- groep, Amsterdam, the Netherlands.

Colquhoun, I., 2004. Design Out Crime, Creating Safe and Sustainable Communities. University of Hull, Hull, UK.

Carter, R.L., Hill, K.Q., 1979. The Criminal's Image of the City. Pergamon Press, New York, NY, USA.

Chainey, S., Ratcliffe, J., 2005. GIS and Crime Mapping. Wiley, USA.

Cisneros, H.G., 1995. Defensible Space: Deterring Crime and Building Community. US Department of Housing and Urban Development, Washington, DC, USA.

Clarke, R.V.G. (Ed.), 1997. Situational Crime Prevention: Successful Case Studies, second ed. Harrow and Heston, Albany, NY, USA.

Clarke, R. V. G., 2001. Crime Prevention Through Environmental Design, paper presented at EU conference in Sündsvall, Sweden.

Clarke, R.V.G., Cornish, D.B., 1985. Modelling offenders' decisions: a framework for research and policy. In: Tonry, M. Morris, N. (Eds.), Crime and Justice, vol. 6. University of Chicago Press, Chicago, IL, USA.

Clarke, R., Hope, T. (Eds.), 1984. Coping with Burglary (Research Perspectives on Policy) Kluwer/Nijhoff, Dordrecht, the Netherlands.

Clarke, R.V.G., Mayhew, P., 1980. Designing Out Crime. HMSO Home Office, London, UK.

CLRAE, 1987. Conference of Local and Regional Authorities of Europe, Local Strategies for the Reduction of Urban Insecurity in Europe. Barcelona, Spain.

CLRAE, 1997. Conference of Local and Regional Authorities of Europe, Crime and Urban Insecurity in Europe: The Role and Responsibilities of Local and Regional Authorities, Erfurt, Germany.

Coleman, A., 1985. Utopia on Trial (Vision and Reality in Planned Housing). Hilary Shipman, London, UK.

COPS, 2005. Crime Opportunity Profiling of Streets (COPS); A Quick Crime Analysis—Rapid Implementation Approach. Building Research Establishment BRE, Garston, Watford, UK.

Cornish, D.B., Clarke, R.V.G., 1986. The Reasoning Criminal. Springer-Verlag, New York, NY, USA.

Cozens, P., 2005. Designing Out Crime, From Evidence to Action. Office of Crime Prevention, Department of Premier and Cabinet, Sydney, Western Australia.

Crowe, T.D., 1991. Crime Prevention Through Environmental Design: Applications of Architectural Design and Space Management Concepts. National Crime Prevention Institute, Butterworth-Heinemann, Boston, MA, USA.

Davey, C., Wootton, A.B., Cooper, R., Press, M., 2005. Design against crime: extending the reach of crime prevention through environmental design. Secur. J. 18, 39–51.

DOE, 1994. Planning Out Crime Circular 5/94. HMSO, London, UK.

DETR, 1999. Towards an Urban Renaissance, Final Report of the Urban Task Force.

ENV 14383-2, 2004. European Standard on Crime Prevention by Urban Planning and Building Design (also available in every national Standardization Institute), later converted to TR 14383-2, CEN, Brussels, Belgium.

European Sourcebook of Crime and Criminal Justice Statistics, 2003. ESC France, Home Office UK, WODC The Netherlands, Boom Juridische Uitgeverij Meppel, the Netherlands.

Duclos, D., 2006. Retour sur la grande Révolte des banlieues françaises, Le Monde Diplomatique.

Farrington, D. P., and Welsh, B. C., 2002. Effects of Improved Street Lighting on Crime: A Systematic Review, Home Office Research Study 252, Home Office, London, UK.

Felson, M., 2002. Crime and Everyday Life. Sage Publications, Thousand Oaks, CA, USA.

Flight, S., van Soomeren, P. Design Against Kerb-Crawling: Tippelzones (Vice Zones) - European Experiences in Displacement, paper presented at the 9th ICA Conference 2004, Brisbane, Australia.

Flight, S., van Egmond, P., 2011. Hits en hints: De mogelijke meerwaarde van ANPR voor de opsporing (with English summary). DSP-groep Amsterdam/Rotterdam, the Netherlands.

Florida, R., 2008. Who's Your City? How the Creative Economy Is Making the Place Where You Live the Most Important Decision of Your Life. Basic Books, New York, NY, USA.

Gardiner, R.A., 1978. Design for Safe Neighborhoods. National Institute of Law Enforcement and Criminal Justice, US Department of Justice, GPO, Washington, DC, USA.

Gensch, V., und B. Zimmer, 1980. Gewalt gegen Frauen in Kassel, Arbeitsbericht des Fachbereichs Stadt- und Landschaftsplannung, Gesamthochschule Kassel.

Gill, M. (Ed.), 2003. CCTV Perpetuity Press, Leichester, UK.

Hajonides, T., et al., 1987. Buiten gewoon veilig, Stichting Vrouwen, Bouwen Wonen, Goossens/Mets, Rotterdam, the Netherlands.

Handel, C. van den, van Soomeren, P., 2009. Hoe doen ze het toch? Modus operandi (MO) van woninginbraken. Ministry of Interior/DSP-groep, the Haag/Amsterdam, the Netherlands.

Heal, K., Laycock, G. (Eds.), 1986. Situational Crime Prevention: From Theory into Practice. HMSO, London, UK.

Hesseling, R., 1994. Displacement: a review of the empirical literature. In: Clarke, R.V.G. (Ed.), Crime Prevention Studies, vol. 3. Criminal Justice Press, Monsey, New York, NY, USA.

Home Office, 1997. Police Architectural Liaison Manual of Guidance. Crime Reduction College, York, UK.

Hough, M. en P. Mayhew, 1982. Crime and Public Houding (proceedings of a workshop held in September 1980). Research and Planning Unit Paper 6, Home Office, London.

ICVS, 2000. Kesteren, J. van, P. Mayhew, and P. Nieuwbeerta (2000). Criminal Victimization in Seventeen Industrialized Countries (key findings from the International Crime Victims Survey), WODC, Ministry of Justice, the Hague, the Netherlands.

ILE, 1999. Guide for Crime and Disorder Reduction Through a Public Lighting Strategy (Author: K. Painter), and Lighting and Crime (Author: K. Pease), Warwickshire, UK.

Jacobs, J., 1961. The Death and Life of Great American Cities. Random House, New York, NY, USA.

Jeffery, C.R., 1971. Crime Prevention Through Environmental Design. Sage, Beverly Hills, CA, USA.

Jongejan, A., 2007. Urban Planning in the Living Environment Using the Dutch "Police Label Secured Housing," Madrid, Spain.

Jongejan, J., and Woldendorp, T., 2012. (in press) A Successful CPTED Approach: The Dutch "Police Label Secure Housing," special edition *Journal of the Built Environment*, Rachel Armitage (ed.), International Perspectives of Planning for Crime.

Keizer, K., Lindenberg, S., Steg, L., 2008. The spreading of disorder. Science, 1681–1685.

Korthals Altes, H.J., van Soomeren, P., 1989. Modus operandi woninginbraken. Bureau Landelijk Coördinator Voorkoming Misdrijven, the Haag, the Netherlands.

Korthals Altes, H.J., Woldendorp, T., 1994. Handboek Politiekeurmerk Veilig Wonen. Stuurgroep Experimenten Volkshuisvesting, Rotterdam, the Netherlands.

Kube, E., 1982. Städtebau, Wohnhausarchitektur und Kriminalität: Prevention statt Reaction. Kriminalistik-verlag, Heidelberg, Germany.

Landry, C., 2000. The Creative City: A Toolkit for Urban Innovators. Comedia/ Earthscan, London/Sterling, VA, USA.

Landry, C., 2006. The Art of City-Making. Routledge, Earthscan.

Loef, C.J., 1985. Aanranding en verkrachting. Gemeente Amsterdam, Bestuursinformatie, afd. onderzoek en statistiek, Amsterdam, the Netherlands.

López, M.J.J., Veenstra, C., 2010. Een veilige wijk, een veilig gevoel. RCM-advies and Experian, the Haag, the Netherlands.

Manière de Voir, 2006. Banlieues, trente ans d'histoire et de révoltes. Manière de Voir, numéro 89, Oct.-Nov. 2006.

Mawby, R.I., 1977. Kiosk Vandalism: a sheffield study. Br. J. Criminol. 17 (1).

Mayhew, P., Clarke, R. V. G., Hough, M., Sturman, A., 1976. Crime as Opportunity, Home Office Research Study No. 34, HMSO, London, UK.

Metz, G., Rijpkema, H., 1979. Mythen en feiten over verkrachting. Groningen, the Netherlands.

Michael, S. E., Saville, G., Warren, J. W., 2012. A CPTED Bibliography: Publications Related to Urban Space, Planning, Architecture and Crime Prevention Through Environmental Design, 1975-2011, Safe Cascadia, Port Townsend, WA, USA.

Nauta, O., 2004. De effectiviteit van het Politie Keurmerk Veilig Wonen®. DSP-groep, Amsterdam, the Netherlands.

Newman, O., 1972. Defensible Space: Crime Prevention Through Urban Design. MacMillan, New York, NY, USA, (republished by Architectural Press, London, in 1973).

Newman, O., 1996. Creating Defensible Space. US Department of Housing and Urban Development, Office of Policy Development and Research, Washington, DC, USA.

Newman, O., 1973. Architectural Design for Crime Prevention. Law Enforcement Assistance Administration, US Department of Justice, GPO, Washington, DC, USA.

Newman, O., 1975. Design Guidelines for Creating Defensible Space. GPO, Washington, DC, USA.

Newman, O., 1979. Community of Interest. Doubleday, New York, NY, USA.

Newman, O., Franck, K., 1980. Factors Influencing Crime and Instability in Urban Housing Developments. National Institute of Justice, GPO, Washington DC, USA.

Painter, K.A., 1996. Street lighting, crime and fear of crime: a summary of research. In: Bennett, T.H. (Ed.), Preventing Crime and Disorder: Targeting Strategies and Responsibilities. Institute of Criminology, University of Cambridge, Cambridge, UK, pp. 313-351.

Painter, K., Farrington, D.P., 1997. The dudley experiment. In: Clarke, R.V.G. (Ed.), Situational Crime Prevention: Successful Case Studies, second ed. Harrow and Heston, Albany, NY, USA.

Pascoe, T., 1992. Secured by Design: A Crime Prevention Philosophy. Cranfield Institute of Technology, Cranfield, UK.

Pascoe, T., 1993a. Domestic Burglaries: The Burglars' View. Building Research Establishment (BRE Information paper 19/1993), Garston, Watford, UK.

Pascoe, T., 1993b. Domestic Burglaries: The Police View. Building Research Establishment (BRE Information paper 19/1993), Garston, Watford, UK.

Parker, J., 1997a. Safe Cities 3: Relationships between Crime, Urban Insecurity and the Built Environment. Council of Europe International Conference—Crime and Urban Insecurity in Europe: The Role and Responsibilities of Local and Regional Authorities, Erfurt, Germany.

Parker, J., 1997b. Urban Environment and Crime: Some Pointers Towards Policies and Action. Council of Europe, Congress of Local and Regional Authorities of Europe, Strasbourg, France.

Parker, J., 2000. Safer Spaces and Places: Reducing Crime by Urban Design. Council of Europe international conference on the relationship between the physical urban environment and crime patterns, Szczecin, Poland.

Ratcliffe, J., 2012. The Spatial Extent of Criminogenic Places on the Surrounding Environment: A Change-Point Regression of Violence Around Bars. Geographical Analysis.

Pawson, R., Tilley, N., 1997. Realistic Evaluation. Sage Publications, London, UK.

Pease, K., 1992. Preventing burglary on a British public housing estate. In: Clarke, R.V.G. (Ed.), Situational Crime Prevention: Successful Case Studies, first ed. Harrow and Heston, Albany, NY, USA.

Police Label Safe/Secure Housing, 1998. van Zwam, C., van Bakel, B., Jongejan, A., van de Kant, F., van der Nat, C., Reijnhoudt, P., Scherpenisse, R., van Soomeren, P., Vroombout, M. Police Label Secured Housing® New Estates, (Politiekeurmerk Veilig Wonen® Nieuwbouw Trans. from Dutch), Steering Group Experiments Public Housing (SEV), Rotterdam, the Netherlands.

Poyner, B., 1981. Crime prevention and the environment: street attacks in city centres, In: Police Research Bulletin, No. 37, London, UK, pp. 10–18.

Poyner, B., 1983. Design Against Crime (Beyond Defensible Space). Butterworth, London, UK.

Poyner, B., 1997. Situational crime prevention in two parking facilities. In: Clarke, R.V.G. (Ed.), Situational Crime Prevention: Successful Case Studies, first ed. Harrow and Heston, Albany, NY, USA.

RPD: Rijksplanologische Dienst, 1985. Maakt de gelegenheid de dader? Rijks Planologische Dienst, Ministerie van VROM, Staatsuitgeverij the Hague, the Netherlands.

Ramsay, M., 1982. City-Centre Crime: The Scope for Situational Prevention, Research and Planning Unit Paper 10, Home Office, London, UK.

Rhodes, W.M., Conly, C., 1981. Crime and mobility: an empirical study. In: Brantingham, P.J., Brantingham, P.L. (Eds.), Environmental Criminology. Sage, Beverly Hills, CA, USA.

Saville, G., Cleveland, G., 1998. 2nd Generation CPTED: An Antidote to the Social Y2K Virus of Urban Design. School of Criminology and Criminal Justice, Florida State University and Toronto District School Board.

Selm, E., van, A., Lodder, M., Buitenhuis, Arkenstein, M., 1985. Eng op straat. Wageningen, the Netherlands.

Shaw, C.R., 1929. Delinquency Areas. University of Chicago Press, Chicago, IL, USA.

Shaw, C.R., McKay, H.D., 1931. Social Factors in Juvenile Delinquency. Government Printing Office, Washington, DC, USA.

Shaw, C.R., McKay, H.D., 1969. Juvenile Delinquency and Urban Areas. University of Chicago Press, Chicago, IL, USA, 1942 (revised edition: 1969).

Skogan, W.G., Maxfield, M.G., 1981. Coping with Crime, Individual, and Neighbourhood Reactions. Sage, Beverly Hills, CA, USA.

United Nations, 1995. Economic and Social Council, Resolution 1995/9, 49th plenary meeting 24 July 1995, Guidelines for the Prevention of Urban Crime, Annex, Guidelines for Cooperation and technical Assistance in the field of Urban Crime Prevention.

van Dijk, A.G., van Soomeren, P., Walop, M., 1980. Vandalisme in Amsterdam. Universiteit van Amsterdam, Amsterdam, the Netherlands.

van Dijk, A.G., van Soomeren, P., Walop, M., 1982. Vandalism in Amsterdam: An Ecological Approach. International Colloquium on Vandalism, Sorbonne, Paris.

van Soomeren, P. (with P. de Savornin Lohman, H. Caron, L. de Savornin Lohman and B. van Dijk; 1987) Gebouwde Omgeving en Criminaliteit, Ministerie van Volkshuisvesting, Ruimtelijke Ordening en Milieubeheer, the Hague, the Netherlands.

van Soomeren, P., 1995. Dream, Nightmare and Awakening: Experiences at the Crossroads of Town Planning, Architecture, Security and Crime Prevention, Paper The International Forum on Promoting Safer Cities and Secure Housing, September 1995, Tokyo, Japan.

van Soomeren, P., 2001. Situational Crime Reduction in Partnership Theory, Proposal to EU Oisin program, Van Dijk van Soomeren en Partners, Amsterdam, the Netherlands.

van Soomeren, P., Woldendorp, T., 1996. Secured by Design in the Netherlands. Secur. J. 7, 185–195.

van Soomeren, P., Wever, J., 2005. Review of Costs and Benefits Analysis in Crime Prevention. European Crime Prevention Network (ECPN), European Commission, Brussels, Belgium.

Vanderveen, G., 2006. Interpreting Fear, Crime, Risk and Unsafety (Conceptualization and Measurement). Research School Safety and Security in Society, BJu Legal Publishers, The Netherlands.

Vollaard, B., van Ours, J.C., 2011. Does regulation of built-in security reduce crime? Evidence from a natural experiment. Econ. J. 121, 485–504.

Voordt, T. van der, Wegen, H. van, 1990. Sociaal Veilig Ontwerpen. Technische Universiteit Delft, Delft, The Netherlands.

Wekerle, G.R., Whitzman, C., 1992. Safe Cities: Guidelines for Planning, Design, and Management. American Planning Association Book Service.

Wood, E., 1961. Housing Design, A Social Theory. Citizens, Housing and Planning Council of New York, New York, NY, USA.

Important Websites:

European Designing Out Crime Association: www.e-doca.eu
Designing Out Crime Association UK: www.doca.org.uk
International CPTED Association (worldwide): www.cpted.net
CPTED Latin America: www.cpted.cl

13

CHECKLIST FOR A PROGRAM OF SUCCESSFUL CRIME PREVENTION THROUGH ENVIRONMENTAL DESIGN

Susan Geason, Ph.D. and Paul W. Wilson, Ph.D.

CHAPTER OUTLINE

It is 2013 and Design Out Crime (DOC) has become well known as a crime-prevention measure, not only across Australia but also internationally. It cannot be claimed, however, that it is adopted and implemented as much as many of us would like. Nevertheless, characteristics of programs using CPTED that we outlined many years ago are as relevant today as they were then.

Signs of a Successful CPTED Program

The following factors are characteristic of a CPTED program. The greater number in operation in your neighborhood or housing development, the more successful the program will be and the less likely you will be burgled or assaulted.

- Houses and apartments are situated where they are easily observable.
- Exits and entrances can be seen from the street.
- There is sufficient lighting to deter intruders.
- Solid-core doors have been used on all exterior exits.
- All residences have security locks and one-way viewers.
- Children's play areas can easily be seen from windows.
- Rooms for family use are positioned for surveillance of the outside.
- Streets are wide and straight enough to give patrolling police an unobstructed view.
- Houses and apartments are clearly numbered.

- Residents have off-street parking and can see it from their houses.
- Cul-de-sacs control the way in and out of the residential areas.
- Garages are totally enclosed.
- Chain-link fences rather than privacy fences are used and are 7 feet tall.
- Landscaping is designed so intruders cannot hide behind shrubbery.
- Police patrol cars can easily reach all sides of a building.
- Keys or entry phones control access to buildings.
- In apartment buildings, there are sufficient security guards, building maintenance is adequate, and the landlord has a fair eviction policy.
- Tenant storage areas are located in secure places.
- The building, house, or apartment expresses a sense of defensible space, e.g.:
  - Buildings are set far enough back from the street to create a semiprivate space than can deter an intruder from entering.
  - Houses have been clustered and buildings are small enough to create social cohesion and defensible spaces.
  - The intended use of spaces is clear.
  - The incompatible use of spaces has been avoided.
  - Landlords and town planners have provided enough recreational facilities to create social cohesion.
- Recreational areas are enclosed by chain-link fencing.
- Adequate social services and crisis and intervention services are available.
- There are sufficient self-help activities such as tenant associations.
- Sufficient security surveys and inspection programs have been carried out.
- Adequate crime-prevention programs exist.

Broader Planning Strategies

A number of criminologists have looked at the wider planning aspects of crime prevention through environmental design. In *Design Against Crime: Beyond Defensible Space* (1983), for example, Barry Poyner makes the following suggestions:

- Privatize residential streets
- Limit pedestrian access
- Separate residential from commercial uses
- Limit access to the rear of houses
- Block access from open land
- Arrange apartment doors and windows carefully
- Allocate residential child density
- Favor pedestrian overpasses rather than underpasses

- Make sure schools are visible from other buildings
- Keep school buildings compact
- Encourage resident caretakers in schools

In interviews with Marcus Felson in 1987, Brantingham and Brantingham also described planning strategies to prevent crime, including:

- Siting a youth hangout in view of an all-night taxi stand
- Letting recreation center caretakers live in
- Building crime-impact planning into early design stages
- In high-rise buildings for the elderly, siting recreation rooms on the first floor with a direct view of the doors
- Regulating the flow of adolescents by carefully siting fast-food shops and electronic games arcades

Felson also reported the following suggestions from James Wise:

- Minimize obstructions and use bright pastel paints to protect flows through parking structures.
- Carefully position bank tellers, doors, and flows of customers to discourage bank robberies.
- Site bars and pubs in such a way as to create informal social control.
- Provide specific crime-prevention training for facilities managers.

Other ideas cited by Felson include:

- Design parks and parking lots in long strips to maximize visibility from passersby.
- Do away with open-campus designs.
- Use telecommunications and computers to reduce the size of offices and to develop "scattered site" business practices.
- Reduce the size of facilities catering to young males—high schools, for example—to maximize adult surveillance.

14

CPTED IN THE TWENTY-FIRST CENTURY[1]

Timothy D. Crowe, Ph.D. and Severin Sorensen, CPP

CHAPTER OUTLINE

Over the years CPTED concepts have been examined, researched, and refined, and CPTED is now applied in more types of places. CPTED practitioners must continually update their strategies to adapt

[1] Originally from Crowe, T. (2000) *Crime Prevention Through Environmental Design in the Twenty-First Century*, Butterworth-Heinemann, Boston, MA, USA. Updated by Severin Sorensen CPP (2012) *The Handbook of Loss Prevention and Crime Prevention* (5th ed.), Elsevier, Amsterdam, the Netherlands.

to new technologies, regulations, standards and guidelines, and crime challenges that impact use of space. Consequently, CPTED in the 21st century requires as much attention to the future use of properties and settings as it did in the past. But the transition to this new century is one that points toward an explosion of technological and space management advances in the use of the environment to promote behavior that is desirable and conducive to human existence.

Leadership in Energy and Environmental Design

As with CPTED, some of the leadership in energy and environmental design (LEED) concepts complements security concerns, whereas other facets conflict with physical security principles. The LEED Green Building Rating System represents an effort to provide a national standard for what constitutes a "green building." It aims to improve occupants' well-being as well as buildings' environmental performance and economic returns using established and innovative practices, standards, and technologies.

The Transition to the Future of CPTED

Although CPTED is a self-evident concept that seems like common sense to many, there is a great deal of science behind it suggesting that there are particular ways that CPTED can be applied to obtain the greatest benefits in reducing crime opportunity and fear of crime. Research and assessment of CPTED since 1973 has confirmed the utility of many CPTED aspects; however, criminal justice research has also challenged conventional wisdom. CPTED concepts are not easily blueprinted and should not blindly meet all requirements; rather, CPTED concepts are more of a cookbook of strategies whereby certain strategies are appropriate for specific types and uses of places. One recommendation does not fit all situations.

The greatest impediment to the widespread use of CPTED is ignorance and lack of unity in technical approaches. Now, after nearly 40 years of CPTED experimentation, many individuals have heard of CPTED; however, its principles are not applied consistently throughout all domains or geographies. Many schools of CPTED thinking have evolved, from the simple to the scientific:

1. Oscar Newman (the Newman School) introduced the formal concept of defensible space and crime prevention through environmental design. His early work focused on the use of natural "access control, surveillance, and territoriality."

2. Tim Crowe (the Crowe School) later examined Newman's concepts and formalized CPTED into its current orthodoxy. The Crowe interpretation of CPTED incorporated Newman's earlier work and moved beyond natural access control, surveillance, and territoriality to include natural, mechanical, procedural means. Crowe also introduced the concepts of "image maintenance and situational activity support."
3. The next generation of CPTED practitioners (called the Florida School) found new ways of applying CPTED to specific locations and were some of the first practitioners to get CPTED adopted into formal codes and planning guidelines. Some of these CPTED practitioners have more recently coined the phrase *Second-Generation CPTED* to distinguish their recent work from the original work.
4. Several research-based CPTED scholars, most notably from the UK Home Office and Rutgers University (Ron Clarke), found that CPTED is an important part of a much larger rubric of "situational crime-prevention" strategies. There are many other contributors to CPTED from Australia, Canada, the United Kingdom, and the United States, but the previously listed schools represent the primary threads of thought on CPTED today as well as ASIS International, Facilities Physical Security Measures, ASIS GDL FPSM 2009 Guideline.

In this chapter, the authors relate what is typically considered CPTED orthodoxy, or the school of thought promoted by the late Timothy Crowe, Ph.D. According to Crowe, these are the factors necessary for CPTED to make the transition to wide acceptability and use:

- *Education and training.* CPTED must be included in professional and academic education and training. Legislators, planning board members, and professional societies need to become oriented toward CPTED immediately so that their future decisions reflect a commitment to its concepts.
- *Codes.* Current codes, regulations, standards, and guidelines governing all aspects of the physical environment need to be improved to incorporate CPTED concepts.
- *Design review.* CPTED concepts need to be included in an expanded concept of design review, which emphasizes interagency and interdisciplinary approaches to making better decisions about the design and use of the environment.
- *Code enforcement.* The uneven and inconsistent enforcement of existing codes is a major cause of the deterioration of our communities. Interdisciplinary approaches to code enforcement must be used as a tool in prevention of decay and in revitalization of those communities.
- *Litigation.* The courts are rapidly becoming a tool for forcing people to make better decisions about human space. It is human nature to overlook all the good reasons for doing things right in

the first place (e.g., quality of life, profit, aesthetics, reduced victimization, and loss) and wait for civil law to require that changes be made, often at great cost.
- *Documentation.* CPTED successes must be documented in multimedia presentations that ensure a wide dissemination of the concepts and a permanent record of how to use those concepts to avoid repeating past mistakes.

CPTED Definitions

The definition of CPTED used by NCPI is:

> *... the proper design and effective use of the built environment can lead to a reduction in the fear and incidence of crime, and an improvement in the quality of life.*

Put simply, CPTED is the design or redesign of the built environment to reduce crime opportunity and the fear of crime at a specific place. CPTED is most favorably implemented by multidisciplinary teams of stakeholders focused on reducing crime opportunity and fear of crime at specific places. Desirable secondary benefits of CPTED are lower crime rates, greater sense of community, more beautified properties, and higher property values.

CPTED in the New Millennium

New technologies, new challenges, and new uses of spaces will create additional need for CPTED strategies to reduce crime opportunity and fear of crime.

Modern advances in technology and building management systems will enable an explosion of technological and space management advances in the use of the built environment. The following are a few of the many topics related to CPTED that will be part of the ongoing development of human experience in the early 21st century.

Information and Communications Technology

The emergence of the Internet, embedded computing devices, and high-speed network communications has created opportunities and challenges for the security professional. More information and methods to secure places are available; however, the use and application of CPTED concepts remain germane and important to best practices in the industry. Areas where CPTED concepts apply include reducing crime opportunity in these new ways:
- Protecting and discouraging crime on information system superhighways.

- Protecting mobile places and situations where geography is variable, such as is now made available through the merger of radio, telephone, smart phone, and television technology.
- Protecting the personal identity and financial information of an estimated 365 million Apple 5 mobile devices and 650 million Android devices currently in consumer hands (*USA Today,* July 12, 2012).
- Audio loops for the hearing impaired and the incorporation of other ADA hardware into security applications such as voice-activated entry and security systems.
- Microspace implants of microchips for digital tagging and information storage and retrieval.
- IP advanced access control and surveillance technologies enabling more "eyes on the street."
- Texting (SMS), Facebook, Twitter, LinkedIn, YouTube, and other social networks will increase connectivity of individuals but will also introduce additional security risks that can be mitigated by CPTED concepts.

Housing

- Higher density housing in cities
- Higher numbers of housing in rural and resort areas enabled by virtual work and virtual employee opportunities
- Property reuse and repurposing challenges requiring shuffle-housing for changing needs of second and third generations of extended families
- Co-housing for the maintenance of identity and control for family and near-family groups
- Detachable housing for changing urban scenes
- Collapsible housing for unattended protection and storage
- Adjustable room size for smaller, more defensible space
- Movable yards with window or dumbwaiter access
- Floating communities

Transportation

- Electric vehicles, hybrids, hover vehicles
- Service/frontage and residential pass-through roads
- Adjustable streets
- Instant cul-de-sacs
- Automatic speed/collision controls
- Robotics
- Digital camera-controlled autopilot for hands-free navigation
- Infrared and radar for collision avoidance

- Integrated gas- and battery-operated vehicles for fuel efficiency of up to 200 miles to the gallon
- Standard use of GPS and concierge service for obtaining directions and monitoring the safety of the vehicle and occupants
- Particle-beam conversion of humans and transport
- Virtual reality trips for shopping, medical care, and recreation

Institutional

- Biospheres
- Closed school campuses, lockdowns, badges for students, and close-circuit television (CCTV)
- Behavioral space management/design
- Remote services/monitoring/treatment
- Robotics/bionics

Commercial/Retail/Industrial

Disposable businesses

- Disposable centers
- Remote shopping
- Instant products
- Information/communications

Social Recognition/Control

- New social networks
- Behavior incentives
- Visual accessibility
- Property values/rights
- Legendary health rediscoveries (e.g., kudzu)

Materials/Construction

- Pre-built modular construction advances
- IP connected devices on formerly analog or nondigital hardware
- Electronic implants in construction
- Durable materials
- Adjustable walls and windows
- Behavior-directed products/devices
- Behavior/threat-directed stand-off controls

Projected CPTED challenges in the 21st century similar to those just listed will have dramatic effects on the reduction of exposure of people to victimization. With the introduction of each new technology, there is the possibility of new, unpredicted exposures to victimization. Accordingly, it will be a continuing challenge to CPTED planners and specialists to be involved in the development and application of these new technologies. One way or another, the technologies will develop. The CPTED perspective can help improve the overall value of new technologies and social change.

Downtown Streets and Pedestrian Areas

- From the 1950s through the 1990s, the growing dominance of the vehicle over pedestrians resulted in off-street parking, one-way streets, synchronized traffic signals, and shrunken sidewalks to accommodate cars and trucks.
- Pedestrian-oriented businesses have failed or chased the buyer to outlying shopping centers and malls. As businesses moved from downtowns, there was less pedestrian activity, which forced even more businesses out.
- Narrow pedestrian footpaths increased conflict and fear between vagrants and other abnormal users of space and normal users. Normal users avoided these streets, thereby reinforcing the decline of business and normal downtown activities.
- Downtown streets became "no man's land" at night and on weekends.
- Pedestrian malls were created to replace the vehicle with people, but most failed because the designers lost track of their Three-D aesthetics.
- Upgrade in lighting and CCTV.

Commercial and retail establishments have always used the physical environment to affect customer perceptions and behavior. CPTED adds a new dimension by incorporating these elements into space design and management:

1. *Natural access control.* Your space should give some natural indication of where people are allowed and are not allowed. Don't depend on locks and security officers; make security part of the layout.
2. *Natural surveillance.* Again, traditional factors such as good lighting are important, but do not overlook a natural factor such as a strategically placed window or the placement of an employee workstation.
3. *Territorial reinforcement.* This is an umbrella concept, embodying all natural surveillance and access control principles. It emphasizes the enhancement of ownership and proprietary behaviors. Using features such as landscaping and planting of small bushes and shrubs, pavement surface design, gateway treatments, and fences defines property lines as well as helping distinguish private from public spaces to promote territorial reinforcement.

These concepts can be more important than you suspect. There is one individual, for instance, who has owned five convenience stores for about 20 years. He always felt that environmental concepts were a lot of hogwash. But the neighborhood changed and disintegrated, and he failed to keep up with it. Now, almost too late, he realizes that you must design your space to cope with your environment.

There are many applications of CPTED to commercial environments. Perhaps the greatest and most valuable lesson to be learned is that good store design and merchandising are not incompatible with effective security. Both objectives may be achieved and enhanced through space planning and behavioral concepts.

The CPTED concept—assumption that the proper design and effective use of the built environment can lead to a reduction in the fear of crime and the incidence of crime and to an improvement in the quality of life—translates into many practical and useful applications.

Crime Prevention Through Environmental Design[2]

Crime-prevention practitioners are recognizing the importance of considering design and physical planning in crime reduction. The crime-prevention officer has an opportunity to influence the design of facilities through the installation planning board. However, to be effective, the CPTED planner must understand a number of concepts about the relationship between the physical design of buildings and crime occurrences. These include the concepts of territoriality, natural surveillance, and defensible space.

Territoriality

Historically, a single-family home on its own piece of land and somewhat isolated from its neighbors (but often by as little as a few feet) has been considered the typical family's territory. The single-family home sits on a piece of land buffered from neighbors and the public street by intervening grounds. At times, symbolic shrubs or fences reinforce a boundary. The positioning of lights in windows that look out on the grounds also acts to reinforce the claim.

Unfortunately, as the population has grown and the need for housing has increased, the trend toward developing single-family units has been paralleled, if not surpassed, by the development of row houses, apartment buildings, and various high-rise structures. Architects, planners, and designers involved in developing structures have not paid a great deal of attention to crime control or the need for an individual or a family

[2] *Field Manual*, Department of the Army, Appendix B, FM3-19, 30; 1979, pp. 18–22.

group to identify with its home in a manner that might affect crime. Therefore, most families living in apartment buildings consider the space outside their apartment door to be distinctly public. In effect, they relegate responsibility for all activity outside the immediate confines of their apartment to public authorities. A question is whether environmental design can be used to extend the boundaries of these private realms, subdividing public space outside living quarters so that more of the common space comes under the resident's influence and responsibility.

Through extensive research of efficiently functioning housing developments, a number of mechanisms have been identified that may be used in the design process (or may be added after construction). These mechanisms encourage the residents of multifamily dwellings to identify more with the ground or area around their immediate home site and to assume responsibility for its protection. Presented here is a brief discussion of a number of these mechanisms:

- *Site design.* If the grounds around a set of quarters can be directly identified with a particular building and the residents of that building take a personal interest in the use or upkeep of that area, they will play a role in protecting it. Through proper site design, a recreational area adjoining a building may be used as a buffer zone by providing play equipment for young children and seating areas for adults. The fact that children play and adults sit in these areas serves to increase the resident's concerns with the activities taking place there. Strangers are usually recognized and their activities come under observation and immediate questioning.
- *Street design.* Research has shown that by the placement, enclosure, or rerouting of streets and traffic, the nature of a particular area can be changed and the crime rate reduced. For example, a particular portion of a street might be closed to vehicular traffic, and play equipment and seats may be added. In a number of areas where this technique has been used, it has been found that most residents know or at least recognize people up and down the block and strangers on the street are identified. Similar approaches that involve rerouting traffic, using one-way streets, or blocking off streets have lowered the crime rate in some areas.
- *Symbolic barriers.* The types of barriers that planners can use in laying out an area include open gateways, light standards, low walls, and plantings. Both physical and symbolic barriers serve the same purpose: to inform an individual that he is passing from a public to a private space. Symbolic barriers identified by residents as boundary lines serve as defining areas of comparative safety. Many places warrant the use of symbolic barriers, including transition points between a public street and the semipublic grounds of a building; an area between a building's lobby and its corridors; or hallways on particular floors of a building.

- *Internal design.* Although economics may sometimes enter the picture, a building's interior may be designed for specific groupings of apartment units and shared entrances. These factors may cause the residents of these apartments to develop a concern for the space immediately adjacent to their dwelling. For example, on each floor of an apartment building, two to four families might be required to share a common corridor area. The apartment doors would be grouped around that common corridor, and access to elevators or stairs might be screened by a glazed partition. The net effect would be that the floor's residents would adopt the corridor as a collective extension of their dwelling unit and would take an increased interest in its maintenance and use.
- *Facilities and amenities.* The location of particular facilities (such as play and sitting areas and laundry facilities) will tend to give an area a high intensity of use and support the idea of territoriality. The presence of residents involved in various activities (children at play and people chatting or engaged in other types of activities) allows for casual surveillance by concerned members of the family and screens out possible intruders.

Reducing the number of apartment units grouped together to share a collectively defined area and limiting the number of buildings that comprise a housing project are important factors for creating an environment that residents will help protect. Research has documented the fact that housing projects comprised of fewer high-rise buildings (two to four) have lower crime rates than projects containing a larger number of buildings. Based on this finding, it is argued that there appears to be much less freedom of movement in the public spaces of the smaller high-rise projects. Unlike buildings and large developments, every building of a small grouping usually has an entrance directly off a public street. These dwellings more closely resemble middle-income, high-rise developments and look more private.

As a crime-prevention officer, you might not be in a position to directly use these techniques. However, your familiarity with these approaches and the value of their use in the crime-prevention process are important elements in your arsenal of tools to create public involvement in reducing crime. In particular, the purpose of outlining these tools is not to equip you to be a designer but rather to equip you to communicate with those who are involved in that profession.

Based on these conditions, a number of mechanisms have been identified that can be used to design the grounds and internal areas of apartment units, housing developments, and other residential areas to facilitate natural monitoring of activities taking place. By providing opportunities for surveillance through the positioning of windows in relation to stairs, corridors, or outside areas, continual natural observation will be maintained and crime will be deterred. If such steps are taken, the security of observed areas will be understood by the potential criminal, making him think twice before committing a crime.

The first of these natural surveillance mechanisms involves the positioning of service areas and access paths leading to apartment buildings to facilitate surveillance by residents and authorities. For example, buildings might be designed so that their entries face and are within close proximity of a street, so that well-lit paths lead to the front door or the lobby, so that the lobby is arranged to afford good visibility from the street. Other related steps focus on the strategic placement of windows, fire stairwells, lobby lights, and mailboxes so that they can be easily viewed from the street. Elevator waiting areas on each floor can also be designed so that they can be seen from the street level. Research has proven that if steps such as these are taken, residents will be more likely to become involved with protecting the facility, patrols will be in a better position to observe what is going on, and criminals will be discouraged from vandalizing the site.

A second technique that might be used to increase surveillance is to design facilities so that people within them will naturally view commonly used paths, entries, and play and seating areas during their normal household activities. This concept also focuses on the strategic placement of windows, lighting, and open areas so that natural surveillance by residents is improved.

Another mechanism involves the subdivision of housing areas into small, recognizable, and identifiable groupings that improve visual surveillance possibilities. Research has shown that in housing developments where the surveillance of a neighbor's outside activities was possible, residents were found to be very familiar with everyone's comings and goings. The overall effect was to cement collective identity and responsibility through social pressure.

Defensible Space

Defensible space is a term for a range of combined security measures that bring an environment more under the control of its residents. A defensible space is a residential environment that inhabitants can use for the enhancement of their lives while providing security for their families, neighbors, and friends. The physical mechanisms suggested to create safety and improve upkeep (as part of the defensible-space concept) are self-help tools wherein design catalyzes the natural impulses of residents rather than forcing them to surrender their shared social responsibilities to any formal authority.

Research has revealed investigative techniques that might be used to modify existing housing areas to make them more secure. The following methods may require alteration or adaptation to the particular situation at your installation:

- Widening major pathways and using colored decorative paving
- Differentiating small private areas (front lawns) outside each dwelling unit from the public path with low, symbolic walls
- Adding public-seating areas in the center of public paths far enough from private-dwelling units to eliminate conflicts of use but close enough to be under constant surveillance by residents
- Designing play areas as an integral part of open space
- Adding new and decorative lighting to highlight various paths and recreation areas at night and extending the residents' surveillance potential and feeling of security
- Adding seats and path networks to recreational facilities where large, central court areas exist. This increases the interest and usability of the areas
- Redesigning parking and play areas around buildings to create the illusion that the buildings are grouped where natural opportunities exist
- Modernizing building entrances to create breezeways into building courts and to accommodate a telephone intercom for opening entry doors to the lobby
- Providing video surveillance of public grounds and central paths by security of public monitors
- Installing audio and video surveillance capabilities in elevators and at the doors of residences

The Crime-Prevention Model

The model for crime prevention through environmental design is based on the theory that action must be taken to counter crime before it occurs. The critical element in this model is the environmental engineering component. It provides both direct and indirect controls against criminal activity by reducing the opportunity for crime through science and technology and the use of various urban planning and design techniques. The crime-prevention model explains what environmental engineering is and how it supports crime prevention. With this information, you may be in a better position to understand and respond to questions and discussions on how urban design and planning can have an impact on your installation's criminal element.

The Environmental Influence on Criminal Behavior

The basic theory that supports crime prevention through environmental design is that urban environments can influence criminal behavior in two ways. First, the physical surroundings in which people live have an effect on each individual. These physical characteristics include noise, pollution, overcrowding, and the existence and unmonitored spreading of refuse and other unsightly waste. The second element that must be dealt with in the environmental engineering formula concerns the social characteristics of the community that provide individuals with social relationships to which they must respond. Characteristics such as alienation, loneliness, anxiety, and dehumanization are seen as keys to criminal behavior.

The following examples of CPTED strategies for low-income and public housing are grouped under the three primary CPTED concepts of natural surveillance, natural access control, and territorial reinforcement.

Natural Surveillance

- Provide magnets for watchers or gatekeepers by increased outdoor use of space (e.g., porches, yard assignment, and gardening).
- Reduce light pollution on bedroom windows to influence residents to leave curtains and blinds open or partially open to create the reality and perception of surveillance.
- Install windows in dead walls on the sides of buildings.
- Install automatically controlled porch lights to create a sea of light at the human scale to allow for better visual identification of faces and to reduce light pollution through the reduction of the use and intensity of overhead mast-mounted lights.
- Place car parking in the line of sight of units or, preferably, immediately in front.
- Install central HVAC to eliminate the use of window units that block natural surveillance; this also significantly improves the quality of life.
- Remove walls and hedgerows that produce impediments to natural surveillance; replace dumpster enclosures and perimeter fencing with transparent materials.
- Bushes should be 3 feet or less in height and the first branch of a tree should be 8 feet off the ground to obtain good natural control and natural surveillance.

Natural Access Control

- Control vehicle traffic to reduce nonresident through access; this may include closures, one-way streets, or other designs.
- Install traffic chokers and speed bumps to reduce speed and to improve pedestrian safety.
- Install entry monuments to celebrate the identity of the community and to signify the movement from public to private space as a warning to potential abnormal users.
- Segment parking areas to create enclaves for fewer cars in each and to create one way in and out to promote the perception of potential entrapment for abnormal users of space.

Territorial Reinforcement

- Reduce the number of people sharing a common entrance or stairwell access.
- Reduce the number of people sharing a common balcony or gallery.
- Reduce the number of people sharing a common green area.
- Reduce the number of people sharing a common parking area.
- Increase the assignment and active use of yard space.
- Relocate parallel sidewalks away from close proximity to individual units to create more defensible space for the residents.
- Site area redesigned if necessary.
- Create psychological barriers.

The following nine major CPTED strategies may be used in any number of combinations:

1. *Provide clear border definition of controlled space.* It is a common-law requirement that space must be defined to preserve property rights. Boundaries may be identified physically or symbolically. Fences, shrubbery, or signs are acceptable border definitions. The underlying principle is that a "reasonable individual" must be able to recognize that he or she is passing from public to private space. The arrangements of furniture and color definition are means of identifying interior spaces. Plaques and pictures on walls in hallways help define ownership and are powerful environmental cues that affect the behavior and predisposition of owners and normal users and abnormal users alike.
2. *Provide clearly marked transitional zones.* It is important to provide clearly marked transitional zones on moving from public to semipublic to semiprivate to private space. As the transitional definition increases, the range of excuses for improper behavior is reduced. The user must be made to acknowledge movement into controlled space.
3. *Relocation of gathering areas.* It is appropriate to formally designate gathering or congregating areas in locations with good natural surveillance and access control. Gathering areas on campuses may be placed in positions that are out of the view of undesired users, to decrease the magnetic effect or attraction.
4. *Place safe activities in unsafe locations.* Within reason, this strategy may be used to overcome problems on school campuses, parks, offices, or institutional settings. Safe activities serve as magnets for normal users who exhibit challenging or controlling behaviors (e.g., staring) that tell other normal users that they are safe and tell abnormal users that they are at greater risk of scrutiny or interventions. Some caution must be used to ensure that a safe activity is not being placed in an unreasonable position it cannot defend.

5. *Place unsafe activities in safe locations.* Positioning vulnerable activities near windows of an occupied space or within tightly controlled areas helps overcome risk and make the users of these areas feel safer.
6. *Redesignate the use of space to provide natural barriers.* Conflicting activities may be separated by distance, natural terrain, or other functions to avoid fear-producing conflict. For instance, the sounds emanating from a basketball court may be disruptive and fear producing for a senior citizen or toddler gathering or play area. The threat need not be real to create the perception of risk for the normal or desired user.
7. *Improve the scheduling of space.* It has been found that generally the effective and productive use of spaces reduces risk and the perception of risk for normal users. Conversely, abnormal users feel at greater risk of surveillance and intervention in their activities. Well-thought-out temporal and spatial relationships improve profit and productivity while increasing the control of behavior.
8. *Redesign or revamp space to increase the perception of natural surveillance.* The perception of surveillance is more powerful than its reality. Digital cameras that are clearly mounted and visible are more likely to be a deterrent to crime than hidden cameras. Indeed, hidden cameras do little to make normal users feel safer and, therefore, act safer when they are unaware of the presence of these devices. There are times for hidden or covert cameras, but these devices are designed to capture activity rather than deter activity. Likewise, abnormal users do not feel at greater risk of detection when they are oblivious to surveillance potentials. Windows, clear lines of sight, and other natural techniques are often as effective as the use of mechanical or organized (e.g., security officers) methods.
9. *Overcome distance and isolation.* Improved communications and design efficiencies increase the perception of natural surveillance and control. School administrators have learned to carry portable radios to improve their productivity as well as create the perception of immediate access to help. Restroom locations and entry designs may be planned to increase convenience and reduce the cost of construction and maintenance.

Conclusion

Moving forward, aside from all the theory, bells, and whistles, we must:

1. Continue to have the police and the community work together in partnership.

2. Continue to establish neighborhood-oriented policing and neighborhood watch programs to assist with the solving of crime problems, create zero tolerance for specific crimes, and reduce the fear of crime.
3. Lower poverty levels through employment opportunities.

Additionally, it's not just law enforcement in these partnerships with the private sector to utilize CPTED concepts in urban areas—it's the Department of Planning and Zoning, the Health Department, the Housing Authority, and so on. The point is to improve the total quality of life, not just reduce crime and the fear of crime.

References

Crowe, T., 2000. Crime Prevention Through Environmental Design in the Twenty-First Century. Butterworth-Heinemann, Boston, MA, USA.

Fennelly, L., 2012. Handbook of Loss Prevention and Crime Prevention, fifth ed. Elsevier, Amsterdam, the Netherlands.

APPENDIX A: BROWARD COUNTY SCHOOL CPTED MATRIX*

Table A.1 Broward County School CPTED Matrix.

Crime Environment	Crime Environment Problem	CPTED Strategies	CPTED Design Directives
School grounds: Assault Bicycle theft Breaking and entering Vandalism	Design of and procedures for bus-loading areas prohibit teacher surveillance, increase supervision ratio, impede pedestrian traffic flow, and cause congestion. Confrontations, thefts, and vandalism occur.	Redesign bus loading zone and revise procedures to increase surveillance area for natural surveillance, control pedestrian flow, and decrease ratio of students to supervisors.	Create one zone in a surveillance area for loading and unloading students, limited in size to a maximum of 4–5 buses.
			Require bus drivers to allow students to enter or leave their bus only when in a specified loading zone. Create a bus-queuing zone for waiting buses that is convenient to the unloading zone.

(*Continued*)

*This Matrix was designed by Tim Crowe and updated for this edition to reflect current technology in CPTED. It was originally designed for the Broward County, Florida, School System, but it can apply to any primary school or college setting.

Table A.1 (Continued)

Crime Environment	Crime Environment Problem	CPTED Strategies	CPTED Design Directives
			Require teachers on monitoring assignment at the bus-loading zone to direct the movement of buses and to disperse each group of students from the bus-loading area before allowing another group to load or unload.
	Location of informal gathering areas (natural and designated) promotes the preemption of space, interferes with traffic flow, and prohibits natural surveillance. Assaults occur.	Relocate informal gathering areas near supervision or natural surveillance.	Move benches and physical amenities that support informal gatherings from undefined areas to courtyards.
			Relocate the student smoking zone to the interior courtyards.
		Redesign informal gathering areas to promote orderly flow and break up the preemption of space by groups.	Remove conventional picnic tables and benches.
			Install new tables and benches that physically divide space and the size of groups.
			Position amenities to create multiple access and passageways.
			Place ticket booths in problem areas.

(*Continued*)

Table A.1 (Continued)

Crime Environment	Crime Environment Problem	CPTED Strategies	CPTED Design Directives
	Design, use, and location of facilities have created isolated and blind-spot areas that are difficult to survey (due to design and/or nonuse because of fear or avoidance). Assaults, thefts, and vandalism occur.	Provide functional activities in unused or misused problem areas to promote natural surveillance, increase safe traffic flow, and attract different types of users.	Create mini-plazas in courtyards.
			Organize a student/faculty committee to assist in the design and coordination of mini-plaza activities.
	Design and border definition of campus creates unclear transitional zone definition. Breaking and entering, theft, and vandalism occur.	Provide clear border definition of transitional zones for access control and surveillance.	Install low hedging, flower beds, or ornamental fencing along borders.
			Organize a student/faculty committee to assist in the design and coordination of border definition activities.
	Location and positioning of school physical plant prohibit natural surveillance (off-hours) by local residents and passersby. Breaking and entering, theft, and vandalism occur. (One-half of vandalisms are incident with breaking and entering.)	Provide functional community activities on school campus (off-hours) to increase surveillance through effective use of facilities.	Create a police "school precinct" office.
			Install audio burglar alarm system.

(*Continued*)

Table A.1 (Continued)

Crime Environment	Crime Environment Problem	CPTED Strategies	CPTED Design Directives
		Overcome distance and isolation by improving communications to create rapid response to problems (and its perception) and more effective surveillance.	Provide portable radios to deans, school resource staff, and custodians.
	Design, use, and location of bicycle compounds or parking areas on school grounds prohibit natural surveillance and limit proper use because of students with variable hours. Thefts of bicycles occur.	Redesign bicycle parking areas to provide levels of security consistent with variable access needs of students.	Create a fenced bicycle parking area (secure area).
			Create an open bicycle parking area located in a place with good natural surveillance (nonsecure area). Assign bicycle students to either secure or nonsecure parking area on the basis of schedule. Install ground-level locking devices in each bicycle parking area. Set a policy requiring students to utilize a bicycle locking cable or chain.

(*Continued*)

Table A.1 (Continued)

Crime Environment	Crime Environment Problem	CPTED Strategies	CPTED Design Directives
Parking lots: Assault Theft Breaking and entering Vandalism	Location and design of student parking near bus-loading areas without restricting borders promotes unmanaged pedestrian use of parking areas, promotes preemption of space by groups, and prohibits natural surveillance. Assaults, breaking and entering, thefts, and vandalism occur (affected by bus-loading procedures).	Relocate and/or redesign bus-loading and parking lot access procedures to reduce necessity for pedestrian use of lot, reduce congestion in transitional zones, and support strict definition of parking lot use.	Switch locations between student parking and driver education range.
			Designate access ways to the student parking lot that avoid the bus-loading zone.
	Design and location of parking lots provide unclear definition of transitional zones and unmanaged access by vehicles and pedestrians, students, and nonstudents. Breaking and entering, thefts, vandalism, and trespassing occur.	Provide natural border definition and limit access to vehicular traffic in student parking to clearly define transitional zones, to reroute ingress and egress during specified periods, and to provide natural surveillance.	Install hedges around parking lots.
			Install aesthetically pleasing gates on vehicular access points.
			Set policies to limit student pedestrian use of parking lots.

(*Continued*)

Table A.1 (Continued)

Crime Environment	Crime Environment Problem	CPTED Strategies	CPTED Design Directives
			Secure gates at external vehicular access points during school hours; leave internal access points open.
			Organize a student/faculty committee to assist in the design and coordination of the border definition and parking lot access control activities.
	Location of informal gathering areas designated as smoking zones in open corridors adjacent to parking lots and visible from public thoroughfares prohibits natural surveillance, attracts outsiders, and is an impediment to school policies restricting student use of parking lots during school hours. Breaking and entering, thefts, and vandalism occur.	Relocate informal gathering areas to places with natural surveillance that are isolated from the view of public thoroughfares and designed to support informal gathering activities.	Create mini-plazas.
			Relocate the student smoking zone to the mini-plazas.
			Organize a student/faculty committee to assist in the design and coordination of the mini-plaza activities.
	Isolation of student parking lots (some locations) prohibits any natural surveillance. Variable student hours limit use of fencing and gates.	Relocate all (or part of) student parking to areas with natural surveillance and/or relocate safe activities in juxtaposition with student parking to increase natural surveillance.	Switch locations between student parking and the driver education range.

(*Continued*)

Table A.1 (Continued)

Crime Environment	Crime Environment Problem	CPTED Strategies	CPTED Design Directives
	Breaking and entering, thefts, and vandalism occur.		
		Redesign parking lots to provide levels of security consistent with variable access needs of the students.	Create a fenced parking area (secure) that is locked during school day.
			Create an open parking area (nonsecure) in a place with good natural surveillance.
			Assign parking to either the secure or nonsecure area on the basis of student schedule.
			Reroute vehicular access to nonsecure parking area through internal parts of school ground before entering the parking lot.
			Set policy limiting student pedestrian use of parking lots.
Locker room: Theft Breaking and entering	Design and use of lockers (by multiple assignment) disperses students throughout area, reduces surveillance, and increases territory for teacher supervision. Breaking and entering and thefts occur.	Redesignate use of space to increase territorial concern, to increase the defined purpose of space, and to reduce area requiring surveillance.	Assign lockers by section separately for each class.
	Similar design of lockers creates confusion and decreases natural surveillance by creating unclear definition of transitional zones.	Provide clear definition of transitional zones and use of space for easy recognition of bona fide users.	Uniquely color-code locker sections for each class.

(Continued)

Table A.1 (Continued)

Crime Environment	Crime Environment Problem	CPTED Strategies	CPTED Design Directives
	Breaking and entering and theft occur.		
	Isolation of locker area while class is in gymnasium or on playing field eliminates natural surveillance. Breaking and entering and thefts occur.	Provide functional activities in problem areas to increase natural surveillance.	Relocate a teacher planning area to the physical education offices.
			Assign teachers to the planning area during all classes.
Corridors: Assault	Design and use of corridors provide blind spots and isolated areas that prohibit natural surveillance. Assaults, threats, and extortions occur.	Provide functional activities (or redesignate use) in blind spots or isolated areas to increase natural surveillance (or the perception thereof).	Relocate teacher planning areas.
			Redesign blind spot areas to provide storage spaces for clubs and/or school administration.
		Remove obstacles to natural surveillance (increase perception of openness).	Install windows in walls along problem corridors.
			Install windows in walls of exterior stairwells.
	Class scheduling promotes congestion in certain areas at shift changing that decreases supervision capabilities and produces inconvenience. Assaults and confrontations occur.	Revise class scheduling and management procedures to avoid congestion, decrease supervision ratio, and define time transitions.	Provide a 3- to 5-minute shift change hiatus between lunch periods.

(Continued)

Table A.1 (Continued)

Crime Environment	Crime Environment Problem	CPTED Strategies	CPTED Design Directives
	Location of benches and/or other amenities in corridors creates misused space and congestion. Corridor locations are lacking in natural surveillance because of design. Assaults and confrontations occur.	Relocate informal gathering areas to areas with natural surveillance that are designed to support that activity.	Remove benches and other physical amenities from crowded corridors.
	Location and use of corridors for functions other than pedestrian passage, such as smoking zones, promotes preemption of space by groups and unsurveillable misused space. This misused space supports behavior that attracts outsiders to the external corridors designated as smoking areas. Assaults, confrontations, and other illegal activities occur.	Relocate activities and functions from misused space to areas designed to support these activities and to provide natural surveillance.	Move the student smoking zones from corridors to mini-plazas.
			Revise school policy to restrict student use of the outside corridor previously designated for smoking.
			Provide cafeteria food at the gymnasium snack bar.
			Provide multiple access to the snack bar and install queuing lanes.

(Continued)

Table A.1 (Continued)

Crime Environment	Crime Environment Problem	CPTED Strategies	CPTED Design Directives
	Design and definition of corridor areas do not support a clear definition of the dominant function of that space (i.e., passage). Unclear transitional zones produce behaviors conducive to assault and confrontation.	Provide clear definition of the dominant function (and intended use of space) and clearly define transitional zones to increase territorial concerns and natural surveillance.	Place graphic designs in stairwells and corridors defining the intended functions of these spaces.
			Color-code various sections of the school and use graphics and art designs uniquely for each functional component of the school.
			Organize student/faculty committees by functional component to select and coordinate the graphic design and color-coding activities.
Restrooms: Assault Extortion	Location of restrooms near external entrances and exits isolates them from normal school-hour traffic flow and prohibits surveillance. Assaults occur.	Limit access to isolated areas during specific times for access control and to reduce the need for surveillance.	Install collapsible gates at restroom entrances for locking during problem periods.
	Privacy and isolation required for internal design provide blind spots that reduce surveillability on the part of students and supervisory personnel (i.e., exterior door and anteroom wall). Assaults occur.	Remove obstacles to natural surveillance to decrease fear, increase use, and increase risk of detection.	Remove entrance doors to restrooms.

(*Continued*)

Table A.1 (Continued)

Crime Environment	Crime Environment Problem	CPTED Strategies	CPTED Design Directives
			Eliminate unnecessary portions of anteroom walls.
Classrooms: Assault	Design requirements for classrooms produce isolation of individual classes, resulting in high student-to-teacher ratios and little external natural surveillance (real or perceived) when class is in session. Assaults occur. Theft occurs when classrooms are empty.	Remove obstacles to natural surveillance to increase risk of detection and to reduce perception of isolation.	Install windows in classroom walls and doors.
		Overcome distance and isolation by improving communications to create rapid response to problems, the perception of rapid response, and more effective surveillance.	Provide portable radios to deans, school resource staff, and custodial personnel.
			Install audio alarm systems in problem classrooms for after hours.
	Location and design definition of multiple-purpose classrooms produces unclear transitional zones, decreases territorial concern, and decreases natural surveillance. Thefts occur.	Extend the identity of surrounding spaces to multiple-purpose space to increase territorial concern and natural surveillance.	Color-code and graphically identify multiple-purpose classrooms with adjacent spaces.

(*Continued*)

Table A.1 (Continued)

Crime Environment	Crime Environment Problem	CPTED Strategies	CPTED Design Directives
		Provide functional activity in problem areas to increase territorial concern and natural surveillance.	Relocate a teacher planning area to each multipurpose classroom.
	Class-shift procedure during lunch hour produces unclear time transition and definition of groups, decreases control, and increases student-to-teacher ratio. Many classroom thefts are committed by class-cutters.	Revise class scheduling and movement procedures to define time for class shifts, making surveillance and supervision of class-cutters easier.	Provide a 3- to 5-minute shift change hiatus between lunch periods.

APPENDIX B: SCHOOL CPTED SURVEY

School Security Survey/Assessment

A CPTED assessment attempts to evaluate the physical setting of facility and maintenance factors that affect the safety and crime quotient capability of a particular school. Environmental factors such as the types of neighborhoods, housing facilities, businesses, streets, and institutions surrounding the school affect the school's operation.

Classrooms, security systems, lighting and color design, accessibility, and quality of maintenance are all evaluated to determine their effect on school climate, natural supervision, defensible space, and differentiated space. The survey items are to be rated as satisfactory (S), unsatisfactory (U), or not applicable (NA).

Thirty points to review*:

1. Poor visibility at entry to site
2. Easy vehicular access onto grounds
3. Off-site activity generator
4. Inadequate distance between school and neighbors
5. Easy-access hiding places
6. Area hidden by planting
7. School adjacent to traffic hazard
8. Portion of building inaccessible to emergency vehicles
9. Secluded hangout area
10. Vegetation hides part of building
11. Site not visible from street
12. No barrier between parking and lawn
13. Gravel in parking area
14. Dangerous vehicular circulation
15. Enclosed courtyard conceals vandals
16. High parapet hides vandals
17. Trees located where visibility required
18. Pedestrian/vehicle conflict
19. Structure provides hideout

20. Building walls subject to bouncing balls
21. Parts of bus shelter not visible
22. Mechanical equipment accessible
23. Stacked materials and downspouts provide roof access
24. Recessed entry obscures intruders
25. Portions of building not visible from vehicle areas
26. Walkway roof eases access to building roof
27. Recess hides vandals
28. Skylight provides easy access
29. Mechanical screen conceals vandals
30. Access through equipment

*Prepared by Timothy D. Crowe.

C. Ray Jeffrey, in his classic theoretical work *Crime Prevention Through Environmental Design* (1971)[1], written before Jeffrey became aware of the works of Newman and others, proposed a threefold strategy involving not only physical design but also increased citizen participation and the more effective use of police forces. He contended that **the way to prevent crime is to design the total environment in such a manner that the opportunity for crime is reduced or eliminated**. Jeffrey contends that both the physical and social characteristics of an urban area affect crime patterns. Better physical planning is a key to unlocking the potential for improved physical security and the potential for development of informal social control. He also argues for high levels of precision in the analytical stages that precede physical planning for crime reduction:

> *One of the major methodological defects in ecological studies of crime rates has been the use of large units and census tract data as a basis for analysis. The usual units are rural-urban, intricacy, intercity, regional, and national differences... Such an approach is much too gross for finding the physical features associated with different types of crimes. We must look at the physical environment in terms of each building, or each room of the building, or each floor of the building. Whenever crime rates are surveyed at a micro level of analysis, it is revealed that a small area of the city is responsible for a majority of the crimes. This fact is glossed over by gross statistical correlation analysis of census*

[1] Jeffrey, C. R. (1971) *Crime Prevention Through Environmental Design*, Sage, Beverly Hills, CA, USA.

tract data, which ignore house-by-house or block-by-block variations in crime rates. For purposes of crime prevention we need data that will tell us what aspects of the urban environment are responsible for crime, such as the concentration of homicide or robbery in a very small section of the city.[2]

Risk Assessment and Application

This step involves identifying risk due to intentional or unintentional threats that have the potential of direct or indirect consequences on an organization's activities, assets, operation, function, and stakeholders (threats, vulnerability, and critical analysis).

Security Maintenance Checklist

How often are the doors and windows checked?

Doors and Locks

1. Are the doors of metal or solid core construction?
2. Are door hinges nonremoval from outside?
3. Are there windows in the door or within 40 inches of the lock?
4. Are there auxiliary locks on the doors?
5. Are strikes and strikeplates securely fastened and doors a tight fit?
6. If there are no windows in the door, is there a wide-angle viewer or voice intercom device?
7. Can the lock mechanism be reached through a mail slot, delivery port, or pet entrance at the doorway?
8. Are all exterior entrances lighted and working?
9. Can entrances be observed from the street or public areas?

Badges and Key Controls

Key Controls

Whether a school complex has physical keys or access control, key control or badge control is an extremely important inclusion in a CPTED assessment. Check whether the managers are in the habit of picking up physical and electronic keys from employees at their termination and if they have an accurate record of who has which keys. Within a few short minutes, you should realize whether or not the recipient of your survey has a problem. Almost every organization has some sort of master key system, because many people must have

[2] Jeffrey, C. R. (1975) *Behavior Control Techniques and Criminology*, Ecology Youth Development Workshop, University of Hawaii School of Social Work, Honolulu, HI, USA.

access to the building without the inconvenience of carrying two dozen keys around every day. Master keys are required for executives, middle managers, and the security department as well as the maintenance department. Access badges not in use within 30 days should be deleted from the system.

Objective: To determine whether badges, locks, and key program controls are adequate to deter and detect misuse. These requirements are only applicable to facilities where there is exclusive control of all keys providing access to space.

Approach: Review the latest version of the security manual related to lock and key controls.

1. Validate that master-level keys (for example, grandmaster keys, building-master keys, and floor-master keys, as defined in the security manual) are adequately controlled and only specific authorized people have *Master* access on their badges.
   a. Daily and/or shift accountability is maintained.
   b. Keys are restricted and controlled.
   c. If more than six master access keys are available, site security manager documents approval every 12 months.
   d. Process to control access to master keys is kept outside of security to allow management or fire/emergency response personnel access.
2. If fireman access boxes, Knox lock boxes, or a Morse watchmen key control or badge process is used:
   a. Verify that these boxes are alarmed to a security control center or constantly staffed workstation.
   b. Determine whether duplicating hardware is secured when not in use.
   c. Validate that all duplicate, blank, and unissued keys are properly secured when not in use.
   d. Determine whether key codes and pinning combinations are secured and available on a need-to-know basis.
   e. If key operations are contracted, verify they are audited against requirements every 12 months.

Access Controls and Badge Designs

Objective: To determine whether the processes and technology in support of physical access are operating effectively.

Approach: Review the latest version of the security manual related to access controls and badge designs.

1. Determine whether badges are issued per requirements. For example:
   a. Documentation of management authorization for noncompany personnel was obtained prior to the badge being issued.

   b. Proof of identity was obtained prior to a badge being issued to noncompany personnel.
   c. Temporary contractor badges are authorized by a manager, purchasing buyer, coordinator, or authorized predesignated contract company supervisor. Visitor identity (those requiring escort) must be validated by the person authorizing the visit.
   d. Badges are in compliance with the security manual design requirements (e.g., sealed, white photo background with a postage-guaranteed post office box return address on the reverse).
2. Validate that all badges have an expiration date in the database.
   a. Determine whether badges that are not returned on the due date (e.g., temporary or visitor badges) are deactivated.
   b. Determine whether badges reported as lost have immediate action taken to place the badge in lost status and whether the profiles are kept in the database for six months.
3. Validate that all hardware, badge stock, and other components of the badge process are secured when not in use.
4. Validate that user IDs are assigned to all operating personnel in compliance and authorization reviews are performed every six months.
5. Verify that an effective process is in place to remove employee access in a timely manner:
   a. Category manager reports are distributed to category managers every 90–95 days.
   b. Every 30 days Security must match database to the HR database.
   c. Process must be in place to deactivate lost badges or termed individuals within 24 hours.

Windows

Windows come in a variety of shapes, sizes, and types, each of which presents a different type of security problem. Windows provide an inviting entryway for a burglar who does not like to break glass because the noise may alert someone. On double-hung sash-type windows, drill a hole through the top corner of the bottom window into the bottom of the top window. Place a solid pin into the hole to prevent the window from being opened.

All ground-floor windows must meet the following criteria, depending on their accessibility to an intruder:

1. Do all windows have properly fitted and working locks?
2. Opening is protected with burglar-resistant glazing or decorative grill?
3. Broken windows have been replaced with burglar-resistant glazing?

4. Is additional security provided for window openings with air conditioners?
5. Are basement windows protected with security grilles?
6. Are trees and shrubbery kept trimmed back from all windows?

Exterior Lighting

1. Is the lighting adequate to illuminate critical areas (alleys, fire escapes, ground-level windows)?
2. How many foot-candles is the lighting on horizontal at ground level?
3. Is there sufficient illumination over entrances?
4. Are the perimeter areas lighted to assist police surveillance of the area?
5. Are the protective lighting system and the working lighting system on the same line?
6. Is there an auxiliary system that has been tested?
7. Is there an auxiliary power source for protective lighting?
8. Is the auxiliary system designed to go into operation automatically when needed?
9. Are the protective lights controlled automatically by a timer or photocells, or is it manually operated?
10. During what hours is this lighting used?
11. Does it use switch box(es) or is it automatically time secured?
12. Can protective lights be compromised easily (e.g., unscrewing of bulbs)?
13. What type(s) of lights are installed around the property?
14. Are they cost-effective units?
15. Are the fixtures vandal-proof?
16. Is there a glare factor?
17. Is there an even distribution of light?

Digital Closed-Circuit Television

Digital closed-circuit television (CCTV) is a valuable asset to any school security package and an even more valuable tool if hooked up to a digital video recorder (DVR). Analog video recorders are still used in some applications, but the merits of DVRs and IP video systems have trumped analog video system components. CCTV is a surveillance tool that provides an added set of "eyes." Whether the video system is actively monitored or merely recorded for follow-up depends on the application and requirements for security. If this equipment is on the site you are surveying, it is your job to evaluate its operation and effectiveness, as follows:

1. Is it working properly? Is the video quality sufficiently clear to determine the identity of individuals or detect activity in the field

of view? Are all the cameras working? Is the system set up for triggered events (e.g., on motion, door opening, or other dry-contact prompt)? Are the pan-tilt-zoom cameras commissioned for a purpose (e.g., with preset camera-view positions at critical areas)? Are privacy zones set up where appropriate?

2. How is the scene being monitored or recorded, and is the video data being saved for the appropriate number of days? Typically 30 days of storage was the standard for digital video recorder applications; however, 90 days of storage has become the norm for digital video storage, with the capability to save video events on the digital storage permanently as required. You will find that auditors will want 90 days to be available as a minimum.
3. Are the camera fields of views placed where they will be most beneficial?
4. Are the lighting levels in the areas being video monitored sufficient for the setting, place, and activity to be detected?
5. Is the security recording hardware system secured in a locked cabinet or enclosure?

Intrusion Alarms

If the site you are surveying already has an alarm system, check it out completely. Physically walk through every motion-detector unit. Evaluate the quality of the existing alarm products versus what is available to meet the needs of the client. I surveyed a warehouse recently that was only five years old. It was interesting to note that the warehouse had a two-zone alarm system. The control panel was to the right of the front door, which was about 15 feet from the receptionist.

Both alarm keys were in the key cylinders, and according to the president of the company, "The keys have been there since the system was installed." My point is, for a dollar, another key could be duplicated, and then the area would be vulnerable to attack. Another time, while I was doing a survey of an art gallery in New York, the security director stated that he had not had a service call on his alarm system in two years. We then proceeded to physically check every motion-detection unit and magnetic contact. You can imagine his reaction when he found out that 12 out of the 18 motion-detection units were not working.

In conclusion, intrusion alarms come in all shapes and sizes and use a variety of electronic equipment. It is advisable to be familiar with the state of art of electronics so that you can produce an effective report. It is also advisable to test your systems to make sure they are working.

Landscaping

A simple CPTED guideline regarding landscaping is:

1. All bushes must be between 18 inches and 3 feet.
2. The first tree branch must be 8 feet from the ground.

These guidelines assure not only a safe but an aesthetically pleasing landscape. By careful design of your landscaping you will create visual surveillance.

Walkways

I recently conducted a school assessment where the pathways were overgrown with hedges, weeds, trees, and vines. I took pictures and included them in my report (which I rarely do) and asked the question, "Can you see the person behind the bushes?"

Recreational Areas

Remember that unobstructed views give you good visual surveillance. A fenced-in basketball court with chain-link fence provides security and visibility.

Bike racks should be in areas that are highly visible—all the more reason for low hedges and greater view. If bikes are not secured properly, parts of two bikes will be stolen to make one bike.

School Gymnasiums

Basketball players love their game; I know some who would play 24/7 if they could. Let's assume that your gym is the only court in town. The lock is broken, the latch is jimmied, now the players have access. If this is the case, consider new solid-core doors, heavy-duty hardware, and an intrusion alarm system.

School or Town Libraries

DVDs or CDs have become big in recent years, as have research books and general texts. Most libraries have special collections, restricted areas, turnstyles, fire and intrusion alarms, valuable paintings in the reading room, and active library personnel. Their issues are a bit different from other institutions, but physical security issues are the same. Theft of rare books is nothing new. I was called once to a library for assistance in investigating the theft of nine books. "Nine books," I said to myself; "Why am I wasting my time on nine books?" Then I saw the titles of these books and said to myself, "*Wow.*" Even the investigation become different, more than simply listing them on police computer.

Computer Labs and Equipment and Music Rooms

All costly equipment must be properly secured with cables and bolts and protected by intrusion alarms as well as being placed in a secured area.

Lighting

Improved lighting provides another school or residential area security measure. Although some studies documented crime reduction after improved lighting systems were installed, these studies typically have not accounted for displacement effects.

Even if individuals living in a residence reduce the likelihood of a burglary by installing better lighting, they may only be displacing the burglary to another, less well-lit area.

By definition, a *foot-candle* (fc) is a unit of illuminance or light falling into a surface. It stands for the light level on a surface 1 foot from a standard candle. One foot-candle is equal to one lumen per square foot. Here are recommended lighting levels for some types of facilities:

- 0.5 fc for perimeter of outer area
- 0.4 fc for perimeter of restricted area
- 10 fc for vehicular entrances
- 5 fc for pedestrian entrance
- 0.5–2 fc for roadways
- 0.2 fc for open years
- 0.2–5 fc for decks on open piers
- 10–20 fc for interior sensitive structures
- Open parking light levels are a minimum of 0.2 fc in low-level activity areas and 2 fc in high vehicle activity areas; if there is cash collection booth, the light level is a minimum of 5 fc
- Loading docks: 15 fc
- Loading docks interior: 15 fc
- Shipping and receiving: 5 fc
- Security gatehouse: 25–30 fc
- Security gatehouse interior: 30 fc

For pedestrians or normal CCTV cameras, here is the minimum level of light for:

- Detection: 0.5 fc
- Recognition: 1 fc
- Identification: 2 fc
- Parking structures: 5 fc
- Parking areas or open spaces: 2 fc
- Loading docks: 0.2–5 fc
- Loading dock parking areas: 15–30 fc

Conclusion

The CPTED applications in the featured cities achieve the following:

- Reduce opportunities for crime and fear of crime by making schools and open areas more easily observable and by increasing activity in the neighborhood.
- Provide ways in which neighborhood residents, businesspeople, and police can work together more effectively to reduce opportunities and incentives for crime.
- Increase neighborhood identity, investor confidence, and social cohesion.
- Provide public information programs that help businesspeople and residents protect themselves from crime.
- Make the area more accessible by improving transportation services.
- Improve the effectiveness and efficiency of governmental operations.
- Encourage citizens to report crimes. The steps taken to achieve these objectives include:
  - Outdoor lighting, sidewalk, and landscaping improvements
  - Block watch, safe homes, and neighborhood cleanups
  - A campaign to discourage people from carrying cash
  - A major improvement and expansion of public transportation
  - Improved street lighting
  - Public transportation hubs that are purpose built

These improvements have enhanced the quality of life and provided an atmosphere of improvement in each of the communities featured in this book. The application of CPTED to school design has been promoted in a number of locations through the work of local practitioners and in cooperation with school district personnel.

APPENDIX C: CPTED DESIGN DIRECTIVES FOR DORMITORY AND STUDENT LOUNGES

Table C.1 Interior Spaces Matrix.

Environment	Environment Goal	CPTED Strategies	CPTED Design Directives
Rooms	Increase surveillance of room entrances.	Promote natural concern for room entrances with neighbors.	Avoid isolating an individual entrance at the end of a hall or head of stairs.
Hallways	Enhance territorial concern for hallways.	Provide a clearly identifiable zone that is shared by a small number of rooms.	Reduce the number of rooms sharing a common hallway.
			Provide transitional definition moving from stair landings, lounges, and restrooms to residents' rooms.
			Assign wall space to immediate residents for decoration and territorial identity.
	Increase natural surveillance of hallways.	Promote natural surveillance to increase the perception of risk by abnormal users.	Place window walls at ends of hallways to increase natural illumination and visibility.
			Place windows in doors of stair landings.
			Position lounge areas to provide direct line of sight to hallways; use windows in walls.
			Illuminate walls in hallways to increase perception of width and safety.
Stair systems	Increase natural surveillance of stairs.	Increase the perception of surveillance of interior stairs to make abnormal users feel more subject to scrutiny and challenge.	Design wrought-iron or see-through wood railings for stairs and landings to increase visibility.

(*Continued*)

Table C.1 (Continued)

Environment	Environment Goal	CPTED Strategies	CPTED Design Directives
			Provide landings with visibility to lobby areas.
			Place windows in landings of all stairs (outside).
Restrooms	Enhance natural surveillance and access control.	Increase convenience of access.	Place restrooms in central areas.
			Reduce the number of residents sharing a common restroom.
		Increase the perception of natural surveillance and access control.	Install maze entrances to restrooms; avoid double-door entry systems.
			Refrain from placing restrooms near stairs or exterior doors.
Lounges/study areas	Enhance the territorial nature and identity of dormitory lounge areas.	Assign lounge areas to define groupings of rooms.	Reduce the number of people sharing a common lounge.
			Involve residents in the decoration and adornment of their lounge areas.
	Increase the natural surveillance of lounges and contiguous hallways.	Place lounges in strategic locations with visibility of hallways and stairs.	Install windows in inner and outer walls of lounges.
		Increase the use of lounges through enhancements to decor, amenities, and environmental systems.	Design lighting systems and select window coverings to limit the desirability of closing blinds.
			Install floor, wall, and ceiling systems to reduce the effects of noise.
Laundry	Enhance the effect of laundry usage on natural surveillance and access control.	Increase convenience of laundry locations.	Place laundries in central locations near major activity areas. Refrain from isolating laundries in remote areas.

(*Continued*)

Table C.1 (Continued)

Environment	Environment Goal	CPTED Strategies	CPTED Design Directives
		Increase perception of surveillance.	Maximize the use of glazing in outer walls.
			Provide intense illumination.
			Increase number of machines to reduce the need for late-night or odd-hour usage.
Resident assistant room location	Increase the perception of natural surveillance and access control on the part of abnormal or undesired users of the space.	Place safe activities in potential problem locations.	Place apartments in strategic locations; place windows in walls overlooking entrances and lobbies.
		Improve accessibility between managers/ resident assistants and students.	Place resident assistants' rooms at the entry points of each floor.
			Provide a visible sitting and waiting area in front of manager's apartments.
Lobbies/ vestibules	Increase the transitional definition of movement from public to semipublic to private space.	Make potential abnormal users feel less comfortable and more subject to scrutiny by acknowledging transition through space.	Create minor obstacles or passage points to prevent easy movement from very public areas to lobbies.
			Change the texture, width, and border definition of sidewalks as they move from parallel passages to building approaches.
	Improve natural access control.	Increase proprietary concern by residents over general use and access areas.	Assign lobby walls and vestibule areas to dorm residents for reasonable decoration/ adornment.
	Increase natural surveillance.	Increase the perception of visibility from and to buildings.	Maximize the use of glazing and wall-mounted lighting.

(*Continued*)

Table C.1 (Continued)

Environment	Environment Goal	CPTED Strategies	CPTED Design Directives
Telephones/ telephone rooms	Reduce the tendency for public telephone locations to increase vulnerability of normal users and to legitimize loitering behavior of abnormal users.	Place unsafe activities in safe locations to extend the natural surveillance of the safe location over the unsafe activity (telephones).	Locate public telephones in well-used hallways and controlled areas away from restrooms.
		Provide natural barriers to conflicting activities.	Refrain from placing public telephones in or near entrances to buildings.
Apartment units	Enhance natural surveillance of individual room doors and restrooms.	Provide direct view from living room and kitchen areas.	Design bedroom and restroom entrances to cluster around living rooms and kitchens.
	Increase natural access control of main entrances to individual apartments.	Orient entrances toward high-activity areas.	Provide windows at each apartment that are directed toward entry door(s).
	Increase territorial identity of common exterior entrances, foyers, landings, and shared hallways.	Reduce number of residents sharing a common exterior entry.	Separate landing and exterior stair systems to emphasize access to a small number of apartments.

Table C.2 Exterior Spaces.

Environment	Environment Goal	CPTED Strategies	CPTED Design Directives
Entrances	Enhance territorial identity of entrances.	Provide transitional definition of approaches to main entrances to identify movement from public to private space.	Set back sidewalks that are parallel to buildings to provide distance as transitional definition.
			Ensure a reasonable length for approach sidewalks.
	Increase surveillance of entrances.	Provide observation from room windows and approaches.	Increase the length of line of sight from approaches to entrances.
			Place windows overlooking entrances.
			Use glazing material in entry doors and adjacent panels.
	Increase natural access control of entrances.	Control building access through space management strategies and juxtapositioning with safe activities.	Reduce ingress/egress to one entry during vulnerable times.
			Architecturally celebrate and define the preferred and primary entry point.
			Place a job function or other safe activity near primary entry points.
Windows	Increase perception of natural surveillance from windows.	Increase opportunities for occasional surveillance through the planning of window locations.	Place windows in walls overlooking isolated areas.

(*Continued*)

Table C.2 (Continued)

Environment	Environment Goal	CPTED Strategies	CPTED Design Directives
		Increase the perception of natural surveillance through the management of window blinds and lighting.	Place windows in all external stair systems.
			Use adjustable Venetian or mini-blinds on all windows, including bedrooms.
			Direct outdoor lighting away from windows, especially in the bedroom, to influence residents to leave windows loosely curtained or blinds partially open to increase the perception of surveillance from apartments.
Balconies/galleries	Enhance natural surveillance of pathways, isolated areas, and parking lots.	Increase the perception of surveillance from balconies, patios, and galleries.	Install balconies and open galleries as often as possible.
		Increase the visibility of patio/balcony entry points to rooms/apartments from ground levels and adjacent buildings.	In place of walls or continuous wood fencing, use railings that allow visibility.
			Orient patios, balconies, and galleries to allow for direct line of sight to outdoor pathways and areas.
Outdoor stair systems	Increase perception of natural surveillance.	Increase visibility of stairs and landings by open design.	Use wrought-iron or wood railing to improve visibility.

(Continued)

Table C.2 (Continued)

Environment	Environment Goal	CPTED Strategies	CPTED Design Directives
	Increase natural access control.	Orient stair/landing directions to route people past surveillance opportunities.	Place stairs in direct view of windows or activities.
Loading/passenger drop-off zones	Enhance territorial concern and natural surveillance through the strategic placement of loading/ drop-off zones.	Increase visibility of loading zones from building entrances.	Identify a special loading zone for each building.
			Provide for direct line of sight from building entrances to loading zone.
Lighting	Increase natural surveillance through effective use of lighting.	Increase the perception of natural surveillance to make normal users feel safe and abnormal users feel at greater risk.	Provide for standard levels of light for all paths, sidewalks, bicycle parking, and isolated areas.
	Ensure that lighting enhances human activities and does not become an impediment.	Set lighting levels to meet the objectives of each human activity in terms of effective illumination and perceptions of safety.	Reduce lighting glare on bedroom and living room windows to ensure that residents do not obscure their windows at night from the view of walkways, open entrances, and parking.

Table C.3 Immediate Vicinity.

Environment	Environment Goal	CPTED Strategies	CPTED Design Directives
Building groupings	Increase territorial identity of housing areas.	Orient buildings into distinctive clusters.	Face buildings toward courtyards with entrances in line of sight of all buildings; keep number of buildings sharing a common courtyard to a minimum.
		Provide natural border definition of controlled space.	Plan landscaping and topographical features to reinforce borders of building clusters.
	Overcome isolation of building groups through improved natural surveillance.	Provide for natural surveillance of perimeter areas of building groups/ clusters.	Orient balconies and windows to provide effective overviews of unassigned space.
Courtyards	Enhance territorial identity of building groups through the use of individualized courtyards.	Design courtyards to serve as the focal point for access to buildings.	Route all pedestrian approaches through courtyards.
		Increase natural surveillance and access control through courtyard planning.	Identify and celebrate entrance points to courtyards to provide a sense of arrival that signifies movement from public to semipublic space.
Sidewalks	Increase the safety of sidewalks through natural surveillance.	Increase the reality and perception of natural surveillance through sidewalk route planning and landscape maintenance.	Route sidewalks close to roadways and/or high-activity areas.
			Reduce landscape impediments to sidewalk visibility.
			Provide transitional thinning of underbrush and foliage, especially in curves and bends.

(Continued)

Table C.3 (Continued)

Environment	Environment Goal	CPTED Strategies	CPTED Design Directives
	Enhance territorial concern through the routing of sidewalks.	Use the public sidewalk to define the perimeters of controlled space.	Refrain from placing parallel sidewalks near bedroom windows or entrances to residential units.
Landscaping	Enhance territorial identity through landscape planning.	Define pedestrian approaches with landscape.	Install landscaping to define borders of private spaces and to signify transitional movement from public to private space.
	Increase natural surveillance through landscape planning and maintenance.	Reduce barriers to visibility through routine trimming and maintenance of trees and bushes.	Establish maximum height standards for bushes and shrubs; establish minimum height standards for tree foliage (lower level).
Bicycle shelters, racks, and posts	Enhance natural surveillance opportunities for bicycle storage areas.	Provide convenient access to bicycle parking.	Implement landscape management procedures that require periodic thinning and replacement at the end of the useful life of the plant, shrub, or tree.
		Increase natural surveillance of bicycle parking by effective placement and design.	Integrate illumination planning with landscape maintenance activities to enhance and maximize the free flow of light.
Bicycle shelters, racks, and posts	Enhance natural surveillance opportunities for bicycle storage areas.	Provide convenient access to bicycle parking.	Install bicycle racks and posts near all building entrances.
		Increase natural surveillance of bicycle parking by effective placement and design.	Relocate existing bicycle shelters, racks, and posts to locations that are directly in view of ongoing activities.
Lighting pedestrian ways and approaches to buildings	Enhance natural surveillance and safety through illumination of pedestrian ways.	Provide lighting of all pathways and building approaches at the human scale.	Increase lighting at the ground level without overilluminating upper-floor windows.

(*Continued*)

Table C.3 (Continued)

Environment	Environment Goal	CPTED Strategies	CPTED Design Directives
		Plan lighting to direct pedestrians along areas with high-volume activities.	Create corridors of light along roadways and other pedestrian paths connecting colleges, the student center, and library facilities.
	Increase territorial identity through illumination of controlled spaces.	Plan for specific areas to become "islands of light."	Illuminate the lower levels of buildings and adjacent grounds, extending the light to perimeter areas.
Coffee shops	Increase natural surveillance of college grounds through the effective location, design, and management of coffee shops.	Place coffee shops in central locations to serve as a magnet for evening activities.	Maximize the use of windows and glazing material to increase visibility from and into coffee shops.
			Illuminate the immediate area of the coffee shop to provide an "island of light" for students.
Trash bins/ disposal areas	Increase natural surveillance of trash-disposal areas.	Improve the accessibility of trash-disposal areas.	Place trash bins in prominent locations within view of windows and high-activity areas.
		Increase the visibility of trash bins.	Design trash-bin enclosures to psychologically screen instead of physically obscure.
			Refrain from isolating trash bins by location and design.
Outdoor amenities	Enhance natural surveillance of outdoor picnic and sitting areas.	Ensure visibility of outdoor sitting areas by locating them near activities.	Install amenities in direct view of windows.
		Increase the accessibility and convenience of picnic areas to ensure high levels of use.	Install amenities in college courtyards.
			Refrain from designing or installing any features that block natural surveillance.

Table C.4 General Area.

Environment	Environment Goal	CPTED Strategies	CPTED Design Directives
Parking	Increase natural surveillance of remote parking lots.	Place safe activities in areas that have few opportunities for natural surveillance.	Relocate guard booths from perimeter entry points to the intersections of the entrances of remote lots.
		Remove obstacles to natural surveillance.	Redesign landscape plans to reduce the negative effect of foliage and topographical features on direct visibility from adjacent streets and structures.
	Increase natural access control of parking areas located near buildings.	Provide border control and clear transitional definition in movement from public streets and semipublic access roads to private parking areas.	Design and manage parking lots so that some ingress/egress points may be closed during vulnerable periods to reduce the possibility of cruising by abnormal users.
	Increase the perception of risk of detection and scrutiny of abnormal users of parking areas.	Plan for new parking areas to be located in areas of high visibility.	Place parking in front of buildings and windows, and landscape appropriately to provide minimal screening for aesthetics.
Traffic levels/ direction	Increase natural access control through traffic management.	Reduce vehicular access to controlled points at night.	Route all traffic past guard booths.
Sidewalks and pedestrian paths	Increase natural surveillance along sidewalks and pedestrian paths.	Remove obstacles to natural surveillance.	Provide transitional landscape control along all wooded and obscured pedestrian paths to increase fields of view.
	Increase accessibility and convenience to sidewalks along roadways.	Develop a pedestrian pathway master plan.	Install intense lighting at the human scale along all critical pathways.
			Install sidewalks along all roadways.

APPENDIX D: CONVENIENCE STORES AND GAS STOPS CPTED ASSESSMENT FORM

Date____________________

Name of Reviewer______________________________________

Natural Surveillance (NSU)
Natural Access Control (NAC)
Territorial Concern (TER)

Twenty-Six Risk Assessment Points

1. Propane tank storage secured
2. Light level adequate
3. Number of employees on duty (at least two)
4. Store hours
5. Mirrors inside store
6. Digital CCTV and 90-day recorder
7. Good cash-handling policy
8. Drop safe and type of safe
9. Security officer ever on duty?
10. Store location
11. Level of crime in area
12. Landscape
13. Doors, locks, key control, and windows
14. Restroom access
15. Level of protection needed
16. Graffiti
17. Signage
18. Traffic direction
19. Fire-suppression system
20. Panic button to police
21. Silent intrusion alarm
22. Location of cashier within store
23. What training do employees receive?
24. Roof access
25. Fence and perimeter
26. Crime area data

Now let's look at this situation from the robber's point of view. What is he concerned with?

1. The location: How close to another business?
2. Lighting and visibility, parking lot entrance, walkways
3. Windows: Are they covered with sales information or can you see inside?
4. Doors: Clear view to cash register and its location
5. Alarms
6. Number of employees and their alertness
7. When is change of shift and store hours?
8. CCTV units inside and outside?
9. Signage
10. What are my chances of pulling it off?

The answer should be "not too good."

I. Demographics
   A. Name of site
   B. Location
   C. Jurisdiction
   D. Customers

Type/#	Repeat	Nonrepeat
Resident	_____	_____
Nonresident	_____	_____
Drive	_____	_____
Walk	_____	_____
Commuter	_____	_____
Visitor	_____	_____

   E. Police services____________________
   F. Fire services____________________
   G. Number of employees____________________
   H. Hours of operation____________________

I. CPTED/security

Advantages____________________

____

____

Disadvantages ____________________

____

____

Precautions____________________

____

____

Recommendations ____________________

____

____

II. Neighborhood/area
   A. Residential %____________________
   B. Commercial/retail ____________________
   C. Industrial ____________________
   D. Streets by type ____________________

____

Private__________ Residential__________
Service__________ Subcollector__________
Collector__________ Major collector__________
Expressway__________ Interstate__________

E. Proximity to expressways __________

F. Access to transportation (by type)__________

G. Lighting __________

H. Demographics__________

I. Vehicle approaches __________

J. Pedestrian approaches __________

K. Other__________

L. CPTED/security
   Advantages__________
   Disadvantages __________
   Precautions__________
   Recommendations __________

III. Site plan
   A. Acreage__________
   B. Topographical features __________
   C. Green areas
      Public__________
      Semipublic __________
      Private __________
   D. Recreation __________
   E. Landscape __________
   F. Access to contiguous properties __________
   G. Fences/walls/natural barriers __________
   H. Border definition __________
   I. Lighting (type, mounts, location) __________

J. Type of store ______________________

K. Parking ______________________
L. Pumps (visual access) ______________________
M. CPTED/security
Advantages ______________________

Disadvantages ______________________

Precautions ______________________

Recommendations ______________________

IV. Buildings/exterior
A. # by type ______________________
B. Station (by type) ______________________
C. Scale (# of buildings, size, volume) ______________________

D. Use patterns/users ______________________

E. Sitting/gathering areas ______________________

F. Vehicle approaches ______________________

G. Vehicle drop-off ______________________

H. Pedestrian approaches ______________________

I. Telephones ______________________

J. Lighting—public areas ______________________

K. Lighting—service areas ______________________________

L. Doors/entrances/exits ______________________________

M. Windows/openings ______________________________

N. Service areas ______________________________

O. Public transit stops ______________________________

P. Connections/other buildings ______________________________

Q. Life-safety codes/issues ______________________________

R. Trash enclosures ______________________________

S. Carwash (visual access, glazing) ______________________________

T. Other ______________________________

U. CPTED/security

Advantages ______________________________

Disadvantages ______________________________

Precautions ______________________________

Recommendations ______________________________

V. Parking
   A. Type(s) ______________________________
   ____
   ____
   B. Characteristics
      Ingress/egress ______________________________
      ____
      ____
      Surface ______________________________
      ____
      ____
      Enclosures/structures ______________________________
      ____
      ____
      # units (by type) ______________________________
      ____
      Access to public ______________________________
      ____
      Visual access ______________________________
      ____
   C. Porch design/size ______________________________
   D. CPTED/security
      Advantages ______________________________
      ____
      ____
      Disadvantages ______________________________
      ____
      ____
      Precautions ______________________________
      ____
      ____
      Recommendations ______________________________
      ____
      ____

VI. Interior
   A. Layout/type ______________________________
   ____
   B. Scale ______________________________
   ____
   C. Waiting/seating ______________________________
   ____
   D. ATMs ______________________________
   ____
   E. Other businesses ______________________________
   ____
   F. Movement areas/corridors ______________________________
   ____

G. Observation areas/opportunities
   Offices ____________________
   Windows ____________________
   Balconies/terraces ____________________
   Stairs ____________________
   Other ____________________

H. Decorations (fountains, planters, sculptures ____________________

I. Gondolas/shelves/racks ____________________

J. Cashier location/work area (risers, barriers) ____________________

K. Food service—seating ____________________

L. Food service—movement areas ____________________

M. Restrooms
   Locations ____________________
   Entry design ____________________
   Layout/fixtures ____________________
   Materials ____________________

N. Telephones ____________________

O. Lighting ____________________

P. Service/maintenance ____________________

Q. Administration offices (location, access, fenestration, proximity, and visual access) ____________________

R. CPTED/security

Advantages ____

____

____

Disadvantages ____

____

____

Precautions ____

____

____

Recommendations ____

____

____

VII. Materials

A. Interior ____

____

B. Exterior ____

____

C. Paint ____

____

D. Lighting

Type ____

Mount ____

Comments ____

____

____

E. Other ____

____

____

F. CPTED/security

Advantages ____

____

____

Disadvantages ____

____

____

Precautions ____

____

____

Recommendations ____

____

____

VIII. Security

A. Systems (alarms, safes, timers, mirrors, EAS) ____

____

____

B. Security officers (proprietary, contract, etc.) ______

C. Lessee/concession ______

D. Police ______

E. Key control ______

F. Access control ______

G. Cash control ______

H. Training ______

I. CPTED/security

Advantages ______

Disadvantages ______

Precautions ______

Recommendations ______

IX. Crime patterns/security incidents (attach reports/maps to Section XII)

A. Crime report ______

B. Crime map (spot map of incidents) ______

C. Fear map (spot map of fear locations) ______

D. Land-use map (local area) ______

E. Pedestrian activity map ______

F. Vehicle parking/movement map ______

G. Other ______

H. CPTED/security

Advantages____________________

Disadvantages ____________________

Precautions____________________

Recommendations ____________________

X. Priority recommendations

Physical space

A. Replace____________________

B. Repair____________________

C. Remove____________________

D. Install ____________________

E. Reallocate ____________________

F. Other____________________

Management

A. Policies ____________________

B. Procedures ____________________

C. Personnel ____________________

D. Neighborhood programs ____________________

E. Other ____________________

XI. Security plan

A. Neighborhood ____________________

B. Perimeter ____________________

C. Grounds ____________________

D. Parking ____________________

E. Building access ____________________

F. Building exterior ____________________

G. Building interior ______________________________

H. High-value areas ______________________________

I. Protection of people ______________________________

J. Special events ______________________________

K. Others ______________________________

XII. CPTED matrices and drawings (attach to this form and provide any comments in this section) ______________________________

APPENDIX E: MALLS AND SHOPPING CENTERS CPTED ASSESSMENT FORM

Natural Surveillance (NSU)
Natural Access Control—NAC
Territorial Concern—TER

I. Demographics
   A. Name of site ________________
   B. Location ________________
   C. Jurisdiction ________________
   D. Type: Mall________ Strip________ Neighborhood________ Intermediate________
      Regional__________ Renewal (downtown)__________ Urban village__________
   E. Customers/visitors

Type/#	Repeat	Nonrepeat
Resident	_____	_____
Nonresident	_____	_____
Drive	_____	_____
Walk	_____	_____
Commuter	_____	_____
Visitor	_____	_____

   F. Police ________________
   G. Fire ________________
   H. EMS ________________
   I. Number of employees ________________
   J. Hours of operation ________________

II. Area/neighborhood
   A. Residential % ________________
   B. Commercial/Retail ________________
   C. Industrial ________________
   D. Streets by type ________________
      Private________________ Residential ________________
      Service________________ Subcollector ________________
      Collector________________ Major collector ________________
      Expressway________________ Interstate________________
   E. Proximity to expressways ________________
      ____
   F. Access to transportation (by type)________________
      ____
   G. Lighting ________________
      ____

- H. Demographics__________
- I. Vehicle approaches __________
- J. Pedestrian approaches __________
- K. Other__________

III. Site plan
- A. Acreage__________
- B. Topographical features __________
- C. Site plan __________
- D. Footprint __________
- E. Green areas
  - Public __________
  - Semipublic__________
  - Private__________
- F. Recreation __________
- G. Landscape __________
- H. Access to contiguous properties __________
- I. Outlot uses__________
- J. Reservoir roads__________
- K. Ring roads __________
- L. Fences/walls/natural barriers __________
- M. Border definition __________
- N. Lighting (type, mounts, location) __________
- O. Parking __________
- P. Other__________

IV. Buildings/exterior features
- A. # by type __________
- B. Scale (# of buildings, size, volume)__________
- C. Use patterns/users __________
- D. Sitting/gathering areas __________
- E. Vehicle approaches __________
- F. Vehicle drop-offs__________
- G. Pedestrian approaches __________
- H. Telephones and Wi-Fi access__________
- I. Lighting—public areas__________
- J. Lighting—service areas__________
- K. Doors/entrances/exits__________
- L. Windows/openings __________
- M. Service areas __________
- N. Public transit stops__________
- O. Connections/other buildings__________
- P. Life-safety codes/issues__________
- Q. Trash enclosures__________
- R. Other__________

V. Parking
- A. Type(s) __________

B. Characteristics ______
 Ingress/egress ______
 Surface ______
 Enclosures ______
 # of units (by type) ______
 Access to public ______
 Rights of reasonable public access ______
 ______
 Visual access ______
 Islands ______
 Walkways ______
C. Other ______
 ______

VI. Interior
 A. Layout/type ______
 B. Scale ______
 C. Waiting/seating ______
 ______
 D. ATMs ______
 E. Arcades ______
 F. Food courts
 Seating ______
 Pathways/movement areas ______
 Service areas ______
 Restrooms ______
 Telephones ______
 G. Theaters ______
 H. Clubs/entertainment ______
 I. Movement areas/corridors (main, approach) ______
 J. Observation areas/opportunities
 Offices ______
 Windows ______
 Balconies/terraces ______
 Stairs ______
 Escalators ______
 Elevators ______
 Other ______
 K. Decorations (fountains, planters, sculptures) ______
 L. Vendor carts ______
 M. Special events ______
 N. Restrooms
 Locations ______
 Entry design ______
 Layout/fixtures ______
 Materials ______
 O. Telephones (location, proximity to seating, planters) ______
 ______
 P. Lighting ______
 ______

Q. Service/maintenance access ______
R. Administrative offices (location, access, fenestration, proximity, and visual access) ______

______

______

S. Other ______

VII. Materials
A. Interior ______
B. Exterior ______
C. Paint ______
D. Lighting
Type ______
Mount ______
Comments ______
E. Other ______

VIII. Security and crime problems
A. Systems (alarms, safes, timers, mirrors, EAS, etc.) ______

______

B. Security officers (proprietary, contract, etc.) ______

______

C. Lessee/concession ______

______

D. Police/security ______

______

E. Key control ______

______

F. Access control ______

______

G. Cash control ______

______

H. Training ______

______

I. Other ______

______

IX. Crime patterns/security incidents (attach reports/maps to Section XII)
A. Crime report ______

______

B. Crime map (spot map of incidents) ______

______

C. Fear map (spot map of fear locations) ______

______

D. Land-use map (local area) ______

______

E. Pedestrian activity map ______

______

F. Vehicle parking/movement map ______

______

G. Other ______

______

X. Priority recommendations

Physical space

A. Replace ______

B. Repair ______

C. Remove ______

D. Install ______

E. Reallocate ______

F. Other ______

Management

A. Policies ______

B. Procedures ______

C. Personnel ______

D. Neighborhood programs

E. Other

XI. Security Plan

A. Neighborhood

B. Perimeter

C. Grounds

D. Parking

E. Building access

F. Building exterior

G. Building interior

H. High-value areas

I. Protection of people

J. Special events

K. Others

APPENDIX F: APARTMENTS, CONDOS, AND PUBLIC HOUSING CPTED ASSESSMENT FORM

Date____________________
Name of Reviewer____

Natural Surveillance (NSU)
Natural Access Control (NAC)
Territorial Concern (TER)

I. Demographics
   A. Name of site ____
   B. Location ____
   C. Jurisdiction ____
   D. # of units ____
   E. Residents ____
   F. Age % under 18______ 18–25_______ 26–45______ 45–65______ over 65______
   G. Race/sex/ethnic origins

	Female	*Male*
Anglo	______	______
________	______	______
________	______	______
Hispanic	______	______
________	______	______
________	______	______
African Am.	______	______
________	______	______
________	______	______
Asian	______	______
________	______	______
________	______	______

   H. Police services____
   I. Fire services____
   J. CPTED/security
      Advantages ____
      ____
      ____
      Disadvantages ____
      ____
      ____
      Precautions____
      ____
      ____

Recommendations ____________________

II. Neighborhood
   A. Residential % ____________________
   B. Commercial/retail ____________________
   C. Industrial ____________________
   D. Streets by type ____________________

Private ______	Residential ______
Service ______	Subcollector ______
Collector ______	Major collector ______
Expressway ______	Interstate ______

   E. Proximity to expressways ____________________
   F. Access to transportation (by type) ____________________
   G. Lighting ____________________
   H. Demographics ____________________
   I. CPTED/security
      Advantages ____________________
      Disadvantages ____________________
      Precautions ____________________
      Recommendations ____________________

III. Buildings
   A. Flats high/garden ____________________
   B. Townhouses ____________________
   C. Maisonettes ____________________
   D. Single family ____________________
   E. Duplex or higher ____________________
   F. Stairs ____________________
   G. Elevators ____________________
   H. ADA (e.g., ramps) ____________________
   I. CPTED/security
      Advantages ____________________

Disadvantages ______________________________

____

____

Precautions ______________________________

____

____

Recommendations ______________________________

____

____

IV. Grounds

A. Acreage ______________________________

B. Topographical features ______________________________

____

C. Yards

Public ______________________________

Semipublic ______________________________

Private ______________________________

D. Recreation ______________________________

E. Gardens ______________________________

F. Landscape ______________________________

G. Access to contiguous properties ______________________________

____

H. Fences/walls/natural barriers ______________________________

____

I. Border definition ______________________________

____

J. Lighting (type, mounts, location) ______________________________

____

____

K. Signage ______________________________

L. CPTED/security

Advantages ______________________________

____

____

Disadvantages ______________________________

____

____

Precautions ______________________________

____

____

Recommendations ______________________________

____

____

V. Interior streets

A. Pattern ______________________________

B. Ingress/egress (to outside) ______________________________

____

C. Parking
 Ingress/egress ______
 Street ______
 Court ______
 Cluster ______
 Pads ______
 Enclosures/roof ______
 Conflict ______
 ______
 # per unit ______
 Proximity to units ______
 Access to public ______

D. CPTED/security
 Advantages ______
 ______
 ______
 Disadvantages ______
 ______
 ______
 Precautions ______
 ______
 ______
 Recommendations ______
 ______
 ______

VI. Units
 A. Floor plan ______
 B. Private space—balcony/patio/stoop ______
 ______
 C. Pedestrian approaches ______
 ______
 D. Sidewalks and proximity ______
 ______
 E. Fenestration
 Doors and frames ______
 Windows ______
 Screens ______
 Materials ______
 Comments ______
 F. Locks
 Doors ______
 Windows ______
 Storage areas ______
 Other ______
 G. Materials
 Interior ______
 ______
 ______

Exterior ______________________________

____

____

Paint ______________________________

____

____

H. Lighting
   Type ______________________________
   Mount ______________________________
   Comments ______________________________

I. Visual accessibility ______________________________

____

J. CPTED/security
   Advantages ______________________________

____

____

   Disadvantages ______________________________

____

____

   Precautions ______________________________

____

____

   Recommendations ______________________________

____

____

VII. Security

A. Systems ______________________________

____

B. Security officers ______________________________

____

C. Neighborhood watch associations ______________________________

____

D. Police/sheriff ______________________________

____

E. Key control or access control ______________________________

____

F. CCTV ______________________________

____

G. CPTED/security
   Advantages ______________________________

____

____

   Disadvantages ______________________________

____

____

Precautions________________________________

Recommendations ________________________________

VIII. Common buildings
  A. Office________________________________
  B. Meeting________________________________
  C. Recreations ________________________________
  D. Laundry ________________________________
  E. Maintenance ________________________________
  H. CPTED/security

Advantages ________________________________

Disadvantages ________________________________

Precautions________________________________

Recommendations ________________________________

IX. Crime patterns/security incidents (attach reports/maps to Section XIII)
  A. Crime report ________________________________
  B. Crime map (spot map of incidents) ________________________________
  C. Fear map (spot map of fear locations) ________________________________
  D. Land-use map (local area) ________________________________
  E. Pedestrian activity map________________________________
  F. Vehicle parking/movement map________________________________
  G. Other________________________________
  I. CPTED/security

Advantages ________________________________

Disadvantages ________________________________

Precautions____
____
____

Recommendations ____
____
____

X. Priority recommendations

Physical space

A. Replace____
____
____
____
____

B. Repair ____
____
____
____
____

C. Remove____
____
____
____
____

D. Install ____
____
____
____
____

E. Reallocate____
____
____
____
____

F. Other____
____
____
____
____

Management

A. Policies ____
____
____
____

B. Procedures____
____
____
____

C. Personnel ____

D. Neighborhood programs ____

E. Other ____

XI. Security plan

A. Neighborhood ____

B. Perimeter ____

C. Grounds ____

D. Parking ____

E. Building access ____

F. Building exterior ____

G. Building interior ____

H. High-value areas ____

I. Protection of persons ______________________

J. Special events ______________________

K. Others ______________________

XII. CPTED matrices and drawings (attach to this form and provide any comments in this section) ______________________

INDEX

CPSIA information can be obtained
at www.ICGtesting.com
Printed in the USA
BVHW081913051220
594509BV00009B/87